GROWING UP GLOBAL

University of Minnesota Press / Minneapolis • London

GROWING UP GLOBAL

Economic Restructuring and Children's Everyday Lives

Cindi Katz

All photographs in the book were taken by the author.

Copyright 2004 by the Regents of the University of Minnesota

Published by the University of Minnesota Press
111 Third Avenue South, Suite 290
Minneapolis, MN 55401-2520
http://www.upress.umn.edu

Library of Congress Cataloging-in-Publication Data

Katz, Cindi, 1954–
  Growing up global : economic restructuring and children's everyday lives / Cindi Katz.
    p. cm.
  Includes bibliographical references and index.
  ISBN 0-8166-4209-5 (hc : alk. paper) — ISBN 0-8166-4210-9 (pb : alk. paper)
  1. Rural children—Sudan—Social conditions. 2. Globalization—Social aspects. 3. Human reproduction—Social aspects. 4. Economic development—Social aspects. 5. Economic development—Environmental aspects. I. Title.

HQ792.S73K38 2004
305.23'09624'09734—dc   20044017577

Printed in the United States of America on acid-free paper
The University of Minnesota is an equal-opportunity educator and employer.

12 11 10 09 08 07 06   10 9 8 7 6 5 4

For my mother, Phyllis Katz,
who gave me humor,
and my father, Arthur Katz,
who taught me to sing
without words.

Contents

Preface

A screaming comes across the sky.

—Thomas Pynchon, *Gravity's Rainbow*

This book is about the disintegrative effects of "development." Development—always uneven—is less a process imposed by one place on another than the uneven motion of capital finding, producing, and reproducing places and people in particular and differentiated relation to peculiar strategies of accumulation. If its signal form in the second half of the twentieth century demarcated a specific relationship between the global north and south or between the "first" and "third worlds"—indeed producing them as such—development might more usefully be imagined as a process occurring at various scales within and across these different spheres, whose distinction is riddled with similarities. Development is the iterative flux of capital moving across space in time, making and unmaking particular places; structuring and restructuring social relations of production and reproduction; and being met, engaged, and countered by social actors whose own histories and geographies enable and call forth broad and differentiated material social practices. These practices and the social relations associated with them may embrace, rework, and be disrupted by the encounter.

Growing Up Global examines the processes of development and global change through the perspective of children's lives. At its core is a longitudinal ethnographic study of rural Sudanese children growing up in Howa,[1] a village in central eastern Arabic-speaking Sudan that was included in a large state-sponsored agricultural project in 1971, the year they were born. It follows a small number of children intermittently from ten years of age to early adulthood, focusing especially on their acquisition and use of environmental knowledge. In teasing out how "development" transformed the grounds on which these young people came of age, I hope to provide a textured analysis of the meaning of knowledge and the consequences of knowing in an economic, political-ecological, and cultural context in the throes of significant change. In tracing the effects of and responses to capitalist development over a generation, I found several creative strategies that people used to stay afloat and even reformulate the conditions and possibilities of their everyday lives. I have categorized these responses as *resilience, reworking,* and *resistance* in an effort both to provide a more nuanced account of responses to significant political economic change and to offer a constructive critique of the contemporary literature on resistance. In pairing development and development—children's coming of age and the structured transformation of their local environment—the book demonstrates how childhood and its material social practices are shot through with the effects of social, political, and environmental change, while making clear that children are social actors in this process. Their work and play not only intersect with and are altered by these processes, but they have the capacity to further or frustrate them as well. Neither form of development can be understood fully without the other.

The theoretical questions at the heart of this project concern social reproduction. Social reproduction, as the name implies, encompasses that broad range of practices and social relations that maintain and reproduce particular relations of production along with the material social grounds in which they take place. It is as much the fleshy, messy, and indeterminate stuff of everyday life as it is a set of structured practices that unfold in dialectical relation to production, with which it is mutually constitutive and in tension (Katz 2001c, 710). Among other things, social reproduction entails the reproduction of the population and the means by which people produce their subsistence. It encompasses daily and long-term reproduction, both of the means of production and the labor power to make them work. At its most basic, it hinges on both the biological reproduction of the labor force (both generationally and on a daily basis through the acquisition and distribution of the means of existence, including food, shelter, clothing, sanitation, and health care) and the physical conditions that make ongoing production possible. Social reproduction is, of course, much more than this. In Marxist theory it also involves making a labor force at a certain (and fluid) level of differentiation and expertise. Not only is this process historically and geographically specific, but its very contours and requirements are always contested. Up for grabs are what constitutes being skilled, what kinds of knowledge are admissible and useful, what work attitudes are acceptable, and by whose authority these are determined.

As the preceding description might suggest, social reproduction embodies the whole jumble of cultural forms and practices that constitute and create everyday life and the meanings by which people understand themselves in the world. It is interesting and important, then, as the arena wherein the future is shaped, the conditions of production are forged, and the relations of production are both made and naturalized, through an amalgam of material social practices associated with the household, the state, civil society, the market, and the workplace. Yet social reproduction is a critical practice in the sense that Henri Lefebvre understood everyday life (Lefebvre 1984, 1987; Kaplan and Ross 1987). The possibilities for rupture are everywhere in the routine. If *rupture* in the efflorescence of cultural forms and practices that make up social reproduction hegemony is secured, so, too, might it stumble. These possibilities, together with the elemental nature of the work of social reproduction, inspired my project.

Growing Up Global focuses on the sorts of mundane things through which people make themselves and the historical geographies in which they live, but it was impelled by a politics intent on locating practices that scratched at, and under certain conditions might completely break down, hegemony. This is no easy task, but I thought it might be easier to do during a period in which broad-scale, and largely imposed, political-economic, environmental, and cultural changes were under way, such as was the case in Howa. With so much up for grabs, contradictions were apparent everywhere. People incorporated and adjusted to new patterns of work and social relations as they mourned the loss of their more autonomous farming practices and the landscapes with which they were associated. At the same time, and not necessarily contradictorily, they scrambled to get a leg *scrambled* up in the new social formations in which they and their village were cast, and thus in myriad small ways reformulated them as well. In this flux, which I have come to call (after a Russian friend's inadvertent slip) the "recent future" because of its backward tugging wrench forward, I wanted to see what kinds of knowledge—particularly work knowledge—parents shared with their children, children learned on their own, and children were taught in more formal contexts, figuring that it would be in the production, exchange, and use of knowledge that resistance to the new forms of production might be located. But if that kind of resistance proved hard to locate, my focus on children provided a peculiar and wonderful vantage point on the nexus of the creative and recuperative impulses that are at the heart of social reproduction and that drive my project.

For children, one of the things that began to fall apart with Howa's incorporation into capitalist relations of production and more forceful ties with the national and global economy was an easy unity between work and play in their everyday lives. While the contours of this shift are addressed in chapter 3, I raise it here to note the mimetic logic of children's play and the ways it anticipates and echoes the contradictions and possibilities embraced by social reproduction (cf. Benjamin 1978a). Children's play— even their dramatic play—is never simply imitative but is also inventive. If in their play children are engaged in making meanings, then the very act of playing encompasses new possibilities for making sense or nonsense of the world. It is precisely this imaginative and potentially subversive aspect of play that redounds in social reproduction, but as play is severed from work in time, space, and substance, its meanings and potential consequences for children and the broader society are altered.

As a meditation on the disintegrative effects of capitalist development, this book is inevitably global in its concerns, even if its purview is quite local. To that end, I have not so much conducted an ethnography of a particular place—though I have done that—as attempted what might be called a critical ethnography of global economic restructuring (see G. Hart 2002). Because economic restructuring simultaneously produces and is the outcome of uneven and spatially interconnected material social practices, I have found it instructive to look comparatively at how it works and is reworked in two very different historical geographies, Howa and New York City. I have framed this project as a "countertopography," which draws on a close study of the relationship between capitalist globalism and social reproduction in Howa refracted in parallax from the vantage point of New York City. This strategy is meant not only to draw out the structural similarities between the two places—focused around children's learning and therefore social reproduction—but in doing so, to make sense of restructuring in a different manner than is customary. In examining global processes in their particular historical geographies, my project disrupts the seemingly contradictory assumptions that the imperatives of global capitalism are homogenizing, while at the same time their effects in one locale are separable from their effects in another. These processes are spatially as much as socially intertwined, and while their effects are of course differentiated in diverse historical geographies, their often startling similarities offer interesting common grounds for political response.

The work in Sudan is based on several periods of fieldwork between 1980 and 1995. I spent a year in the field from late 1980 through late 1981, and returned for brief visits in 1983, 1984, and again in 1995. The long hiatus between visits was in part because of the political instability in Sudan during the late 1980s and early 1990s, the renewed civil war and its ghastly toll on the south and the nation as a whole, and the policies of the Islamic fundamentalist government of 'Umar al-Bashir and Hassan al-Turabi, which came to power in 1989 and in the course of entrenching itself prosecuted the civil war with a vengeance, shattered civil liberties, and promulgated a version of Islam that seemed antithetical to the more ecumenical rhythms and practices of Islam familiar in Sudan. Part of my resistance to returning was deeply personal. The Bashir government had imprisoned or forced into exile many of my friends as it set up a thick web of military surveillance, making it unconscionable for me to return.

Apart from these political motivations, I did not return to Sudan because I wanted to address the issues my research raised in a different location, one much closer to home. Among the findings of my initial research was that children were not being prepared for any future they were likely to face. They were learning the skills and knowledge associated with agriculture, but they were unlikely to have access to land as they came of age. At the same time, they were acquiring an exquisitely detailed knowledge of how to use the local environment even as its resources appeared to be under erasure. One of the signal effects of "development" in Howa was the "deskilling" of young people, who, it seemed to me, were unlikely to have the knowledge and skills necessary to make it in the futures that seemed possible. Something quite similar seemed to be going on in New York City, where I lived by 1986.

As New York was reconfigured by the flight of manufacturing starting in the 1960s and the turn to a service and financial economy by the 1980s, young people, particularly working-class children, no longer seemed prepared for the employment futures that awaited them. The toll of economic restructuring was apparent in the prospects of young people who were rendered unskilled and ill-prepared for the futures that seemed most likely, just as the grounds on which they came of age grew increasingly inhospitable. If similar things were happening to such vastly different populations of young people, a focus on their coming of age—and in particular on the forms and practices of social reproduction associated with it—would offer critical insights into the workings of contemporary capitalist-driven globalization. In a number of studies and collaborations focused largely on social reproduction in Harlem, New York City, with particular attention to children's everyday lives, I tried to address the concerns that arose in the course of my work in Sudan. This project was not comparative in a strict sense, but was intended to draw out the structural similarities between the two sites.

Thus in chapter 6 I ratchet the focus from rural Sudan to look at New York City. The strategy is intended to juxtapose the circumstances of children in both places in the wake of global economic restructuring, at once "de-exoticizing" Howa as some sort of remote object of globalization and exposing common effects of capitalist globalism in both settings. The broader intent of *Growing Up Global,* then, is to situate children's lives in these two vastly different places within the shifting configurations of global economic restructuring, both to examine the ways these shifts have transformed their everyday lives and prospects in sometimes startlingly similar ways, and to make global capitalism sensible in a different register than is usually the case. In working out these "topographies" of global capitalism, I am hoping to develop a nuanced account of how the encroachments of capitalism are engaged and responded to across disparate geographies. While I initially understood this comparison temporally, as an examination of the sorts of displacements children can suffer in the transition from an agricultural to an industrial economy and from an industrial to a postindustrial economy, what I realized in the process was the importance of their simultaneity.[2] The perspective offered by doing a topographical analysis affords me a more productive and spatialized understanding of the problems and their coexistence. Drawing out the structural similarities between these two sites and examining how particular children are deskilled and marooned within them is a means of forging a different geographical imagination, one that might enable new forms of political identification.

My framing of this project as a countertopography is both methodological and political. Topographies are simultaneously the detailed description of a particular landscape and the landscape itself. They suggest, therefore, that nature and space, as much as our understandings of them, are produced (and thus could be otherwise). But topographies can be mobilized as a research methodology; a means of producing "thick descriptions" of social relations, material social practices, and the construction of meaning as constitutive of and constituted by particular historical geographies. But beyond such descriptions, which are the traditional purview of ethnography, topographies as method can produce "thick descriptions" of abstract social relations and processes, such as those associated with global economic restructuring or the advance of capitalist relations of production, or at a different level of abstraction, deskilling or the disinvestment in social reproduction. If topographies offer a means for examining these processes closely in a particular historical geography, the notion of countertopography is meant to invoke the connections among particular historical geographies by virtue of their relationship to a specific abstract social process or relation, such as restructuring or deskilling. New political economic formations can be mobilized along "contour lines" connecting particular places (or topographies). The politics sparked and informed by countertopographies—by making perhaps unexpected connections among disparate places—can produce spatialized abstractions akin to those fostered by the permutations of globalizing capitalist production that are my concern here. In mobilizing similar abstractions like these, countertopographical analysis may have the fluidity to match the deft moves of capital and its attendant social relations, and thus expose their wily ability to produce uneven developments across space and scale in ways that eclipse and hide common grounds in a welter of difference and inequality.

The perspective offered by doing a topographical analysis of Howa and New York, for instance, affords a productive and spatialized means of understanding the sorts of displacements children can suffer in the course of broad-scale political economic change. Not only does this kind of analysis reveal the simultaneity of different kinds of disruptions but, making good on John Berger's brilliant insight that it is now "space not time that hides consequences from us," it reveals the intertwined consequences of globalizing capitalist production in ways that demand a different kind of politics (Berger 1974, 40; cf. Soja 1989). My argument is that if the disruptions of social reproduction in Howa and Harlem are two effects of a common set of processes, and I think they are, then any effective politics challenging a capital-inspired globalization must have similar global sensitivities, even as its grounds are necessarily local. This is different from a "place-based" politics. It is not merely about one locale or another, nor is it a matter of building coalitions between such diverse places, vital as that is. Precisely because globalization is such an abstraction, albeit with varying forms, struggles against global capital have to mobilize equivalent, alternative abstractions. I offer this countertopography as one such mobilization in the hopes that it invigorates the sort of political imagination able to counter the disabling effects of globalized capitalism.

The book is structured in four parts. The first part, "Fluid Dynamics," opens with an evocative chapter that details a child's day and concludes with a brief discussion of the concerns of the book. The second chapter provides an overview of Howa and the changes brought about by its inclusion in the Suki Agricultural Project. The next part, "Social Reproduction," encompasses two chapters on children's work, play, learning, and knowledge, and a third on the disruptions in production and social reproduction associated with changes under way in the village. Part III, "Displacements," consists of two chapters. The first offers a displacement across space, presenting an analysis of disinvestments in social reproduction in New York City that mirror and refract the circumstances in Howa, providing a parallax view of each setting. The second displacement is across time. This chapter distills my findings from a return visit to

Howa nearly fifteen years after the original study to excavate a historical geography of the intervening period and to catch up with the now-grown children to see how they were faring in the circumstances of their young adulthoods. The final part, "Topographies of Global Capitalism," includes two chapters. The first discusses the ongoing reformulations of rural life in Howa as it was drawn more fully into the social relations associated with global capitalism and other global networks, such as Islam. The concluding chapter works out a critique of resistance by analyzing the responses I encountered in Howa and Harlem as material social practices better thought of as "resilience," "reworking," and "resistance," and returns to the questions of mimesis that infuse my concern with children and social reproduction more generally. The section is framed "topographically" to underscore that this is an ethnography of process and to call attention to the connections between the disparate sites of my concerns.

With a bit of poetic license these disparate sites came forcibly together on September 11, 2001 (and its ongoing aftermath), in a diabolical arc that recalls Thomas Pynchon's "gravity's rainbow," describing the trajectory of Germany's V2 rockets on Britain. Extreme and horrific, the events—from the terrorist strikes themselves to the U.S. retaliations for them—threatened to override and obliterate the common interests of people in both of the places that have been my concern, rerouting them into old binaries as fatal as they are fatuous; "the West and Islam," "modernity and tradition," "good and evil." To refuse the "screaming across the sky" that day and since as something that connects young people in both places has made it all the more important to me to work out the nature of their common concerns while remaining mindful of their differences. In describing the geographical arc of global economic restructuring and some of its common effects on young people in rural Sudan and at the heart of global capitalism, this countertopography gestures toward novel sorts of spatial and political consciousness and different kinds of political projects that might disturb and exceed the assumptions of local, national, and identity politics. Working those grounds not only spurns the deadly arc of "gravity's rainbow," but insists on developing political responses that do not eat the young to make the future.

PART I
FLUID DYNAMICS

1. A Child's Day in Howa

Morning

An Errand. Almost every morning as the sun reached the horizon Ismail awoke, slipped into his flip-flops, and trundled off to the butcher shop to get meat for his family. On most days mutton or goat was available from at least one of the two butchers who worked in the village. Demand almost always exceeded supply, and unless it was one of the three or so days a month when a cow was slaughtered, Ismail needed to be early to get any meat at all.

Although located on different sides of Howa, neither butcher shop was more than a few minutes' walk from Ismail's house. It seemed that slight proximity and family preference combined to favor the butchery of Abdel Monim, and unless passersby advised otherwise, Ismail checked there for meat first. By the time he reached the wood-and-grass shed that served as the butcher shop, Ismail was likely to find a jostling crowd pressed up against its open side. He pushed through men waiting to be served and joined other children, who, having done the same, stood up front, arms out-stretched holding money and papers or empty food packages to receive the meat, shouting to Abdel Monim to attract his attention. The butcher chopped the carcass with a knife and an ax, weighing out portions on a balance using brass weights.

At ten years old, Ismail seemed fascinated with trucks, and often propelled him-self around the village as if he were one himself. After securing meat for his family, Ismail was likely to make the sound of an engine revving and charge back up the nar-row dirt road to the combination of mud and mud-brick walls, thorn branches, and buildings that defined the perimeter of the *hosh*, or houseyard, of his extended family. Most extended families in Howa were patrilocal, and the household of Ismail and his relatively small family of five was located within the hosh of his paternal grandfather.

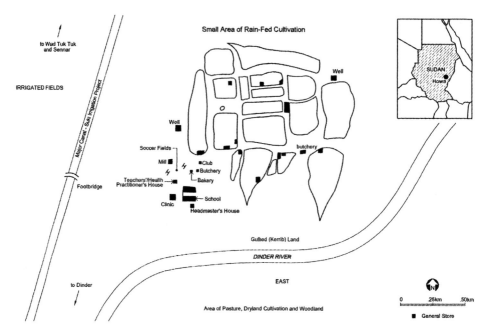

Figure 1. Sketch map of Howa Village, showing clusters of settlements separated by paths, main common structures, and surrounding features.

From the end of 1980 through most of 1981 I lived in this hosh—six months of the time with my then-partner, Mark—in a mud house that had been abandoned recently by a household moving to a newly constructed brick house. Each morning Ismail bought meat for us as well. We heard his "engine" above the sound of braying donkeys and bleating sheep a few moments before he peeped around the rag rug and thorn branches that served as a door to our grass enclosed "veranda." He gave me a handful of goat meat wrapped in the last pages of a *Time* magazine bought months ago. His pleasure was apparent as he unwrapped the paper and showed us a relatively unstringy and boneless quarter kilo.

Off to School. Sometimes Ismail stayed to have tea and cookies, but on this day he declined; having been long at the butcher shop he did not want to be late for school. He picked up the package of meat for his family and crossed the small yard between our houses. At home he found some sweet milky tea his older sister had prepared for him waiting on the embers of their charcoal stove. He gulped down the tea, slipped his blue ankle-length cotton *jallabiya* (caftan) over his coarser knee-length muslin one, grabbed his cloth book bag and raced back down the road to the village elementary school, where he was in second grade.

From the school yard one could see the butcher's shed, a few dry goods stores, and the mud oven of the bakery, which produced bread during only part of the year. A road formed between these mud-and-grass buildings and led out past the gristmill, through some acacia shrubs to the major canal of the Suki Agricultural Project and the agricultural fields lying on the other side of it. In June, by seven o'clock, when the teachers

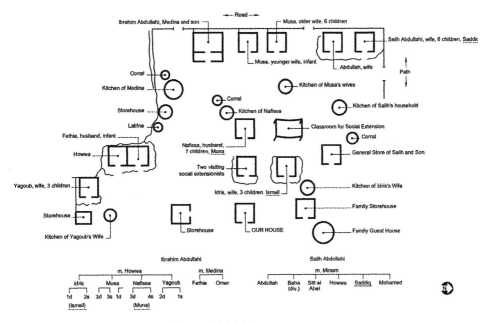

Figure 2. Houseyard (hosh) and kinship relations of Abdullahi family.

began to call the children to attention, most farmers were long gone, clearing their fields and cleaning the irrigation ditches along them in anticipation of the planting season, which began with the rains in late June or early July.

With the hottest months of April and May over and the first rains beginning, the summer solstice brought about a time of renewal during good years in Howa. In a few days school would close, in part to allow the teachers to return to their home districts during the rainy months from July through September, and in part to free students to help their families with the agricultural tasks of this busy season. In the coming weeks, for example, Ismail and most other children nine to twelve years old would spend their mornings in the fields planting groundnuts, sorghum, and cotton in rows drilled by the digging sticks of their fathers and older brothers.

Herding. The ground was still parched, however, and even after a few rains there was only a hint of new green vegetation. June was an especially difficult time for the animal population of Howa. Even dry vegetation of minimal quality was sparse by this time of year, and shepherds had to go out with their flocks from dawn until dusk so that an adequate diet could be maintained. The long days of grazing notwithstanding, milk production had all but stopped and several animals in the village had died of starvation-related causes.

Ismail's eleven-year-old cousin, Saddiq, was the shepherd for his family's flock of approximately fifty goats and sheep.[1] In these weeks of extreme heat, when daily maximum temperatures averaged over 40° Celsius (104°F) (Ferguson n.d., 20), Saddiq's parents often saw to it that he did not herd all day, but rather was relieved for part of the time by his slightly older, but less reliable, brother, Mohamed.

One day when I went shepherding with Saddiq, Mohamed came along. We set off at six-thirty in the morning. Saddiq made Mohamed guide the animals over the footbridge spanning the major canal of the irrigation project bounding the settlement. With a series of special clicking and yelping noises, Saddiq then led the animals to drink briefly from a small canal south of the bridge before continuing southwest to a depression he had heard was green because a broken irrigation ditch had flooded the area. The depression or *maya* was indeed green, and Saddiq and Mohamed let the animals graze, joining two friends who had met them along the way to play *shedduck,* a game in which players hop holding one leg behind them, madly attempting to knock down their opponents while remaining standing themselves. The boys played several rounds along with some other active games and then sat in the as-yet unplanted fields talking. Finally they rounded up the animals and led them to an area of *Acacia seyal.* Because of the dearth of green vegetation, Saddiq and the other herdboys scaled some trees and, with axes brought along for this purpose, lopped off branches for fodder, clicking and calling to the animals as they did.

By nine o'clock the sun was high in the sky and the boys were ready for breakfast. One of them brought out an old enamel bowl, another had a wad of sorghum porridge. Saddiq ran from sheep to goat to sheep squeezing a bit of milk from each one. With Mohamed holding the hind legs of the unwilling and rather dry animals, Saddiq

Figure 3. Shepherds not only were attentive to watering their flocks and ensuring that they circulated through various pastures (at once a means of maintaining grazing areas and diversifying their animals' diet) but also were sensitive to their overall look—making sure no animal was missing, watching their gait, and checking whether they showed any symptoms of distress. Here a shepherd removes a thorn from the foot of a sheep as they head out of the village along the major canal just after the rains had begun.

managed to get enough milk for the five herdboys then present. The boys added the porridge to the bowl of milk and gathered around it to eat in a bit of shade cast by one of the trees.

Breakfast for Ismail. At about the same time, the schoolchildren were dismissed for breakfast. They spread out quickly along the fan of dirt roads that extended from the school area. Ismail's fifteen-year-old sister, Selwa, had prepared a typical breakfast of sorghum porridge and a soup of reconstituted pulverized dried okra, spices, and water. Ismail and his seven-year-old brother, Ali, who had just started first grade, washed their hands to join their father for breakfast. They squatted around a common bowl to eat in the shade of their grass-covered veranda and followed their meal with hot sweet tea. Selwa and the children's mother ate their breakfast from a separate bowl. The two groups sat near one another and conversation flowed freely between them.

An Errand. Ismail was still drinking his tea when his mother asked him to go get three piasters'[2] worth of green coffee beans, enough for the several small cups of strong spicy coffee that she and her husband, like most adults in Howa, enjoyed after breakfast. He took the money from her and somewhat begrudgingly trudged off to the nearest dry goods store likely to be open. Along the way he stopped to watch some men building a mud house and became so absorbed that only after a few minutes did he remember the coffee and continue on his way. He bought the coffee beans and again stopped to watch the men at work. When some boys passed him on their way back to school, he set off quickly for his house. Screeching to a halt in front of his mother, he dropped the small newspaper cone of coffee beans, grabbed his book bag, and raced back down the road to school.

Domestic Chores. In his haste Ismail barely noticed his ten-year-old cousin, Muna, standing between their houses holding her infant brother. Muna, who envied Ismail for being in school, glared at him as he ran by. Muna was the daughter of Ismail's father's sister and the fourth of seven children. Her thirteen-year-old sister, Ajba, was the oldest girl in the family and shouldered most of the responsibility for helping the children's mother with domestic work, including cooking, child care, getting firewood, and fetching water. Because of Ajba, Muna was not directly responsible for many of the tasks undertaken by girls of her age in Howa. Despite her relative freedom, Muna's parents had not seen fit to send her to school, largely because they did not think school was important for girls and also because they seemed to feel it was not proper for girls to study side by side with boys.

Muna often helped out in the other households within the family compound. She assisted her grandmother and one of her aunts, whose three children were all under six years old, with domestic chores such as sweeping and dishwashing. In her own household, Muna ran errands for her parents, swept, and helped to take care of her two younger brothers, who were four years and eighteen months old. In recent months, as Ajba neared puberty and thus the beginning of restrictions on her mobility associated with *purdah* (the seclusion of women from public observation), Muna had begun to take greater responsibility for some of her sister's tasks in anticipation of the elder girl not leaving the houseyard unnecessarily and probably marrying. Muna helped her older sister and mother wash clothes, occasionally accompanied her grandmother to glean charcoal from abandoned kilns around the village, and was learning to fetch water from the village well, in part by bringing water to her grandmother in gallon-size containers.

Fetching Water. After Ismail passed on his way to school, Muna went to the well to fill a small, plastic jerry-can for her grandmother. Because Ajba had been largely responsible for this task, Muna was not as adept at fetching water as many of her peers. Some girls of ten years rode donkeys to fetch as much as ten gallons of water. With only minimal assistance, they lifted the full five-gallon jerry-cans, each weighing forty pounds, onto the wooden bar that crossed the saddle of their donkeys. Other girls this age were able to carry a full five-gallon vessel on their heads, but most were not yet strong enough. Most of these girls carried one- or two-gallon containers on their heads. Muna, however, was inexperienced and not yet able to balance even a small jerry-can on her head for the two hundred or so meters between the well and her house.

When Muna reached the well she was reticent to move forward into the throng of people that usually surrounded the water taps during the well's limited hours of operation. While Muna's hesitation may have been a result of her inexperience, it also may have been a considered response to the pushing and shoving that often occurred at the well. Others with considerable experience were timid when faced with the crowded water table.

Certainly it was a question of style rather than experience with ten-year-old Sofia, who went to the well frequently. Sofia was the oldest of five children and got water for her family everyday, sometimes several times a day. One day I accompanied her to the well just after it had opened and found it already crowded. Most of the crowd was made up of kids who pushed and shoved one another in an attempt to get water before anyone else. Sofia was quite timid compared with most of the children. She waited several minutes before going near the meter-high table with its four overhanging spigots. In the interim the jockeying and jostling intensified. After several more minutes, during which she frequently looked over with a mixture of bemused helplessness, exasperation, and loathing on her face, she made her move and climbed onto the concrete table that supported the pipe and spigots. On the edge of the wet table Sofia looked a lot smaller than most of the other kids. After another few minutes, she succeeded in getting her bucket under a spigot. When she removed it in order to rinse it out, someone grabbed her spot. With a bit more pushing her foothold became more tenuous. Her balance was thrown off further because she was hanging onto her bucket. With another shove in her direction, Sofia fell off the table and splash-landed sitting upright in the mud puddle that surrounded it. She seemed to have scraped her leg along the edge of the cement table as she fell, and she looked shocked, hurt, and sad when she landed. Sofia's older and tougher female cousin took her bucket and filled it as Sofia wrung her dress and stood crying at the end of the table. She took the full bucket from her cousin, gingerly put it on her head and, still looking a little defeated, walked off with a group of sympathetic friends.

Given this sort of scene, Muna's cautious approach to filling her jerry-can was well founded. She went up to the table during a lull in activity and pushed her plastic jug up to the faucet. She managed to hold her own until it was full, then slogged through the mud and ankle-high water around the well, holding the heavy jerry-can with her extended arm. Once on dry ground, Muna put the jug down, wiped her face with her wet hands, and headed up the slight incline toward home, holding the full container in both hands. Carrying things on the head was a task children learned by doing, and once Muna was up the hill and out of sight of the other girls she put the tightly closed one-gallon Mobil Oil container on her head and attempted to balance it as she walked. She wobbled while walking and more than once had to steady the jug with her hand, but she seemed proud that it never fell, wearing her aching neck around like a badge of glory.

An Errand. After pouring the water in her grandmother's clay water container, Muna ran the short distance back to her house. Her mother was in their thatched round kitchen-house preparing the afternoon meal on the same fire she had used for the morning porridge. When she heard Muna, she called her to come in the kitchen. It took a few seconds for Muna's eyes to adjust from the bright sunlight to the kitchen, which was lit only by the fire and a few small windows in the thatch. As she stood in the doorway her mother gave her two piasters and asked her to buy some garlic to season the okra-based stew. Muna took the money with little enthusiasm and a touch of pique at being asked to do another chore. As she headed across the houseyard to the metal gate next to her grandfather's one-room mud-brick house, her mother called her back. Muna found her digging a few piasters out of the old leather wallet she wore on a leather string around her neck. She handed Muna four more piasters and told her to get a package of cookies as well. This time Muna sang and walked with an occasional skip down to the shops near the schoolyard. When she returned, she took one of the cookies and, without being asked, gave the remaining ones to her younger sister and two younger brothers.

Domestic Chores. Muna found the wooden mortar and heavy metal pestle and began to pound several cloves of garlic to add to the gumbo. Keeping an eye on her youngest brother, she squatted in the shade in front of the house and pounded deftly and swiftly until the garlic was a smooth paste. She gave it to her mother who had finished making the day's *kisra* (sorghum pancakes) and was beginning to fry onions for the gumbo.

Midday

Play. Muna picked up her eighteen-month-old brother and walked over to the adjoining yard of her great uncle—Saddiq's father—to seek out his daughter, nine-year-old Howwa. The two girls, fast friends, spent some time hanging out and talking in the shade of Howwa's family's veranda. After a while they began to gather bits of material, found objects, and homemade straw dolls to play "house." Just as they began to demarcate a place for their play, a teenaged relative of the girls came over holding her baby and told them that her father—Muna's grandfather—wanted help shelling groundnuts to be planted in the coming weeks. In one move the girls dropped their things, Muna picked up her brother, and they sped across the yard to join in the nut shelling.

Shelling Groundnuts. In the two months preceding the planting period, each of the 250 or so local tenants of the state-sponsored agricultural project needed to shell several sacks of the previous year's groundnut crop for seed. Every household accomplished this task with the assistance of child labor. Most children were paid for shelling groundnuts, even within their own extended families. There was no difficulty in finding ready hands for the task because everyone seemed eager for a little pocket money.

When Muna and Howwa reached the house, they found about ten of their cousins and neighbors already at work in the shaded veranda. Muna's grandfather handed them a large bowl brimming with unshelled groundnuts and each girl took another bowl for the shelled nuts. They found a couple of spots on the earthen floor and sat down. Muna plunked her brother down next to her and gave him a handful of shelled nuts to eat. The girls worked quickly, talking, singing, laughing, and eating as the unshelled nuts disappeared, the bowls of shelled nuts filled, and the husks scattered over all exposed surfaces. After a couple of hours, her brother having long since wandered home on his own steam, Muna brought her bowl to her grandfather, who was seated in his vinyl-strung chair at the back of the small veranda. He used a small tea glass to measure the shelled nuts. The going rate was a half-piaster per five-ounce tea glass, and in two hours, Muna had earned three piasters. She immediately went to buy one piaster's worth of candy and then gave the other two piasters to her mother.

Relaxing. Muna returned to her house in the heat of the day and found her mother and three of her aunts sitting in the veranda drinking coffee, talking, and tossing cowrie shells. The women of Howa often passed the time telling fortunes and exchanging information, gossip, and advice based on their interpretations of the patterns made by six cowrie shells tossed in turn by each participant. Certain women were considered expert interpreters and fortune tellers, and it was usually their presence (and their shells) that sparked a session. Muna sat quietly near the women and listened to them talking as she absentmindedly ate a handful of sugar given to her by her mother as she sweetened the coffee.

While the women talked, Muna's father napped on the other side of the veranda. He had spent the morning clearing their tenancy in preparation for planting. When he stirred, the women began to leave and Muna's mother prepared to serve the midday meal.

Dinner. In Howa, men, women, and young children ate separately. With his oldest son studying typing in the town of Sennar, approximately forty kilometers away, and his next oldest son attending junior high school in Dinder, the district capital, about twenty-five kilometers away, Muna's father ate alone. Although Muna sometimes ate with her mother, grandmother, and sister, Ajba, she usually ate with her three younger siblings. Before eating, she helped the two youngest wash their hands and had a minor squabble with her six-year-old sister when she questioned Muna's authority on such matters. The children squatted on the ground to eat from a tray of neatly folded sorghum pancakes and a bowl of gumbo. The three older children pulled off pieces of the pancakes with their right hands and dipped them into the hot gumbo. Muna helped her youngest brother by dipping small pieces of pancake into the stew and putting them into his right hand to eat by himself once they had cooled. Every few days when the family had meat, each child got one or two small chunks of it, and quarrels sometimes erupted over who got more.

Domestic Chores. After the black sugary tea that followed dinner, Muna picked up the short straw broom and, beginning in the back by the wall of the house, swept the whole veranda clean. She picked up the sweepings with an old metal sheet and, because most of it was organic, tossed it to their donkey, who ate most any scraps.

Play. The intense heat of midday precluded strenuous activity. After taking their main meal most adults napped, visited, or took care of more sedentary chores, such as mending, rope making, mat making, and accounting. Almost everyday during this quiet time, ten-year-old Rashid, who had just begun third grade, led his mostly male and slightly younger friends in one of three dramatic-modeling play activities. The content of each game is suggested by its name: *dukan* (store), *hawashaat* (tenancy), and *bildat* (subsistence fields). These games involved the children in elaborate enactments in miniature of the behaviors and tasks associated with each of these settings.

One day I found Rashid in his family's houseyard sitting under a shade tree, just putting the finishing touches on a toy tractor he had made with the help of his fourteen-year-old brother, Adam, who was home on vacation from junior high school. It had been Rashid's idea to build the tractor, and he had completed most of the work on it himself. When I arrived he was pushing it back and forth while Adam made a plow to attach to it.

The tractor, which measured about eleven by eighteen centimeters and just over eleven centimeters high, was a good example of the ingenious motor vehicles fashioned by children in Howa from things that would be considered junk to the untrained eye. The chassis was a piece of wood bridged by two strips of metal that arched across it one-third of the way from each end. The tires were circles cut from the soles of old plastic thongs and turned on axles of thin metal rods. Its headlights were made from the circular nubs that rivet the straps of flip-flops into their soles. The final touch was a plow fashioned from a thin sheet of rusted metal that was attached to the rear of the tractor.

Once the plow was attached, Rashid and two male friends about nine years old, along with two boys about four years old, began to play hawashaat (tenancies). They rolled the tractor to the shady area in front of the men's sitting house and began to play by modeling the dirt into raised squares about twenty-five by forty centimeters. These raised plots were their agricultural fields, and each boy plowed his field with the tractor, occasionally using his fingers to form ridges when the finicky plow became too much of a bother. After the rows were completed they made *teganet,* the impoundment ridges that run across groups of furrows and control the flow of water from the irrigation ditches to the crops. When the ridges were in place, the boys planted groundnuts by

Figure 4. In almost daily games of "hawashaat" and "bildat," Rashid and his friends worked through the agricultural sequence of irrigated agricultural and rain-fed subsistence cultivation, respectively. Playing out the discrete work activities of cultivating various crops, the games also embraced the political-economic and social arrangements associated with the two forms of agriculture.

sticking date pits they had collected and saved for this purpose vertically into the plowed rows. Although sometimes they used limited quantities of real water, on this occasion they "watered" the crop by sprinkling sand on it. The boys were aware of the method of irrigation in the real fields, and seemed to enact this knowledge by watering only in the furrows between the rows, as if the water had flowed there from the canals.

When they finished irrigating, the boys began to weed the fields using miniature short-handled hoes that closely resembled those used in the working fields. Each boy made his own hoe from a short piece of thick straw and a small piece of thin metal broken into the customary wedge shape. When the weeding was completed, the boys harvested the groundnuts by piling the date pits in the center of the field. During the harvest in Howa, the whole groundnut plant is pulled and piled similarly in the center of each field. The children used tomato paste cans as sacks and filled them with the harvested date pits. They loaded the sacks onto the tractor and carted them several meters to the shade tree that was their storehouse.

They repeated this complete agricultural cycle, and then in the third round grew cotton as well, which they represented, perhaps not accidentally, with goat dung. After the cotton harvest Rashid went to each boy's field, counting and weighing the crop in the tomato paste cans. He paid the boys shards of "china money" according to the size of their yields. While the going rate for a sack of groundnuts mirrored the market price during the preceding season, the children's price for a sack of cotton was considerably less than the actual price. This confusion may have been rooted in the obscurity of cotton prices for adults in Howa as well. Tenants did not sell their cotton on the open market as they did their groundnuts. Not only did they not receive direct payment for their product, but they were paid by the Suki Project authorities only after all agricultural, service, and marketing expenses had been deducted. It was difficult for most tenants to determine the precise rate at which they were paid, and it follows that cotton prices may have been less accessible to children as well.

The quiet hot hours of early afternoon were almost all spent by these boys playing several rounds of "tenancies," or a variation called bildat (rain-fed subsistence fields) in which they reenacted the dryland cultivation of sorghum and sesame that characterized the village before the Suki Project. The boys also played another dramatic-modeling game called "store," where they spent those shards of china on everyday commodities represented by found objects, like bits of metal and glass, battery tops, and scraps of packages. While the village rested, these children carried on its work at a miniature scale—playing with their possible adult roles—using the debris they found around them.

Late Afternoon

Fetching Water for Sale. As the day became cooler, the village began to burst with activity and by four o'clock people were up and about as if it were morning all over again. Since diesel fuel was expensive and not easy to come by, the village well was generally

Figure 5. In playing "dukan" (store), Miriam and other children enacted a riot of consumption that in its intensity far exceeded existing commercial patterns in Howa but certainly anticipated what was to come. "Found objects" (otherwise known as garbage) made up the merchandise, and shards of broken crockery, "china money" (sometimes earned playing "tenancies" and crossing over to games of "store") provided the medium of exchange.

open only a couple of hours in the morning and again in the late afternoon. I often knew that it was time to resume working outdoors when I heard the first child coming up the road hawking water. About fifteen boys and girls between ten and fifteen years old sold water regularly in Howa. Many of these young people had donkeys of their own for this purpose, while others relied on the availability of their families' animals.

In a typical morning or afternoon a youngster selling water made at least one trip for his or her own family and returned to the well four to eight more times to fill a pair of five-gallon jerry-cans and hawk them in the village. Each pair sold for the equivalent of about twelve cents, and children generally contributed their earnings to their households. Indeed, Talal, who was a regular water seller in Howa and the oldest child in his family, had withdrawn from school midyear in part to provide this income for his family and in part to work with his father in the fields and at other tasks.

Making Charcoal. The hour before sunset was also a time when people, young and old, went to collect or cut firewood. Ten-year-old Sami, the middle child of three and the oldest boy in his household, went in search of firewood almost daily in the late afternoon with his elderly but quite energetic father and his thirteen-year-old sister. Sami's father was not a tenant and earned an extremely modest living primarily from the sale of charcoal he produced, lumber he cut, and vegetables he cultivated on the riverbank during the rainy season, supplemented with earnings from his occasional agricultural labor during the season. Until the rains soaked the ground and the Dinder

Figure 6. About 10 percent of boys and girls in the village supplemented their households' income through the sale of water. Drawing water from the wells, the river, and even the irrigation canal, young people like Talal hawked their ten-gallon loads for about a penny a gallon to households that either were too busy or were without child labor to provide their own.

River again flowed, Sami's father produced charcoal almost biweekly from an earth-mound kiln he fashioned beside his house. Each day, in the early morning or late after-noon and sometimes both, he and his children crossed the dry riverbed in search of wood suitable for charcoal production. Because the wood supply around Howa had diminished in recent years, most such wood—which only a few years before would have been considered too small—was at least a half hour's walk away.

On a typical day, Sami's father took along Sami, his daughter, Maha, and a nephew about Sami's age. Any number of little ones might tag along, and on one of the days I accompanied them, two boys and a girl less than six years old joined the procession. From the family's round grass house we followed a deep gully to the riverbed. We main-tained a swift pace as we trooped across the sandy river bottom and up its steep east-ern bank. On the other side, we headed further east through a large and still bare depression that, once the rains came was an area of sorghum cultivation for a neigh-boring village, until we came upon a stand of *Acacia seyal.*

Sami's father immediately began chopping down a relatively large tree. Within a few minutes Sami took his cousin's ax and began to chop down an acacia, about seven centimeters in diameter, designated by his father. Although far from being as deft, fast, and strong as his father, Sami made good progress cutting down the tree and was clearly familiar with the work. Before Sami was done chopping, his father sent him, Maha, and their cousin to a nearby area to collect wood they had chopped on a previous day.

After about ten minutes the children returned, loaded with wood. When they did so, Sami's father, who had continued to cut down trees and branches, was ready to head back to the village. They would have left with Sami's half-chopped tree to be finished another day, except that I asked if I could see him finish. He accomplished this swiftly, and then they all left, leaving the newly cut tree to be collected at another time.

On the trip home each of them was loaded to capacity with wood. The girls carried the wood on their heads, while Sami's father and the boys carried their loads on their shoulders and backs. The children bore their heavy loads without complaint for the half-hour walk home. Even the youngest girl, who was no more than four years, carried her large load with grace and assuredness. At home, they added their wood to the pile.

After about seven days of this back and forth, there was enough wood to make a charcoal mound. Sami and Maha participated in this part of the task as well. The children helped their father to pile the wood tepee-style around a mound of dirt and dried grass. After building a large cone of wood, Sami and Maha helped their father cover it with a thick layer of straw. While their father raked up straw near the kiln, the children went further afield to gather handfuls of straw fallen from the grass walls, fences, and roofs near their house. Once the wood was completely covered, their father shoveled a layer of dirt over the whole pile. The children rarely assisted with this part of the task. From a small opening in the dirt at the base of the mound, which by then was at least waist high, Sami's father ignited the grass with a hot coal. Once the straw began to burn, he raked some dirt over the opening and left the wood to smolder for two to three days. The earthen kiln was checked throughout this period to ensure that it continued to burn and that no flames erupted through breaks in the dirt. When the wood was completely carbonized, Sami's father spread it outward with a rake and covered it completely with dirt to stop it from burning further. After the charcoal cooled for a day or so, the children helped their father pile it into large burlap sacks. The sacks were sold within or outside the village for the equivalent of between US$2.50 and $3.75 apiece.

Most families in Howa could not afford to use much charcoal, and relied almost exclusively on wood for cooking. The labor of children was integral to procuring a sufficient wood supply for most households. Nine-year-old Awatif, the youngest child in a household with three other daughters twelve to sixteen years old and a son of thirteen, generally collected firewood with her friends a couple of times each week. Awatif was one of the few girls in Howa who attended school, and therefore could only collect wood in the late afternoon and on days off from school.[3]

Play. Much of the time, Awatif's twelve-year-old sister, who did much more household work than she did, collected the fuelwood supply. Thanks to her sister's work, Awatif was often free to play dolls and "house" with her friends. On many days when I visited in the late afternoon, I found these girls playing with dolls in the dramatic-modeling game of "house."

One day I found Awatif and two friends playing along the wall of the veranda with dolls they had made of two sturdy pieces of straw crossed so that the horizontal piece served as the arms, and the vertical piece the head to toe. Each doll had a name

and was dressed in scraps of fabric. The dolls were male and female and of all ages. The girls manipulated them in and around houses that they established with dividers made of shoes, mortars, pestles, bricks, and pieces of tin cans. They used all manner of found objects for props, including an enamel cup, a knife fashioned out of a tin can, shards of glass and crockery, can lids, battery tops, small bottles, grass, razor-blade wrappers, a soap carton, a hollowed-out D battery, empty food tins, dirt, charcoal bits, and cardboard.

Awatif and her friends used these props to play out a range of domestic activities. As I watched, one girl had her doll prepare sorghum pancakes and stew by spreading dirt on a can top, then breaking up pieces of grass and leaves and putting them in a shard of glass. In the course of the afternoon the dolls cooked, cleaned, ate, went to the well, ran errands, and visited. The girls clearly enjoyed this game, in which they experimented with both their present tasks and potential adult roles. They played "house," or a per-mutation of it without dolls, at least four times a week. They stored all their treasures carefully in boxes and added new found objects as they came upon them.

As I walked home from Awatif's house, I passed by the schoolyard where the teachers, the village medical practitioner, and several other young men were playing soccer. Nearby, and inspired by their example, several boys between nine and four-teen years old played soccer using a wad of socks and rags as their ball. During the relative cool of the hour before darkness, the streets of Howa usually filled with reg-ular "sock soccer" games. Most boys ten and older participated at least occasionally in these localized games.

Evening

The sun was setting as I made my way home, but since it was almost a full moon, night merged with day rather than snuffing it out. The full moon is a special time in villages without electricity, and all of Howa seemed to be up and moving around in the moonlight. Whenever possible, people celebrated weddings and circumcisions during the full or waxing moon. Even without a special occasion, children danced, sang, and played well into the evening bathed in the moon's bright light. On one of these nights we stood quietly outside our house and heard makeshift jerry-can drums played by girls and boys throughout the village. After several glasses of tea we took a walk and came upon about ten boys in the street singing loudly and accompanying themselves by drumming on a jerry-can and clapping. Elsewhere, we found about fifteen girls in a household compound singing, drumming, and taking turns dancing. I danced one long song with Sofia and a friend of hers. It was fun and felt almost magical to establish the old and familiar communion of dancing with the children.

A Child's Day in Larger Perspective

The acquisition and use of environmental knowledge are key aspects of children's socialization. These practices are particularly important in agricultural settings, where environmental knowledge is basic to the productive use of resources and where children's labor figures centrally. Enduring production pivots on the social acquisition of such knowledge as a critical aspect of social reproduction. Political-economic and political-ecologic change of the sort affecting Howa after its incorporation in the Suki Agricultural Project can disrupt these material social practices, as well as the social relations that bind production and reproduction. Acquired knowledge may no longer be apposite, bodies of knowledge may be altered and recomposed more intensely than usual, modes of sharing knowledge may be displaced, and sources of knowledge may be discredited.

This book examines the production and exchange of environmental knowledge in Howa following its inclusion in a state-sponsored agricultural development project geared to production for the world market, and the play of these material social practices over a number of years as the children who are its protagonists and focus came of age. The content, acquisition, and use of environmental knowledge are addressed as mutable cultural forms and practices, structured and shared within a particular socioeconomic matrix and inseparable from the labor process and its underlying relations of production. My aim was to discover and illuminate not only the nature and structure of these cultural forms and practices and their imbrication with political-economic and environmental changes in Howa, but also their meanings for children and their families. By locating this study in a rapidly changing society, I hoped to develop a more dynamic understanding of the relationship between a particular material social practice—the production and exchange of knowledge—and the evolution of the relations and processes of social reproduction. My underlying concern was with resistance and persistence in everyday life.

This project has been long in the making and my initial approach to it grew out of the social theories of Marxism and feminism, and my frustration with the way most Marxist work at the time either subsumed social reproduction to production or imagined it solely as a function of the state, and thus failed to theorize or interrogate it adequately (see Dalla Costa 1972 for a notable and compelling exception). With the obvious exception of the work associated with feminist theory, as well as with the Birmingham Centre for Critical Cultural Analysis and the Social History Workshop, the critical practices of everyday life—wherein social relations were enacted, maintained, and altered—were either invisible, assumed to be unproblematic, or presented in a functionalist manner in most analyses of social life or the operations of political economy.[4] The concern with social reproduction among those scholars who did address it was commonly intertwined with a search for resistance, as was the case for me. But as interest in resistance blossomed in various quarters, its definition became increasingly amorphous and the measure of its effect ever more slight. The attenuation of resistance was compounded by the ascendance of poststructuralism during the 1980s and 1990s as many authors appeared to suggest that the material grounds of production no longer mattered. Yet in the critical practices of everyday life—among other aspects of social reproduction—the conditions of production are ensured. If the terrain of their possibility is profoundly material, so, too, are their operations and effects. One of my aims, then, is not only to examine the workings of one aspect of social reproduction closely, but in the process to problematize the very notion of resistance, defining it more rigorously and differentiating its various forms analytically and practically. This project is taken up in chapter 9.

As suggested in the preface, social reproduction encompasses that broad range of practices and social relations that maintain and reproduce particular relations of production along with the material social grounds on which they take place. Social reproduction has political-economic, cultural, and environmental aspects, each of which bears on the geographies of children's everyday lives. The political-economic aspect of social reproduction encompasses, for example, the reproduction of work knowledge and skills, the practices that maintain and reinforce class and other categories of difference, and the learning that inculcates what Pierre Bourdieu refers to as the habitus, a set of cultural forms and practices that works to reinforce and naturalize the dominant social relations of production and reproduction (Bourdieu 1977; Bourdieu and Passeron 1977). If the political-economic aspect of social reproduction takes place in some combination of the household, the market, the workplace, "civil society," and the state, the relationship and balance among settings varies across time, space, class, and nation, among other things. The gender division of labor within the household, which is itself historically and geographically contingent, commonly presumes women's responsibility for most of the work of reproduction, including, for instance, child rearing, food collection and preparation, cleaning, laundering, and other tasks of "homemaking." With wealth and "development," an increasing number of these tasks may be provided through the market and purchased, depending on household circumstances and other socioeconomic factors. Prepared foods, domestic assistance, child-care services, and the like may lessen household work for some and "free" some women's time for participation in the paid labor force or other activities, but they do not alter the gender division of labor or the social relations of production and reproduction that undergird and are sustained by it. Likewise, the state has historically played a role in social reproduction. From state-subsidized electrification, water supplies, and sewage treatment, to schools and health-care services, as well as a variety of goods and services associated with the welfare state, the state has long been implicated in social reproduction. The varying role of the state across history and geography also affects the balance among the various constituencies in how social reproduction gets carried out. While in some instances, certain aspects of social reproduction, such as child care or meals, are provided through the workplace or through organizations associated with "civil society," it remains that women, almost everywhere, fill whatever gaps are left in ensuring their households' reproduction and well-being.

In Howa most of the work associated with the political-economic aspect of social reproduction was accomplished within the household or the extended family. Seeds of change were evident, however. For instance, the role of formal schooling increased dramatically during the course of my study, decentering the household as a source of work-related knowledge. Less dramatic, but quite significant, the social extension program associated with the agricultural project introduced a nursery school, encouraged formal schooling, and sponsored a women's literacy class, among other activities that began to shift some of the weight of social reproduction from the household to the state.

There is a blurred boundary between these practices that I have associated with the political-economic aspect of social reproduction, and those associated with its cultural aspect. Here I include the cultural forms and practices associated with knowledge acquisition broadly understood, not just in relation to work or the workplace. Also included is the learning associated with becoming a member of particular social groups. All people are, of course, members of multiple and overlapping social groups, and social reproduction entails acquiring and assimilating the shared knowledge, values, and practices of the groups to which one belongs by birth or choice. Through these material social practices, social actors become members of a culture and construct their identities. In these activities, young people (and others) are both objects and agents, acquiring cultural knowledge and reworking it through the practices—intentional and otherwise— of their everyday lives. Here again, household forms and their fluid gendered and generational divisions of labor have as much bearing on how cultural reproduction is enacted as on its contours and what it is socially understood to encompass. These relations are both the "medium and the message" of social reproduction, and thus their particular form is of important political-economic and sociocultural consequence.

Other arenas of social reproduction that are primarily cultural include that broad category of cultural production categorized as "the media," "mass culture," and those institutions associated with religious affiliation and practice. "Culture" is made within these broad arenas, and in this interchange, the social relations of production and reproduction that characterize a particular social formation at a given historical moment and geographical location are encountered, reproduced, altered, and resisted. For instance, the spiritual practices associated with Islam, especially those of Sufism, were of particular significance in Howa. Islamic practice was so much a part of everyday life that children appeared to absorb it by osmosis—virtually all adults prayed five times a day, there was no alcohol available in Howa, not even the homemade beer that was widely available in many similar villages, Sufi paths and the sheikhs associated with them were a common topic of conversation, and people routinely visited religious sheikhs in and outside of the village for counsel and treatment of all manner of problems. Children played at praying, climbed rubble heaps or whatever height they could muster to bellow the call to prayer, sang ballads about religious heroes and leaders as readily as they sang popular songs, and were often entranced by the exchanges among their elders and various religious sheikhs. Important as these practices associated with the cultural realm of social reproduction were, I paid much less attention to them than to the material practices associated with work. Ironically, or perhaps not, the cultural practices associated with religion may have proven a more fruitful arena in the search for resistance than the ones I pursued, especially as Howa grappled with the differences between the familiar Sufi paths and the more rigid version of Islam propounded by the state beginning in the mid-1980s.

Finally, apart from these cultural arenas, there are the material grounds of reproduction—its environmental aspect. All modes of production produce and are enabled by particular political ecologies. This fact is so obvious that it often goes unremarked, but the environmental toll of centuries of capitalist production, and its increasingly global nature, has been enormous. The widespread and serious environmental problems that are symptomatic of capitalist relations of production have received plenty of public attention, but not necessarily as problems of social reproduction (although see O'Connor 1994). In Howa, these issues of political ecology could be seen quite directly in the landscape produced by the agricultural project, which, among other things, required chemical inputs and reduced available grazing and wooded areas, all of which compromised ongoing production. Environmental degradation—in this case part and parcel of "development"—undermines sustained productivity. In Howa there was a particular and direct toll of degradation upon children, who frequently worked in the fields. The health of children in Howa was compromised by their exposure to pesticides that were sprayed in the fields without warning while they and others were working; by their direct contact with herbicides that often covered the "weeds" they picked as greens for a family meal; and by their vulnerability to schistosomiasis from wading into the irrigation canals where young boys swam and girls and boys fetched water on days when the village well was closed.

In the course of "development" the relationship between production and social reproduction is thrown open and reconfigured. Along the way, the material social practices and cultural forms associated with social reproduction are altered. So, too, is the balance among settings where social reproduction takes place. These processes are contested and uneven, but looking closely at them should render clearer what is at stake in contemporary "development." Refracting the social development of the children through the "development" imposed on their community, and vice versa, reveals the promise and perils of the "recent future." The recent future, a time-space of becoming and imma-nence, is produced in the routine practices of everyday life, such as children's work and play, as much as by larger social and political-economic forces, such as those associated with global capitalism. I try to keep both in tension in this work because it seems to me that if we are ever to begin to undo the operations of capitalism, global and otherwise, we will have to understand how it roosts in the routine, and how it does not.

The focus of my project is children's work, play, and learning, and the content and organization of their knowledge about the physical environment, including knowledge of agriculture, animal husbandry, botanical and animal resources, land use practices, and environmental degradation. I emphasize that body of knowledge concerned most directly with sustained productive use of the local environment. Environmental knowl-edge is not only fundamental to enduring production in Howa, but with the shift from the largely subsistence dryland cultivation of sorghum and sesame to the irrigated cul-tivation of cotton and groundnuts for the world market brought about by inclusion in the Suki Project, it had became a fulcrum of struggle. Not only was the traditional sub-stance of environmental knowledge threatened with obsolescence or erasure, but the means of its acquisition started to butt up against and jostle with other forms of learn-ing. The ensuing shifts and struggles altered children's daily lives as producers in their community and their prospects as adults. I hope to render specific the abstract forms and practices associated with the production and exchange of knowledge and tie them to the particular historical, geographical, and socioeconomic conditions of Howa vil-lage as a means of both grounding my analysis of the social, cultural-ecologic, and political-economic change underway there and providing a framework to clarify the meaning and significance of everyday practices amid such transformations.

The heterogeneity and vitality of cultural forms and practices point to the inde-terminate nature of social transformation. If capitalism roosts in the routine, so do the possibilities for its disruption; the chance for diversion speckles well-worn paths. These may come from any quarter. The elaborate and embedded nature of the children's everyday practices, only hinted at in the first part of this chapter, makes clear that the outcomes of externally imposed socioeconomic change are not determined, however powerful they may be, but rather are forged in the dynamic and often contradictory juncture of social, cultural, political, and economic practices composing production and social reproduction.

Capitalism is often depicted as a deluge that sweeps away and drowns all that comes before it. Yet it is, of course, more complicated than that. As Stephen Jay Gould (1982) pointed out years ago, Darwin was drawn to study earthworms because their mundane and incremental actions transform the world. As I began to see in this study, capitalism works more like Darwin's worms than a deluge. But it doesn't have the earth to itself. Peo-ple encounter, oppose, and absorb the transformative effects of capitalism in the course of producing their identities, doing their work, playing, imagining themselves, constructing alliances, and carrying out their everyday lives. The incremental dislocations, reinventions, and removals inherent in such daily routines reveal—and create—a world of difference.

2. The Political Economy and Ecology of Howa Village

It would appear that some inducement would be needed to divert these people from their traditional subsistence economy.

—Sir M. MacDonald and Partners, *Roseires Soil Survey, Report 9*

Howa before the Suki Project

The village of Howa was established in the late nineteenth century on the ephemeral Dinder River, which provided a year-round source of water either from subsurface wells or the stream in flow. The village is approximately twenty-five kilometers from the nearest market town, Dinder or al-Gueisi, which also serves as an administrative center for the district. Forty kilometers west is Sennar, a market and provincial administrative center on the Blue Nile in central eastern Sudan. Howa was established by pastoralists (predominantly Kawahla, Hamada, Sherifa) about twelve years before the Mahdiya, a brief period of Islamist independence in Sudan ushered in by the victory of Muhammad Ahmad al-Mahdi over the Turco-Egyptian forces led by Charles Gordon in 1885 and ending with the Anglo-Egyptian "reconquest" in 1898 that established the so-called Anglo-Egyptian Condominium.

From the time of its settlement, Howa's economy was rooted in agriculture and animal husbandry. Most men in Howa cultivated sorghum on a largely subsistence basis, supplementing it with sesame they sold to passing traders or pressed into oil and marketed to meet their limited needs for cash. As Howa's pastoralist beginnings might suggest, livestock was important to the subsistence and, whenever possible, the savings of the newly sedentarized farmers. According to local residents and historical accounts of the region, most families kept at least a few goats and sheep for milk and occasional

Figure 8. Map of Sudan. From "Fueling War: A Political Ecology of Deforestation in Sudan," in *Producing Nature and Poverty in Africa*, ed. V. Broch-Due and R. A. Schroeder (Nordiska Afrikainstitutet and Transaction Press, 2000): 321–39. Reprinted courtesy of Nordiska Afrikainstitutet.

meat, and many households kept flocks of ten to fifty small animals as well as a small number of cattle, and even a camel or two (see Tothill 1948; Gelal el Din 1970; Ahmad 1974; O'Brien 1978; Gruenbaum 1979; Duffield 1981). Many families maintained close ties with relatives who remained exclusively pastoralist, not only having their herds travel with them for part of the year, but renewing and maintaining familial relations through the occasional intermarriage between villagers and their contemporaries still leading a life of pastoral nomadism. Indeed, the dry season grazing routes of at least three pastoral groups transected the area around Howa. In contrast to many agricultural villages in northern Sudan, especially those along the Niles, ties to pastoral populations were both more common and more economically significant in Howa than ties to labor migrants, even as late as the mid-1980s (see Bernal 1991).

Prior to 1971 when the Suki Agricultural Project was established, the area around Howa was characterized by *bildat* agriculture, the rain-fed cultivation of sorghum and sesame on small, often scattered, plots around the village (see Tothill 1948; MacDonald et al. 1964; Lebon 1965; Gelal el Din 1970; O'Brien 1978). Some villagers also had small *jeref* (riverbank) gardens that they cultivated along the ephemeral Dinder River as its waters receded in the latter months of the year. Jeref cultivators grew vegetables for household consumption and for sale. Agriculture was routinely complemented by animal husbandry and forestry on a modest scale.

Villagers reported that in Howa land was historically held in common. Local administrative sheikhs were responsible for allocating parcels from this land to residents for cultivation. Cultivated land remained in the hands of individual farmers as long as it was worked, and individual plots might stay in a family for generations. According to local farmers, the land around Howa had been adequate for them to cultivate enough sorghum and sesame for their annual consumption and cash needs until the time when the system was disrupted by the founding of the Suki Project (cf. Bernal 1988). They indicated that as new households were formed[1] young male farmers were allocated fallow land from village or family holdings. As Howa grew, these plots were often further afield, but few were at distances beyond an hour's walk from the settlement, and those acquired from the customary holdings of the young farmers' extended families were generally closer. These fields often were cultivated for upward of fifteen years with no appreciable declines in fertility. By some accounts, soils were productive for twenty-five to thirty years of continuous cultivation[2] (MacDonald et al. 1964). Soil fertility was maintained largely through crop rotation and having livestock graze on crop residues. As soils did become exhausted, however, farmers cleared new or fallowed areas and left their former fields fallow for several years. When these fields were brought back into cultivation, they were cleared by burning after the first rains (see Tothill 1948; Gelal el Din 1970). Not only did the burning provide substantial organic matter to the soil, but it cleaned it of weeds and forestalled the possibility of weed infestation substantially.

Prior to the Suki Project, the local environment sustained a combination of agriculture, forestry, and animal husbandry. Cultivation took place on individual allocations from the common lands, while forestry and animal husbandry were accomplished largely within common and fallowed lands near the village. Under the socioeconomic conditions that prevailed through the first two-thirds of the twentieth century, production was determined and constrained more by the physical and economic limits of available labor and other resources than by external political-economic relations, such as those associated with the Suki Project, which not only circumscribed the land available for cultivation but determined who had access to it and under what conditions. Access to land had been by customary right, with distance, elevation, and soil type most crucial in determining the gradations between individual holdings. Most farmers cultivated at least two plots in different areas around the village to mitigate losses in case of crop destruction by pests, disease, flooding, or water shortage. The total land cultivated by most village farmers ranged between two and ten *feddans* (approximately two to ten acres, or one to four hectares).

Under the system of mixed land use that prevailed prior to the Suki Project, many areas around Howa were forested. Trees and bushes were interspersed with fields and fallowed areas. In our conversations, most farmers indicated that during this time it was easy to cut firewood after working in the fields. Women and children also gathered and cut wood from areas just a short walk from the village. By all accounts, a wide variety of tree species existed in the area during this period and were used for a range of purposes. In the initial land and soil survey for the Suki Project, for instance, Hunting Technical Services (MacDonald et al. 1964) had reported "thick" woodlands along the Dinder. Likewise, Barbour (1961, 193–94) notes that although certain areas in the vicinity were allotted for charcoal burning, no use was made of them. He remarks that the *Acacia arabica* (*sunt*) along local watercourses, including the Dinder River, went uncut despite their attracting so many birds that cultivation in the immediate vicinity was largely abandoned. Nearly a decade later, Gelal el Din (1970) found natural regeneration in the region adequate to enable residents to fell wood for various purposes from areas within a day's walk of their villages. Yet, within ten years of the Suki Project's encroachments on the area, one stately tamarind tree—part landmark, part source of pride, but nevertheless coppiced heavily—was just about the only tree that stood along the Dinder in Howa, and before long it, too, was gone.

Until the mid-1960s most of the houses in Howa were round thatched roof *tukls* or *gutiyas* constructed of tall grasses, stalks, and wood poles. Construction materials were procured easily from local fields and forests. When people built the square, flat-roofed, mud-and-dung houses that predominated in Howa by the 1970s, the wood

Figure 9. Within a few years of the Suki Project's founding, the banks of the Dinder River near Howa were stripped of all but the largest trees, themselves coppiced heavily. Just twenty years earlier, geographer Kenneth Barbour (1961) described the banks as so thick with acacias that cultivation was frustrated because of the number of birds they attracted. By 1995 not even the much revered tamarind, the last of the large trees, remained.

necessary for beams, rafters, and building posts was available in nearby forests and along the river. The tall, sturdy center posts in most village houses were *doleib* (*Borassus aethiopicum*) or sunt (*Acacia arabica*), trees that by all accounts were abundant in the vicinity of the village, particularly along the river.

Several species that grew in the area were used for fodder and a few provided fruit treasured by the local population for their own consumption. Most important were *nubg* from *Ziziphus spinachristi*, *lalob* from *Balanites aegypiaca*, and doleib fruit. While these fruits were not a critical component of the diet, they were a favored source of variety from the usual fare, and in times of duress could be used as a famine food source (see Ferguson n.d.; Tothill 1948). Various cosmetic, medicinal, and household products were also collected from nearby forests by the local population. These goods, which included roots, seeds, bark, wood, and fruit, were readily available around Howa until the clearings for the 36,000-hectare Suki Project began during the late 1960s. Without these formerly wooded areas and the fallowing associated with the earlier land-use system, the remaining forests decreased rapidly. Deforestation was exacerbated by the increased demand provoked by a growing population (brought about in part by the resettlements associated with the Suki Project), and a rising need for cash that was often met by the sale of wood or wood products.

Trade and commerce were fairly limited in Howa prior to the agricultural project. The manifestations of mercantile capitalism prior to the twentieth century were little felt in the rural areas of the Blue Nile region of Sudan. While during the Funj Sultanate (1504–1820) and the Ottoman *Turkiya* (1820–81), the surrounding areas were encompassed in trading and tributary networks that included animals, grain, and slaves in which pastoralist forebears were likely to have been encompassed, there were few settlements in the area between the Blue Nile and Dinder Rivers during these periods, and Howa itself was not established until the 1870s, as Ottoman rule was coming to an end. Unlike areas to the south, where the slave trade was more active, other parts of Sudan, where gold and other valuable ores were mined, or the Nile Valley with its access to communication, the economy of this area was disrupted only minimally, if at all, in the initial period of contact between what became Sudan and the centers of trade and empire in Western Asia, the Arabian Peninsula, and Europe. This situation was not altered dramatically during the Anglo-Egyptian Condominium, and seems to have persisted with Howa's subsistence agricultural economy through the early years after independence in 1956. Full monetization and more active economic exchange between Howa and the larger economy developed only gradually after 1956.

Within Howa the development of commerce was likewise minimal through the first couple of years after inclusion in the Suki Project. There was no grain mill, butcher stall, or bread bakery until the 1970s. Grain was ground at home by women and girls, the occasional butchered goat or sheep was shared in a *karama* among family and friends, and bread was not part of the diet; the staple was sorghum porridge or large paper-thin sorghum pancakes made daily by women over a three-stone fire. There were only one or two dry goods shops in the village, which were stocked with a narrow range of goods that, in the main, were produced regionally if not locally. Within ten years of Howa's inclusion in the Suki Project, the number of shops more than quintupled. They carried thongs from Hong Kong, tea from Tanzania, flashlights from China, and small tins of tomato paste from Bulgaria, as well as an array of nationally produced consumer goods from cigarettes and biscuits to kerosene and wash tubs. Until the advent of the Suki Project, which all but stopped the local cultivation of sesame, there was a camel-driven wooden oil press in the village that produced sesame oil largely for local consumption. With sesame gone after the project, the press met its demise. Within a couple of years, few households could afford sesame oil, instead using poor quality peanut oil pressed at factories in the region and elsewhere in Sudan.

When sesame was still cultivated in the village, truck-traders visited after the harvest and purchased the crop from individual farmers. They traveled on rough roads all but impassable during the rains. Virtually all transportation from the village to towns further than twenty-five kilometers away depended on these passing trucks, which were either traveling between market towns or visiting rural areas to purchase sesame seed and other agricultural products. Except for these passing trucks, most communication between Howa and Dinder Town (al-Gueisi)—the nearest commercial, service, and administrative center, twenty-five kilometers away—was by camel until the mid-1960s. Villagers told of riding the better part of a day a couple of times a year to sell livestock, stock up on provisions, and/or buy goods for a bridewealth. There was no motorized transportation serving the village directly until the first market lorry—an old Bedford—was purchased by a resident in the mid-1960s. The number of trucks owned and operated out of Howa has increased slowly but steadily since then.

Village infrastructure was similarly limited. Unlike many small villages in Sudan, Howa did not have a Quranic school operating on a regular basis. Some boys studied the Quran with local religious leaders and a few were sent to other villages for short periods to further their formal religious training. A secular primary school (grades one through six) funded by the national government was built around 1959 as part of a nationwide campaign for universal primary education, which was not yet achieved forty years later. This school was attended almost exclusively by boys, and only a minority of school-aged boys was enrolled, a situation that persisted until the 1980s.

The only other physical infrastructure that existed prior to the agricultural project was a diesel-powered artesian well constructed by the regional government in the mid-1960s. The well was constructed in response to a self-help initiative by the village, which paid for most of the construction costs out of the proceeds collected by adding a few piasters to the cost of each pound of sugar sold in the village cooperative. Before the well's construction, the only source of water in Howa was the ephemeral Dinder River. During the eight months of the year that the river is dry, water was drawn from shallow wells (*jemmam*) dug in its sandy bottom. The filtration through the sand of this subsurface water made for a relatively clean, if silty, water supply. Jemmam provided safer water than the river in flow, which, racing from the highlands of Ethiopia to the Blue Nile, was full of debris and massive quantities of silt. Jemmam water was also safer to procure. The river and its shallow wells remained crucial to Howa years after the well was built because the well was unreliable thanks to fuel shortages, the absence of spare parts, and the schedule of the part-time well operator.

The Suki Agricultural Project

Theoretical Shifts

For most of its first century, then, Howa was characterized by a mix of animal husbandry, rain-fed agriculture, and modest forestry. Its economy was largely subsistence-oriented and connections with the broader economy of Sudan were minimal. What cash was required—for taxes, to buy things like sugar, tea, clothing, tobacco, and for special events or crises—was earned largely through the sale of sesame and sesame oil, animals, and handicrafts. All this changed in 1971 when Howa was included in the state-sponsored Suki Agricultural Development Project. The project, which was funded multilaterally by Kuwait and Japan among others, was the first agricultural project of President Ja'afar al-Nimeiri's "May Revolution," which had come to power in 1969. The Suki Project provided an early opportunity for Nimeiri to demonstrate his commitment to agricultural development, though in its focus on cash crops, particularly cotton, the project was typical of the sort of agricultural development that had characterized Sudan since the colonial era and had in fact been in the works prior to Nimeiri's coming to power.

Small by Sudanese standards, the Suki Project embraced a nearly 1,600-square-kilometer swath of central eastern Sudan between the Blue Nile and the Dinder Rivers. Approximately 7,500 tenants were enlisted in the project to cultivate cotton and groundnuts on ten feddan (4.2 hectare) allotments. Their irrigated cultivation, geared to the export market, disrupted and largely displaced the dryland cultivation of the staple food crop, sorghum, and sesame produced for the domestic and international markets. The project also disturbed the pastoralism that had characterized the region. Seasonal grazing areas that abutted and ran through the area were typically marked as "uninhabited" in the land-use survey commissioned by those planning the Suki Project (see MacDonald et al. 1964). Although displaced pastoralists were offered tenancies, most refused. The Suki Project incorporated a number of existing villages in the area between the rivers and created a number of new villages to resettle western Sudanese brought in to assume tenancies when the pastoralists rejected them. The disruptions in the area's political ecology were substantial and ongoing.

Inclusion in the Suki Project also exacerbated trends toward monetization and capitalist means of organizing production that had been underway since the earliest years of the century. Howa's economy, for instance, was shifting from a subsistence orientation, characterized by the simple circulation of commodities (C-M-C), where commodities (C) are exchanged for money (M)—selling in order to buy—to one characterized by M-C-M, where money is transformed into commodities and then changed back into money—buying in order to sell. Money circulating in this manner is incipient capital. Used for purposes of exchange and not consumption as in the form

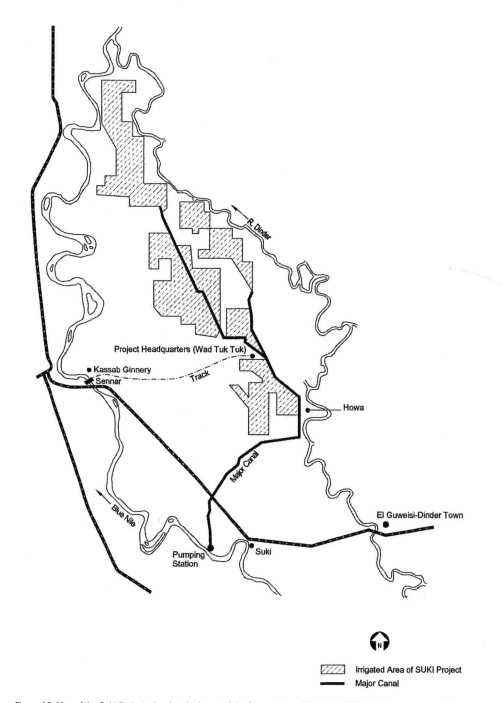

Figure 10. Map of the Suki Project, showing the layout of the four sectors of irrigated cultivation. Howa was near the southeastern terminus of the project close to the Dinder River.

C-M-C, money may be accumulated and eventually available for production, wherein its owner can secure particular means of production and purchase the labor power of others who lack access to these means of production (see Marx 1967, 1:146–55). Similar transformations have resulted historically in the dislocation of the household as the center of both production and social reproduction, in the redefinition of social relations within the household—notably gendered and generational divisions of labor—and eventually in the proletarianization of much of the population. Socioeconomic marginalization and differentiation are attendant upon these changes.

In more abstract terms, as capitalist relations of production confront an existing economy,[3] its general motion separates producers from their means of production and removes most productive activities from the household to central and specialized sites. In this process—which in Howa was most decisively propelled by inclusion in the Suki Project—things once produced in the household for members' use (what Marx called use-values) are produced increasingly for exchange. This shift, often referred to as commodification, increases the need for cash and often drives the proletarianization of independent producers. At the same time, the household is reformulated as a site of reproduction untethered spatially and formally from the process of production. In essence, the disruption of largely subsistence economies such as Howa's by the social relations and practices associated with capitalism is associated with three linked processes: the interruption of household production, commodification, and socioeconomic differentiation. These processes, in turn, are accompanied by fundamental changes in the social relations and cultural practices with which they are mutually constituted.

According to Marxist theory, the decisive moment in the capitalist penetration of an economy is when the unity between production and reproduction is disrupted. In every case, the monetization of certain components of the preexisting economy is central to its destruction. Although each case is historically specific, in "Notes on Capital and the Peasantry," Bernstein presents such familiar examples of this process as the imposition of taxes, the use of *corvee* labor by state and private capital, and the forced cultivation of certain cash crops (Bernstein 1982, 162). In Howa, the preexisting economy was undermined largely through the last of these when the village was included in the Suki Agricultural Project in 1971. After that time, the majority of households in Howa were required to cultivate the cash crops of cotton and groundnuts as part of the terms of their tenancies. This process reoriented the local economy from the production of use-values to the production of crops and eventually other commodities for exchange. The change led to the gradual and uneven substitution of commodities for goods that previously were produced by households for their own consumption or that had been commonly held or freely available. Citing Pierre-Philippe Rey and Claude Meillassoux, Bernstein indicates that "this process involves the erosion of an entire culture of production and the 'disqualification' of many traditional production skills particularly in non-agricultural activities" (162).

This erosion, the nature and meaning of the "disqualification" it engenders, and the forms of response to it—from the intertwined processes of deskilling and reskilling to the remaking of geographies that disable or enable certain kinds of work—are a central focus of my project. Neither the direction nor the pace of such transformations are determined. These changes are grounded in a particular historical and geographical context, and evolve in the relation between production and reproduction as material social practices. My project deals particularly with those aspects of this relation that are associated with the production, exchange, and use of environmental knowledge, and by extension with the dislocation or reformulation of the household as a center of production and reproduction.

Three aspects of this transformation are of particular relevance to my project and will be addressed throughout the work. The first, referred to above, is the decline in the ability to produce or procure household subsistence through historic or conventional means. This problem was becoming apparent in many Howa households within a decade of its inclusion in the Suki Project and was partially attributable to the sundering of production and reproduction in the household, which was fundamental to the project's advance. The dislocation of the household as a principal site wherein production and reproduction are joined, and the deterioration of households' ability to procure the means of existence through traditionally available channels, have a direct effect on the nature and allocation of household labor time, and therefore change the role of children as actors and objects in the material social practices associated with production and reproduction. Second, the shifts in household social relations associated with the transformation of Howa can be understood schematically as a renegotiation of the relationship between patriarchal relations of production and reproduction and those of an evolving rural capitalism. The particularities and reverberations of this unfolding affected children's everyday lives and prospects in obvious and unanticipated ways. Finally, the transformation underway in Howa, which was changing the role of children as it altered the nature and content of their socialization—including their acquisition and use of environmental knowledge and its associated skills—appeared to be leading to a disharmony between what children knew and the skills and knowledge that were likely to be useful in their adulthoods. This disharmony was not only of importance for the children themselves, but in the broadest sense, had serious implications for the stability of Sudan as a whole. These three themes—the dislocation of the household as the center of production and reproduction, the changes this dislocation engendered within the household and beyond, and the disharmony between what children learned and what they were likely to need to know as adults—propelled and undergirded my inquiry. Because these transformations were set entrain most decisively by the Suki Project, I want to spend the rest of this chapter looking at how the political-ecological and political-economic terrain of Howa were altered by the project.

New Political Ecologies

The Suki Agricultural Project altered the fortunes of Howa, literally changing the grounds of everyday life as it accelerated political-economic and cultural shifts that were already underway. With the project, the subsistence-oriented economy of the village was undermined; money increasingly began to define social life and local land-use patterns were transformed. This change was marked directly on the landscape when the major canal of the project (running northerly from the Blue Nile at Suki town, forty-four kilometers, to Wad Tuk Tuk near Howa) was dug and created a fixed boundary between the people in the village and their (newly created) fields.[4] Practically, incorporation in the Suki Project meant that almost all of the dryland fields and much of the pasture and wooded land in the vicinity of the village were cleared, graded, and divided for the irrigated cultivation of cotton and groundnuts for the world market. This change all but precluded cultivation of the staple food crop, sorghum, severely reduced wooded areas nearby, and sharply curtailed the grazing land available to the small herds of goats, sheep, and cows held by villagers. Independent cultivators became farm tenants, no longer producing grain for household consumption but cultivating cash crops for international exchange under conditions set by the Ministry of Agriculture through the management of the Suki Project.

As the project was established, 250 tenancies of approximately 4.2 hectares (10 feddans) were distributed to residents of Howa (mostly male household heads) for cultivation beginning in 1971. Until 1981, when tenants lobbied for the right to add sorghum to the rotation, each tenancy was divided in two: half cotton and half groundnuts planted in a system of 100 percent rotation each year. The Ministry of Agriculture, through the project administration, set the schedules, standards, and accounting criteria for the project. It determined what crops would be grown and which cultivation practices and tools were appropriate. The Suki Project pioneered the use of an individual account system that effectively put all the economic risk on the tenant with few prospects for gain. With this system, all of the expenses associated with an individual tenancy, e.g., for seed, fertilizers, herbicides, pesticides, water, and mechanized plowing, were deducted automatically from the tenant's gross receipts from cotton. In other agricultural projects in Sudan, the receipts and expenses were historically calculated for the whole project or project subdivision, with each tenant getting an even share of the net receipts (see Barnett 1977; Bernal 1991).

The "individual account system" resonates with moves toward "Post-Fordism" or flexible specialization taking place in industrialized countries at the same time. Project administrators argued that the system would provide greater incentives for each tenant. However, it proved to be so difficult to derive any income at all from cotton that few tenants produced at a level where incentives might have come into play. In any case, some years tenants were not paid even what little they were owed by the project, and poorer tenants were forced to borrow money just to acquire the supplies necessary to begin the next season (see Hummaida 1977, who reports tenant distrust of the Suki management after it failed to pay farmers following the 1973, 1974, and 1975 seasons). Likewise, even though the labor demands of the harvest were high, and most tenants relied on hired assistance, they had difficulty paying the field workers without advances from the Suki Agricultural Corporation, which were often slow in coming. The empty-handed project manager's response was to encourage the use of family labor power (Y. Mahmoud 1977).

The project largely supplanted sorghum cultivation. In theory, tenant earnings were to have been sufficient to allow for the purchase of foodstuffs grown more efficiently elsewhere in Sudan (notably the rapidly expanding mechanized grain-growing areas to the northeast). In practice, tenant income was frequently inadequate for that purpose, particularly in the face of often drastic increases in sorghum prices after 1971. Not only had the vulnerability of each farm family increased in the absence of their traditional grain stores, but Sudan as a whole began to experience food deficits in the 1980s, despite its productive capacity and the dramatic expansion of mechanized sorghum cultivation in eastern Sudan. These periods of food insecurity, and even famine, did not stop the politically powerful mechanized farmers from exporting their harvests to Saudi Arabia and the Gulf States, often as camel fodder. Their unseemly business decisions, unfettered by any government restriction, contributed to increasing food insecurity and fueled domestic price increases for sorghum.

During the 1970s, for instance, the price of sorghum rose from the equivalent of US$2.50 per sack (about 95 kilograms) to as high as US$50.00 per sack. The average household used upward of twenty sacks of sorghum each year, so this increase was an assault on household budgets across Sudan. The price increase was particularly difficult for the former subsistence cultivators of Howa, because their burden was double-edged; not only were they forced to purchase sorghum at prices inflated by as much as 2,000 percent, but they were frustrated that they were no longer able to grow sorghum, the surplus of which they might have sold at these astronomical prices.

Because of the difficulties and frustrations presented by the price increases, the Suki Farm Tenants Union agitated for, and in 1981 received, permission to cultivate sorghum in their tenancies at their own discretion. The twist was that they were only allowed to do so on one hectare of the portion of their fields allocated to groundnuts. Although groundnut prices were quite high that year, most tenants opted to replace half of their crop with sorghum as soon as it was permitted by the Ministry of Agriculture beginning in the 1981–82 season. Their eagerness testifies to the difficulties most tenant households faced in procuring subsistence under the conditions of production associated with the Suki Agricultural Project, even in years when their cash crops fetched lucrative prices. Many tenants, however, frustrated with the difficulties of cultivating cotton and the lack of earnings from it, wanted to change the Suki crop rotation to include wheat and possibly other food crops in addition to the sorghum and groundnuts, and if necessary, cotton. They were not successful in these efforts.

If, in the first few years of the project, most tenants were able to garner an income from cotton, few were able to do so by the close of its first decade in 1981. The reasons for this are threefold. First, the adjusted world price of cotton had declined since the project's first year of operation in 1971. Second, the price paid to tenants was established each year by the government marketing board below world-market rates. Third, all expenses associated with the tenancy, including those for groundnuts, were

Table 1. Economics of Cotton Cultivation, Suki Agricultural Project, 1980/81

Average income from cotton production	
Average price per qantar = $38.70	
Average yield = 2.156 qantar/feddan	
Average total output on 5 feddans = 10.78 qantars	
Average total gross income = $417.19	

Costs of production	
Per feddan	
Land and water for cotton	$20.00
Land and water for groundnuts	15.00
Pesticide spraying	48.71
Urea	26.02
Marking materials	2.61
Sacks for cotton	1.41
Total (Deducted per feddan of cotton cultivated)	$113.75
Total deductions on 5 feddans	$568.75
Total deductions excluding cost of groundnut cultivation	$493.75
Per qantar	
Sacks for seeds	$ 1.02
Ginning	7.98
Transport to ginning	.98
Interest on loans	3.13
Social services and auditing fees	1.79
Herbicide, extension services, rat protection, cotton classification, guarding, and employee bonuses	1.55
Total (Deducted per qantar of cotton produced)	$16.45
Total costs on average yield (10.78 qantars)	$177.33

Total income	
Average total costs (producing 10.78 qantars of cotton on 5 feddans) = $746.08	
Average net income/(loss): $746.08 deducted from $417.19 = ($328.89)	
Average net income/(loss), excluding costs of groundnut cultivation = ($252.33)	

Note: All amounts given in U.S. dollars, 1981 exchange rates. 1 feddan = 1.038 acres. 1 qantar = 100 pounds of ginned or 315 pounds of unginned cotton. All costs of groundnut production are deducted from cotton accounts.

Source: Figures from the Offices of the Suki Agricultural Corporation in Wad Tuk Tuk given to the author by the assistant director of the project, Abdel Rahman Mohamed Abdel Rahman. Price figures from the *Official Prices Paid by the Cotton Public Corporation,* obtained from its offices in Khartoum, Sudan.

deducted from the cotton account and these had risen as cotton prices had remained stagnant. By 1981 production expenses were so high that a tenant had to produce 5.11 qantars of cotton per feddan (547 kilograms ginned cotton per hectare) simply to break even (see Table 1). The average yield across the Suki Project was less than half that. The exploitation concealed in these figures becomes clear with reference to the original feasibility study for the project, conducted by Hunting Technical Services in the early 1960s, which estimated yields of 4.5 qantars per feddan *under good conditions* (MacDonald et al. 1964, 92). Conditions had not been "good." From 1971–81 the average yield exceeded 4.5 qantars only twice. The figures in Table 2 make clear the difficulty tenants faced in earning income from cotton. Even under the well-funded and intensively supervised colonial administration of the Gezira Project, the average cotton yield between 1912 and 1946 was 3.78 qantars per feddan, and only exceeded 5 qantars per feddan in three of these thirty-five years (Tothill 1948, 786). The Suki tenants were impoverished by the very premises of the "development" project in which they were enmeshed.

Reflecting on these economic relationships, many tenants volunteered that they put relatively little effort into their cotton crop in comparison to their groundnuts. Few tenants expressed concern, for instance, if they learned that their cotton field was damaged or destroyed by grazing animals, crop pests, or irrigation problems. The contrast with the level of attention, effort, and concern for groundnut cultivation was marked. Likewise, many spent time growing sorghum on the margins of the agricultural project or in their old bildat fields when these had not been incorporated in project lands (Hummaida 1977). For these reasons, among others, cotton yields in the Suki Project declined steadily from a high of 6.65 qantars per feddan in the 1976–77 season to an all-time low of 2.156 in 1980–81 (see Table 2). Subsequent years have been similarly dismal. Throughout Sudan, however, cotton yields have declined since the 1970s because of lowered world prices, a lack of supplies and spare parts, the increased costs of inputs following oil shocks, labor shortages, acts of neglect, and infrastructural difficulties. In contrast, there was no decrease in the average yield of groundnuts in the Suki area between 1971 and 1981 (see Table 3).

One factor contributing to low crop yields in the Suki Project was the production schedule established for cultivating cotton and groundnuts. The timetables for sowing, weeding, and harvesting both crops were virtually identical. The overlap had been predicated on groundnut cultivation being highly mechanized. However, almost since the project's inception, breakdowns of machinery worsened by a severe lack of spare parts thwarted the mechanization of groundnut cultivation. Moreover, most farmers could not easily afford or were reluctant to pay the fees charged for using available equipment; they preferred to do the work themselves with the assistance of household members or hired day laborers.

The failure to mechanize groundnut farming, along with the increased attention given to the crop by tenants who stood to make substantial private gains from its sale, drained attention from the cotton crop. This imbalance was likely to be further exacerbated in years when the world price for groundnuts was inflated. Such was the case,

Table 2. Cotton Cultivation in the Suki Agricultural Project, 1971/72–1980/81

	1971/72	1972/73	1973/74	1974/75	1975/76	1976/77	1977/78	1978/79	1979/80	1980/81
Total number of tenants	7,345	7,174	7,268	7,523	7,847	7,782	7,771	8,000	7,700	—
Total number of active tenants	7,345	7,143	7,232	7,434	7,689	7,702	6,346	6,228	7,700	—
Total number of productive tenants	5,942	6,703	6,691	6,935	7,366	7,702	6,345	6,228	6,226	—
Total area (in feddans)	36,730	35,870	36,340	37,615	39,237	38,910	38,855	40,000	38,500	—
Prepared area (in feddans)	36,730	35,715	36,160	37,170	38,443	38,510	38,800	37,842	38,500	33,930
Harvested area (in feddans)	29,712	33,515	33,455	34,675	36,831	38,510	31,730	31,140	31,130	27,670
Acreage yield (qantars/feddans)	2.9	3.5	4.1	3.78	4.01	6.65	6.02	4.01	2.63	2.156

Source: Records of the Suki Agricultural Corporation in Wad Tuk Tuk, Sudan.

Table 3. Groundnut Cultivation in the Suki Agricultural Project, 1971/72–1980/81

	1971/72	1972/73	1973/74	1974/75	1975/76	1976/77	1977/78	1978/79	1979/80	1980/81
Total number of tenants	6,193	7,177	7,325	5,723	7,413	5,707	5,887	7,374	6,311	—
Total number of active tenants	3,940	4,776	3,265	4,391	4,702	4,414	4,633	5,046	5,964	—
Total area (in feddans)	34,565	35,885	36,626	28,615	37,065	28,536	23,167	36,870	31,555	29,580
Total productive area (in feddans)	19,700	23,730	16,325	21,955	23,510	22,070	29,435	25,230	29,820	15,093
Average yield (100 pound sacks/feddan)	4.13	6	6.03	10	24	26.5	25	26	30	24

Source: Records of the Suki Agricultural Corporation in Wad Tuk Tuk, Sudan.

for example, in 1980 and 1981, when the price of groundnuts had risen fivefold from US$2.50 to $12.50 a sack. This high price, combined with depressed cotton prices and the general deterioration of project equipment and infrastructure, helps to explain the steady decline in cotton yields and the relative stability of groundnut yields across the Suki Project from 1976 to 1981, when despite its lucrativeness, groundnut cultivation was sacrificed for sorghum.

Regardless of productivity levels, the labor requirements for both cotton and groundnut cultivation were significant. As many tenants pointedly noted, they were substantially higher than those associated with the dryland cultivation of sorghum and sesame. Most tenants relied on a mix of labor from family members and hired hands. With almost all tenants being men, the increased labor demands of cultivating in the Suki Project conscripted wives', children's, and other relatives' labor time so that tenant households could stay afloat. My research suggested that the Suki Project drew children from school to the fields more intensely than farming before the project had. While access to land and other productive resources in Howa was mediated by men's participation in various social networks—however changed these networks might be as a result of the Suki Project—their access to labor was individualized, and the project was predicated on tenants mobilizing household and family labor (see Berry 1993, 17). Indeed, preference was given to larger families when tenancies were first allocated, and during labor crunches, when the project management was unable to advance tenants money to pay hired hands, they explicitly encouraged the conscription of family labor (Hummaida 1977; Y. Mahmoud 1977).

The major agricultural tasks were clearing, planting, thinning, weeding, irrigating, and harvesting. The agricultural season began in late May with clearing the fields. Crops were sown in June and early July and from then until November there was almost constant work as the plants were thinned, weeded, and irrigated. The groundnut harvest began in early November, and about six weeks later cotton was ready to be picked. By the end of January the bulk of the year's agricultural work was finished. Tenants who had not yet marketed their crops generally did so in February. Following the agricultural season was a time for celebration. Marriages and circumcisions were commonly celebrated in Howa during March and April because both time and money were relatively plentiful.

Rarely did a tenant finish an agricultural task without the assistance of household members. Their efforts were supplemented in some instances by communal work parties (*nefir*) or hired laborers. While wealthier tenants could afford to hire either day laborers from the village or seasonal laborers from elsewhere in Sudan (usually the south or far west), most tenants kept hired labor to a minimum, and relied instead on family members, except during the height of the labor-intensive harvest period, when work was accomplished almost entirely by village women and children, especially girls, working for hire or in the fields of their own households.

For the average tenant, then, most agricultural tasks were completed by family members. Fields were generally cleared by the tenant, sometimes with the help of teenaged sons or other adult male relatives. During the planting period, children between eight and thirteen years old provided most of the assistance to their fathers (and occasionally grandfathers or uncles without their own children to assist them). Thinning, weeding, and irrigating were completed by tenants themselves, often with the help of adult male relatives and sometimes with communal work parties or hired labor. Of these tasks, weeding was the most labor-intensive, and young boys frequently assisted their fathers and uncles. The communal work parties (*nefir*), which had long been a mainstay of Sudanese agricultural life, had become labor exchanges by the time of the Suki Project. A group of men (often relatives) would work for one tenant or another in exchange for a return of the favor and possibly a meal. In this way, people pooled their resources during labor-demanding periods apart from the harvest. Since the harvest was accomplished largely by local women and girls or migrant laborers, and women's earnings were considered separate from household (and by extension tenancy) earnings, their labor did not exchange in the same way that male tenants' did.

The harvest was the most labor-demanding period of the agricultural year. In many tenant households, the whole family worked from dawn until sunset, breaking only during the hottest part of the day. Some families even built temporary shelters (*cambo*) near their fields to maximize their labor time. In the nearby Rahad Project, estimates were that one laborer was necessary to pick each feddan of cotton (Jansen and Koch 1982). Yet, as Jansen and Koch note, after the establishment of the Rahad Project in 1978, the number of agricultural laborers who turned up was hardly more than half of what was required in any given year. Such localized labor shortages have been common in many parts of rural Africa, and are exacerbated as more people leave the country- side in search of more permanent or lucrative employment (cf. Berry 1993). Likewise in Howa, where, according to Jansen and Koch's figures, the equivalent of about 1,250 cotton pickers would be required each season. Nowhere near that number of migrant workers was available, and the harvest was routinely accomplished by local women and girls working intensively from tenancy to tenancy.

Traditional agriculture had not given way completely to the irrigation project in Howa, although the total time and space devoted to it was small compared with irri- gated cultivation. With most of the arable land surrounding the village incorporated into the project, little land was available for rain-fed cultivation. Some people still man- aged to have bildat (dryland fields) where they grew sorghum and occasionally millet. When the cultivation of sorghum was permitted in the irrigated fields in 1981, the area devoted to rain-fed sorghum cultivation was reduced further, although there is evi- dence that this made room for the renewed cultivation of sesame, albeit on an extremely limited scale. Others grew a few vegetables, either in *juruf* on the riverbanks or along the margins of their irrigated fields. Given the steepness of the Dinder's banks, just one or two old-timers attempted to cultivate horticultural crops there. A few more grew vegetables and sweet sorghum (*Sorghum spp. graminae*) in the margins of their tenancies or (surprisingly rarely) in kitchen gardens, where loofa gourds often sprawled exuberantly in the rainy season. Most of these crops were for household consumption.

Figure 11. Wild okra grew in the interstices and along the margins of the project fields. Picking the thorny crop was rough going and was frequently left to children, like Ismail, armed only with a rag to dampen the spikes' effects.

Figure 12. Wild okra was routinely sliced into disks and left to dry in the sun. The quickly desiccated slices were then pounded into a fibrous powder that thickened the daily stew. Using wedges of tin cans, sharpened into cutting blades, and a log as a cutting board, these girls chop the daily harvest in the midst of the routine activities of their houseyard.

Any surpluses were hawked by children in the village. *Weka,* a wild variety of thick-skinned okra that grew in both dryland and irrigated fields around the village, was a dietary staple in Howa. The sticky, thorny pods were picked primarily by women and children, and then cut and sun dried for daily household consumption and for sale in regional markets. Weka, like beans, was considered a women's crop, and was sold at their discretion. Women were entitled to the full proceeds from these sales and were under no obligation to share their earnings with their husbands or households. Sesame was rarely grown in the vicinity of Howa after the Suki Project. However, young men from the village frequently traveled to sesame growing areas further south to work as field hands during the harvest.

New Political Economics

The political-economic changes associated with the project had direct effects—of exclusion as much as inclusion—on nearly every household in Howa. Two hundred and fifty tenancies of approximately ten acres each were allocated to residents of Howa in 1971. When I conducted a village-wide survey ten years later, 225 of the 324 households responding indicated that they held tenancies. Of these 225 households, which represented just over two-thirds of the village, 16 held more than one tenancy. While some of the approximately 99 nontenant households had declined or were disqualified from participation in the project at its outset, most were households that had formed since 1971. As the village continued to grow (local growth rates were approximately 3 percent a year), an increasing percentage of its population lacked access to productive land and were compelled to seek work outside the village or as laborers or sharecroppers in the tenancies of others. This is, of course, a common and even expected feature of agricultural development projects, as is a certain measure of intensification. However, given the hobbled nature of Sudan's economy since the project was established in 1971, off-farm employment possibilities have not only failed to materialize and grow, but have disintegrated as people from all over Sudan have left the countryside in search of earnings.

While socioeconomic differentiation in Howa had its origins well before the establishment of the Suki Project, the project sharpened existing differences and brought forth new ones, first by instantiating and controlling access to the new key means of production—farm tenancies—and then by distributing a fixed number of tenancies within the village. These conditions were made worse by the project administration's failure to develop other integrated economic activities in the area, despite initial plans to establish an oil and soap factory and later a dairy, and by a shortage of capital among villagers to promulgate such developments themselves.

Nevertheless, nothing so neat as proletarianization was taking place. Young disenfranchised men worked in their fathers' fields, picked up work as day laborers both in the fields and in nearby towns (mostly loading and unloading trucks), dabbled in petty trade, and started to look further afield for more permanent work options. They did not leave the village in droves, as I had imagined they might, but straddled multiple worlds of production and possibility in order to get by. With a fixed number of tenancies allocated to Howa and over half the village population under fifteen years old, the number of men turning to nonagricultural employment both near the village and further afield was sure to grow as those born after the project was established came of age. These demographic shifts, among other changes, were sure to heighten the contradictions between production and reproduction in Howa.

In 1981 most of those employed as nonagricultural workers were employed in the workshops and offices of the project headquarters in Wad Tuk Tuk, only a few kilometers from Howa. These wage laborers were generally young men who worked as mechanics, drivers, messengers, guards, and clerks. They commuted to their jobs each day on market trucks heading to Sennar or other points. Their wages ranged from levels equivalent with the going daily rate for agricultural labor (between US$1.25 and $1.90 per day) to twice that for skilled jobs, such as drivers, mechanics, or clerks.

This nearby labor market was pretty much saturated within the first decade of the project. As the availability of nonagricultural jobs in Wad Tuk Tuk decreased, some young men began to seek work in the regional centers of Sennar, Dinder, and Suki. Some of these men found work as casual laborers doing unskilled jobs, such as loading trucks or assisting construction crews. A few of them found permanent work in factories, workshops, service establishments, and offices. Most of these young men were single and stayed with friends and relatives in the towns. The remittances they sent to their families were a relatively new phenomenon in Howa. Only about 5 percent of the households in the village reported earnings from a member working in an urban area. A very small number of young landless men from Howa began to venture to urban areas as far away as Khartoum in search of work in the industrial and service sectors. Many of these men were poorly prepared for city life and unqualified for most of the few jobs available. Their migrations often did little to help their families back in Howa, who relied on their earnings. Equally problematic, their presence in the cities contributed to the serious infrastructural and employment problems in Sudan's burgeoning urban areas.

While the agricultural project marked a watershed of sorts in the social history of Howa, it would be a mistake to infer that economic life in Howa was focused narrowly around farming. Survival would have been impossible if this were so. Indeed the multiplicity of economic activities in which the local population of all ages engaged, coupled with the contempt shared by so many of them for cotton cultivation, suggests that a perspective viewing villagers simply as farm tenants would not only miss important distinctions of gender, age, and class, but would present a deracinated portrait of everyday life in Howa.[5] Victoria Bernal (1991) makes much the same point in her study of Wad al Abbas, a village on the Blue Nile about thirty miles from Howa. Within the matrix of economic activities and the webs of connections between them, however, it was important to make some distinctions in order to assess both the process of socioeconomic differentiation underway in Howa and what impact, if any, parental occupation had on the children's activities that were my immediate concern and focus.

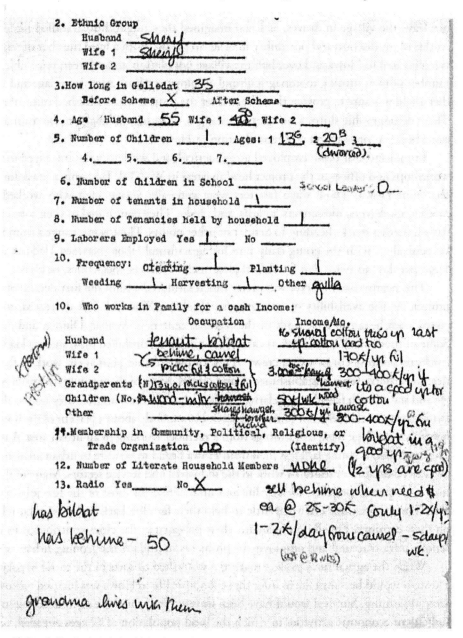

Figure 13. Proud of having included multiple wives and grandparents in my household survey forms, I quickly stumbled on having provided only one line to encompass their multiple and seasonally varied occupations.

I identified four socioeconomic/occupational groups in Howa on the basis of my 1981 household survey. Each of these groups, which are rough conglomerations at best, was defined by a distinct relationship to the means of production. For obvious reasons, one of the axes of difference between groups was membership in the project. Slightly over two-thirds of the households in Howa were tenant farmers when the survey was completed. As the village continued to grow, the percentage of tenant households

dwindled proportionately. While agriculture was a central productive activity for tenant households, most of them engaged in numerous other economic activities, sometimes at the expense of their agricultural responsibilities, but usually as a complement
to them, both seasonally and on a shorter-term basis.

The nature of these complementary activities was the basis for dividing tenant
households into two groups: those whose household heads engaged in wage labor
and/or the petty production and trade of commodities, such as fuel, food, crafts, and
animals (53 percent of village households); and those who had accumulated sufficient
capital to engage in trade, invest in production, or lend money on a regular basis (16
percent). While this distinction between supplementary economic activities was often
more like a fuzzy continuum than a sharp division, tenant-merchant households usually had investments in things like trucks, shops, storehouses, substanial livestock holdings and more recently, in productive activities such as the new brickworks in Howa.
The male heads of such households did not engage in wage labor or participate in the
self-employment activities listed above, but other members of their households, including wives, commonly did. The elderly matriarch of one of the wealthiest and most powerful families in the village, for instance, spent several mornings during the hottest part
of the year gleaning charcoal bits from spent "kilns" around the periphery of the village. After several days, assisted by her grandchildren, she accumulated enough charcoal to fill a sack to sell for the equivalent of about US$3.00. Likewise, the junior wife
of this family grew *lubia* (white beans) and weka (dried okra), which she sold to provide herself with independent means. Their husband worked in his fields and supervised the family's commercial interests, including part ownership of a truck, but he left
most of the physical labor to his youngest son, still a teenager.

Bolstered by the record prices received for groundnuts following the 1980 harvest,
most tenant-merchant households appeared to be accumulating capital steadily during my initial stay in Howa. As was common in many parts of Sudan (see Ali and
O'Brien n.d.; Barnett 1977; Bernal 1991; F. Mahmoud 1984; and O'Brien 1978), several
tenant-merchants seemed to be profitably involved in extending credit and lending
money to poorer tenants and nontenants in the village through the illegal practice of
crop-mortgaging (*shayl*), as well as through other means.[6]

Nontenants composed almost one-third of the households in Howa by 1981. I
divided nontenants into two groups as well, distinguishing between those who earned
their money as merchants or full-time laborers (11 percent of village households), and
those who worked occasionally as wage laborers or who were petty commodity producers (20 percent). The latter characterized most nontenant households, wherein the
means of existence were secured by the labor of members as agricultural wage workers,
small-scale traders, and petty commodity producers. However, a growing minority of
nontenants were employed full-time—at all levels of skill—in the village, at the project headquarters, or elsewhere, including nearby towns. Most of these wage laborers
were men who worked for the Suki Project in the fields as tractor drivers, overseers, or
guards, or in its workshops and offices six miles away. A very small number were

employed full-time in the village, at the clinic, the school, the grain mill, or the bakery. A few of the nontenants were merchants who participated in the same range of commercial enterprises as the tenant-merchants. The distinction between these two groups of nontenants—"merchant/full-time laborer" and "occasional wage laborer/petty commodity producer"—though somewhat unwieldy and artificial given the multifold nature of their economic activities, parallels the distinction made between tenants.[7]

The process of socioeconomic differentiation was still in its early stages during the early 1980s, and there was tremendous fluidity over time and contemporaneously in the socioeconomic distribution of households. Most notably, because the number of tenancies allocated to the village was fixed, the proportion of nontenant households was growing as new households were formed faster than older tenants retired. According to my census, over 52 percent of nontenant households in Howa were formed since the village was included in the project ten years prior. Nontenant households on the whole were either younger or older than average. Several of the older households lacked tenancies because they had passed theirs on to newly married sons. The growing number of nontenants in Howa and the nature of the response to land disenfranchisement in general suggest that the pace of proletarianization was increasing there and would continue to do so. But alongside and interstitial with this process was the tendency of residents to engage in multiple economic activities straddling not only diverse aspects of the agricultural economy, but urban activities as well. This sociospatial and sectoral straddling became an increasingly prominent and critical means of survival in the years that followed.

As suggested above, such multiple engagements were not new to local residents, who were long-time "jugglers." Their very multiplicity was evidence of the contemporaneous fluidity between occupational categories as well. The political-ecologic and socioeconomic changes underway in Howa all but required a multiplicity of livelihood strategies for tenants and nontenants alike. Each person was likely to engage in a number of income-producing activities that varied individually, daily, seasonally, and as particular circumstances arose. Individual flexibility and agility, along with great porosity in the boundaries between economic activities, were hallmarks of the local political economy for everyone, no matter what their gender, age, class, or so-called "primary" occupation. Children grew up learning to negotiate and be accomplished in the multiple political-economic and political-ecologic terrains that composed their everyday environment.

No matter how adept the local population was in working through the political-economic circumstances in which they found themselves, the level of household earnings in Howa remained low for most. According to the responses to my 1981 survey, I estimated the average annual per capita income in Howa to be approximately US$285.[8] Given an average household size of just over five members, the mean household income was about $1,476, although at $1,015, the median household income in Howa was substantially lower. Using the prices that prevailed during my field stay I estimated the absolute minimum annual costs of basic household subsistence (including sorghum, cooking oil, tea, coffee, sugar, and spices) for an average household to be approximately $850.[9] Minimalist estimates notwithstanding, over 42 percent of the households in Howa reported an income less than adequate to cover these basic goods. While my experience and observations suggested that indeed many households in Howa were just eking out their subsistence—relying on extensions of credit from local merchants, receiving loans and gifts from family members, foregoing certain items such as meat or new clothing, and/or selling animals if possible—these figures were still probably exaggerated due to underreporting of income, either systematically or through the omission of some of the odd jobs undertaken throughout the year.

The conditions that had engendered marginalization and differentiation in Howa were met with active resistance by many tenants. Of most consequence was the successful popular effort led by the tenants union to allow the cultivation of sorghum on project lands. Another arena of resistance was seen in the relative inattention of many tenants to cotton cultivation and their general lack of concern with yields, particularly in relation to livestock predation. Some families seemed to consider cotton nothing more than high-quality fodder, and even instructed their sons to graze the animals in their own fields, which would otherwise be economically marginal. These tactics could have fairly high stakes. They forced herdboys to evade guards stationed in the fields by the project, or to risk having their animals impounded and being punished themselves. One boy told me that he fled from a gun-wielding guard who had chased him all the way to the major canal. This wily herdboy jumped in and swam across, confident that guards never pursue their quarry into the water. He knew, of course, that they would never shoot anyone either. But as this game of cat-and-mouse suggests, other kinds of differentiation were underway in Howa. Some of the guards were fellow villagers—the same disenfranchised young men who found work with the project were now representing its interests against those of their neighbors or maybe even their own households. Along a different axis of evasion and punishment, if a herdboy's animals were impounded by project authorities, he would be responsible for his costly oversight. Each animal caught had to be bailed out from the project's pound for a fee, and this was not appreciated in any household; as likely as not, the cost would be taken out on the hide of the unfortunate shepherd.

The tangle of interests in tenant households among agriculture, animal husbandry, and other economic activities reflects in many ways the peculiar relation between capital and the peasantry in the wake of an agricultural development project. As Bernstein (1982) noted, the peculiarity is engendered because tenant producers are not completely separated from the means of production and because the individualized production of the household remains largely intact—it is not displaced by a socialized production process. Given this relationship, Bernstein surmises that two of the main struggles between farmers and project authorities are over the conditions of labor in the sphere of production and the distribution and realization of the product (173). Thus, Bernstein suggests, farmers may resist the encroachments of capitalist agriculture by refusing to grow certain crops or reducing the area of their cultivation, and by sabotaging new cultivation practices.

Both of these strategies were evident in Howa, and to some extent they limited capital expropriation from the village. Using the first strategy, farmers in Howa reappropriated cultivation of a subsistence food crop at the expense of a sanctioned cash crop. This move both limited the local market for large-scale mechanized sorghum farmers operating elsewhere in Sudan and diminished onerous cash expenditures by the local population for their means of existence. The second strategy—sabotaging new cultivation practices—limited the amount of cotton furnished to the project, thus reducing the rate of capital accumulation by the state.[10] Many others, of course, have found similar instances of foot-dragging, sabotage, and outright resistance in other rural settings. James Scott (1985) most famously recounts numerous examples of similar and bolder strategies of resistance and sabotage among the Malaysian rice cultivators with whom he worked; he champions these strategies as viable means of undermining hegemony and subverting notions of "false consciousness." Nevertheless, as Gillian Hart (1991) astutely points out, Scott's analysis brackets so many things, most notoriously gender, ethnicity, religion, and the role of the state, that it fixes its (male) protagonists as peasants resisting "'external' forces in order to remain a peasant." There is no sense in his analysis of the webs of gendered, classed, and raced social relations within which these social actors are embedded and produce their identities, or any hint that they may have ambivalent feelings about their lives as peasants and the possibilities that lie outside of agricultural life. The shifting grounds of production and reproduction in Howa were precisely that, shifting, and the means people developed for negotiating them and producing their identities were ambiguous, fluid, and up for grabs. Sometimes what made these transitions endurable were practices that fell short of what might unambiguously be thought of as "resistance," but that nevertheless reworked new situations so that they became manageable and even productive.

Shifting Currents

Although the changes brought about in the wake of the Suki Agricultural Project were substantial and in some instances pivotal, I want to be careful about constructing too sharp a divide between "before" and "after." While the project expanded and intensified the nature of capitalist penetration in the village—transforming local relations of production and reproduction, increasing the monetization of the local economy, sharpening socioeconomic stratification, and altering the productive basis of the area— these changes were already underway. In some instances the project hastened change; in others it appears to have altered its course. Indeed the conditions remained highly fluid years after the project had been established, and some of the most profound effects of capitalist penetration in general and the Suki Project in particular only began to be felt in Howa decades later. Even then, the ongoing flux in material conditions—broad and local—and the fluidity with which they were experienced and responded to resulted in a much fuzzier terrain of practice and possibility than is often assumed. Although the major canal might have cut sharply between village and fields, the project's other cuts, though often deeper, were more diffuse.

Labor

The role of labor migration in the village economy was a case in point. Unlike many villages in Sudan, in Howa outmigration to towns, cities, and abroad was minimal until the mid-1980s. Before that time, almost all of the labor migration had been agricultural and seasonal. Prior to the Suki Project, migrant laborers frequently worked in the tenancies of the Gezira Project to the north or in the private pump schemes along the Blue Nile west of the village. Some of the men from Howa who worked in the private schemes eventually acquired tenancies in them. When these cotton-growing schemes, established following World War II, lost their importance after the spread of large state-sponsored endeavors, such as the Suki Project, young men and other nontenants migrated to other agricultural areas in the Blue Nile Province, searching for work from tenant farmers or in dryland areas where sesame was still cultivated.

Wage labor was also not a stranger to people in Howa. It had long provided a secondary source of income in the event of poor crop yields or unusual expenses. In years when the rains failed or were inadequate, larger numbers of dryland farmers sought outside work (see O'Brien 1978, 8). Likewise, when irrigated cultivation failed or proved inadequate in the years after the project, the number of people looking for work as day laborers and migrant laborers increased again. Many men who lacked tenancies or whose tenancies provided insufficient household income also worked in the tenancies of others in Howa, as well as further afield. During the harvest, of course, women and girls in Howa did the vast majority of the work. The labor demands of the harvest were so enormous that the bounds of purdah were relaxed, except for married women in their prime childbearing years, roughly between fifteen and thirty-two. Women and children not only picked cotton and pulled groundnuts in their households' tenancies, but they also were hired to harvest others' fields. Both activities were poorly paid, but nevertheless, in providing women and girls with a seasonal income, gave them some financial autonomy they might not otherwise have had. Likewise, the demands of the Suki Project altered the gender division of labor in Howa by drawing heavily on the labor time of women and girls.

The changes provoked by the project, then, called forth new labor arrangements, such as women's fieldwork, altered older patterns of work, such as men's day labor, and intensified rather than created patterns of labor migration, which by and large were short term, temporary, and fairly localized. A generation later, however, the saturation and inadequacy of these patterns resulted in new migration strategies (though still largely of young men) that were more far-flung, urban-oriented, and enduring. Even then, labor migration configurations were more provisional and fluid than might be imagined.

Trade

The situation was similar with trade. While people in Howa had long been part of trading networks in the region and further afield, the Suki Project's effects broadened and deepened local people's commercial interchanges at all levels. Just as wage labor became more important after the project so, too, did trade, which became a source of supplemental income both in response to, and as part of, the process of Howa's incorporation into the national economy. With the establishment of the project, access to many goods that had been commonly held, self produced, or freely available was restricted. For example, with farmers no longer cultivating sorghum, virtually every household had to purchase this dietary mainstay. In addition, the process of land allocation associated with the project took a significant bite out of wooded areas in the vicinity. As firewood and other wood products became more difficult and time consuming to procure with household labor, some households began to purchase them. Likewise, meat had become more of a commodity with the decline in pasture areas and the monetization of the economy. As more freely held or formerly self-produced goods became commodities, the need for cash increased. Though this process was underway in Howa long before the Suki Project, the environmental and economic effects of the project accelerated local commercialization tremendously. Monetization was compounded by the introduction of an increasingly wide array of consumer goods in Howa, fostered by the growing number of merchants and occasional traders there, and the galloping globalization of exchange.

The need for cash in increasing amounts became more pressing as time passed. In some households this need was met with regular trading trips to Sennar or Dinder, the main market towns serving Howa. On these trips, which might occur two or three times a month, villagers—almost always men—sold animals, agricultural and forestry products, and handicrafts produced by women in their families. They often returned from town with something to sell piecemeal in the village. For example, because there were no fresh fruits and few fresh vegetables produced in Howa, an individual might visit Sennar, sell a goat, and purchase several dozen lemons with part of the proceeds. Back in the village he would sell the lemons at a slight markup from a burlap cloth spread on the ground in front of one of the general stores. Most of these casual traders bought in quantities small enough to sell out their entire stock within a few hours.

While some villagers traded at this level regularly—weekly or even more frequently at certain times of the year—and a few even derived the better part of their income from petty trade, most families in Howa engaged in trade only when a particular need for cash arose, or to sell goods made specifically for sale, such as straw mats. Mats were plaited by virtually every woman in Howa. Like certain other goods, such as white beans, wild okra (weka), and dairy products, women controlled the sale and the proceeds of mats they produced, though they rarely marketed them directly themselves. Their husbands, brothers, fathers, and sons sold the mats in town and also purchased the various kinds of straw and dyes necessary to make the next ones. A small number of women also made clay *zirs* (water jugs), griddles, and charcoal stoves, but they tended to sell them locally themselves.

Most petty trade was undertaken to provide the trader's family with enough cash to purchase those basic needs, goods, and services that the family did not produce. Several people in Howa, however, were engaged in trade at a slightly higher scale. Among these traders were the owners of Howa's general merchandise shops. These stores, which by 1980 numbered thirteen or so, stocked a growing range of goods to whet and satisfy the increasingly cosmopolitan tastes of Howa. In addition to the basic foodstuffs such as (black market) sugar, coffee, tea, oil, garlic, spices, rice, lentils, and tomato paste, these stores sold such things as cigarettes, candy, kerosene, plastic thongs, flashlights, batteries, razor blades, aspirin, and school supplies. Most households bought these supplies in extremely small quantities only as needed, keeping their daily expenditures to a few piasters, making trips to the shop (by children and men) frequent, and increasing the margins of shopkeepers.

The merchants who owned and operated these stores earned incomes well above those of the average tenant farmer in Howa. Since most of the shop owners were tenants as well, their total earnings were among the highest in the village. Many merchants in Howa appeared to be accumulating capital at a steady pace. While some of them invested their earnings in livestock, several expanded or diversified their business operations: building a new shop, enlarging their stock, or buying a used truck to further

Figure 14. Howa supported more than a dozen small general merchandise stores. Microcosms of global trade, the stores offered batteries and galvanized aluminum products from China, tea from Tanzania, tomato paste from Bulgaria, soap made in Sudan and abroad, cigarettes from Egypt, locally grown onions and garlic, unroasted coffee beans from Kenya, and black market sugar, among other sundries. People purchased these goods in the smallest possible units—a single packet of cookies, a pot's worth of coffee beans, a single cigarette, and a few cloves of garlic were typical.

their commercial ambitions. One merchant family (with several tenancies, large animal holdings, a shop, and a market truck) had invested some of their capital to develop a brickyard just outside the village where they made the fired clay bricks used increasingly in local construction. As wealthier families began to trade up from mud-and-dung to clay-brick houses, local builders started to learn the masonry techniques that would enable them to capitalize on this trend, rather than have the work go to outside builders, as had been the case with the first brick constructions in Howa.

In addition to the general merchandise stores, there was a privately owned grain mill and a bread bakery in Howa by the 1970s. Both were owned by people from outside the village. For different reasons, the profitability of these two operations, particularly the bakery, was dicey enough to result in sporadic closings during the year. The mill was used by every household in Howa. Its financial difficulties were based more on mismanagement than lack of demand. Prior to the establishment of the mill, women and their daughters ground their own sorghum by hand each day. Once it was available, mechanical grinding became such a commonplace that many women had their grain ground in other villages or towns on days when the village mill was closed. Others returned to the grinding stone that remained in every village kitchen. The bakery faced a different problem. Wheat bread was a recently introduced commodity in Howa and had made few inroads on the sorghum pancakes and porridge that were the basis of the local diet. At the equivalent of almost eight cents for a small round, bread was seen as a luxury, and the demand for it was insufficient to keep the bakery open consistently. The bakery operated regularly only during the agricultural season, when sales were buoyed by the influx of agricultural laborers and when women's work in the fields increased the local need for convenience foods.

The butcher stalls were relatively new to Howa. There were two locally owned butcher shops, each of which slaughtered a locally raised goat or sheep almost daily. A cow was butchered every two weeks or so by one of the butchers. While many families did not eat meat every day, village demand usually exceeded the meat supplied by two small animals so the butcher stalls were crammed with men and children in the early morning, just after the animals were slaughtered. The meat was sold out long before breakfast was served around nine o'clock. Demand was low enough, however, that beef was sold over a two-day period. Given the lack of refrigeration, cattle were rarely slaughtered during April and May, the hottest months of the year. Until the 1960s, meat was not part of the regular village diet. When it was eaten, meat was distributed traditionally through a sharing practice known as *karama* (generosity) in which a family who slaughtered a sheep or goat—usually to commemorate something or give thanks—would share the meat with their extended family, neighbors, and friends. Through an informal system of reciprocity, the average family ate meat approximately two or three times a month, but as meat was commodified, *karama* became more ritualized than routine.

Apart from these businesses, several people in Howa worked as independent artisans on at least a part-time basis. Approximately five men in the village owned sewing machines and worked occasionally as tailors. Several men were professional builders, some skilled in grass-and-thatch construction and others in mud-and-dung. Some of the latter had begun to learn the skills associated with brick construction. Several women were potters and made clay water jugs, griddles, and stoves for local sale, and almost all women plaited grass mats that men sold in nearby towns or weekly markets. Others in Howa produced and sold charcoal, cut and sold firewood, or hired themselves and their draught animals out to haul things for a fee. One man washed and ironed for a piece rate, and children and teens sold water in the village. The income derived from each of these activities was generally significant to household earnings over part if not all of the year.

A small number of men in Howa were engaged in trade at the regional and even the national level. Approximately eight households, either individually or in partnership, owned a used Bedford or Austin truck. These market lorries, which are modified in Sudan to withstand rugged driving conditions, were used to transport people, animals, and merchandise between villages, between Howa and regional centers, and occasionally between urban centers. The truck owners not only profited from the fees they charged for transport, but also from the spontaneous trade they engaged in as the opportunity arose on the road. Some of them had made substantial sums of money from these commercial opportunities. Some worked as groundnut brokers, plying back and forth between the harvest areas and the market towns daily during the harvest period. Others bought charcoal during the dry season, when it was relatively cheap, and sold it at a tremendous markup in the towns during the rainy months, when demand was highest. Like the village shopkeepers with whom they overlapped, many of these trucker-traders were accumulating capital at a steady pace, and some had begun to diversify their operations both within and outside of Howa.

Infrastructure

Infrastructure—provided by the government or through self-help initiatives—was fairly basic in Howa. By the time of the project there was the government-run school, a clinic staffed by a government-paid medical technician, a diesel-powered artesian well, and little else. A second artesian well on the other side of the village was constructed in 1981, both to compensate for various problems with the first well's operation and to mitigate crowding as the village population grew. Like the first well, it was funded by a self-help initiative by Howa's village council. A couple of years later they initiated the installation of pipes throughout the village to be fed from the artesian wells. The standpipes saved substantial labor time, particularly for children.

The village council, which was tied to the ruling Sudanese Socialist Party, negotiated local and more far-flung social, political, and patronage networks to get village improvements like these. Their accomplishments were impressive. In just two years they raised the US$7,500 necessary to pay for the pipes and their installation. They got the district government in Dinder to pay $1,250, while $6,250 of the cost was raised from the sale of approximately 91,000 pounds of sugar from the cooperative in Howa between 1981 and 1983.[11] The council attributed its success raising these funds to its aggressiveness in ensuring that Howa got its full quota of sugar from the district center in Dinder, and to its careful management of the collected funds. Even before the pipes were laid, the council had begun saving sugar proceeds to construct a girls' school in Howa. "Sweetness and power" indeed! (*pace* Mintz 1985).

Integration into the Suki Agricultural Project, and with it the larger economy, resulted in many tangible improvements in Howa. First, the communication and transport infrastructure between the village and the regional centers improved markedly. Second, health and social services were made available to Howa, where none had been before. Finally, as noted above, the infrastructure within the village, particularly around water resources, was developed substantially after 1971. These improvements were the result of both inclusion in the agricultural project and the self-help initiatives of the village council and local tenants union.

One of the most significant changes after 1971 was the development of Wad Tuk Tuk, a few kilometers away, as headquarters for the Suki Project. This development meant not only employment opportunities in the workshops and offices of the project, but also the establishment of a small market and service center. In 1981, for example, there were boys' and girls' primary and lower secondary schools in Wad Tuk Tuk, as well as a small hospital staffed with two doctors and several other health practitioners. Prior to the project's development, the nearest doctors were in Dinder and Sennar, and secondary school students had no choice but to board in Dinder or another regional town to continue their education. The development of Wad Tuk Tuk as an administrative center for the project also increased the visibility of the area to the district government, and integrated it more fully at the provincial and national levels.

Wad Tuk Tuk was also socially influential in Howa. Almost everyone from the village had visited Wad Tuk Tuk, and many went there regularly. They not only took advantage of the commodities and services offered in the town, but when there, they observed the life of the educated middle-class Sudanese who ran the project and its affiliated programs and services. One of the most influential observations, for example, was that the elite sent their daughters to school. Another was the advantage of electricity in daily life.[12]

As part of the integration of Wad Tuk Tuk into the regional political economy, the road between it and Sennar, approximately forty kilometers away, was graded and improved after 1971. In the past, this track had been impassable for much of the rainy season, but the project administration made every effort to keep it open throughout the wet season, though heavy clay soils often stymied them for days at a time. In 1988 an external review of the by-then tottering Suki Project renewed the call for paving the road to ensure speedier and all-season communication (Euroconsult 1988). Paving the track had been in the original plans for the project, but as late as 1999 it remained unpaved. This enduring problem notwithstanding, area roads had been improved and better maintained since the project, and as mentioned earlier, the number of trucks in

Howa had multiplied. These trucks, in addition to the many that passed near the village on the road from Suki that paralleled the major canal, had made the region much more accessible to people in Howa, and vice versa.

Health and social services had also improved dramatically in Howa. A clinic was built in conjunction with the project's development, staffed with a health practitioner paid by the regional government. This much sought after *hakim* could tend to the most common health problems in the village; gastrointestinal disease, malaria, superficial wounds, minor infections, and everyday aches and pains. The more complicated cases, or those for which the necessary medication was unavailable, were referred to the hospital in Wad Tak Tuk, which was staffed by two physicians. A government-trained and supported midwife was affiliated with the village clinic. The government midwife, who had moved to Howa in 1978 after completing her training, had replaced, for most, the traditional village midwives in assisting at births and performing female circumcisions with higher sanitary standards than had prevailed previously.[13] She also dispensed lots of middle-class health and child-care advice and was a sympathetic ear for village women.

Beginning in 1980, as part of the social extension service of the agricultural project, there were one or two social extension workers (*murshida*) living in Howa running classes for women in basic literacy, home science, and market-oriented craft making. These young women—school leavers or secondary-school graduates from more urban areas—were supervised by three female social extension workers based in Wad Tuk Tuk. The resident murshida taught reading, writing, cooking, child care, and sewing, and offered ideas for home improvements to a daily class of almost fifty dedicated young women. Most people in Howa seemed pleased and proud that these courses were taught in their village. The local value placed on this three-year program was seen not only in the women's consistent class attendance—sometimes against husbands' and fathers' wills—but in their attentiveness and diligence in completing their course work.

Like Wad Tuk Tuk and the government midwife, the social workers had more subtle impacts on everyday life as well. Leila, the first resident murshida, and her supervisors significantly influenced the ideas and opinions of people, especially young women, in Howa. After only one year, the social workers' active support for female education, as well as the example they set for others, seemed to have encouraged at least some village families to send their daughters to school. With so much resistance to female education, the significance of this program and its associated effects cannot be overestimated. Within two years of the social extension program's 1981 arrival, the village council was discussing plans to construct a girls' school in Howa during the next couple of years.

Conclusion

Incorporation in the Suki Agricultural Project transformed the local economy of Howa from one geared largely to production for consumption to one based on production for exchange and ultimately the accumulation of profit. This transformation propelled socioeconomic differentiation in Howa, exacerbating existing differences between households' earnings and assets as it created new ones. Because it altered people's relationship to the primary productive resource in the area, land, the Suki Project changed not only the socioeconomic status of the local population, but class relations there as well. In addition, the project dramatically transformed the cultural and political ecology of the area, with serious consequences for people's everyday lives, household labor dynamics, and the local resource base.

These intertwined processes represent not so much a sharp divide between what had been and what was new, but a congeries of imbricated forces and practices that subtly but surely altered the makeup and meaning of work, play, knowledge, and learning in the village and its surroundings. The fluid form of these shifts was the outcome of local, national, and global forces and practices, and mutually constituted them in turn. Negotiating these shifting grounds, the local population developed new social relations within and between households; new definitions of work, authority, property, and exchange; and a broadened palette of practices undertaken to survive.

PART II
SOCIAL REPRODUCTION

3. Children's Work and Play

It's mid-July and everybody is weeding. Tenants, their sons, nephews, brothers, and hired hands are immersed in the first of four weedings. Ismail has been assisting his maternal uncle Said in their groundnut fields for the last couple of weeks. On one of these mornings he met up with his uncle at his grandparents' compound just before seven o'clock and they went together to his tenancy, just near the major canal. Getting to the fields around seven-thirty, Ismail and his young uncle set to work up and down the rows. They used the short-handled hoe (*kedunka*) mandated by the project administration to hack out the weeds. These hoes were made by local carpenters, who also made shorter handled tools for children's use. Ismail's hoe was one of these. Said was more skilled and speedy than Ismail, but Ismail worked hard and well, modeling his actions upon those of his uncle. They occasionally stopped to clean the clayey soil from the blades of their hoes, using a piece of scrap metal that Said had picked up on the way out. Weeding along the last planted row near the feeder canal, Ismail did not recognize some recently sprouted *onkolib* (sweet sorghum, *Sorghum spp. graminae*) until his uncle stopped him from weeding it. Ismail said that he thought it was *adar*, a tall grass in the same family (*Sorghum vergatum*) that was considered a weed in the fields, although it was a source of fodder. In general Ismail was good at discerning cultivated from unwanted plants and could recognize most of the horticultural things planted along the edges of the field, including lentils, haricot beans, and corn. Now he recognized onkolib.

After weeding about half an acre, they found the rest of the ground too wet to continue and left it for another day. Moving to a section that had already been weeded, they neatened a part of it by clearing the few remaining weeds. By about eight-thirty they were ready to return home, but Ismail's mother had requested that he bring back some *mulayta* (*Picridium trigitanum* Desf.), a green that grew profusely along the canals. People in Howa relished the bitter green—eaten fresh—and often asked their children to gather some when they went to the fields. Ismail picked greens for about twenty minutes, filling a bag the size of a pillow that he had tied around him as he picked. He gave two-thirds of the mulayta to his grandparents and brought the rest home.

Environmental knowledge is practical knowledge. In Howa it included knowledge of the local terrain, available resources, land-use practices, and environmental processes fundamental to production and reproduction. Like all knowledge it was learned in a community of practice (Lave and Wenger 1991). Adults and teenagers shared this knowledge with children through a variety of means—conscious and not—starting in early childhood. Through direct oral instruction, stories, songs, riddles, demonstration, apprenticeship, guided practice, and shared activities, adults ensured that their rich and evolving store of knowledge about the environment was passed on as a routine part of everyday life. Children also acquired environmental knowledge in the course of their autonomous activities with peers and older children. Their routine activities and everyday interactions—both work and play—offered opportunities to acquire, try out, use, master, reimagine, and alter environmental knowledge. Each of these material social practices was important for the continuation of village life and helped shape the children's impending adulthoods.

Work and play were key and critical means through which children reproduced themselves and the social and economic life of their village. Play and work were intertwined in the time-space of children's everyday lives in Howa with deep resonances between the two. An element of play was almost fused with the work of children—they worked at play and played at work—temporally, metaphorically, and imaginatively. They worked while they played and played while they worked, they worked around their play and they played in the interstices of their work, they participated in tasks that were playful and play that was "workful," and they engaged in play activities whose focus was work.

The unities that bound work and play in the children's everyday lives frayed under the impress of the changes brought about by the agricultural project and its attendant social relations. One of the obvious reasons for this unraveling was the increase in children's work time resulting from the intensified cultivation requirements of the project, the decreased availability of wood and the deterioration of nearby pasture areas, and the heightened monetization of the local economy. Still, the ties that joined work and play in Howa were numerous and durable, in part because even as children worked more, it was hard to the drain the play out of them. Nevertheless, some of the fine weave between certain work and play practices was worn thin by the uncertainties for the future posed by the project. Yet this is precisely why the children's work and play activities and their intertwinings were of so much interest to me. If in their work and play children encountered, made sense of, and tried to prepare themselves for the world, they also encountered and engaged the inchoateness of the ways that new and old social relations and cultural forms and practices clashed in that world. Their playful work and workful play were not only ways of making sense of and negotiating these shifting conditions, but they offered glimpses of creative possibilities that were new and different.

In this chapter, I examine the unfolding of the children's work and play as material social practices, looking at their meanings for both the village and the children themselves and suggesting how these activities and the relations between them were changed in the encounter with the new political ecologies of everyday life in Howa. The discussion describes how play and work and their relationships were altered in the political-economic transformation that was taking place in Howa and offers them up as a way to imagine and even produce something different of it.

Work and Play in Howa

It's just after six o'clock on a June morning and Merwan is rounding up his flock, making shepherd sounds (a series of clicks, "sshts," and high-pitched "ayes" that the animals respond to) and using his long stick to prod and hit the animals into motion. His uncle helps him get the animals out of their houseyard and moving toward "the East" (an open forest savannah to the east of the still-dry river). Within minutes Merwan is heading back carrying two lambs that were to stay behind. He quickly returns to his flock of about sixty small animals, mostly sheep, and energetically keeps them moving, making lots of shepherd sounds and scampering around them. He spots a friend on the horizon and waits at the riverbank for him and a couple of other boys to catch up so they can hang out together while their animals graze. The flocks get mingled as the boys work together—making noises and hitting the animals—to get them to descend the steep bank. As the animals graze along the riverbed the boys do acrobatics in its soft sandy bottom. . . .

After making themselves a breakfast of fresh milk and porridge brought from home, the boys move the animals up the steep eastern bank and over to a maya (depression) about a ten-minutes' walk away. Compared to Saddiq and his friends, these herdboys seem relaxed about getting the animals to the maya, and don't seem too worried about whether any of them might have wandered off or been left behind. As they reach the slightly more vegetated maya, the boys immediately begin searching for camel dung so they can play *mala,* a game similar to jacks that uses camel dung as the playing pieces. Each boy finds his twenty pieces and they begin to play in the shade of an acacia as the animals graze around them. The animals eat their way about one hundred meters to the east and every once in a while one of the boys casts an eye toward them. Their mala is spirited, full of pinching cheeks and hitting vanquished opponents, cheering at one's own successes, and chomping on fingers in a performance of nervousness after dropping playing pieces. Amid the good-natured arguing about various moves, I notice Merwan cheating—he distracts one of his friends while simultaneously slipping the boy's pieces into his own pile. The move is unnoticed and the boys continue to play for about forty-five minutes, during which time the animals drift back to the river. One boy is delegated to go after them, and with a shower of shepherd noises and the occasional use of his whip, he rounds up all of the animals and leads them back to the maya. Not long after, the boys themselves head off to play again in the sandy river bottom, leaving the animals to continue grazing in the depression.

Work, Play, and Environmental Knowledge

In their work and play, ten-year-old children learned, integrated, mastered, and used many of the environmental skills and much of the knowledge fundamental to the agriculture, animal husbandry, forestry, and resource use that dominated the economic life of Howa. The range of activities in which they engaged or manipulated the physical environment was extremely broad and varied. Many of these tasks were considered children's jobs, and by ten most children exhibited mastery or near mastery of the knowledge and skills required to carry them out. These tasks included herding, drawing water, gathering fuelwood, and collecting certain wild foods.

In other activities children assisted adults. In these, children may have mastered one part of a complex process, and as they carried it out learned other aspects of the task as a whole. Such was the case with farming. Children's labor was essential to most agricultural chores, but at ten they had not yet mastered the interrelationship and sequencing of the complex processes of agricultural production, even as they learned discrete aspects of these processes in the course of their everyday tasks. In agriculture, as with most other environmental activities, children learned by doing, watching, and receiving something like on-the-job training from their elders, siblings, or peers. Some skills, like the specialized use of certain local resources, were taught to children more formally by adults.

Most environmental knowledge was shared less formally, however, as part of the give-and-take of everyday life. As children played, worked, and explored the village and its surroundings, they often asked peers or elders to explain or identify objects or processes they were curious about. For their part, adults often imparted information about the environment casually or as it was appropriate, pointing out which trees to cut, guiding a child's hand as she reconstructed a shallow well in the riverbed, or instructing a young boy on ways to trap and kill birds. Adults and older kids were also careful to correct children's mistakes in identifying, understanding, and using local resources as these instances arose, just as Ismail's uncle did when he mistook the sweet sorghum for a weed (see, for example, Fortes 1970; Raum 1940; Middleton 1970; Modiano 1973; Ruddle and Chesterfield 1977; Porter 1996). Idle hours around the houseyard were sometimes spent puzzling through riddles (*hajwa*) or reciting rhymes that often as not conveyed environmental information (see Hurriez and Bell 1975).

It was late April and the dense and steamy heat of *sayf* (summer) was upon us. Finally grasping what it was about "mad dogs and Englishmen," I sat out the midday sun in the shaded *rakuba* (grass veranda) of Ismail's family. As I sunk into a seat on one of several rope beds arrayed around the "veranda," Ismail told me that he'd seen a *simbriya* (Abdim's Stork, *Ciconia abdimi*) that morning. That means it will rain soon, he let us know, because simbriya come during *kherif,* the rainy season. With the mix of sweetness, excitement, and wisdom that was his trademark, he launched into a nursery rhyme that marks the stork's role as a harbinger:

> Al Simbriya Um Guddoum
> Aysh Aboui Bigoom
> Mitaya Bitgoom Bakir
> Ma' al Asakir

> The Abdim's stork with its long bill
> My father's sorghum sprouts
> It will grow tomorrow
> With the dawn [literally, "With the army"]

This released a barrage of riddles and rhymes. Ismail told some to his relatives, while others were inflicted upon him. The next also involved a bird, the white stork (*Ciconia ciconia*), which he called *Um al jeday,* though elsewhere in Sudan they are referred to as *Ab al Jebar,* a reference to their enormous size. "Um al Jeday," Ismail sang out, "Hannini e dai, Hannini kour ai!" (hennaed hands, hennaed feet). Our talk wandered back to the simbriya and I asked what they ate. His great-aunt immediately answered sorghum, prompting Ismail to ask, "Don't they eat grass too?" And she assured him that they did. The conversation moved on to vultures and Ismail provided a vivid—even lurid—description of carrion. Habiba, his younger cousin, who loved all things gory, made sure to tell us how the vultures ate the eyes of their quarry. This prompted yet another bird-identifying rhyme, about a carrion-eating bird, "Hourab Hourab, Kubba addum, Gal Hurrum" (Hourab, Hourab, spills blood, swears its might). Jumping along, Ismail got on the subject of *hidaya* (*Elanus caeruleus,* black shouldered kites), letting me know that they eat chicks. The assembled contributed a few more riddles about animals and everyday life, and Ismail concluded with one about *kakool,* the gum that oozed from acacias in places where the bark was disturbed: "If you take one today / another will grow tomorrow." He had learned this and some of the other riddles from his herdboy cousin, Saddiq. Children and others out in the brush often pulled wads of kakool off acacias to chew. With little taste but a lot of texture, kakool is similar to gum arabic, which comes from *Acacia senegal,* but it has no economic value.

Everyone enjoyed exchanging hajwa, though they were considered largely the province of grandmothers. They were so much a part of cultural learning in Sudan that radio and television programs for children had adopted the form, and—so people in Howa told me—were gradually putting grandmothers out of business. Play was another means through which children acquired, internalized, and integrated environmental knowledge. It offered them a way to practice their environmental skills, while providing an arena in which they could "romance" about what they were learning, imagine alternate outcomes, and even make up aspects they vaguely understood or had yet to learn.

The following examination of the key environmental activities of children in Howa weaves together descriptions of the practices themselves, discussions of the variety of connections between work and play in the children's lives, and analyses of how these activities were connected to the larger political economy and ecology within which they occurred. As the examples woven through this discussion demonstrate, the interrelationship and balance among children's work, play, and learning, and the back and forth between the adults' and children's practices were striking.

Time-Economics of Children's Work

The porous border between commodity and subsistence production in Howa had an interesting effect on children's participation in various work activities. In the initial year of this project, I documented the full range of activities—work and play— of a group of seventeen ten-year-old children. My analysis of their work revealed that socioeconomic factors, such as parental occupation and household socioeconomic status, influenced children's participation in work undertaken to produce income or to further household capital accumulation, such as agriculture, animal husbandry, and charcoal production; on the other hand, individual demographic characteristics, such as gender or birth-order position, were more influential for their participation in tasks of household maintenance and reproduction, including the procurement of water, fuel, and noncultivated foods for household consumption. Because reproductive work took place in every household regardless of economic status, these daily tasks drew heavily on the labor of children across the board, whether from poor or relatively well-off households. Other forms of work, by contrast, required particular assets, such as animals or a tenancy. The availability of such assets affected whether or not children worked, and resulted in my somewhat counterintuitive finding that children in wealthier households often worked longer hours and at more tasks than children in poorer ones.

While this distinction was true overall, children's work activities were, of course, influenced by a number of factors whose relative importance varied largely according to the task. Neither the variables nor the tasks themselves were mutually exclusive. It goes without saying, for instance, that a family must have animals to require a child to work as a shepherd, but in Howa this socioeconomic factor intersected with the gendering of herding as exclusively a boys' task. Once a boy was a herder, however, the constancy of his work precluded him from assisting with most other household chores. In other words, children's customary tasks exerted their own influence upon their participation in other activities. These distinctions are often missed in analyses of children's work, which tend to look at particular demographic or socioeconomic variables and assess their impact on work participation, rather than examining the interweave between tasks, household economics, and the particular characteristics of the children. The significance of the analytic distinction between work that was reproductive and work that was undertaken for exchange or in relation to capital accumulation and how that distinction affected children's responsibilities and use of time was striking. Also striking were the intrahousehold effects of gender, age, birth-order position, and customary responsibilities.

In a related vein, as was noted above, the children of wealthier households tended to be more encumbered than others. Because of the diversification of the household economy, children from wealthier households tended to work more hours than those less well off, mostly because herding and, to a lesser extent, farming were so time consuming. Although children from the poorest families were often forced by circumstances to work at many tasks, their households lacked the resources that would have employed them over long hours. Instead they worked at a range of subsistence and income-generating activities that did not depend on household assets, such as land and livestock. Thus, while children from poorer households in Howa tended to work at a greater array of activities, those in wealthier households tended to work longer hours. But more than this, it appeared that the economic diversification that characterized wealthier households led them to employ their children more intensively than others did in the village. There was also a tendency among these families to groom their children—more accurately, their sons—to tend particular areas of the family's operations. Thus one son might take care of the animals and learn the ins and outs of animal husbandry, another might specialize in agriculture, a third might work in the family store or assist on their truck and so learn to be a merchant, while yet another would be formally educated through secondary school and beyond, if possible.

In his work on children's labor in Char Gopalpur, Bangladesh, Mead Cain (1977, 219) also found that the children of better-off families tended to work at different activities than their peers from poorer households. In Char Gopalpur, as in Howa, boys from richer households were more likely to work at tasks such as herding and crop production, while those from poorer households were more likely to work at fishing or wage labor. Cain found, as did I, that children from wealthier households also worked at an earlier age than those from poorer households on tasks that required assets, such as agriculture and animal husbandry. These tasks were inaccessible to poorer children except through wage labor, the opportunities for which were limited for very young children. In Howa, it was even the case that young children who worked as paid field hands were more likely than not to be from tenant households. Although access to land was through the agricultural project, and tenancies were not neatly correlated with wealth, it seemed that a familiarity with the tasks developed from working in the tenancies of their households and chance encounters with other tenants while out in the fields made these children more likely than others to pick up agricultural work at an early age.

Finally, my work revealed an interesting relationship between school attendance and work. While school attendance did not preclude children's participation in most of the environmental work practices of their community, it certainly structured their time differently and made extra-household demands on them. Although I found extremely low rates of school enrollment in Howa (42 percent among boys between seven and twelve; 4 percent among girls of the same age), I also found low rates of absenteeism. Once a family made a commitment to send their child to school, they appeared to respect the restrictions that attendance made on him or her, and did not interfere by demanding that the child work during school times. Children who were students participated in all the agricultural tasks that took place during the three-month school holiday, which coincided with the rainy season, but they participated much less frequently in the tasks of clearing and harvesting because these took place during term. Even though harvest work was particularly labor-demanding, parents did not pull their children from school to participate. Harvest work was usually done by women and girls, however, and girls' school enrollment was so small that its effects on participation in this activity were relatively negligible. Nevertheless, in later periods of my study I learned that one of the reasons girls left school was to participate in cotton picking, which was seasonally lucrative. Others suggest an opposite trend. David Landy (1959) and Marta Tienda (1979), working in Puerto Rico and Peru, respectively, found much higher levels of school enrollment than I did (80 percent in rural Puerto Rico and 77 percent in rural Peru), but more frequent absenteeism when children were needed for labor-intensive agricultural or other tasks.

In Howa, on the other hand, where school enrollment was only 24 percent over-all, households made every attempt to manage without the assistance of school children, even during the busiest periods. However, when children's labor was important across a range of tasks, or for an essential year-round activity such as herding, they either were never enrolled or left school before completion. This was often the case in Howa. Among the seventeen children working with me, eleven were not enrolled in school. Of these, the work of seven was essential to their households. The low levels of school enrollment in Howa were a clear reflection of the importance of children's labor to their households.

Talal, for instance, was one of the hardest working children I knew. He worked more than four hours a day all year long, participating significantly in animal husbandry, procuring water and fuel, assisting in the fields, and gathering wild foods. His labor contributions to agriculture and fetching water were particularly critical. Both activities were necessary not only to his household's reproduction, but to its economic well-being. When I first met Talal at the beginning of 1981 he was a student in the third grade. His work time was governed largely by the school schedule, which allowed time each afternoon and on Fridays to fetch water or gather fuelwood for household consumption. During the summer holidays he participated in the agricultural tasks of planting and weeding, but because of school, not in the bulk of clearing and harvest activities. Talal was the oldest child in his family, and at ten he was mature and strong enough to help significantly with a range of tasks, either working independently or alongside his father. By early 1981 the need for his labor, as well as the money he was able to earn daily from selling water (the equivalent of approximately US$1.00), outweighed for his parents the advantage of keeping Talal in school. After the school break in April he did not return to school. At first he and his family denied that this situation was permanent and indicated that he would resume after the summer holidays that ran from June through September. I came to realize that the family was humoring me, if not themselves. Given their precarious economic existence and Talal's consistent hard work across a range of tasks, school had become an unaffordable luxury for them.

Unities of Work and Play

Talal's withdrawal from school should not be scripted as entrapment in a grim life of constant toil, however. Work and play remained tightly bound in many ways in the children's lives, and Talal was no exception. One of his myriad projects, for instance, involved the construction of a small kitchen for his mother. The many intrinsic pleasures of the activities involved were as obvious as their purposiveness: Talal and his friends energetically demolished a nearby crumbling mud house and carted back the dirt to build the kitchen, went to the woods to find just the right saplings for its door, and built and fussed over the finishing touches to the (unrequested) simple structure. This was typical. Children's work time was often imbued with playfulness, while their play was often goal directed and worklike—all of which raise profound questions about the nature of work and play in children's lives in Howa and beyond.

The ties between work and play were multiple and varied. Work and play were bound temporally; activities associated with each were simultaneous, overlapping, or punctuated by one another. Much work was playful, especially that which took the children on journeys outside the village, and a lot of play activities were "workful," such as Talal's kitchen project or other boys' bird-snaring. Still other forms of play—such as the endless dramatic games of "fields"—rehearsed work activities that the children engaged in at other times, while some play involved toying with likely future work activities, such as the girls' games of "house." These unities—and the threats against them—are addressed in the discussions of the children's activities, below. The activities, which encompass the material social practices of animal husbandry, fetching water, procuring fuelwood, agriculture, and collecting wild food and other resources from the surrounding environment, cover almost all of the most important ways children in Howa spent their time outside of school. However, my focus on activities that were particularly environmental downplays household domestic labor, in which children's role was often substantial. Activities such as child care, cooking, cleaning, running errands, and other household chores absorbed a substantial amount of children's time. These activities dot the periphery of the descriptions that follow, but their importance—both in consuming children's time and in the significance of children's contribution to their getting done—was anything but peripheral.

Herding

Herding was one of the principal activities of children. All of the shepherds in Howa were boys. They ranged in age from about ten to eighteen, but a few continued to herd until their early twenties. Not only was this crucial aspect of animal husbandry solely a young person's task, but going out every day of the year from dawn until dusk inevitably separated herdboys from all others. Once a boy became a shepherd (as early as eight, but more commonly around ten), care of the family's livestock away from the houseyard was solely his responsibility. The task was not passed down successively among brothers and the responsibility was shared with them only because of illness, exhaustion, or extreme heat during the hottest part of the year, when staying out in the sun all day could be dangerous even for the young and accustomed. Because it was a daily task, engaged in by a stable group of boys who spent long hours together every-day over several years, herding was understandably a cliquish arena in which work and play were often simultaneous and overlapping.

Three of the ten boys with whom I worked were shepherds. A fourth, Rashid, herded his family's ten animals on his days off from school. Otherwise, they were grazed by a paid herdboy. Two others took care of their family's donkeys; one watered the donkey used by his father, and the other, Talal, watered, fed, and cleaned the corral of the donkey that he used for collecting wood, fetching water and other activities. When families had small numbers of animals, children often led them to pasture and left them to graze on their own. While girls were not shepherds in Howa, many led their families' animals to and from these nearby grazing areas. Two of the seven girls with whom I worked were frequently responsible for this task. In Howa, almost all milking was done by women, and I rarely saw children milk except when they wanted a drink while out with the flocks.

Shepherds exhibited an extraordinary level of care and responsibility in their work. They were also responsible for cleaning the animals and their quarters, ensuring the safety of their charges, and preventing their families' flocks from roaming, which some shepherds did with less vigilance than others. In the course of their work, herdboys developed and used a finely detailed knowledge of local microenvironments and vegetation to ensure adequate and appropriate grazing for their animals each season. In the course of an interview with Saddiq, for instance, I sketched a map laying out about forty discrete grazing areas that he identified within a four-kilometer radius of the village. His intricate geographical knowledge was typical of herdboys in Howa. With some guidance from their fathers, these boys were able to manage the diverse grazing areas around Howa to maximize limited and declining pasture lands. In daily exchanges the boys told their parents which areas were wet, overgrazed, vegetated, or otherwise, and then negotiated the day's grazing to optimize the resources of the wet and dry seasons and ensure that the animals had access to vegetation with various properties. Of course they might change the plans en route for any number of reasons, including news of flooding, friends' plans, exhaustion, or whimsy. Most accounted for their trajectories each evening, when they were often grilled about whether the animals were watered and what they had grazed upon.

When I was out grazing with Merwan one day in late September—just about the most verdant time of the year—he identified (at my behest) thirty-five distinct plants, mostly grasses—over the course of a two-hour ramble, and informed me about each plant's properties as fodder or as risks to the animals. The variation was splendid and Merwan knew a lot of the plants. On a couple of occasions he said he didn't know the name of something and a couple of other times he identified a plant incorrectly. On each of these four occasions other shepherds nearby, usually older, provided the correct information.

> We sat in the shade of a tree for a while as I scribbled madly, trying to get down all he'd said, but after a while Merwan said that the animals had roamed off and we had to go round them up. In pursuit of the flock, we meandered through the greenery, joining up with others and then parting ways just as casually. Eventually we made our way to a maya (depression) which was by now quite full—knee- to waist-high water filled the expanse so that it looked like a shimmering pond. Grasses and other greens were growing in it along with many—at present very lush—trees. Birds were abundant near the water, and the kids identified about a dozen of them. When they spotted the bird *Ab Gambour,* one of them called out, "Ab gambour, hella jour!!" Ab gambour, it turned out, was not just the name of a bird, but also the nickname of one of the boys, and revealing this let loose an incredible discussion of nicknames. Each boy had at least one and sometimes several nicknames known to their extended group of friends—all herdboys. The names were funny, derivative, and affectionate; defining an in-group and excluding all others. In learning them, I felt that much more in the club. They, in turn, were completely amused at my writing down the names—about thirty in all—and got me to read them out loud at least six times throughout the day.

Though herdboys might leave home each day with a plan, their movements were often influenced by social and other interests. Apart from serendipitous encounters with other herdboys and children out collecting wood or wild foods, or working in the fields, shepherds often traveled together from the start of the day or arranged to meet and play during their long days. Particular sites such as the riverbed, waterlogged depressions (maya), and the canal were favored for these encounters. During the heat of the day, the boys often headed for the shade of the few remaining large trees dotting the open land surrounding the village. In these favored spots herdboys played while they worked. Not only was the fusion between work and play marked in their daily routines, but it was often difficult to distinguish what was play and what was work.

> Later that same day with Merwan and his friends we came to a maya full of *suteb,* the potato-like root of a local variety of water lily. Suteb are a shepherd delicacy, if for no other reason than that almost nobody else can get to them, and they were growing thickly in the middle of this particular pool. No sooner had we gotten there but the boys were stripping down to their shorts and racing into the water. They darted for the middle and began ducking down to yank the suteb from the mud. There were

about six or seven boys out there and they stayed out for about a half hour, horsing around as they filled the aprons of their shorts or shirts with the roots. In the interim, a slightly older shepherd arrived and one by one drove his sheep into the water to bathe them. After Merwan returned from his dunking expedition he helped the older boy in immersing and scrubbing each sheep. Eventually he returned to the shore with about a dozen suteb tucked into his pants waist. Other kids had similar yields. Merwan immediately rinsed one and ate it raw, but suggested I wait for the real delicacy— boiled or roasted. One boy had matches and kindled a fire, another filled an enamel bowl with water. As the roots cooked, Merwan changed back into his short caftan and rinsed out his wet clothes, all the while checking on the whereabouts of his flock.

The frolics, shared meals, songs, riddles, stories, word games (which included making up cascades of names for one another), bird watching, hunting, swimming, wrestling, and more organized action games were routine parts of a shepherd's day. These activities overlapped and were often continuous with the work of herding. While the animals wandered—sometimes too far—the boys played circle games, made themselves into "trains" running through the sandy riverbed, swam, sang songs, or gathered seasonal foods to eat. The environmental content of some these activities, such as bird watching or food gathering, the lyrics to songs, and the content of some riddles and tales were important for acquiring or reinforcing environmental knowledge. But more than that, the easy overlap between work and play helped the boys to pass the long hot days with a minimum of tedium and with obvious pleasure.

The cooperativeness and camaraderie among the shepherds were impressive, even in a village where both of these qualities were instilled in children from an early age. These characteristics were also crucial to their work. The herdboys' affinities were forged in the long days spent together, in the shared responsibility for their families' wealth, in their adventures discovering new grazing areas and daring the guards of the irrigation project, and in the special things, experiences, and information shared only among shepherds. These exchanges appeared to give herdboys the sense that they were different from other children. Their sense of uniqueness and solidarity was reinforced by their cultural practices, including, for instance, shared beliefs, lore, and values, and the encoding of much of their knowledge in a specialized language that included nicknames known only to themselves. As is often the case with youth "gangs" or cliques, these markers of self-definition were used smugly if not derisively against outliers, especially students, who were often scripted as knowing nothing.

> Merwan and I were sitting under a tree, trying to stay cool in the middle of June while the animals grazed on the eastern side of the Dinder, when a couple of herdboys approached. "They're good kids," he told me, taking pleasure in their approach. "All shepherds are good kids," he went on. I wondered about other kids. "Nah," he said with obvious disdain and a little bit of chauvinism, "students are no good."

The self-conscious reproduction of herdboy culture was integral to their work. This culture sustained the boys daily and over the years, but within it there was great autonomy. The boys who herded in Howa, almost to a one, were independent, inventive, and self-confident. Those who were not, such as Mohamed, another of the herdboys who worked with me, were neither accepted in the group nor as successful at their work as those who were. The lack of camaraderie could have tragic consequences. Mohamed, who was a solitary shepherd and a bit of a loner, fell into the swift currents of the Dinder River in flood and drowned because he could neither swim nor pull himself up on the shore. While the Dinder can be quite strong, and the presence of fellow herdboys would not have guaranteed survival, it is most likely that had other boys been around, they would have managed to save Mohamed if only by screaming and running for help.

The comprehensive social network and strong social bonds among shepherds were important, then, because they facilitated the work of animal husbandry and eased the psychic and physical burdens on individual herdboys. Herdboys who, for whatever reason were outside of these social networks, missed out on the play and camaraderie that made the long hours pass more pleasantly. Mohamed, who generally spent his days herding alone, tended to return home in the afternoon. As a result his family had to hire a herdboy to keep the animals out the rest of the day. Likewise, Rashid, who took his household's small flock out on school holidays, worked pretty much alone and was not enamored with the tedious prospect of herding all day. Isolation also limited the lone shepherds' access to the information shared easily within the moving clusters of herdboys concerning the best grazing sites or problems in certain areas, and decreased the likelihood they would receive warnings about guards in areas off-limits to livestock.

The centrality of children's role in animal husbandry did not mean that they determined any of its economic aspects. Here, their fathers were firmly in control. Livestock was an adult investment, and usually represented the bulk of family wealth, however great or small. The seriousness of the investment was seen in the deep and constant concern of animal owners that their animals were well-fed and watered, safe from physical harm, prevented from grazing on potentially injurious fodder, and out of the way of both police and thieves. Parents carefully selected which of their sons would be the family herdboy. Shepherds were supervised closely through intensive questioning at the end of each day as to where the animals grazed, what they grazed upon, and whether any problems were encountered.

Adults were perennially concerned that their sons would be distracted playing and let the animals wander off, graze on harmful vegetation, or get caught in project lands and end up being impounded and incurring fines. Though the shepherds did indeed get absorbed in play, they almost never let the animals slip away entirely. The punishment was such that they were not likely to let it happen too often. On one occasion Saddiq, a scrupulously responsible herdboy, was hit several times when he arrived home at the end of a long day because his father had learned (from Saddiq's older and far less responsible twelve-year-old brother) that one of their animals had been impounded. Despite his general responsibility, Saddiq's costly error was not taken lightly. In fact his father was so steamed that he waited at the edge of the village to have at him the moment he returned. Of course, like many parent-child tiffs, there was a bit of cognitive dissonance at work. In interviews and casual conversations with me, many men recounted their own playful transgressions as herdboys in the same breath that they admonished their sons for doing the same. Such are the interweavings of work and play in time, space, and memory.

Fetching Water

> Late afternoon and the girls as usual are playing dolls in the shade of a wall enclosing the houseyard. The homemade grass dolls have cooked, cleaned, and entertained guests. Now Suad is maneuvering her doll to go to the well. She carries her to a nearby *zir* (large clay water jug), fills a small cup of water, and carries the doll back to the makeshift dwelling the girls have crafted against the wall, all the while balancing the cup of water over the doll's head.

No matter what else was going on, hauling water was an integral part of every day's activities. Fetching water was another arena of work where children's contributions were pivotal. In most areas of Africa, and indeed in many parts of Sudan, women have primary responsibility for providing both fuel and water. But in this part of Islamic Sudan, women in their prime childbearing years (between approximately fifteen and thirty-two) were discouraged from working outside their household compounds during the day because it was not considered proper for them to be seen in public.[1] It is logical, then, that in Howa and probably in many other areas where Islam predominates, children have greater responsibility for providing the means of existence, such as water and fuel, than they do in areas where women are able to carry out these tasks. What I found in Howa dovetails with Enid Schildkrout's (1981) conclusion that it was the labor of children that enabled purdah, the seclusion of women, to persist in Islamic urban Nigeria.[2] Through the course of a year, children in Howa made literally thousands of trips to get water from the village well, the river or its dry bed, and the irrigation canal. Although both women and men in Howa fetched water routinely, children were the predominant figures at each water source.

Children began drawing water for their households when they were as young as seven, making repeated trips to the well or river—often in the tow of older siblings—and carrying small buckets or plastic containers, as their size allowed. My findings suggest that children and adolescents of both sexes were responsible for drawing 80 percent of the water consumed each day in village households. Thirteen of the seventeen children with whom I worked fetched water for their households and extended families at least some of the time. Five of these children were responsible for fetching all or most of the water used in their households. One child, Talal, sold water regularly in the village and Miriam sometimes did. She was especially active during the agricultural season, when demand was higher because people spent so much time in the fields. The figures derived from the children working with me were representative of the village as a whole, where more than 75 percent of all ten-year-olds drew water for their households and about 6 percent of the ten-year-olds sold water regularly.

Gender and birth order exerted a strong influence on participation in these tasks. Girls were more important for providing household water than boys, and oldest children in a household, especially girls, tended to take on the task earlier and keep it longer than younger siblings. Among the children with whom I worked, four of the five who fetched most or all of the water for their households were girls. The sole boy was, significantly, the oldest child in his family. Three of the four girls who fetched most of the water in their households were, likewise, the oldest girls in their households. The fourth had an older sister close in age with whom she shared most tasks, including drawing water. The sisters as often as not switched off between fetching water and caring for their baby brother. On the other side, all four of those who never fetched water were boys with older sisters who were largely responsible for the task. Similarly, in those households where the child who worked with me fetched water only some of the time, it was an older sister who took care of most of the rest.

> The well is closed again so I wander down to the riverbed. It's a hive of activity—a young teenage boy had just collected a sack of riverbed sand to use for plastering a house and is hoisting it onto his donkey when it spills out. As he refills the sack, five teenage girls pass by on their way back from "the East" with huge bundles of wood on their heads. Two women follow with equally hefty loads, theirs topped with axes. They are accompanied by five little children; the four girls, who are about five years old, have small bundles of twigs on their heads while the boy—who looks about four—carries a small bowl of twigs on his head. Two seven- or eight-year-old boys pass carrying axes and large bundles of wood on their backs. On the steep western bank the wood gatherers merge with people getting water. It being close to sunset, there is a steady stream of people coming up from the river with water. A man on a donkey, a seven-year-old boy with a two-gallon container, two women with five-gallon containers on their heads, and four young girls—about eight years old—carrying small buckets on their heads are steadily climbing up the slope. I count thirty-two people still in the riverbed, twenty-five of whom are women or girls. Among them are two women doing their laundry in the stagnant water near the banks where animals drink and people paddle about, cooling off and cleaning their feet. Near the shallow wells in the center, it is noisy as people draw water and wait their turns at the jemmam. People splash and play with the water, taking pleasure in the cool wetness and the soft river bottom sand. As the sun sets, more people arrive, taking advantage of the relative cool to get one last bit of water for the evening and early morning.

The river was frequently abuzz, while the wells—scenes of bedlam during their brief opening hours—were all too often silent. Shuttered for any number of reasons, the two diesel-pumped artesian wells (one longstanding and the second completed toward the end of 1981) were luckily backed up by three other sources: jemmam or shallow wells dug in the subsurface of the ephemeral river that bordered the village, the

Dinder itself when in flow during the rainy season, and the major canal of the agricultural project, which separated the village from the fields.

Both wells were within village bounds not much further than half a kilometer from any houseyard. The water was not only the cleanest of all the available sources, but also required the least labor time for its procurement. During my stay in Howa, however, the second well was under construction and the original well did not operate an average of one in four days, either because of mechanical breakdown or because it lacked spare parts, diesel fuel, or a well operator, who, it turned out, had a wife in another village. When the well was closed, most households returned to Howa's original source of water—the Dinder River, an ephemeral stream alongside the village. Some turned to the newest and least sanitary source of water—the major canal of the irrigation project. For most, the choice of alternative water source when the well was closed was determined by proximity and the labor requirements of drawing water from it, rather than the quality of the water.[3] These decisions were often made by children.

> Talal was at the canal around eight in the morning getting water for his family when he was commissioned to get water for another household. But before he did he had to deliver his own family's water, where unexpectedly he got enmeshed in totaling the groundnuts being shelled by a bunch of kids working in front of his family's house. He registered each child's name and total so that his father could later pay them for their piece work. Talal eventually remembered to get water for the other household, but almost four hours had elapsed since the request. By then the well was open, but since the family who had requested the water lived on the edge of town close to the canal, Talal opted to get canal water because it was much less time consuming. He could draw the water in minutes and deliver it much more quickly from that end of town. He saddled up his donkey, topping it with a cross pole holding two large containers—one tin, the other plastic, each holding about five gallons—and headed to the canal with his brother riding on back. Dismounting quickly, Talal waded in up to his thighs to fill the plastic jug. The can had sprung a leak, and Talal deliberately patched the hole with some mud before wading back in with it. After filling the repaired can he struggled to get the pair balanced across the patient donkey's back. He hooked the rope to the first can, went round to the other side of the donkey and had to use all his weight—his two feet pressed against the donkey's side as he yanked on the pole, neck muscles visibly straining—to cantilever it up and bring the cross pole down to the other jug. After all that struggle he was surprised to discover that his prospective customers had—of all things in four hours—already gotten water. Undaunted, if slightly disappointed, Talal rode to the bakery to see if they were interested, but it being canal water, they were not. He rode off to hawk the water in the village, confident that someone would buy it, even though it was murky canal water. Indeed, in all my time in Howa I never saw anyone— not the social workers, the teachers, or the health practitioner—refuse canal water when alternatives were unavailable. Though everyone probably thought I was somewhat hysterical on this question, I preferred the prospect of slowly dying of thirst.

Prior to the construction of Howa's first well in the mid-1960s, the Dinder was the sole source of water. During that time, as later when the well was closed, people fetched water from the river in flow during the rainy months from July through October. This water was silty but "clean" because of the swiftness of the river in flood. But this swiftness made the water hazardous to procure, and young children were not sent to negotiate the steep riverbanks. As the river receded each November, people dug shallow wells called jemmam in the sandy riverbed, shunning pools of standing water for animal consumption. Although jemmam were no longer in constant use after the well was built, the well was closed so often that one could almost always find them dug in the riverbed. The location of these shallow wells shifted as the river receded, with people digging new holes following along where the subsurface water was closest. When children and others fetched water from the riverbed, they usually had only to clean and drain an existing jemmam to begin drawing water.

Reaching the moister area of the riverbed, Sofia chose a fairly large jemmam with about five centimeters of water at its bottom. She kneeled on the damp sand surrounding the hole and reached down to neaten its walls using the edge of her small enamel bowl to smooth the sides. She walked through the well in order to neaten its other side, and then scooped out all of the water in the hole and poured it onto the sand. A girl of about thirteen years old joined her at the edge of the shallow well. Sofia and this girl spent the next couple of minutes scooping out the water as it filtered into the jemmam. They continued this procedure, taking turns using Sofia's bowl until the water was relatively free of sediment. Sofia then drew two bowls of water in order to wash her bucket. As she did this, the far wall cracked. At this, she and the older girl, with the older child in the lead, broke the wall down further and expanded the well. They smoothed the new wall and scooped out the loose dirt. The whole process took about ten minutes. The older girl cleaned the jemmam again, scooping out the water until it cleared.

In the meantime, Sofia cleaned her feet by slogging through the pools of standing water nearby. She also cleaned her bucket thoroughly by scrubbing it with mud and standing water and then rinsing it with jemmam water. She then ran about twenty-five meters to another shallow well. Tasting and smelling the water to see if it was good, she quickly spit it out. "It's gross, and there's pee in it" she told whoever was listening, and ran back to the original well, where the older girl was still drawing water, trying to get rid of the sediments. The girls worked in tandem to fill the elder one's five-gallon jerry-can. The older girl scooped up the water as it trickled into the jemmam, and poured it into Sofia's bucket. Sofia scooped it up from there and decanted it into the jerry-can. Their careful procedure minimized turbidity. Whenever she inadvertently scooped up some sand, the older girl paused to pour out little mud figures that with time crouched along much of the jemmam's top edge. When the older girl's container was full, Sofia filled her own bucket neatly and carefully by herself. She lifted the bucket to her head and balanced it with grace and surety as she walked through the streambed and up its steep and gullied banks a few hundred meters to her house.

Figure 15. Children like Nowal learned the delicate art of drawing water from older children and women. Jemmam, the shallow wells dug in the sandy river bed as the water receded and disappeared, were once the main source of water in Howa. Even after the construction of two artesian wells, jemmam remained important as a backup water supply whenever the wells were closed, which was all too frequent.

As Sofia's experience attests, drawing clean water from the riverbed was a skill that required meticulous care and patience. Girls did this task more often than boys. Moreover, perhaps because of the skill required, it seemed that more women than usual drew water on days when the artesian well was closed. Procuring jemmam water was often a group effort in which children learned the technique and the qualities of a good well by observing and sharing the work with more experienced children or adults. I often observed adults guiding, instructing, and correcting children as they drew water from the riverbed. With several trips to fetch water in a day, children had the opportunity to constantly practice and develop their competence.

Drawing water from the artesian wells was a simpler task, involving gritty determination more than exacting skill. Children fetching well water were not required to make assessments about water quality or to construct and maintain a safe source. They had only to jostle with the crowds that attended the well during its limited operating hours and secure a place near one of the spigots. As with fetching water from the river or canal, physical skill and strength were required to lift and carry the containers back home. For children of ten years, vessels might be one-gallon plastic jugs—courtesy of Mobil Oil— buckets of a similar size or slightly larger, or five-gallon jerry-cans of plastic or tin. Girls generally transported these containers on their heads, although some of them used donkeys to carry home a pair of the large jerry-cans. Head portage was not a skill learned by men in Howa, so when boys of about ten and older fetched water, they tended to use a donkey with a pair of five-gallon containers. Girls from a young age, on the other hand, started practicing carrying things around on their heads, and by ten years of age many were already quite adept at it, though not all were yet large enough to carry the five-gallon containers that women customarily used. Head bearing required girls to lift the vessels over their shoulders and relied on strong neck and shoulder muscles, along with well-developed balance. Using donkeys, on the other hand, embroiled boys and girls in tough games of seesaw as they cantilevered their loads on and off the donkey's back.

The importance of children's labor to water provision, and of water provision to the round of daily tasks that secured the reproduction of everyday life, cannot be overestimated. Of all the tasks in which children engaged, their labor was most significant here. Fetching water was unique among tasks associated with providing the means of existence because the contribution of children outweighed that of adults in the total time spent at the community level.[4] Perhaps it was the routine nature of the task or maybe it was the sheer volume of work involved, but fetching water was in some ways the least playful of children's tasks. Of course, in the heat of the day it was simply fun to get wet, and everybody always got wet whether from treading in the puddles around the wells, jockeying for a place near the spigots, wading into the canal, or splashing their faces with the cool water of the jemmams. But these playful aspects of the task were subdued and so much a part of the work—which was fairly constrained, either because of the crowds at the well or because of the limited number of jemmams and the need for meticulous care in using them—that they went almost unremarked. Of course, with children involved, nothing—not even getting water in an arid land—was utterly serious.

Figure 16. Even the most essential tasks were toyed with by children, whose irreverence permeated their routines.

Gathering Fuelwood

Collecting firewood was another matter entirely. While woodfuel was one of the crucial provisions supplied in large part by children, and consequently a task that absorbed much of their time, its procurement—almost always from outside the village bounds—left room and time for play.

> It's mid-June and the sun is finally getting low in the sky. Everyone emerges from their shaded grass verandas to get one last chore in or share a bit of leisure. (Pick-up soccer games were popular with young men and boys late in the day, and it was the hour when lots of children played in the streets or open spaces of their courtyards.) Miriam and about five other girls were off to get wood in the East. They collected large acacia branches, knocking off the thorns and small branches with a large stick. In the midst of their gathering they ran into Talal and his brother with a couple of friends out chopping saplings for the kitchen Talal was building for his mother. Before too long the children descended into the riverbed together. Quite spontaneously, the boys decided to sing, using my small plastic water jug as a drum. As the boys sang a number of popular songs, the girls danced in the riverbed. The golden light of *'asur* (the hour before sunset) made this rare instance of older boys and girls playing together even more special.

With the exception of small amounts of wood for medicinal, veterinary, or cosmetic purposes, all of the wood burned in Howa was used for cooking. Fuelwood was collected by gathering sticks from the ground around dead or felled trees, chopping down trees or lopping off their branches, or burning charcoal from local trees. Children's labor was most significant in the first of these, collecting dead and felled branches or twigs, although they also helped adults by chopping wood and in the production of charcoal. I estimate that children and adolescents provided about 65 percent of the *gathered* wood used in their households. Here again, girls between eight and fourteen predominated. Ten of the children with whom I worked (six girls and four boys) collected wood regularly. Children were not the sole providers of household fuel, as they often were for water. Because of the nature of the work, children's contributions were augmented routinely with larger pieces gotten by adults and older siblings or through purchase. This is not to say that children's contribution to fuel procurement was insignificant. In most households children or teens provided the bulk of fuelwood consumed. All of the seven children working with me who did not provide fuel for their households—including the herdboys and children who assisted their elders with market-oriented charcoal production or scavenging—had older sisters who procured their households' fuelwood.

There were political-ecologic and task-specific reasons that the children's role in fuel provision was more auxiliary than in other tasks. Women generally cooked over a hot three-stone fire, for which they preferred wood that was over a meter long and more than an inch and a half in diameter. The best wood this size was available only by cutting, and most ten-year-old children could not wield an ax well enough to provide it. Much of this wood was procured by men or older boys, and occasionally by the women themselves. In addition, local deforestation—exacerbated by the Suki Project—had significantly increased the distance traveled and time required for fuel collection in Howa. Children routinely walked between half an hour and an hour to find wood. Moreover, the sort of wood that remained near the village had to be collected more frequently than before because it was from less valued species or smaller trees. These factors of time and distance led to both the increased participation of children collecting wood near the village and the need to supplement it with larger pieces cut further afield by older household members or others. Finally, even without the stress on the local wood supply, the amount of fuel required to cook two or three meals a day, coupled with the average load a ten-year-old child could carry, required children to collect wood about every three days in most households. Given domestic chores, such as child care, errand running, cooking, and cleaning; other responsibilities, such as drawing water, farming, and shepherding; school attendance; and children's need and desire for free time, many children in Howa were unable to collect woodfuel frequently enough to cover the bulk of their household's requirements.

Nevertheless, children's contribution to fuel provision in the village as a whole was substantial. Thirteen of the seventeen children working with me helped provide fuelwood, eight of them routinely. In most households, the branches and sticks collected by children composed at least half of the fuel they used.[5] The land-use changes brought about by the agricultural project, along with other factors, had so stressed the woodlands nearby that there was little else for village households to burn. The altered environs not only had made cooking more arduous (with smokier fires and the extra work required as a result of poorer quality wood, for instance), but had increased children's work substantially. These increases were felt not only by children who regularly collected fuel, but also by children who normally did not. Among the seventeen children working with me, for instance, one boy and one girl were called on in this ad hoc way. When household supplies ran low, each of them was sent to areas on the village perimeter to gather what wood they could. They usually had to resort to small or extremely poor quality bits of wood in these pinches.

Among those who did collect wood regularly, a camaraderie like that of the shepherds lightened the load, figuratively if not literally. Collecting wood, especially among girls, was usually a group activity. Awatif and a small group of her friends, for instance, spent many late afternoons collecting wood together. Living only a few steps from each other's houses made it easy to initiate work or play spontaneously, and these girls did most things together. The girls—three of whom, including Awatif, were students—enjoyed each other's company, and, like the herdboys, seemed to make a good time out of even the most mundane chores. Their pleasure in being together certainly did not detract from their sense of purpose in carrying out their work, however. To the contrary, the opportunity to work with friends ensured that chores would be more readily undertaken. As with herdboys, the girls' sociality worked to their households' advantage; if two or three girls were set to get wood, for instance, one or two others might join them without any prodding from their mothers—and every bit of wood, whether needed that moment or not, was appreciated.

> On an overcast morning in late June, Awatif and her friends head across the canal and north to an area known as the *tulh* (after a small stand of tulh [*Acacia seyal*]). Leaving their houses at six-thirty, the girls walk for about half an hour. They often collected wood from this area bordering the fields of the irrigation project, where trees were commonly felled for charcoal production or construction needs. The chopping left many smaller branches on the ground, which makes the girls' task easier because they need only cover a small area to find plentiful wood. Chatting as they walk, the girls carry rags and lengths of rope. The rope is to bundle the wood, while the rags cushion their load on the way home.
>
> When we reach the open woodland of the tulh, the girls work steadily and swiftly at this familiar task. They make three separate trips to different parts of the site, each time returning to a central spot with full armloads of sticks and branches. After the third trip, each has amassed a tremendous amount of wood. The girls then begin sorting through their piles of wood, knocking off thorns and laying the sticks and branches neatly over long pieces of outstretched rope. Awatif and her friends each tie the rope loosely around her bundle and then work in pairs to tighten it. A girl sits on either side of the bundle holding one end of the rope and pressing the soles of her feet against the side of the wood bundle. Working in tandem, they tug the rope, rocking the soles of their feet against the wood and arching their backs to yank as hard as possible, producing neat and manageable bundles of wood. The girls roll up their rags and place them on their heads, bend over to put their heads down on the wood piles and then straighten up, pressing the wood to their heads. Awatif takes a bit longer to sort her wood, having collected more than she can carry. Even leaving some behind she seems to struggle a bit in lifting her heavy load, and is plagued all the way home by a broken flip-flop that she fixed by tying a string to a twig at the underside of the sole to create a makeshift thong.

Children's work in charcoal production was another matter entirely. Cutting the necessary wood, making and tending the kiln, and "harvesting" the charcoal was an intensive process lasting several days, and virtually no one under eighteen in Howa did this work on their own. Children often assisted their fathers and older relatives with charcoal making. Two of the boys who worked with me helped with the full range of tasks. Another couple of children, boy and girl cousins, occasionally helped their grandmother and great aunt scavenge bits of charcoal from spent kilns up to an hour's walk away in the wooded areas bordering the agricultural lands and further afield.[6] Muna assisted with this task almost every time her grandmother went (two to three times a week during the hot dry months of May and June, when most of the local charcoal production took place), whereas Ismail accompanied her only on occasion, when he didn't have school. Even at that he joined her largely because of his curiosity and the good-natured rivalry between the children over whose experiences and activities were more interesting and wide-ranging.[7] Whatever the reasons that the children

Figure 17. In the absence of an adequate supply of larger wood, girls collected bundles of branches such as these several times a week to fuel their mothers' cooking fires. Compressing the bundles between their feet, the girls carried them on their heads for the half-hour walk back to the village.

accompanied their grandmother, when they were out with her it was hard work, and even when both of them were there, not much play. Over the weeks Muna collected enough charcoal to fill a couple of sacks that she sold, with her father's assistance, for the equivalent of US$2.19 each, giving the proceeds to her mother. What Ismail collected was used in part by his household; the rest was contributed to his grandmother's collection.

Another child, Sami, participated in charcoal production regularly. Sami was from a relatively poor nontenant household. His father was an older man who earned about half of his annual income from the production and sale of charcoal. Except during the height of the rainy season from July through October, when charcoal was not produced and agricultural work was available, Sami accompanied his father almost daily to cut and gather wood for both the production of charcoal and household consumption. They traipsed over an hour away to find adequate supplies of favored species like tulh (*Acacia seyal*) or, more rarely, *hejlij* (*Balanites aegyptiaca*). While Sami and his father cut wood, the latter with considerably more speed and dexterity, Sami's thirteen-year-old sister, Maha, collected felled branches to haul home for household cooking. Besides cutting and transporting wood, Sami and Maha assisted their father every few days when he built an earthen kiln next to their house to carbonize the charcoal. The children also helped their father tend the kiln for the two or three days that the charcoal smoldered and with bagging it for sale either in the village or a nearby town. Even though the children goofed around when they went out each day, their work was not as playful as that of children out only with other kids to collect wood. As assistants to their father, Sami and Maha were not in control of the rhythm of their work or its duration, and unlike the herdboys or children off on their own to do various tasks, these children had few opportunities for "stolen" moments of unattended spontaneous play. Nevertheless, a different form of play erupted around the edges.

July. The rains were starting and charcoal production would soon be winding down. On a bit of a busman's holiday, Sami spent part of the morning building an extraordinary miniature charcoal mound out of small pieces of wood. Crouching on the ground near his house, he made a small mound of grass and then placed the wood teepee-style around it. He covered the cone in another layer of grass and then sprinkled fistfuls of dirt mixed with dung over the whole thing. The whole enterprise took about ten minutes, whereupon Sami ran to get a burning coal from a neighbor's fire. Touching it to the grass through a small opening he'd left, Sami ignited the *comina*. As he covered the opening with a *doleib* stone, Sami announced with great satisfaction that the charcoal would be ready by afternoon. When Sami unpacked the small mound later in the day, he gave the charcoal to his mother—an indulgence she rarely got from her husband's routine charcoal production.

In this activity, Sami, the eternal assistant in making charcoal, had a chance to sequence and control the full range of tasks associated with the activity. His playful work offered Sami a sense of mastery and his workful play produced small amounts of charcoal for his appreciative mother.

Agriculture

Dramatic enactments of work in miniature were most striking in the arena of agriculture. Children like Rashid, described in chapter 1, whiled away languid afternoons absorbed in endless games of "tenancies" and the subsistence version, "bildat." Engaged in the full course of activities associated with both tenant and subsistence farming, the boys played in the shaded areas of their houseyards, fashioning miniature hoes and tractors to work the beds they raised, graded, furrowed, planted, ridged, watered, weeded, and harvested. As with Sami's charcoal kiln, these games gave children the opportunity and pleasure of working out in miniature the sequencing and coordination of tasks in which they generally participated as assistants. Their attention to detail was extraordinary and their resourcefulness with materials exquisite.

The play of agriculture, like Sami's playful kiln construction, ricocheted and intertwined with other aspects of the children's time. In the work of agriculture, which was, of course, the main productive activity in Howa, ten-year-olds worked as auxiliaries, assisting their parents, elder siblings, and others in myriad tasks. None of these tasks—which included seed preparation, clearing, sowing, weeding, and harvesting—was the responsibility of children alone, although most children over eight years old contributed to each of them. Their contribution was particularly significant in the labor-intensive tasks of seed preparation, planting, weeding, and harvesting. All but one of the seventeen children participated in at least one agricultural task during the year; ten participated in seed preparation (shelling groundnuts), three in clearing, eight in planting, eleven in weeding, three in bird scaring, and eight in harvesting. Almost all of the children between nine and thirteen years old from tenant households helped their parents carry out the full range of agricultural tasks, whether in project lands or outside. While children from nontenant households often worked in the fields of members of their extended families or for a wage or piece rate in the tenancies of other villagers, they did not engage in agricultural work as commonly as did the children of tenants, even as paid workers.[8]

Participation of the greatest number of children was facilitated by the long school vacation, which coincided with the rainy season from late June through September. Although school vacations were set by the Ministry of Education to enable teachers in rural schools to return to their home districts during the difficult rainy months, the timing of these vacations was also intended to free children to assist their parents during one of the busiest times of the agricultural season. Given the intensified labor requirements of irrigated cultivation compared to rain-fed, it was critically important that children be available to work during the rainy months. In many families the labor of youngsters was necessary to complete various agricultural tasks, and my research suggests that if these children were unavailable to work because of school, many of them would be forced to drop out. School attendance in Howa traced a knife edge between households' current needs for their children's labor and their attempts to improve the children's prospects for the future. The edge was sharpened by the economic straits brought about by the production relations and generally low incomes associated with the agricultural project. "Development" often takes place on the backs of children, and crop mortgaging was not the only kind of mortgaging that enabled struggling farm tenants to get by.

Farmers in Howa argued that the cultivation practices of the agricultural project were more arduous than those before it had been. There were a number of reasons for this. Cotton, groundnuts, and sorghum, the only crops allowed on project lands (the last, only beginning in 1981), were sown using a digging stick, rather than broadcast, as with sesame. Planting this way was time consuming. Farmers reported, and my observations corroborated, that a tenancy of approximately ten acres took a minimum of several days to plant. Often, as many nine- to thirteen-year-old children as were available in a household would assist their father or older brother with sowing. Eight of the children with whom I worked helped plant their households' and/or extended families' fields. One of these children, Sami, whose father was not a tenant, also did this work as a paid field hand.

> Early July and the rains have started. Awatif and her twelve-year-old sister and thirteen-year-old brother had been going to the fields each day to help their father plant. Their father left at dawn to take advantage of the coolest part of the day and the three children followed just after six. Awatif rode the donkey, sitting atop a large sack of sorghum that rested on a digging stick and an ax. While her brother and sister dropped some grain

at the village mill, Awatif continued straight to the footbridge over the major canal. She seemed quite comfortable on the donkey, even though her small size made it difficult for her to mount it by herself. We zig-zagged along the canal system for about an hour and a half to reach the family's tenancy. The minute we got there, Awatif's brother Osman ran to a wooded area within view of the family's field and set up the net snare he'd brought along to trap birds. Awatif helped him set the trap while their sister joined their father at work clearing the irrigation ditch bounding the field. After the trap was set, Awatif and Osman joined the other two in the field. Osman immediately took up the digging stick and rapidly went up and down the rows making holes about fifteen centimeters apart with every step. His sisters followed his path in different rows, each carrying a small bowl of sorghum from which they dropped several kernels of grain into each hole, covering them up in the same movement by sliding soil in with their feet. They kept a fairly leisurely pace up and down the rows in the wake of the speeding digging stick. Osman ran off repeatedly to check his bird trap. On occasion he didn't return before the girls finished planting all of the holes drilled, at which point they would either take a break or one of them would take up the digging stick and continue in their brother's path. Awatif's sister accomplished this task with considerably more skill than she did. One time as Osman ran off, his father looked up from the irrigation ditch he was cleaning and shouted over, "Are you here to work or play?" Undaunted, Osman checked his trap anyway, but never snared anything that morning.

Figure 18. Just after sunrise Awatif and her sister and brother headed out to their family's tenancy a few kilometers away to assist their father with planting chores. Working early to avoid the hottest parts of the day, the children—if not their father—were usually back in the village by late morning.

Figure 19. Skirting the edge between work and play, bird snaring was a favorite pastime of boys in Howa. Taking a break from planting sorghum (or was it the other way around?), Awatif and her brother set his homemade net trap, hoping to catch a few doves or migratory birds with some filched grain.

Osman's behavior and his father's response point again to the playful nature of much of children's work and the purposive setting for much of their play. Even in early adolescence, when a child's work contribution is relied on by his or her family, Osman was lured to "fall down on the job" by the prospect of trapping a few birds. (See Fortes 1970, 59–61, for an example of the distractions found and created by children in northern Ghana protecting their families' crops from birds, and Ammar 1966 for a description of the parental response to such lack of discipline in Upper Egypt.)

Even more laborious was weeding the cotton and groundnut fields. This demanding effort forced many tenants to tap the labor of their young sons and, on occasion, their daughters. Because the majority of Howa's tenants could not afford to hire people to assist with agricultural tasks on a regular basis (though most hired field hands during the harvest), the labor of children was all the more important in the face of new tasks and work regimes imposed by the project. Eleven of the children working with me, eight boys and three girls (seven of them from tenant households), participated in weeding; three of the boys did so for pay.

Weeding marked a significant departure from pre-project regimes of work. Project regulations mandated not only four weedings, but that the heavy clay soils be weeded with a short-handled hoe (kedunka or *toriya*) that required farmers to bend over as they worked. Unlike the tools that were traditionally used (the *malod ga'ad* [standing hoe] and *malod wagif* [sitting hoe]), the short-handled hoe was back breaking as well as clod breaking, and many complained about it. When children weeded, they usually used properly scaled kedunkas fashioned for them by local toolmakers. Some children, however, used a "sitting hoe," and thus could sit or squat as they worked. Many old-timers also insisted on using pre-project hoes, despite the objections of project authorities.

The arduousness of weeding notwithstanding, harvest was the most labor-intensive part of the agricultural year. Harvest tasks required the labor of almost every ablebodied family member in most tenant households. Some families with tenancies more than a forty-five-minute walk from the village even built temporary shelters in their fields (*cambo*) and moved the household out there for days at a time during the weeks when the harvest work was most intense. Children as young as seven helped their parents, grandparents, and older siblings pick cotton and pull up groundnuts. Here again, children of tenants were more likely to work than others, even among those working for pay. Indeed, all through the village, children, particularly girls ten years and older and most women over thirty-five, worked for a piece-wage during the harvest. Pioneering the public–private partnerships that have become so prevalent in recent years, even the school got into the act. It had become a tradition for the school children and their teachers to spend one week each year picking cotton in the fields of various tenants. In exchange, the school was paid by the Suki Project at the going rate. In the harvest of 1980–81, for instance, the school was paid the equivalent of US$250, which was used to purchase basic supplies.

In September, about a month before the sorghum, groundnut, and cotton harvests begin, many of the vegetables planted around the borders of the tenancies or in the few remaining bildat (rain-fed fields outside of the irrigation scheme) were ripe and ready for picking. Among them was a prickly variety of okra known as weka that thrived in and around the irrigated fields. Weka, a staple of the local diet, was sliced and sun dried on burlap sacks sprawled all around houseyards immediately after it was harvested. The dried rounds were eventually pounded into a coarse powder in large wooden mortars and reconstituted throughout the year to thicken the daily stew. When the pods ripened, women and children were out nearly every day to harvest them.

> Ismail has been picking weka for the past week or so. He's wrapped his hand in a rag to protect it from the minuscule prickly thorns covering the okra. The cloth was cumbersome and made picking somewhat awkward and difficult. Harvesting weka even without the cloth was difficult enough for Ismail because the okra pods had to be yanked hard from the stems and some of the higher ones were out of his reach. He collected only enough to fill an old stew pot brought for the occasion, and all too abruptly called it a day. While after a week of picking, there was not much left on the plants for the time being, it was clear that Ismail simply did not like the task (not many people did) and cut it off as early as possible. He hardly approached it with the quixotic zeal he had when he was trying to catch fish earlier that morning or the cheerful energy he had for most of his chores. He picked reluctantly and left several pods

on the plants either through laziness or boredom, and did not seem to notice or care that some weka remained unpicked.

Ismail's lethargy notwithstanding, the energy expended picking weka from mid-September until late October was impressive. Not only did each household try to harvest enough for its substantial annual dietary requirement, but it was also picked for sale. Women were responsible for its harvest and entitled to any money earned from the sale of surplus supplies. Thus, there was material incentive for women or their agents—most commonly children—to harvest as much of the fast-growing vegetable as possible as soon as it was ripe. These efforts were all the more intense given that the faster weka was harvested, the more pods would reach fruition.

Toward the end of the weka harvest, the sorghum and groundnuts ripened. Following the groundnut harvest in late November and early December, the cotton crop ripened and was ready for picking. Depending on the schedule of other agricultural operations in a given season, the harvests of cotton and groundnuts often overlapped. As was discussed in chapter 2, this overlap was anticipated by the architects of the agricultural project, but was predicated on a mechanized groundnut harvest. For most farmers this had not come to pass, either because of mechanical breakdowns or because it was unaffordable, placing a great strain on family labor.

As all-encompassing as agricultural work was, it was still infiltrated by play. As with herding or wood collecting, children's play and work in the fields often overlapped and intertwined. Children goofed around and meandered aimlessly in getting out to and returning from the fields, for instance, sometimes having a dip in the major canal or wandering off to socialize with other children out gathering wood, herding, or working in their families' fields. More commonly, play punctuated the children's work in the fields, providing a distraction. Like Awatif's brother Osman, many set up handmade bird traps near the fields. Although boys made and deployed the net traps, their sisters were often part of the enterprise. The children would roll the snare into a narrow strip and cover it with dirt, scattering sorghum—usually the very seed they were meant to be planting—on the ground in front of it. Stretching a long cord from the buried net toward where they were working, the children would return to work, keeping an eye out for any birds alighting on the sorghum. If birds were spotted, these wayward field hands would run to pull the cord and snare their prey. While many times the birds were scared off by the children's approach, sometimes they were actually trapped, at which point one of the older boys (usually a teenager) would systematically slit their necks with a small knife or a sharpened piece of tin. While successfully netting what might be a few dozen small birds for later eating would delight parents almost as much as the children, the distraction and constant back-and forth to check the traps could drive adults determined to complete a task around the bend. In these cases, the children's play—which had its own workful elements—might be inhibited by their elders' agendas and impatience. But if trapping was an activity of boy and bird, the call to work enacted a similar dance between boy and man. By my accounts, the boys were ahead in both arenas.

Collecting Wild Foods

While birds trapped by children and young men were something of a rare treat, other wild foods figured more significantly in the local diet according to the season. Children usually picked or gathered these noncultivated foods for their own or their households' consumption. Ten of the seventeen children working with me procured wild foods for their households. Most of these were seasonal fruits and vegetables, although a few children also hunted and one had tried his hand at fishing.

A small number of uncultivated vegetables, among them the greens, mulayta (*Picridium trigitanum Desf*) and *khudra* (*Corchorus olitorius*), and a variety of unculti-vated okra known generically as weka (*Hibiscus esculentus L*), grew in and around the tenancies, and were gathered almost daily during the latter months of the rainy season. Three of the children regularly harvested these vegetables, providing an important addition to their families' diets. The greens were among the only fresh vegetables eaten in Howa over the year. But there was an alarming underside to their consumption. The greens were treated with an herbicide used regularly in the tenancies. In questioning Suki Project authorities about this, I was told that the herbicide, known to them by its U.S. brand name, Zorial®, killed grasses but not broad-leafed plants.[9] While khudra and molayta were broad-leafed, they were sprayed nevertheless with little regard for whether they were consumed by animals, and no regard or seeming awareness that these and other plants deemed "weeds" by the project were consumed and handled by the local population, particularly children. I was disturbed to find children's bare arms, faces, and clothing coated with a fine white dust after they gathered the treated greens. While of course the chemicals, which the children knowingly called *mobeed* (toxin), were washed off both children and vegetables, the risks of exposure through ingestion or contact were unknown to the local population. The bitterness of the greens may go well beyond their taste.[10]

Many of the wild foods favored in Howa came from trees, and were not so haz-ardous to gather or consume. Neither were they as easy to come by as the vegetables that dotted the irrigated areas. Thanks to widespread deforestation in the vicinity, which had affected both the range of species and the number of trees, the availability of preferred fruits, seeds, and roots had by all accounts decreased significantly in recent years. Many of the fruits that in the past had been enjoyed by the entire population during good years and had been a famine food source in bad, had become largely chil-dren's foods. These increasingly rare foods, such as *lalob* (from *Balanites aegyptiaca*), *nubg* (from *Zizaphus spinachristi*), *aradeib* (tamarind from *Tamarindus indica*), and to a lesser extent, *humbock* (from *Capparis decidua*), were eaten almost exclusively by chil-dren who went in search of them or happened upon them in excursions in and around the village. Some fruits that were once freely available, such as lalob, aradeib, and, to a lesser extent, nubg, had become commodities for sale in nearby markets (see Tully 1988, 90, for a discussion of the same phenomenon in western Sudan). To compensate, per-haps, a few *Zizaphus spinachristi* and *Capparis decidua* had been planted in the village by individual residents. In season, their thorny branches dripped with old flip-flops, sticks, and odd shoes, which testified to the sport of children getting fruit by whacking the trees with whatever came to hand.

The most prized wild fruit in the area was the doleib. This large, sticky, sweet, and stringy orange fruit is from the tall fan palm known by the same name (*Borassus aethiopicum*). The locals called it a "Kauli mango" after the nearby area where large stands were found, but I was sad to discover after months of anticipation that, except for the color, doleibs were a far cry from any mango I'd ever had. The doleib tree had grown commonly along much of the Dinder River, but by the 1980s coverage near the village had been reduced to two isolated and relatively small stands a few kilometers away. These treasured groves had been brought under the protection of the Forestry Department and cutting was forbidden. Apart from its fruit, the doleib was an important and versatile tree resource. It was used in construction and fencing, and its various parts were used widely as tools and household implements. Its decline, then, was due to fairly intense cutting for a variety of local uses, as well as extensive felling for commercial purposes. Natural regeneration of the palm was thwarted not only because the fruit was widely collected both to eat and to sell, but also because the succulent root of the doleib seedling was considered a delicacy and young trees were uprooted regularly.

The doleib was also important as a living tree resource. Its tall and graceful beauty was a source of pleasure and pride for people of the area. Doleib groves were special microenvironments that offered shade and shelter to wildlife. The only remaining baboons in the region were found there. The larger of these two groves, known simply as "the doleibs," was on a bend in the river about five kilometers from Howa, just across the river from the next settlement downstream. It was a spot favored by almost everyone in Howa and its significance for people was striking. For months before going there, I heard about the beauty of the trees, about the wonderful fruit that grew there, about how cool it was in the shady grove, and about the baboons who lived in the treetops.

Certainly the biggest attraction of the doleibs was the large and fleshy fruit that ripened during May and June. During these months young and old people alike beat a path from the village to the trees. Most of these trips were to gather fruit for individual and household consumption, but some young men and several children collected fruit to sell back in the village for the equivalent of five to ten cents apiece. Several times in the season local merchants drove their trucks out to the doleibs and hired young men to collect truckloads of fruit to sell in regional markets.

Most children in Howa between nine and fourteen went to the doleibs to eat the sweet fruits as they ripened and fell from the trees, and to collect a few to take home to their families. Seven of the children working with me collected doleibs. For some children, the prospect of all that good eating, combined with their entrepreneurial plans, led to excited flights of fancy about expeditions to the grove. Talal, for example, came over almost nightly at the start of the season to borrow flashlight batteries to carry out his rather grandiose plans to gather and sell doleibs. Each night he had a plan to get up early, ride his donkey out to the groves before dawn, and sleep under a tree while (in his mind) the fruit crashed down around him. He figured this would give him an edge on village slugabeds in collecting the most doleibs. He raved about having the fruit sold before his friends wiped the sleep from their eyes. But even the bright sparkle that lit his eyes each evening could not dislodge the sleep from them come first light, and each morning when the sun was well above the horizon it seems he awoke, surprised to still be in bed and then trundled sheepishly back to return the batteries. Perhaps the planning was more fun than the execution; in any case, Talal never made a killing in doleibs.

For Awatif, ten-year-old Suad, their sisters, and their friends, the planning had been going on for a few weeks, but the execution was spontaneous. One Friday morning when school was out, the girls—twelve in total, ranging in age from eight to fifteen—decided to dispense with collecting wood and go instead to the doleibs. In granting them permission to go there rather than collecting wood, the girls' mothers had requested that they bring back *wekab,* a starchy ash used for thickening bean and other stews, made by burning the calyx-bearing branches of the doleib palm. These branches fell under the weight of the fruit and, along with piles of fronds and crushed fruit, thickly covered the ground under the trees.

> We set off at 6:45 across the hard-packed and sharply dissected *kerrib* land northeast of the well. All of the girls except Awatif were carrying small containers of water and/or larger buckets and containers for carrying back things from the palm grove. The walk was pleasant and cool thanks to the cloud cover and strong breezes. As we moved away

Figure 20. Trips to the doleib palm grove along a bend in the Dinder were a highlight of May and June when the fruits ripened. Making the trek to eat their fill and have an adventure, Suad and her friends collect masses of palm branches to burn. The starchy ash known as wekab was requested by their mothers, who used it to thicken stews.

from the village the terrain changed from the pale gullied kerrib to dark cracked clayey soil dotted with scrub and a few thorn trees. The latter was an area of rain-fed cultivation, but most of these bildat belonged to people in the village across the river from the doleibs, which had not been included in the irrigation project. Nearer to the grove and river the area evolved into an acacia forest that had been almost completely cut despite or maybe because of government protection. Abutting this area of stumps were the doleibs.

The walk took just over an hour. As soon as we arrived the girls ran in all directions looking for and collecting the choicest fruit from the seemingly limitless number strewn about the area. They devoured several fruits apiece, seeming to relish each sticky bite. Finally sated, they began the task of producing wekab for their mothers by collecting fallen branches from all around the grove and bringing them to a small clearing in the trees. In the meantime, Awatif and a few of the younger girls found some baboons high in one of the trees and excitedly pointed them out to us. Awatif followed the lead of some boys who were throwing doleib stones at the baboons. Luckily for the baboons, her throw rose only about three meters toward its target way up in the tree. Growing bored, she continued to wander around the area looking playfully for select fruit while her sister Shaddiya, as well as Suad and several of the older girls kept collecting branches. While they toiled, the younger girls cracked the doleibs open by banging them together or hitting them against the trees. Burying their faces in fruit after fruit, they devoured them with obvious pleasure. After some more feasting they climbed a termite mound nearby and from the top belted out the call to prayer at the top of their lungs for about two minutes.

All this while, Suad and the older girls were off in different directions collecting branches. They returned after about fifteen minutes, loaded down again and were joined by the younger girls, who climbed down from their perch high on the termite mound and ran over to help carry the cumbersome branches back to the clearing. It was 9:00 and we had been at the doleibs for over an hour. Suad piled her branches high, rapidly set fire to them, and ran from the hot flames. While the fires burned, she and the older girls fooled around on the sidelines, their turn to enjoy the fruit.

When the flames subsided about half an hour later, all twelve girls set off for water in the nearby riverbed. They ran down the embankment and diagonally across the riverbed to a deep jemmam near the opposite shore. They washed their legs, hands, and faces before they drank and filled their buckets. An older boy nearby climbed into the jemmam, which was about a meter deep, and got a footing on its wet sandy edge. From there he drew water that the girls used to fill their individual buckets. Buckets splashing, the girls ran back across the river singing, reaching the still smoldering fires at 9:55. Now it was the older girls who set off in search of fruit. Awatif stayed behind, slowly eating a doleib. The others returned five minutes later with more fruit and still more branches that they dropped on the ground. Using branches with fanlike fronds as brooms or rakes, the girls swept the embers outward and sprinkled them with the water. A few minutes later they swept their doused ashes (wekab) into their buckets.

Suad tried to pick up the small bits of ash that the broom missed and burned her hands in the process. She then got a piece of bark to shovel the remaining ashes into her bucket. As soon as the last ashes were in her bucket, Suad went off for still more branches. She returned after a few minutes and set the new pile of branches on fire. While they burned, she ate another couple of doleibs and then completed the whole process again, including another trip to the river.

Throughout this time, Awatif was "chain eating" doleibs, no sooner dropping the husk of one than immediately picking up another. She was a picture of complete absorption, sitting on one doleib with her face buried almost constantly in another. The air was pungent as the sweet smell of the fruit mixed with the acrid smoke of the burning branches and the girls in their bright flowered dresses wove through the clattering layers of branches and fronds on the ground.

With the second fires doused, each girl filled her bucket or bowl with additional wekab and topped the damp pile with several fruits. They lifted these heavy containers onto their heads and set off for the village. On the way out of the grove we ran into Osman, Awatif's thirteen-year-old brother, who had come out by donkey to collect palm branches to use in the construction of shades and verandas. Awatif convinced him to give her a ride back to the village. She, Suad, and a few other girls helped him to load the branches onto the animal's sides. The rest of the girls waited and did not set off for the village until noon. The walk back was hot, but for the first twenty to thirty minutes everyone kept a brisk pace. We rested for a few minutes in what shade we could find under one of the only trees around. After this stop we sprang ahead of the girls and rushed home for rest and water. We reached the village just before 1:00 and turned back to see the girls resting again, this time in the open sun about four hundred meters in the distance.

It is doubtful that any woman in Howa would send a child to get this ash specifically, and only two children working with me procured it over the season. But given the appeal of a trip to the doleibs, that was a moot point. Women had only to take advantage of the opportunity presented by their daughters' eagerness to visit the palm grove. For their part, the girls loved to go in order to eat their fill of doleibs, to bring fruit home to enjoy later with their families, and to have an outing in the treasured and exotic grove. Work, play, and wonder were almost indistinguishable on excursions like these.

If doleibs were a fruit enjoyed by everyone in the village, there were other plants that were consumed solely by children. Among these were *suteb,* the bulbous root of a plant that grew during the rainy season in the drowned mayas. While adults said that suteb could and would be eaten during food shortages, they did not eat them as a matter of course, despite liking them. This was mostly because with shepherds as competition, they did not get the chance. Herdboys sometimes managed to enlist one of the scrawny but speedy herd dogs to snare a rabbit to cook in the field. Like suteb, the rabbits caught by herdboys rarely made it back to the village.

Figure 21. During the rainy season shallow pools formed in depressions all around the village. Determined water lilies soon sprouted in these pools, and even more determined herdboys waded in to pluck them. Boiled or roasted, the lily's starchy roots, called suteb, were a favorite seasonal breakfast for shepherds. Like the rabbits and other delicacies occasionally snared by herdboys, suteb never made it back to the village for the pleasure of others.

Other children hunted, trapped, or fished, although only bird trapping was of any economic or nutritional significance to their households. Three of the children, two boys and a girl, assisted their older brothers or other male relatives in trapping doves and several varieties of small birds that descended on the area during the rainy season. While these bite-sized birds were consumed most often within the extended family, sometimes upward of a hundred birds were trapped in a good day. Boys tried to sell surplus birds within the village for a few cents each. Of the children working with me, only Ahmed, who worked with his twelve-year-old uncle, engaged in trapping at this level. The other two children were still learning the techniques of trapping, and like most adolescent hunters in Howa, where hunting and trapping were not considered economic activities of any import, they and their brothers approached it more as a sport than as an income-producing activity.

Similarly, fishing was not an economic activity of any significance in Howa, and fish did not figure in the local diet at all. Nevertheless, some children in Howa (as well as a few adults) fished in the irrigation canals on occasion. As with hunting or trapping, almost all of those who fished were older than ten years. Among those working with me, only Sami fished during my stay in Howa, and that (fruitless) expedition to the canal was his first time. Ismail, whose uncles fished on occasion, was enraptured one day on his way back from helping with the harvest by the scores of catfish literally jumping from the canal near his father's tenancy. Balanced precariously on the bank of the canal, he had tried desperately to catch some fish by holding a large acacia branch across the canal in the wild hope that they would impale themselves on the thorns. In the wake of his quixotic venture, Ismail made plans for a fishing expedition, with clear delight at the prospect of eating his catch. Like Talal's predawn trips to the doleibs, the outing never quite materialized, but the pleasure of its anticipation was delicious.

I have perhaps dwelled more on these wild food expeditions than on other activities, such as agriculture, that consumed more of children's time and were more important to local production and reproduction. For me, the wildness of these expeditions extends beyond the food sources because they embody the themes that drive my work. The children's diverse strategies of food collection reveal the playfulness of work and the workfulness of play; at the same time they show how children's autonomous and pleasurable practices were woven integrally into their households' productive and reproductive strategies. In another vein, the waning economic significance of children's (and others') strategies of food procurement from wild sources speaks volumes about the nature of changes in the local political ecology.

Work-Play and Social Transformation

The preceding narratives of children's everyday activities make clear that none of the major categories of children's environmental work were separable from play. Play overlapped with, punctuated, and enveloped work in ways that often made the two indistinguishable in children's lives. In other instances, children played at their present and future work in miniature dramatic games like "fields," "store," and "house." Still other times play activities such as building projects, making miniature charcoal kilns, or going on wild food expeditions had a worklike aspect or outcome that nevertheless did not detract from their intrinsic pleasures. While work and play were mutually exclusive at times, their easy mesh in the children's lives was striking. But these unities in time, space, and meaning were threatened by some of the political-economic, social, and political-ecological changes underway in Howa. Within ten years of the Suki Project's inception, for instance, household labor dynamics had been altered substantially, leading, among other things, to increased demands on children's time. The constricted political ecology brought about by the project had begun to change the nature of certain children's tasks, such as procuring woodfuel and herding, because of declines in vegetation. Finally, the restricted land rights of the project ensured that future generations would have limited access to farm tenancies, and this had begun to change perceptions of the significance of formal schooling.

Each of these phenomena individually and collectively changed the everyday lives of children in Howa, impinging on the relationship between work and play in ways that anticipated and seemed to reinforce the stricter delineations between work and leisure time that characterize industrial capitalism. Under these conditions, work is valorized while play is trivialized as something done *only* in childhood or in time *off* from work. But the relationship between work and play is more vibrant and fertile than that, and in Howa its potency was still apparent. Not only did the weave between work and play illuminate the contours of a less alienated world toward which those intent on creating new social relations of production and reproduction in the future might strive, but the exquisite tension between the children's work and play intensified the force of the interpretations and possibilities offered by looking at children's activities through the Benjaminian lens of mimesis (see Benjamin 1978a; Buck-Morss 1989; Taussig 1993). For one, children's playful activities, like play almost everywhere, remained a psychological reservoir, an oasis for imagining things and themselves differently, for experimenting with various social and cultural relations, and for exercising what Walter Benjamin (1978a) called the mimetic faculty, where, in the acts of seeing resemblances and creating similarities, the power of making something utterly new lies coiled. But this open-ended and even promissory quality of play as a means of transformation was made more powerful in this case by its active and intense relationship with work. In the shifting nexus between play, work, and social transformation, much was up for grabs in Howa.

Play as Transformation

While it appears that children almost everywhere engage in dramatic play that enables them to fantasize about and deal symbolically with the social roles and responsibilities they will be expected to assume as adults, these activities are misunderstood if they are seen solely in relation to the reproduction or maintenance of these communities. They are as much, if not more, fantasy and invention as they are social learning. While the script may be one that follows and closely mimics certain familiar material social practices, such as those associated with farming, school, or shopping, each enactment is original. The children are actors, not simply re-actors imitating the life they see around them (see Schwartzman 1978). Anything can happen and it often does. While as in "real life" the tenant farmers tilling in the games of "fields" orchestrated by Rashid did not all make the same income, they did all receive at least some "china money" at the end of the season; a far cry from the adult world around them, this was a world that allowed all comers to continue to play. Despair and exclusion were likewise forestalled by the fact that each iteration of the games had different outcomes; the poor did not always get poorer, nor did the rich always get richer in the children's dramatic play.

But perhaps more potently, the children were not simply rehearsing, or rehearsing for, the social relations they saw around them, but playing with such things as power, control, symbol, gesture, and routine, while being absorbed by their creative projects, social interplay, and imagination of mastery. As Gregory Bateson (1956) suggests in his classic article, "The Message 'This Is Play,'" the processes of role-taking and role-changing in a world of make-believe render play itself a necessary cultural skill. Instead of addressing the texts of play as a means for learning particular skills and social knowledge, Bateson argues that perhaps the key skill acquired in play is the ability to enter an imaginary and symbolic world, because everyday life, as a set of social constructions and material social practices produced, shared, negotiated, and trusted by members of a particular group, is precisely such a world (see Rubin, Fein, and Vandenberg 1983). In a similar vein, Lev Vygotsky, the Soviet developmental psychologist, noted that the essence of play was to "move in a field of meaning" through taking on different roles and experimenting with fantasy. Play, he suggested, creates a fantastic arena of learning that he called the "zone of proximal development," wherein children freely experiment with, abide by, and expand the rules, roles, and meanings that they encounter elsewhere in a more structured and strictured way. These practices—which also include engagements with adults and older children who teach and otherwise assist children in learning new things and reaching other levels of development from their own grounds—are essential to young people's ways of knowing and producing their material social worlds (Vygotsky 1978).

Play and Mimesis

While Schwartzman, Bateson, Vygotsky, and other theorists of play focus on the importance of its transformative aspects, they do so to understand how these work for children as they develop and are incorporated into a symbolic order. In other words, the interest in play and transformation largely concerns how play engagements transform children by fostering cognitive, moral, physical, and social development. Walter Benjamin takes the transformative aspects of play as his starting point and draws from them a larger political message that infuses and is infused by what he called the mimetic faculty. Likewise, as Susan Buck-Morss brilliantly points out, Benjamin's interests in children's cognition turn those of Piaget on their head. If for Piaget, the developmental trajectory of children's lives was such that "childish" thinking was banished in the teleological march toward reason, for Benjamin this thinking was what got drummed out of children in the course of bourgeois education, but lay coiled in socialized adults ready to be sprung as revolutionary consciousness (Buck-Morss 1989; cf. Piaget 1954, 1963, 1975). Benjamin was much more interested in the residues and resurgences of this consciousness than in its erasure as a measure of abstract thought and "development."

Benjamin's notion of the mimetic faculty simultaneously encapsulates what is at the heart of play while pointing to its more transformative implications and possibilities. Quite distinct from mimicry, the mimetic faculty is not simply the ability to both see resemblances and create similarities between things, but the flash of insight made or read off of that process that impels a moment of invention. For Benjamin it is the fugitive and fleeting nature of playing at something that may spark a realization that the original is also made up: not a fiction, but a performance, or more dryly, a social construction, that might also be made different (Benjamin 1978a, 333; cf. Taussig 1993). Michael Taussig, among others, calls attention to the potency of this idea. He begins *Mimesis and Alterity* by pointing out what a stunning insight it was that various aspects of social identity, previously naturalized, were social constructions, and he continues by mourning how little was made of it. Understanding the constructedness of social life, he suggests, should underscore its mutability. It should, he goes on, be the beginning rather than the end of the road, as it so often has been.

Children's play offers a wonderful vehicle for continuing on that road. Children's play is riddled with mimetic activities. Children in Howa, as elsewhere, played at being shopkeepers, farmers, homemakers, parents, consumers, charcoal makers, *muezzin*, and truck drivers. Many times they played at the very activities at which they themselves also worked, but their play almost always worked through those aspects of the activities that were somewhat mysterious or in which children did not figure centrally. They told stories, swapped riddles, called to prayer, sang songs, danced, ran around, cracked jokes, and acted like goofballs, their energy and irreverence vying for maximum expression throughout.

In these everyday practices, the children made and played with their identities, wildly imagining themselves otherwise or just tweaking the details. Play is both a form of coming to consciousness and a way to "become other." In his brilliant writings on play, Lev Vygotsky (1978) notes that even when children play at being themselves or play out their contemporaneous relationships, play provides a vehicle for becoming conscious of those relationships and things that they otherwise enact or engage without thinking. The essences of social relationships and material social practices are distilled and brought to light in the course of play. In playing, children are also able to imagine, enact, and transmogrify "becoming other" with fluidity and grace. Though no player worth his or her salt would conceptualize it in such belabored theoretical terms, what else do the opening gambits "Let's play . . . , "I'll be . . . ," or "Pretend

Figure 22. The fantasy of mobility was shared by many boys in Howa, who dreamed of being drivers or their assistants when they grew up. Most, like Talal, never got further than building toy cars, but these got them pretty far.

Figure 23. (Always) ready for her close-up.

you're . . . ," signify, if not a literal toying with "becoming other," with making up an identity? The becoming other of play is an intrinsic aspect of its pleasure (with far more interesting possibilities than identity politics has offered), and is the grist of the mimetic faculty.

For Benjamin, as for Vygotsky, one of the key attributes of children's consciousness—which he celebrated as mimesis—was an immediate connection between thought and action (see Buck-Morss 1989; Vygotsky 1978). As Buck-Morss (1989, 264) notes, for Benjamin "perception and active transformation are the two poles of children's cognition," and these are severed in the process of bourgeois socialization. Benjamin saw their reconnection and reinvention as the crux of revolutionary consciousness, theorizing that "the relationship between consciousness and society on a historical level was interspersed with another dimension, the level of childhood development, in which the relationship between consciousness and reality had its own history" (Buck-Morss 1989, 265). This consciousness is there to be retrieved in adults and is always already present among children, and Benjamin was interested in the material social practices through which this consciousness might come to the fore. His astute observations of children were directed to this end, and here Benjamin, like Vygotsky, was struck by the fusion of knowledge and action in children's practices. Benjamin's and Vygotsky's perspectives on play were deeply materialist and emphasized how children learned about things by manipulating them and using them creatively, "releasing," in Buck-Morss's words, "new possibilities of meaning" (264). This engagement with things, especially in play, enabled children to learn about and toy with the meanings of things in their social world. For Vygotsky (1978) such engagements showed how consciousness was formed in action. At the same time, as Benjamin emphasized, these engagements offered the possibility of refusing accepted meanings and thus, in a tactile material way, they had revolutionary potential.

This sort of tactility and play with meanings was characteristic of children's activities in Howa. Their play-work traced an interesting and mobile juncture of embodied knowledge, spatial scale, and temporality. For instance, when Sami helped his father build a charcoal mound or Rashid helped his father plant their fields, they simultaneously acquired and used knowledge transacted physically at the scale of adult practice. In the fields and forests, using tools generally designed for adults, the children were relatively small, and this physical relationship to their tools and the space of their actions shaped their knowledge. But when Sami built his play charcoal mound or Rashid modeled and played "fields," they literally created in miniature the entire field of practice and tended it from above. These very different ways of embodying the same realm of knowledge (in one case charcoal production, in the other agriculture) suggest an interesting and peculiar relationship between tactility and mastery, as well as an important suppleness in children's ways of knowing. The children, who neither commanded nor oversaw the sequencing of the operations of charcoal production or cultivation at the scale of adult practice, orchestrated these entirely in their miniature worlds. There was a clear back and forth between the scales of play-work and the kinds of learning, knowing, and mastery that took place in each.

This to and fro traced the productive tension between what Taussig calls "copy and contact." Mimesis, he suggests, involves imitation as well as the sensuous connection between "the body of the perceiver and the perceived." He goes on to suggest that "the nature of their interrelationship remains obscure and fertile ground for wild imagining" (1993, 21). The power of the children's play-work in Howa was not just that they made sense of their everyday lives and produced themselves in them, but also that the play-work provided a means for making these different.

Mostly, though, everyday life was not made that different in the course of the children's work-play. "Habit" held sway (see Taussig 1993, 25).[11] Part of the reason it did might be attributed to the very same tethers between work and play that made the possibilities of change so palpable. As this chapter has emphasized, children in Howa played at work that they not only were likely to undertake as adults, but that also composed part of their contemporaneous labor. When they played, much of what they played was interstitial with their work. When they worked, they often played at the same time or carved time for play out of their work time. Whatever the particular balance between the two, much of the embodied knowledge associated with the children's play and work was imbricated with their future work. While these intertwined practices were certainly shot through with a frisson of transformation, the intimate connections between work, play, and learning in the children's lives and possible futures created a kind of "tactile knowing"—"habit"—that may have produced more of a tendency toward stability than toward its undoing. Such are the entrenched contradictions of tactility, as much as of mimesis itself. Nevertheless, the arena of children's work-play in Howa and elsewhere remains a fruitful area to look for such ruptures.

Play, for instance, was a way for the children to simultaneously learn about, construct, and find ways to live with their social worlds (see Taussig 1993, xi). To paraphrase Marx, they made up their various identities within particular social conditions that they had not made up, or chosen. If most of the time they were trying on roles that readied them to be subjects of capitalism and participants in available worlds of adult work, it is still important to remember that their acts of play were not about copying as much as invention. And in that invention, and the insights it garners and deploys, was the spark of recognition that things, relations, and selves could be otherwise. Making that so is not child's play, of course, but in drawing out the connections between play and the mimetic faculty, I hope to make clear that play is not immaterial to the task.

Children at play encountered the political-economic and sociocultural changes affecting Howa. Just as these changes entered into the children's play in subtle and startling ways, so, too, did their play enter into these historical transformations and offer the possibility of altering them. Taussig refers to this process, playing with a Benjaminian metaphor, as a "two-way street" between the mimetic faculty and history. To this end, the children of Howa played with capitalism quite literally. Their games embraced and toyed with exchange, money, consumership, new modes of local production, and the expanding fields of everyday life in Howa. At the very least they domesticated capitalism as they outfitted themselves as new subjects of its terms. In traversing this street between mimesis and its historical geographies, the play of children in Howa was particularly interesting for its manifold entanglements with their work. The entanglements at once grounded the play and its mimetic aspects in questions of political-economic relations in quite sobering ways and made the possibilities of the inventive flash of mimesis—the playing at work—that much more powerful.

Nexus of Play and Social Transformation

Benjamin was fascinated with children's play in part because he saw in children an inexhaustible ability to use and transform the debris of society in new and creative ways. This insight paralleled directly his antilinear view of history, which he was interested in entering and engaging in order to make something new of its narratives and material forms. He was particularly compelled by the possibilities of reworking the detritus of industrialization and the things of everyday life to completely other ends, as Susan Buck-Morss's *The Dialectics of Seeing* so insightfully explores. The children in Howa played constantly with its debris; virtually nothing was thrown out that did not have a second life in play. For instance in the game of "store" the children used all "found objects" to stand for the commodities in the store. Like the geodramatic games of "fields" or "house," "store" involved the children in producing miniature worlds within which they enacted landscape-appropriate activities and interactions. While many of

Figure 24. By 1995 vehicle construction was an elaborate affair. Unlike the cruder assemblages of a decade earlier (see Figure 22), the late-model vehicles were carefully crafted by children. Tin-can market trucks, such as the one here, were typical. Making them out of all manner of found objects, children filled the trucks with charcoal scraps and other products in rounds of dramatic play.

these material social practices were familiar to the children as observers of village life or as consumers and errand-runners themselves, their enactment involved the children in stretching their knowledge of local commercial exchange and imagining some of its ins and outs. For a start, the game might more accurately have been called "market" because the children clustered several—sometimes up to a dozen—small shops and restaurants together when they played, a scale and intensity of interchange that far exceeded existing venues in Howa.

A typical game involved boys and girls setting up a number of small shops nestled in the base of a tree, along a houseyard wall, or in some other shaded area. The wares included the standard dry goods available in Howa and some more exotic imports, all represented by such things as vials discarded from the village dispensary, tomato paste tins, can and bottle tops, dirt, wads of mud-clay modeled into such things as bread and other foodstuffs, batteries and battery tops, bottles, goat dung, metal scraps, a telegraph pole insulator, shells, wood bits, packages or scraps of packaging, seeds, and shards of glass. In addition to dry goods shops, the commercial enterprises included several restaurants (this in a village with a single commercial eatery that was opened only part of the year), and a well where water was sold at the tap (represented by a large plastic bottle discarded from the clinic). Apart from the several shopkeepers, the well operator, and the restaurant owners, all of whom traded with one another, there were some nonpropertied customers who frequented all the establishments. The medium of exchange was "china money" (shards of broken crockery and dishes). In some cases this money had been earned and carried over from earlier games of "fields"; other times it just materialized as another prop. "Store" was an elaborate and intricate game that absorbed the children completely in the production and exchange of a wide range of products. Children "spent" many afternoon hours completely enthralled in the market worlds they created *and* had the wherewithal to engage.

Akin to the games of "fields," "house," and "store" or the miniature charcoal mounds constructed by Sami, children also constructed miniature mud houses using the techniques and gestures associated with professional builders in the area. This activity was especially popular among boys during the rainy season, when mud was abundant. Like local builders, they mixed sand in the mud and used wood and grass thatch for roofing; and like children all over the world, they learned about building from watching construction projects wherever and whenever they happened (see Benjamin 1978b). For several weeks there was an extensive building project as yet another extended family demonstrated their upward mobility with the construction of a fired mudbrick wall to replace the old mud-and-dung one around their houseyard. Every time I walked by there were children of all ages watching the work. But children in Howa, unlike children in many other parts of the world, also assisted in building projects. Indeed, several children moved from bystander to assistant as the wall project progressed.

One of these boys was Talal, who also took the opportunity to build a small cooking enclosure for his mother adjacent to their house. He and several other ten-year-old boys who had access to donkeys found work as assistants in the wall project. They dug and transported dirt from about two hundred meters away to be used as mortar in the wall, receiving the equivalent of US$.25 for each donkey load. Talal was on hand each of the several days that work was available, carting approximately twelve donkey loads a day. He was particularly keen because this work was more lucrative than his normal routine of selling water. Not only was he paid more than twice as much per trip, but with a ready customer, the effort took much less time. Large-scale building efforts, such as this one, not only provided jobs for young boys and demonstrated construction methods to children who participated or watched, but they were also an inspiration to them. No doubt the wall project inspired Talal to build his mother a kitchen enclosure. In his effort, he not only copied the mud-brick construction methods of the specialists working nearby, but he used the bricks discarded by the masons. More useful, perhaps, than other children's miniature houses, Talal's kitchen was no less a product of imaginative and playful practice than theirs were. The intertwined practices of assisting in adult construction projects and using their debris to build their own provided the boys with an arena for imagining themselves in the construction trades.

Girls playing "house" likewise manipulated objects through which they imagined and played with the practices of their future lives. They constructed dolls out of straw or sticks and clothed them in scraps of cloth. They delineated their houses with bricks, stones, or sticks, and outfitted them with found objects that served as props. When, like Rashid's sister, they were lucky enough to have access to a miniature mud house,

Figure 25. With the rains came clayey mud, and with the mud came opportunity. Never one to miss a chance, Rashid built this house over a couple of days, enlisting a younger friend to help him. They replicated the construction techniques and body language of village builders, and afterward Rashid and his sister played house in their creation.

the girls delighted in playing "house" in and around it. As with the game of "store," treasures like tin cans, batteries, pieces of metal, bits of straw, packaging, stones, dirt, and water were used to create and populate the play landscape. Although girls playing "house" acted out collecting firewood or fetching water, their focus was largely on the domestic environment and the domain of daily activities, which included child care, food preparation, cooking, cleaning, washing, eating, and visiting, as well as the social events that marked important life passages, such as birth, death, marriage, circumcision, and naming ceremonies. Their playfully elaborate participation in these events and the full range of domestic chores associated with them enabled the girls to experiment with and practice future social roles and to learn about and internalize the domestic activities in which they participated as children, but for which they would be responsible as adults.

The same was true in both versions of the agricultural game, "fields." These games were elaborate miniature reconstructions of the environments and agricultural practices associated with both irrigated and rain-fed cultivation. As their play attests, the children were well aware of the distinctions between the two. In "tenancies" they built the ridges characteristic of irrigation in the area; planted the cash crops associated with the Suki Project, cotton and groundnuts; used tractors and other tools and equipment associated with mechanized cultivation; and spent a good deal of time and energy weighing and measuring their play harvests, then distributing shards of "china money" differentially according to each "farmer's" yield. In the dryland version of the game, the children planted the traditional crops of sorghum and sesame, complemented with legumes and vegetables; they did not construct irrigation ditches or ridges in their fields, but sprinkled "rain" on them instead; they built *hahiya,* platforms from which children scared away birds; they threshed the sorghum and sesame manually, saving the stalks for fodder; and, with due reference to the considerable socioeconomic changes taking place in their village, they reserved part of their product for household use, exchanging only the surplus along with sesame, the traditional cash crop.

The acuity with which socioeconomic or political-ecologic relations were absorbed in the play was extraordinary. The recognition of the commodity form of cotton and groundnuts, for instance, was witnessed in the formal measurement of yields and the precise (and unequal) payments for them. Sorghum, on the other hand, was not "weighed," but was trundled to a storehouse and kept for household consumption. The power of money—china or otherwise—worked across games. Compensated farmers exchanged their shards for all manner of goods in the game of "store," which was played simultaneously or at other times. The children's mimetic exchanges embodied, and were embodied in, Howa's lurch toward the monetization of everything.

Along these lines, cars were most popular among the many things that children, particularly boys, modeled or constructed out of mud, clay, metal, or other materials. Literally and metaphorically seen as "tickets to ride," vehicles were constantly made by boys from objects and debris found in and around the village. The romance of the road, and the money it was seen to bring, were expressed by many boys in Howa in the way they constructed and played with these vehicles. As the children in Howa rushed toward their own futures, the imagined paths ahead were different for boys and girls. Of course they played at the gendered work roles common to their elders, but beyond that, boys were more likely to experiment with new roles enmeshed in the commodity world outside of Howa, while girls tended to play at the reproductive activities that characterized their mothers' lives. Whereas boys built cars as well as farm implements, girls made and clothed straw dolls for playing "house," outfitting them with traditional tools, including largely obsolete grinding stones, used by then only when the mill was out of commission. Some girls did, however, play "store" and through it entered the commoditized fray that was increasingly central in Howa.

Each of these forms of play individually and collectively illuminate different aspects of the relationship between play and social transformation: how play is transformed, how play marks social transformation, and how play itself can be transformative. For instance, the variations in the games of "fields" suggest the way *play is transformed* in the course of political-economic and social transformation. The children absorbed and reflected the differences between subsistence and tenant cultivation in the different enactments of their agricultural geodramas, placing in sharp relief such things as the cash nexus, land-use patterns, food security, and production cycles. While in this sense "fields" certainly also *marked local social transformations,* the heightened importance of money that characterized Howa during the arc of these children's childhoods seemed most sharply reflected in their games of "store." Here their play suggested a riot of consumption that certainly outstripped that which was then in place in the village. In fact, the children engaged in buying and selling with such gusto that the game seemed to reflect—or call forth—an almost frenzied ascendence of capitalist exchange in their community. This sense was echoed in the course of one of my research strategies. To get at their environmental knowledge I did a "geodramatic" exercise with the children, giving them toy animals, vehicles, and human figures to enact everyday life in the village. In this exercise, I was struck by how frequently the children put one or another of the animals in the truck and took it to market. The level of animal sales in this exercise far exceeded actual levels in the village during that time, although it tragically presaged the famine-drought years on the horizon.

Finally, as suggested by the discussion of mimesis, *play also transforms the people playing* and opens the possibility for more willful social transformations. While this was true across the range of the children's activities, it was particularly clear in both the games of "house" and in the children's construction activities. In both of these arenas the children playing also worked with the materials at hand, and the two realms of activity infused one another. Many of the girls who played "house" also collected firewood and fetched water, for instance, whereas many village women, whom they were playing at being, did not. In their play, the girls enacted their liminal status between being girls and women, as well as the shifts that were slowly becoming apparent in the gendered division of household labor. Their doll selves went to the fields to collect wood while they also tended to household chores, entertained, and engaged in various rituals and celebrations in miniature. The boys assisting in village construction projects drew on them to imbue their play-work projects with appropriate gestures and techniques. In each aspect—as assistants and in their independent projects—the boys were likely to have sensed the possibility of, and been experimenting with, a different life from that of farming. In both playing "house" and construction, the children were blending genres and weaving together different practices that might open avenues for changing their and their community's practices more broadly.

Despite these lively connections between work and play, and the inventive ways children encountered new social forms and made them their own, it remains that, to the extent that the possibilities of the mimetic faculty celebrated by Benjamin and others worked, it worked to help the children embrace and become subjects of capitalism. The possibilities of inventing something else remained only possibilities, rather than actual instances of social transformation in Howa, though of course the locally ascendent capitalism was certainly calling forth new kinds of identities that the children were inventing in their play and otherwise.

Yet this situation was precarious and indeterminant, in part because the larger economy of Sudan mostly undid political-economic relations in Howa, rather than constructing an alternative to draw children's imaginations and, somewhat paradoxically, in part because the forward motion of capitalism was well entrenched in Howa. It appeared to me that the everyday practices of children in Howa were hurtling toward some kind of undoing in 1981 because of heightened commodification, deteriorations in the local environment, and changed land-tenure relations, among other things. Among the generation of children with whom I worked, there were likely to be significant disjunctures between what they learned as children and what they would need to know as adults, and for those coming up behind them, formal schooling appeared likely to be increasingly important. The increased importance of formal schooling was sure to change the balance of practices that characterized children's everyday lives. Apart from altering the relation between work and play as everyday practices and fields of meaning, the increasing importance of formal education was likely to modify the kinds of knowledge valued in Howa. This, of course, was the intent of the state in promulgating it.

This struggle over work, play, and schooling was going on during my time in Howa. Children were subjects and objects in this encounter over social production and reproduction and the construction of identities. Their everyday lives, as terrains of the struggle and embodiments of ways of imagining things differently, were a powerful way to understand the process and possibilities of change. But the weight of capitalism and abstractions of knowledge were everywhere.

4. Knowing Subjects/Abstracting Knowledge

I know you, you're from Nimrica. You're the people who went to the moon and all you brought back was rocks!

—Beshir, "al Shibe"

The first time I went to Howa was with a Khartoum University geography department field trip. I taught in Khartoum the year before my fieldwork, and during our Blue Nile Province field excursion (with 130 people and all the trappings of a British university field trip, it was more like an expedition), I commandeered a small group of students to accompany me to Howa. While the students fanned out and did a brief field survey (the results of which I foolishly never got), I arranged my future with a sheikh who turned out to be fairly powerless. But that is another story.

At the university that semester I taught two courses, economic geography and map interpretation. The first made sense, but having been schooled in "mental mapping" and the behavioral geographies popular at my own university at the time, it was strange to teach the latter—with official maps of real places to be interpreted with more science than whimsy. Stranger still, though not the least surprising, was that, nearly twenty-five years after independence, the only maps the geography department held in sufficient number for teaching were of Britain. They had dozens of copies of lovely British Ordinance Survey maps of every corner of the old country, and virtually none of Sudan, which, of course, had been mapped in the same Ordinance Survey style and scale, though clearly not for local consumption.

It was just as well that we had all those British maps to use, because the only book available in sufficient quantity for all sixty-three students dwelled on them exclusively.

Without a word about arid lands geomorphology, it referred to contour lines around Coventry, stream channels near Swansea, and nucleated settlement patterns in Oxfordshire. I, the teacher, had no idea where these places were in relation to one another or what they looked like on the ground. Knowledge more abstract and abstracted than this would be hard to find.

I have always thought of that class as colonialism's revenge; teacher and students from colonies that got away—none of us having ever set foot in the mother country—spending so much time poring over the courses of its streams and the gradient of its hills. Ours was a visceral experience of science in the service of empire. The course materials oriented our minds toward the metropole with greater elegance and cost-efficiency than all those district officers could have ever done. Not only was the power of science reinforcing and reinforced by political economic relations, right down to which books and maps were available, but all university instruction was in English; and while we were able to cover Britain thoroughly at one inch to the mile, we had only one (national scale) resource map of Sudan at our disposal. The ties between the discipline of geography and empire are well known, but that map interpretation class suggested other iterations of the (still imperial) power of science. There we were, sixty-four people whose only experience with chalk was on a blackboard, imagining the Cheltenham Chalklands. To this day, I think of Cheltenham. I imagine it as craggy white hills with a fine light dust that gets washed away with each rain. And in Sudan, even decades after independence, geography graduates may have more images of the Chalklands than of the sandy *qoz* lands of western Sudan. Imagined geographies produce powerful and interested "geographical imaginations" (see Gregory 1994; Godlewska and Smith 1994).

The Production and Exchange of Knowledge

This chapter focuses on children's environmental knowledge in the household, peer group, and school. It examines the different kinds of knowledge associated with each setting, and the fluid relationship between abstraction, knowledge, and practice in children's daily lives. My intent is to tease out the consequences of shifts in the content, production, and exchange of knowledge associated with formal school curricula, the less formal curricula of the household, and more diffuse learning practices. I will look at the problems and possibilities of the different kinds of knowledge the children acquired across settings, and examine differences between knowledge that is abstracted from practice and knowledge that is embedded in, inasmuch as it embeds, practice.

Pierre Bourdieu and Jean-Claude Passeron's (1977) analysis of social reproduction offers a useful, if a bit creaky, framework for examining environmental learning. Their focus is in the "antagonistic interests" that come into play in pedagogy and the diverse practices of "pedagogic action." These practices are socially allocated across three broad arenas and include "diffuse education," enacted by all educated members of a social group; "family education"; and "institutional education," which encompasses the pedagogic actions of those formally assigned this responsibility by a particular society (5).

The goal of "pedagogic work," according to Bourdieu and Passeron, is that the more or less arbitrary principles imposed be internalized sufficiently to be perpetuated after a particular "pedagogic action" has ceased. In this accomplishment, pedagogic work inculcates what Bourdieu terms the "habitus" (31). Pedagogic agencies and practices are extremely durable, and considerable inertia is commonly associated with both educational institutions and household learning. Bourdieu and Passeron go so far as to suggest that the family tends to distill the pedagogic impulses from other social settings so as to become a "conservatory of inherited tradition" (32). Perhaps, but households are also the resilient interface between old ways of knowing, diverse affiliations with different and multiple "traditions," and ongoing scrappy attempts to make survivable everyday lives and livable futures for their members and community. Jean Lave and Etienne Wenger's (1991) much livelier formulation of "situated learning" within a "community of practice" gets to the contradictory questions at the heart of these daily forms and practices of social reproduction more fruitfully than do Bourdieu and Passeron.

Bourdieu and Passeron describe certain pedagogic work as "traditional" to the extent that it is less clearly circumscribed as an autonomous practice, and is carried out by actors whose "functions" are more comprehensive and less differentiated. Traditional pedagogic work is described as "a familiarizing process in which the master transmits unconsciously, through exemplary conduct, principles he has never mastered consciously, to a receiver who internalizes them unconsciously" (48). Such practices were characteristic of much household learning in Howa and exerted a strong influence not only on what children learned, but on household members' responses to future pedagogic encounters.

While I appreciate the way this perspective acknowledges the strength and importance of learning that is more global and diffuse than most formal education, Bourdieu and Passeron's formulation of the habitus tends as much toward functionalism as toward mind-numbing jargon. In the routines and "functions" of all their "agents" of "symbolic violence," it is difficult to see where any rupture in the routine is possible. Nowhere in the "habitus" is the lively sense of possibility (and the urgency to actualize it) of Benjamin's "habit," or Lefebvre's and others' critical notion of "everyday life" (Lefebvre 1984, 1987; cf. Kaplan and Ross 1987). Moreover, environmental teaching and learning do not fit neatly into Bourdieu and Passeron's notion of pedagogy, because as working and workable knowledge they are not simply "arbitraries." Indeed, the political and practical importance of the production and exchange of knowledge is that the violent aspects of pedagogy are inseparable from its creativity—teaching and learning are active, empowering, and potentially disruptive material social practices not reducible to the transmission of cultural arbitraries (e.g., Gramsci 1971; Benjamin 1969; Freire 1970, 1985). The political possibilities of this contradiction are undermined when pedagogy is reduced to the transmission of cultural arbitraries or a play of interests on "the terrain of symbolic production" (Bourdieu and Passeron 1977, xvii).

Situated learning, which takes place through what Jean Lave and Etienne Wenger (1991) call "legitimate peripheral participation," provides a more productive way to understand knowledge acquisition in Howa (or anywhere else). In this framework, participation in social practice is the key form of learning (54), and legitimate peripheral participation expresses the relationship between a learner and one with greater mastery in a community of practice. All learning—even formalized instruction—takes place in a community of practice. Indeed, Lave and Wenger suggest that a community of practice is defined in and through the sharing of knowledge. Learning, in their conceptualization, can be discerned through increasing participation in that community, suggesting simultaneously a nonindividualist notion of knowledge and learning (it is precisely *not* internalization) and a completely relational and dynamic sense of what it means to know. In this schema, everyone engages in producing and exchanging knowledge, moving within and altering the makeup of a community of practice as they themselves are changed, and in this process of ongoing exchange, knowledge evolves as well. The simple roles of teacher or learner are routinely exceeded as all members move within a field of knowledge whose durability turns on its mutability. This seeming paradox suggests two issues that Lave and Wenger's theory of learning addresses. First, it suggests that all participants in a community of practice are potentially "peripheral." In other words, peripheral is not a location juxtaposed to central, but rather it defines the fluidity of the learning process and the mobility of its participants. Second, and not unrelated, "Learning, transformation, and change are always implicated in one another, and the status quo needs as much explanation as change" (57). As communities of practice "produce their own futures" (albeit not within conditions they have chosen or can control), they necessarily conserve *and* alter the material social practices that define and enable them, producing new contradictions as they go along.

In these ways and others, Lave and Wenger's formulation gets at the contradictory drift of social reproduction. This drift is first one of social actors—of newcomers becoming old-timers, and old-timers doing themselves out of a position within their communities of practice. The innumerable exchanges among differently situated practitioners or knowers within a community eventually changes the community itself. The continuity of a community of practice is ensured, then, by the displacement and replacement of its members. This contradiction has, of course, been recognized, if not well explored, but what of its broader implications, when what it means to know is itself being altered? This state of affairs, which was increasingly characteristic of Howa, raises a second contradiction of social reproduction in general and of situated learning in particular. The stuff of the exchange itself changes over time. In the provocative words of Lave and Wenger, "[I]f production and the social reproduction of persons are mutually entailed in the reproduction of the social order, the contradictions inherent in reproducing persons within the domestic group and other communities of practice do not go away when the form of production changes, but go through transformations of their own" (1991, 114–15). The contradictory possibilities of this double shift, with its internal contradictions, were precisely what drew me to Howa. Uncovering some of its myriad outcomes, from the debilitating to the simply humdrum, through the exhilarating and potentially explosive, has been a way for me to examine the effects of political-economic and political-ecological changes on a "community of practice," whether writ large—such as Howa itself—or more modestly, on such smaller groups as herdboys, homemakers, or tenant farmers. Given my focus on the production and exchange of knowledge, I have found the work of Lave and Wenger particularly fruitful, and my reading of their project suggests the many common threads in the possibilities of what they present as situated learning, and what Benjamin and others discuss as mimesis.

The tension between reproduction and change was increasingly evident in successive visits to Howa from the early 1980s through the mid-1990s. Children's learning was at the fulcrum of an increasingly intense struggle between social reproduction and the political-economic transformation taking place in Howa during that time. It was not the village school, which had been there since 1959, but the agricultural project, and the national and international economy it represented that provoked a destabilization of previous—albeit precarious—relations, means, and guarantees of social reproduction. Within only ten years of the establishment of the Suki Agricultural Project, households were forced to develop new strategies of social reproduction to ensure their members' sustenance over time. Among other things, the school's responsibility for social reproduction increased vis-à-vis the household, and many households dispersed members to work in new locations, both within and outside of Howa. Still, it was at the scale of the household that these new relationships were worked out. Jostling with the school and the household, young people themselves, often through their mutable peer groups, were a third locus of knowledge acquisition. Each of these settings was imbricated in a welter of mutually constitutive communities of practice that might be overlapping, intersecting, or nested.

Schooling

As a growing number of households abdicated part of their responsibility for social reproduction to government schools, new forms of abstraction and relationships to local knowledge started to take hold. But not abruptly. At school in Howa, for instance, the geography curriculum actually began quite locally. Second graders were taught mapping using a fellow student's body as the teacher demonstrated perspectival difference by showing how a "child's eye" picture of a boy differs from a "bird's eye" "map" of him. The local eventually became just a staging area for a more expansive knowledge and was gradually diminished, if not erased, on the long pedagogic road "to Cheltenham." After "mapping" their colleagues and the water jugs found in every village household, the children moved outward to map the classroom, the school, and eventually the entire village. The primary school geography curriculum in later years was structured around a child's travels to visit other children in various parts of Sudan, neatly covering regional physical and human geography in a fun and embodied way.

Lessons about the local were reinforced by having the children do some fieldwork of their own. A second-grade geography assignment, for instance, had students interview local traders and shopkeepers about their economic activities, including the sources of and destinations for the goods they exchanged. For most children, such assignments deepened their knowledge about local geography in ways different from those who were not in school, but the lessons served other purposes as well. Their explicit intent was to give children an overview of the local economy and thus provide a foundation for learning about geographic and other relationships in the world outside of Howa. But in the concentration on merchants and the exclusion of farmers, not to mention the routine disregard for women's economic practices altogether, the curriculum also taught children that certain interactions mattered more than others, and simultaneously valorized particular kinds of economic rationality, which helped to shape Howa's future.

Of course, school was not necessarily the right place to learn about agriculture and local environmental practices. As many adults in Howa argued, they did not need or want formal educators to do what they already did quite effectively. If their children were to go to school, it would be to learn something different. Thus, the Sudan government's plans for Integrated Rural Education Centres (IREC), proposed during the 1970s and intended to teach agriculture and husbandry, along with a modified standard school curriculum, never made much headway in Howa or elsewhere in Sudan.[1]

Still I do not want to set up false dichotomies between "abstract" formal training and situated "concrete" learning. All learning involves abstractions and concrete experience, the systematic and the complex. And as the examples above suggest, the school's geography curriculum was no exception. Neither were parents' curricula for their children's environmental educations, and this was part of the indifference toward IRECs. But the intentions and practices of formal schooling and more practically based learning are quite different. Somewhat cynically perhaps, Margaret Mead (1970, 3) once summarized the shift from practice-based learning to more formal schooling as a move "from the need for an individual to learn something which everyone agrees he would wish to know, to the will of some individual to teach something which it is not agreed that anyone has any desire to know." Mead's statement brings to mind a distinction Lave and Wenger (1991) draw between teaching and learning curricula. A learning curriculum, they argue, is "a field of learning resources in everyday practice *viewed from the perspective of learners*," whereas a teaching curriculum "is constructed for the instruction of newcomers." A teaching curriculum mediates "the meaning of what is learned (and control of access to it) . . . through an instructor's participation," thereby externalizing "what knowing is about" (97, emphasis in the original).

The everyday forms and practices of learning I encountered in Howa were textbook instances of "learning curricula," with children commonly working from more "circumferential" or piecemeal tasks toward more central, integrated, and comprehensive engagements. On charcoal expeditions, for instance, quite young children went along and initially just watched their fathers cut trees. They sometimes gathered the kindling that got knocked off the branches or carried a single log back to the village. Older children might cut a sapling or two as their elders went for bigger trees, and, like the little ones, carry some of the load back to the village. Back in the village children often helped to assemble the kilns and then bag the coal once their fathers had raked it out and let it cool. Doing these more circumferential tasks they learned about the process as a whole, eventually mastering it in their late teens. As Sami's father, Beshir, explained one day in response to my questions about what Sami knew of the environment,

> He doesn't know anything I know that well. He's still learning about farming—he's not that good at it. I tell him "do this, do that" so that he knows what to do. When we go out to get wood, I cut; he doesn't cut that much. He helps carry it back, he assists. . . . I do the work—I plant, weed with a small hoe—he's learned to weed and helps with that. I tell him what to clear and what to leave. I show him the way to do things. He knows how to ride a donkey and do errands. . . . If I don't know it, he doesn't know it. He only knows what I teach or show him. . . . alone he doesn't know—if I say to do something, he does. I say "do this, do that, do it like this." That's how he learns.

When I asked if Sami learned things from other children, he was disparaging.

> No—what do they know?? What do they do?? They're all from here! . . . What he knows he's learned from me . . . not from his sister or other kids. . . . Young children don't know anything—if there was a fire in front of them they'd walk right into it! They don't know anything [but as they get older] their eyes see.

As Beshir's responses suggest, learning curricula were integral to everyday life, with children learning new things as they took on new activities. Sometimes realizations of what needed to be learned were precipitated by blundering. On many occasions teaching took place through demonstration with very little verbal exchange. One morning in April when the well was closed I went down to the riverbed and found Fatima, a ten-year-old girl, sitting on the edge of a jemmam:

> She was sitting next to a woman who was drawing water. The woman was of no relation to Fatima but scolded her as she tried to get water because she was putting her feet down the well and contaminating the water. The woman continued to draw water, as did a teenage girl who came and went from the opposite side of the well. When the woman's jerry-can was full, Fatima again attempted to draw water and again the woman scolded her for putting her feet down the sides of the jemmam. Fatima could not get at the water without putting her feet in the jemmam itself (for some reason she did not get on her hands and knees as other kids did). This time the woman took Fatima's bucket and swiftly filled it herself. Fatima sat by looking glum and not saying anything. She then attempted to fill her smaller bucket and again the woman berated her for putting her foot down the side of the well and potentially dirtying the water. She told Fatima to come around and sit by her side, and then she filled the small bucket as well. The woman put the bucket on Fatima's head, wiped the sand off her scooping bowl and plopped it on top of the bucket so it bobbed on the water. Fatima picked up the small bucket and walked off looking dejected but a bit wiser for it all.

This sort of peripheral participation—usually without the dejection—was typical. Adults, in this case someone unrelated to the child, taught children through correction and demonstration in the course of their taking on tasks that they had yet to master. Learning was intimately bound up with the ability to carry out tasks successfully. Such "tests" of knowledge are quite different from those associated with teaching curricula that measure not so much "learning to know" as "learning to display knowledge for evaluation." For Lave and Wenger these sorts of tests, associated with formal schooling, commodify learning, producing a contradiction between the use value of knowledge and its exchange value (1991; 112). This contradiction is at the heart of Mead's snide comment.

When formal education is introduced from outside a community, the trouble is multiplied. In Howa the tension was not so much around the content of the curriculum as deference to a different kind of knowledge and modes for its assessment. What was at stake was less the shift from practical to school-based learning (because both forms of learning coexisted and were intertwined), but rather the ways these very different kinds of teaching and learning, and the bodies of knowledge they traded in, were negotiated, reworked, and valorized by people in Howa as the political economy and local ecology changed during the last three decades of the century. The shepherds' scorn for schoolboys, as much as the sly mockery many in the village reserved for their lone university graduate in the early 1980s, both traced the sensitive cusp of power and knowledge. Yet as the political-economic and political-ecological manifestations of the agricultural project intensified in subsequent decades, so did the scramble to change shared knowledge. Here, there was definitely a shift in interests quite contrary to the drift of Mead's comments. To secure their children's futures on these shifting grounds, many adults came to embrace the possibilities offered to their children by school learning. But the shift was no less fraught with tension over power, legitimation, and displacement for having been undertaken and even driven by the local population. The fact that it was necessitated by the changes going on around them, which, in effect, were deskilling their children, made the "desire to know" something different a contradictory move at best.

Yet the desire to know was often confounded. As ever, state-sponsored schools were both gateways and gatekeepers to alternative futures for young people. Delineated largely by strict rules of discipline and a standardized curriculum, formal schooling redefined learning, knowledge, and the measures of its achievement. As Peter Marris (1974) has conceptualized it, capitalist formal education is inherently contradictory because it simultaneously fosters ability as it institutionalizes the allocation of vocational opportunities. While government schools present themselves as "great equalizers," according to Marris, they must deny most children the chance to acquire the knowledge and skills that only a few can exercise, and exams are key to this process. School tests may assess knowledge attained (or the ability to display it), but they also make arbitrary use of this "commodified" knowledge to mystify the sorting of children into different levels.[2] The school exam not only works as a floodgate controlling the number of members of society "qualified" for particular roles, but it naturalizes their selection. The arbitrary nature of this process itself is a strategy to inculcate respect for the authority represented by the school and the educated strata of society. This process in turn helps to advance and justify the social stratification and economic differentiation associated with the dissolution of subsistence economies and the advance of capitalism (see Gramsci 1971; Bourdieu and Passeron 1977; Freire 1970, 1985).

In formal schooling, unlike most of the learning that otherwise took place in Howa, knowledge was purveyed and acquired largely through a process of accretion and in abstraction from its employment. This abstracted style of learning and the kinds of knowledge it produces are important to the reproduction of a complex socioeconomic system where the social relations of production are stratified, work roles are specialized, production in its entirety is no longer undertaken by the majority of producers, and relations between the "concrete" and the "abstract" are mystified. While abstracted knowledge and less integrated means of learning dovetail with capitalist social relations, they serve other ends as well. Such cultural forms and practices had made their debut in Howa in the small Quranic schools (*Khalwa*) that occasionally operated there long before the government-sponsored school was established at the end of the 1950s. To this day Khalwa usually offer religious training through a peculiar form of literacy rooted in the rote memorization of the Quran and the *Hadith* (the sayings and narratives associated with the Prophet Mohamed). In Howa this mode of education was largely displaced by the government school, built in 1959, which taught its own versions of reading, writing, and religion.[3]

This is not the place for an extended critique of formal education; I want only to mark the ways that the production and exchange of knowledge, and their connections with everyday life in Howa, were coming undone by the 1980s. My criticisms are not intended to negate the gains of formal schooling. Not only would this be a denial of my life's work, but it would fly in the face of what I very quickly saw myself about the significance of literacy and numeracy in people's lives, along with the importance of the worlds opened by these skills. As Spengler noted, "Writing is the grand theory of the far."[4] The need to acquire these skills and the kinds of knowledge associated with formal schooling were visceral to people in Howa within a generation of inclusion in the project and it is the pace and extent of that shift—of power/knowledge—that are remarkable. But the potential loss—of ways of knowing, of kinds of knowers, of particular bodies of knowledge—is also enormous and irretrievable.

Household Learning

The household operated as a nexus of production and reproduction in the early 1980s. It was also the center of wider social relations of reproduction involving other institutions and activities. Children were more objects than subjects of the ensuing struggles and negotiations, which encompassed, among other things, school attendance, work roles, and the kinds of free time they had. Although decisions concerning school attendance and children's household or remunerated tasks were the outcome of discussions between their parents and other elders that sometimes included them, in most households the father appeared to have the final—sometimes the only—say. Most women were nonetheless able to assert their "rights" to children's labor time to assist with a host of domestic chores, including water and fuel provision, running errands, and child care.

The household remained the most potent site for the production and exchange of knowledge with children and the most important setting for environmental learning. Much of this knowledge was acquired, assimilated, differentiated, and ultimately integrated through the children's "legitimate peripheral participation" in the work of their households, to borrow Lave and Wenger's term (1991). Their learning often seemed osmotic; a seemingly easy "familiarizing process" into the material social life around them. Of course some aspects of their learning were taught more directly according to parents' more-or-less conscious curricula for their children's environmental learning, but even this knowledge was imparted largely in the course of practice. Knowledge was contextual. Learned in use, it was systematic, with domains of knowledge evolving in a sequence of increasing complexity appropriate to children's abilities and experience; and it was deliberately reproductive, geared primarily to enable youngsters to take their parents' roles. As Sami's father said,

> [Environmental knowledge] is important for working here. If I say get this or that, get water or wood, or go to the store to get oil, he'll know how to do it. He'll take care of it and I don't need to. Right now he doesn't know things on his own, only if I tell him. But when he gets a little older, he'll know on his own. . . . If I die, he'll know everything. Then he'll tell his children and they'll teach their children. This is how they learn. If you don't teach them, their lives won't be good, if you teach them, their lives will be as good as yours. They'll learn like me. It's like studying.

In agricultural communities such as Howa, environmental knowledge forms the basis of productive life, and its acquisition is essential to the physical maintenance and reproduction of the community. Most commonly, children learned by accompanying, observing, and assisting elders (including older children) in their daily activities. Learning rather than teaching was the norm. Children were guided by adults and teens in the practical contexts of work. There was little direct instruction detached from participation. Imbued from the earliest age in work practices and the knowledge associated with them, Howa children rarely asked the sort of "why" questions that can become interminable among the children of industrial societies, whose everyday lives can be at much greater remove from social or natural process (see Fortes 1970, 40; Hogbin 1970, 147; and Rogoff and Gardner 1984). Environmental learning was part and parcel of the work of children in Howa, and they seemed to embrace its means and outcomes quite easily. As Meyer Fortes argued over half a century ago, children's awareness of the socially productive nature of their learning makes it psychologically rewarding for them. Embedded learning, he suggested, "can never become artificial or boring" (Fortes 1970, 58). In Howa this liveliness was seen most clearly in the fluid connections between children's work and play and the weave between household and peer group in their acquisition and use of knowledge.

Children's Environmental Knowledge

The socially productive nature of Howa children's environmental learning was not just "psychologically rewarding." The deep, thick, and multiple connections between what children in Howa did, knew, and needed to know resulted in quite elaborate, comprehensive, and workable bodies of knowledge shared more or less by all children ten years and older. Children who engaged in specialized activities, not surprisingly, shared more intricate knowledges associated with their particular communities of practice. Entwined with social practice, such knowledge was not necessarily revealed or measured by the kinds of abstract tests associated with schooling. It was with no small irony, then, that I consulted Linnaeus to "measure" and categorize—with Latin names no less—what children in Howa knew about the environment. Despite the ironies of the exercise, I want to present a collective taxonomy of the children's plant knowledge—*pace* Linnaeus—as a way of discussing how practice was congealed in knowledge. I am well aware that taxonomies represent particular kinds of arbitraries in the ways they fix knowledge that is more messy, fluid, practical, and processual. The children often struggled to demarcate categories that seemed more fluid or multiply articulated. For some it mattered whether plants were dry or green, for others whether they were cultivated or not, while still others delineated plants according to their structure, how they fruited and produced seeds, or whether they had any economic value. But each child would backtrack on whatever category they created and rework the constellation according to whatever consideration was at hand. It is clear from the agility of their taxonomizing and the almost kaleidoscopic variety of their taxonomies, individually and collectively, that each of the children would recognize the classificatory systems of the others.

One of the primary distinctions drawn, not surprisingly, was between flora and fauna. As Saddiq told me, "[T]hat's blood and that's wood." Despite their obvious distinction, the two were inseparable in the children's engagements with the world and in the physiologies they constructed (as will be discussed later). One way this understanding played out was in how children and adults conceptualized and imagined their physical environment. While in many ways the local environment was understood and encountered essentially as a vegetation complex, it was a complex intimately linked to a range of uses. By the time they were ten years old, children knew the species of trees used for fuelwood, most of the tree resources and herbaceous plants consumed locally, a range of fodder plants, the major plants used in construction, and a smattering of plants used for other purposes, such as medicine, cosmetics, and the fabrication of tools or other utensils. Most plants in the area had a multiplicity of uses, and most children were aware of more than one use for each plant. The composite taxonomy of the children's plant knowledge revealed not only the extraordinary breadth of their knowledge, but some interesting distinctions between their organization of environmental knowledge and that of trained botanists.

The children with whom I worked mentioned collectively a total of 137 cultivated and naturally occurring plants. Almost 28 percent of these were named by five or more of the seventeen children, and it was clear that most children knew many more species than they mentioned. Many known plants, especially cultivated ones, simply did not come up in the course of my interactions with all of the children. In part this was because the plants were not around to observe and discuss. This much became clear after the rains had begun. As the fields, forests, and surrounding lands sprang to life, the children mentioned or were able to identify many additional—30 percent more—plants than they had previously, simply because the plants were again apparent in the environment. In part, of course, their memories were jogged by the plants' presence, but in part this phenomenon suggests that the children's plant taxonomies were less abstract lists than context-dependent reservoirs of knowledge that were deeper still than what I recorded.[5]

The store of (undemonstrated) practical knowledge shared by children was likewise quite extensive. Environmental knowledge was significantly differentiated among the children, however. Along gender lines, for instance, boys mentioned an average of thirty-eight plant varieties in the ethnosemantic interviews, compared with just over twenty-five mentioned by the girls. Of course, the differences reflect gendered "occupational" differences among the children and their different modes of interaction with the environment. But, even if shepherds—whose knowledge of local vegetation was particularly detailed—are excluded from the tally, boys named 34 percent more varieties than girls did. The boys also tended to make finer analytic distinctions between plant varieties, distinguishing, for instance, between grasses and broad-leaved plants based on particular aspects of their propagation and development. The girls instead divided the plants along more functional grounds, such as whether they had economic value.

These differences underscore the relationship between children's everyday work practices, socialization, and environmental learning. But they also point to differences between boys' and girls' participation in the two activities that had the greatest influence on environmental learning: agriculture and animal husbandry. While boys participated in husbandry activities significantly more than girls did, both participated in agriculture at almost equal rates. In the latter, boys predominated in clearing, planting, and weeding, whereas girls predominated in the harvest, and these occupational differences had their effects. Harvesting brought children into contact with far fewer plant varieties than other agricultural activities did. Weeding, for example, required children to discriminate between weeds and cultivars, while clearing introduced them to a range of indigenous and introduced plant varieties. The differences between boys' and girls' knowledge also suggest that elders made gendered discriminations in the kinds of knowledge they made a point of teaching to children. By ten years of age, the boys had begun to learn the knowledge associated with agriculture more systematically than girls did. Differences in their exposure to and interactions with pasture vegetation were also apparent in their learning and knowledge by this time.

Evidence from the Orinoco Delta seemed to bear out the relationships I found between children's work and their botanies, and about the gendered nature of children's knowledge. Boys from four to fifteen in the Orinoco study knew—and were taught—a wider range of species than girls, with the notable exception of kitchen garden plants (Ruddle and Chesterfield 1977). Much as in Howa, boys learned by accompanying and assisting their fathers in the tasks of agriculture and animal husbandry. It took about ten years for boys to master the identification and learn the uses of the full range of local vegetation (Ruddle and Chesterfield 1977, 114). Here, as in Tanzania (Raum 1940) and the Chiapas of Mexico (Modiano 1973), men were often quite formal about teaching their sons, spending five to ten minutes each day instructing the boys about plant varieties. Fathers even tested their sons by asking them to accomplish particular tasks, such as gathering fodder. In Howa, by contrast, instruction was almost always entwined with practice. As boys spent more time assisting their fathers relative to girls, they learned substantially more about environmental resources. Practice was generally the "test" of children's knowledge. When herdboys allowed animals to graze on inappropriate or hazardous plants or girls brought home lesser varieties of wood for fuel, they heard about it from their elders. Pamela Reynolds (1996) found similar practice-based instruction among healers in Zimbabwe who instructed boys and girls in the identification, locations, and uses of various medicinal plants as they accompanied them to gather plants or sat by their sides when these plants were processed and administered. Perhaps because of the practical and participatory nature of this learning—another clear example of "situated learning" and "legitimate peripheral participation"—Reynolds found a shared conviction among many with whom she worked that the botanical and other knowledge associated with healing was not exchanged formally (see Lave and Wenger 1991).

The gendering of children's environmental knowledge suggests the importance of specialized work roles. Specialized workers produced distinctive vegetation taxonomies. More than a quarter of the ninety herbaceous plants identified by the children were mentioned by shepherds alone, and no child was familiar with as many plant varieties as the herdboys. Saddiq, for instance, was able to reel off a total of fifty-seven noncultivated plants, fourteen more than the child with the next highest tally. Numbers alone do not tell the whole story. Adequate pasturage and the availability of decent fodder were of serious concern throughout the village, even in households with a small number of animals. Different varieties of plants had different seasons, uses, and values for grazing that were recognized widely but understood best by shepherds, and this, too, was reflected in their taxonomies. Nevertheless, children's knowledge in this regard was impressive across the board. Most ten-year-olds were familiar with the common grasses and other vegetation grazed upon or collected for fodder, and were able to name at least a few trees browsed by local animals. The children collectively mentioned a total of ninety-one distinct plant varieties used as fodder, but there was only moderate overlap among their lists, suggesting a fairly wide base of knowledge among children of this age. For most of them, though, this knowledge was relatively undifferentiated, whereas herdboys' knowledge of fodder and grazing plants was more elaborate and further specialized. Herdboys knew the microenvironments where particular varieties could be found and had a better sense of their specific qualities as resources. Unlike most other children, shepherds were clear about what plants were better for fattening animals and increasing milk production, and they knew which plants lasted longer after the rains ended, all of which allowed them to maximize grazing resources as a matter of course.

Some of the children distinguished vegetation hazardous to animals. Here again, the shepherds tended to have the greatest awareness. One striking exception was the plant *awire*, which grew in the irrigation canals and was reported by many to be highly toxic if ingested by goats or sheep. One shepherd identified awire as a hazard, but all other mentions came from students in the village school, suggesting that teachers may have been teaching the children about the problems associated with the irrigation project. As regards other hazards, herdboys were aware of the specific problem caused by each plant—skin irritation, reduced milk production, and death, among other things—but they also knew where they were likely to encounter the offending plants. Herders were held responsible for injuries to the animals in their care, and it is not surprising that they shared a greater awareness of the hazards to livestock around Howa than other children, whose knowledge in this regard seemed haphazard at best. Two nonshepherds—a boy and a girl—mentioned a couple of plant hazards, for instance, that local shepherds (and professional foresters) disagreed were dangerous to animals. The differences in the children's knowledge—subtle or striking—were most commonly reflections of differences in their daily practices and routines.

Like the rest of their knowledge, the children's botanies—extensive, rich, and complicated—reflected their work and play relationships with the environment around them. The "tests" of this knowledge—not weeding out cultivars, fattening animals and protecting them from harm, getting the best firewood, and procuring clean water—were very different from the tests of children's knowledge in the village school. The knowledge "assessed" in the former was so embodied in practice that "habit" was the mark of mastery. The consequences of this production and exchange of knowledge—facility in the routines of everyday life—had everything to do with the children's material existence and the well-being of their families.

Although I was keen on developing taxonomies of the children's plant knowledge, these were as much a way of discerning their knowledge of environmental processes as of producing botanical classifications. Ten-year-old children were also aware of a host of environmental processes and ecological relations. From a young age, for instance, pretty much everyone knew that seeds required water to germinate and that some form of irrigation, whether from rain, watering, the river, or the gravity-fed canals of the Suki Project, was necessary for plant survival. The role of the sun seemed less clear, which may not be so surprising for children in a semiarid area, where a day without blazing sunshine was treated like a gift. One day five-year-old Habiba planted some seeds in the floor of my house. She seems to have been inspired by a sorghum seed that had sprouted near the water jug and the availability of a few groundnuts. As she drilled a few holes at the foot of the bed and placed a nut in each, she explained that the seeds would sprout if they got water. As she was doing this, her older sister, Muna, came in and disparaged the project, letting us know somewhat authoritatively that it would be better to grow the groundnuts outside. When asked why, Muna answered that they needed tall grass not a mud wall to grow alongside, and she offered to plant some outdoors. The sun was never mentioned (and the nuts were never planted), though in the meantime Habiba had made a small canal beside the newly planted nuts and watered them. They never received another drop, and so ended the indoor garden experiment.

It makes sense that the children were acutely aware of water's importance to plant growth, living as they did in a semiarid environment where cultivation commenced with the rains as the surrounding landscape seemed to turn green overnight. In this environment, the role of the sun may have been taken for granted. I never heard discussions about photosynthesis and heard very little about the relationship between the sun and plant growth. In the course of a series of ethnosemantic interviews with five of the children (seventeen interviews in all, lasting over eighteen hours in total), only one child mentioned the role of the sun in plant life. Talal was clear that if people wanted to make money from their fields they had to get rid of the tall grasses because they shaded the crops. The ground had to be left sunny, he insisted, or the grasses' shadow (*dul gussub*) would kill whatever was planted. Other plants he discussed as undesirable seemed to be more a matter of cleanliness than shadow casting. Referring to certain weeds as dirt (*wasakh*), he said that the project authorities insisted on their removal, but when I asked why, he only said that the inspectors wanted it that way. In response to further questions, he made it seem beyond explanation by pointing out, "[W]e clean our clothes, don't we?!" The project's logic, as far as Talal was concerned, was that clean fields enabled farmers to earn more from their crops. In a similar discussion, Ismail told me that weeds were cleared because crops needed the air. When I asked why, he reminded me that water in earthen zirs was cooled by the air, and by extension air in the fields would cool the water that the plants drank, and this was better for them. Almost as an afterthought he added that the weeds themselves drank the water as well.

If the relationships among light, earth, air, and plant growth were a bit ambiguous, water was another thing altogether. All of the children were well aware of the relationship there. Adults constantly monitored the weather once they were ready to plant or had planted, investigating any local rainfall and discussing what might be coming as they scanned the sky. Whereas adults were likely to aver that whether it rained or not was the will of God, they easily patched this view together with observations of clouds, winds, and other signs that rain might coming. Children were more likely to invoke God's will than to piece together meteorological evidence in the anticipation of rain. Ismail assured me one day that it rains when God wills it and no one can say when that will happen. On another occasion, when some large cumulus clouds rolled in, I asked him if they had rain in them and shrugging he said that he didn't know. He asked his mother and she assured him that they did. I was somewhat surprised that Ismail didn't seem to know this, and pushed a bit on exploring his knowledge of the hydrologic cycle (see Kates and Katz 1977). In our conversation he revealed no familiarity with the process of evaporation, and despite my prodding, he refused to recognize its existence. In response to my questions, he steadfastly maintained that water remained in vessels left in the sun, on the stove, or outside. When I said that in my experience the water would eventually disappear, quite rapidly in fact if it were boiling, he asked if perhaps things in America were different, and then suggested that the goats might have drunk it.

If in casual conversation the children were sometimes unclear about or disinterested in environmental processes, they were far from ignorant of them. In the course of the ethnosemantic interviews I conducted with five of the children (two girls and three boys) a rich understanding of process and environmental relationships was revealed.[6] For instance, as already discussed, all of the children were clear about the essential role of water in germination and plant survival. They discussed the dormancy phase of plants and trees during the dry months (from December to June) and the ways they seemed to spring back to life and become "soft" and green with the start of the rains. The course they charted consistently wedded vegetation to animal husbandry: the arrival of the rains led to the germination or regeneration of plants, their growth and blossoming, and finally to their consumption as fodder. As this linkage suggests, the children recognized the interrelationships not just between the availability of water and the "happiness" of plants, but between the dessication of plants and the weakening of animals who graze on them. The children connected the slow withering of plants after the conclusion of the rains to the milk of grazing animals running dry. They noted how much more dry vegetation animals had to consume to be nourished, marking the deaths of animals who failed to find enough fodder. The interweaving of these processes was clear to the children, as were their connections to the children's own nutrition and the tediousness of herding during the dry times. Just as the work was tiring, so were the animals "tired" during this time of year. The children were equally clear that as the pastures regenerated with the rains and the ground became "inundated" with water, the animals were easily "full." Too easily it seems; a couple of boys noted that the flocks had to be moved around not just to maintain grazing quality at each site, but to ensure that the animals kept eating and did not laze around. As the interviews made clear, these spatial negotiations also involved an understanding of soil quality. As shepherds juggled the provision of particular kinds of fodder so as to nourish and increase milk production without overgrazing, they routinely took the nature of the ground into consideration. For instance, they avoided mud-clay areas right after a rain because the gummy ground hampered the animals' mobility; they knew all of the accessible maya (seasonal pools); and they sometimes steered toward the eroded kerrib land near the river, which, despite supporting generally poor vegetation, was nearly impermeable and thus always passable.

Apart from plants that "just grow from the ground," which the children routinely associated with grazing or waste, there were also cultivated plants. Again the availability of water was central. The children linked the arrival of the rains to the swelling of the Nile, which in turn allowed the filling of the project's canals and enabled the planting season to begin. The children easily recognized the relationship between irrigation and plant growth, often using the language of "drinking." Not only do plants "drink" the water made available from the ground, but the terminology of drinking is used across categories. The ground and particularly the fields "drink" and then "hold" the water, while plants do the same—both "drinking" the water held in the ground and "holding" their own water so that they can use it when the sources of additional water disappear. This sort of parallelism with obvious anthropocentric associations also played out in the terminology associated with plant growth and development. For instance, when plants blossomed or produced an ear that gave forth fruit or seed, the children, and their elders, described the process as "giving birth" (*bilid, wilid*). They referred to seed sacs as *himla,* a word for "carrier" or "case" with the same etymological roots as pregnancy, and used a single word, *gena,* to refer to seeds and children. One child, explaining plant reproduction to me, opened a peanut and implored me to "look at the two children." These associations are not accidental and suggest a connectedness in the cosmology that joins physiology, botany, and husbandry (see Gupta 1998).

The links between practice and knowledge were extensive and durable. Most of what the children learned in their everyday engagements, whether among their elders or their peers, was important to both the contemporaneous reproduction of their community and its future. But knowledge guarantees nothing. The children's knowledge, whether of plant resources, land-use practices, or variations in the local landscape, was not productive in itself, rich though it was. Their knowledge required particular relations and conditions of production to be useful, even as it in part produced these. By the last decades of the twentieth century, children and their elders were working in and against a forceful set of material social practices that threatened and undermined the viability of their knowledge and showed signs of overwhelming the reproductive nature of local exchanges of knowledge. The irrigation project together with its entailments, for instance, were eroding—if not erasing—the very grounds that the children were learning so well. Yet the knowledge offered at the school was not necessarily putting them in better stead to face the future. The outcomes and significance of children's learning and knowledge—in school or out—were up for grabs in Howa as the social relations, forms, and practices of production and reproduction were unhinged from their previous moorings by the effects of the agricultural project. Whether in or outside school, children seemed to be prepared and disqualified simultaneously for most possible futures. Their everyday lives were negotiations of this edge.

Abstractions of Environmental Knowledge

The Howa school has not, in all likelihood, introduced its budding geographers to Cheltenham or its Chalklands, but they have started down that path. There is no such thing as pure abstraction. If they continue along the path, they are likely now not to find themselves in "mother England," but in the United States, where environmental education is often a crucial part of the geography or social studies curriculum in primary and secondary school. Anyone with even a passing knowledge of U.S. school children knows that many of them share a deep concern for the environment, and that many are virtually consumed with righteous environmentalist rage. They have been bombarded from every quarter—school, the mass media, friends, and families—with messages about environmental doom and responsibility for "saving" the planet. While these concerns have encouraged children and their schools to participate in various environmental projects, from neighborhood cleanups to whale adoption, the responsibility children are made to feel far outweighs their power to do anything. The gap between frustration and moralism is often colonized by low-level eco-fascism (see King 1995).

There is a long history of children's affinity with nature in many parts of the world (Hart and Chawla 1982; R. Hart 1997), but late twentieth-century environmentalism in the United States and Europe was dramatically at odds with the breadth and intensity of environmental destruction there and elsewhere. "Corporate environmentalism" has tended to overemphasize individual, consumption-side "solutions," like recycling and "buying green," while leaving destructive transnational production processes largely intact. There is a certain abstraction from creative environmental engagement, therefore, when children in the urban industrial centers argue righteously—in electrically lit and fossil-fuel-heated rooms—that extreme environmental measures are needed. This critique is not intended to patronize children or disparage their sometimes important environmental activism; the same is largely true for adults in these same places. The key issue here is that northern children commonly learn about the environment through a grid of powerful abstractions from the uses of nature. The contradictions of their own environmental positioning provoke well-intended but often partial and partisan environmental "solutions" that eclipse the social integument of human relations to nature and the ways it is produced.

How different the consciousness of children in Howa, whose knowledge of the environment and its degradation was more immediate, viscerally so. Children in Howa were strikingly aware of the deforestation all around them, for instance. Those with whom I worked commented on it constantly, indicating that trees of all kinds were disappearing from the area. Their own work practices were directly affected by the ever-expanding devegetation. They echoed the often repeated comments of their elders about the erstwhile abundance of several well-known tree species around Howa. Although they themselves had never witnessed this abundance, the historical geographies of earlier plenty were so vivid in the public imaginary that the children spoke as if they had. Most of them knew that there was a government-run reforestation area near the village and knew just as well that Forestry Department restrictions on wood cutting there were frequently flouted by Howa residents and others.

Some of the children had heard of fuel crises in nearby towns, but none described their own dwindling wood resources in crisis terms, although in the ethnosemantic interviews Talal described the creep of deforestation in a nearby area as going from large trees to small, then to scrap and ultimately nothing:

There were [trees], they didn't leave them. If there was a tree, they felled it, they'd burn just a stick, but there was nothing near them. Here there is. . . . Everyone—you know—all of Suki will be burning cartons. You pour kerosene on a box and light it. . . . When there are no trees you make do, you burn boxes. . . . What'll a carton do?!?

Another time he noted the rising prices of wood products for construction and associated these changes with declines in local and regional woodlands. But still these problems were not seen as crises; people went further afield, used smaller wood, paid more money, and otherwise made do, despite the immensity of the loss that everyone saw taking place around them. In any case, their awareness of the lack of alternatives was keen. In one interview Saddiq told me that he'd climb trees (including the sole surviving tamarind on the riverbank) to cut branches for his animals. "You don't love trees," I teased. He was indignant:

How could you say not love!!? In the days of summer the animals are hungry, they have no milk, I have to go up and cut, climb up and cut so the animals can be filled. They need just a little, little, little until the rainy season comes. By the time the rains come, I don't cut anymore.

Perhaps the very dailiness of the fuel shortage, and their own mundane responses to it, made it impossible to construct it as a "crisis," just as the intangibleness of the environmental problems perceived by so many children in the industrialized north enabled them to construct crisis everywhere.

No matter how articulate they were in setting forth the problems of local deforestation, Howa children neither offered nor seemed to think about solutions to the problem, nor did they make plans for using forestry resources less destructively. In this they followed their elders. Virtually all adults in Howa bemoaned eloquently and often the rapid disappearance of trees from the area. Given the economic and political-ecologic constraints upon them, most felt that it was impossible to do anything to stop the process because wood was the cheapest and most commonly available source of fuel in the area. Kerosene and propane were outside the budget of almost all village households, and while kerosene for lamps was sold in small quantities in the village, procuring tanks of propane (not to mention stoves to use them) would have been too expensive and logistically complicated. They also noted the environmental strains imposed by large-scale wood cutters—often refugees from Ethiopia and Eritrea—who were clearing forested areas near the village to produce wood and charcoal for sale in urban areas and other regions of Sudan. While there was a tendency to demonize and blame "the refugees" for deforestation, most adults also understood its connections with the overall land-use changes associated with the agricultural project and the resulting loss of both pasture and wood resources in the area. Most people in Howa, including children, therefore, clearly recognized their own contributions to deforestation, seeing it as a slow inexorable process that under contemporary circumstances they were bringing upon themselves. With no reasonable alternatives to woodfuel and no government or international programs encouraging fuel efficiency via new stove designs or new sources of energy (solar or wind power for rural electrification, for example), there was little alternative but to cut what trees remained. In the industrialized north, where environmental destruction is part of the stealth of everyday life, removed from the view of many, people can advocate noble environmentalist positions more easily than those whose routines enmesh them in environmental destruction to which there are no easy alternatives.

But it is precisely such abstracted environmentalism that drives much of the international and governmental policy and practice that affects the global south and therefore places like Howa. It undergirds World Bank, USAID, and other programs to address "overpopulation" in the so-called "third world," transnational reforestation programs that cannot see the people for the trees, or various "appropriate technology" and "sustainable development" projects that never ask "Appropriate for whom?" or "Sustainable of what?" as they demand those in the global south forego the gains made by technologies that have been so "appropriate" for "sustaining" global capitalism. These issues and concerns point clearly to the political significance of the symbolic practices that construct knowledge and name problems. At the same time, the near total absence of locally derived conservation practices in the face of dramatic and widely recognized deforestation and pasture degradation points to the difficulty of managing resources when securing the means of existence depends on those very resources. These contradictions were the grit of children's everyday learning, and more than just their futures were at stake in the outcomes.

Remaking the Scales of Everyday Life

Another part of the grit was an almost intimate geography of Howa and the area around it. This geography—encompassing an area of about eighty kilometers—was so replete with discrete, if sometimes overlapping, localities, that it made me appreciate how Ismail could ask me one day whether the United States was bigger than Howa. While everyone in Howa, from about eight or nine years on, was readily familiar with this intricate microgeography, together with the work and other activities associated with each location, few had as intricate a local geography as herdboys. Their days were spent moving their animals and hooking up with one another in innumerable discrete pasture areas a few kilometers around the village. Each separate area had its qualities for both children and animals, and these were the focus of daily decisions about where to go. As groups of herdboys headed out each day they determined their destinations among themselves, and when they split up from one another at various points, they would usually plan later rendezvous sites. I was always intrigued with the herdboys' intricate mental maps—the way they parsed areas that looked largely uniform to me. In the course of the ethnosemantic interviews, Saddiq made a map with me of all the grazing areas he distinguished within about a kilometer of the village. He mapped no less than forty separate sites in this area. The detail of Saddiq's knowledge is reflected in the specificity of the names for the pastures: "Tulh of Mohamed Sherif" (Mohamed Sherif's acacia tree) or "Maya of Fadlallah el Khider" (Fadlallah el Khider's depression).

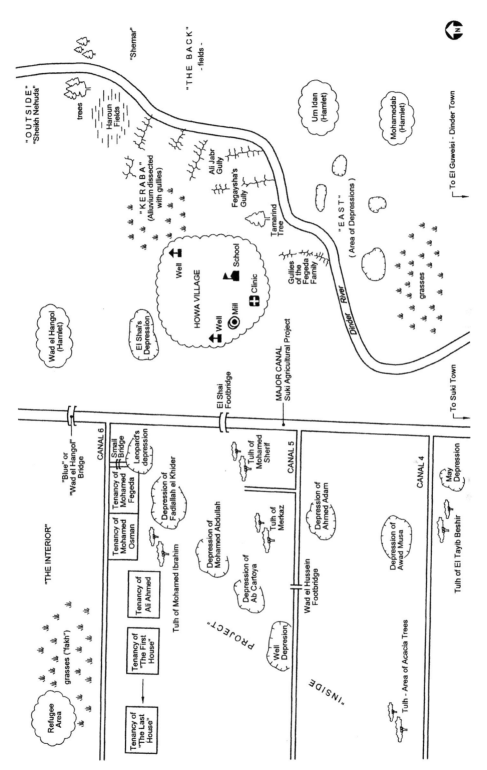

Figure 26. This rendering of a map produced as a sketch in the course of a number of interviews with Saddiq reveals his exquisitely detailed knowledge of local grazing areas in and around the village. Saddiq's knowledge was typical of herd-boys, but many of the pastures he identified were under threat from the environmental degradation associated with the agricultural project.

If his extraordinary map of local knowledge was rooted completely in Saddiq's daily experience herding, it was not idiosyncratic in the least. Just as the children's individual taxonomies were mutually recognizable, albeit different, Saddiq's map traced an intricate cartography familiar to most children his age, even if his map offered more detail than theirs might. In the interviews and otherwise, all of the children displayed an elaborate knowledge of the local geography of work and play. They knew the multiple locales of various kinds of wood resources, the pattern of grazing areas surrounding Howa, where individual tenancies and subsistence fields were located, the location of all the nearby villages, the best places to find wild resources such as fruits and nuts, and various divisions within the agricultural project. Like Saddiq's map, which parsed a seemingly uniform area into dozens of discrete places with specific seasonal qualities, the children's mental maps revealed layers of microgeographies within the project area, the village, and the areas beyond them. Their maps and movements through the local environment revealed constellations of differentiated spaces within an environment that might appear homogenous to outsiders. Moreover, each of these spaces was linked to specific practices whose heterogeneity was easily eclipsed in an undifferentiated view of the local environment. The children's cartographies of everyday life were rich, nuanced, and inseparable from their activities and aspirations. If their maps were rooted in experience, others' were not.

Beshir, Sami's father, also known affectionately as Al Shibe, asked me one day where "Nimrica" (his name for the United States) actually was. He was on a straw mat on the ground, leaning back in total pleasure as he smoked a cigarette we had given him. I drew a map with words. "You go all the way west to the end of Africa—it's thousands of kilometers—and then there's a huge sea called the Atlantic Ocean, you cross that going northwest and then you'll come to the United States. New York is on the water, that's where my mother is." Many of the conversations in Howa concerning distance, time, space, and the relative geographies of Sudan and the United States were somehow anchored by my mother, who understandably was thrilled with the idea. All of a sudden, though, this conversation took a turn for the weird. The Shibe sat up—mid-cigarette—looking disturbed, and asked me if this was past the Maghreb. I said yes. "Past Fez?" Thrilled with the geographic detail, I delightedly nodded yes. Now he was really disturbed. He started mumbling a prayer that went on for so long that he almost seemed in a trance. He flicked his prayer beads between thumb and forefinger, whispering as incantation the anchoring Islamic phrase that there was no God but God. After a couple of minutes he stopped, looked at me calmly, and said, "No, you go to the west of Africa and cross the sea until you come to Nimrica, keep going and *then* comes Fez." "No, Fez *is* the west of Africa," I said laughing. The Shibe was an unusual character and a bit of a prankster, it took me a while to realize he was not kidding—something was really wrong. His words drew the map again with Fez somewhere near San Francisco. I relented, now delighting in the eccentricity of his map and the peculiarity of his relationship to Fez. He relaxed, leaned back, relit the cigarette, and explained that according to the Quran, there was nothing beyond Fez.

The Shibe's map was an abstraction held in place by the very localness of his immediate experience. He was one of the most broadly informed people in Howa. From local history, through traditional land-use practices, to the antics of Americans on the moon—"You went to the moon and all you brought back was rocks!"—he never ceased to impress me with what he knew and how he organized his knowledge. But the abstractions from his reading and what he heard on the radio were kept intact because there was little in his daily experience to unsettle them. The intrusion of my personal geography disturbed his map of the world, but was quickly reinterpreted so that his view could hold. Not an uncommon phenomenon of "worldviews" anywhere on earth. Such abstractions can only take so many assaults by evidence to the contrary before they must bend if not collapse to incorporate them. I was not the first and surely not the last intrusion, but the seeds of unsettling were surely sown and it was not clear what new forms the Shibe's maps of the world might take.

Saddiq's map was as rooted in daily experience as the Shibe's map was abstract, and yet his map was threatened as well. Saddiq's map—and by extension those of the other children—was threatened by practical disruptions at a whole other scale from the Shibe's. The very terrain he mapped was continuously being compromised by the land-use practices associated with the agricultural project. The map of his detailed local knowledge was becoming an artifact—increasingly superceded by new physical forms and arrangements—even as he used it daily. The children constantly referred to places that *used to have* trees, that *had been* cultivated fields or gardens, that *once had* this or that resource. Their maps already traced absences and they were only ten years old.[7] As the deep reservoir of tactile knowledge reflected in their maps was undermined, it was not clear what Saddiq or his contemporaries might do with it, or what alternative maps they might make to chart their way into or out of a different world.

This chapter started with the Cheltenham Chalklands—an abstraction that staged an encounter between colonial history and the postcolonial imagination. Abstraction can be deadening, as can concrete learning and knowledge, but as I have tried to suggest, "wild imagining" (Taussig 1993, 21) can sprout in its interstices. Wild imagining can be drawn on consciously to build on and undo "habit" in ways that rework and remake the world and its social relations in a more willful way. The maps here are parables of the fluid relationships among knowledge, practice, and abstraction in everyday life, and the tenuousness of the ways they are held together at different scales. In unraveling some of the paths that led to Cheltenham, dislodged Fez, or eliminated Mohamed el-Sherif's tulh—each a kind of "wild imagining"—I have tried to make clear the important resonances of these shifting relationships, not just in the children's everyday lives, but for the process of social change itself. Negotiating this ground and reworking its maps were material social practices full of power, problems, and possibilities for the children and their "recent futures."

Stuart Hall tells a story of when he first arrived in Britain from Jamaica and saw fat English cows grazing on a grassy hillside. In a flash, these almost unrecognizable creatures led him to reimagine all the British literature with which he had been steeped.

Figure 27. Saddiq surveys the animals, vehicles, and dolls available for his use in the geodramatic exercise I used to learn about village life from the children. When I bought those perfect British-made animals in an old-fashioned toy store in Harvard Square, the genteel shopkeeper, possibly sensing my urban origins, quietly suggested that camels had no place on a proper farm; perhaps—she suggested—I'd be interested in a few pigs. Later, at a more humble toy store where I went to purchase farm vehicles and toy soldiers (which I clothed as Sudanese men and women for the exercise), I fussed to the garrulous shopkeeper about the relative size of the vehicles and people. "Lady," he said, "when I was a kid I had a bunch of sticks and a cigar box. It ain't gonna make a difference!" The camels were right and so was the second shopkeeper.

Figure 28. Not Jane Austen's cow.

In the imaginary space between those scrawny Jamaican cows he had in his head as he read and the Jerseys Jane Austen probably had in hers as she wrote erupted a spark to reinvent the world. In one of my research methods with the children in Howa, I asked them to make models of Howa and its surroundings on the ground using dirt, sticks, grass, and water—the basic elements of the village. I then gave them a set of miniature farm animals, vehicles, and human figures to enact "geodramas" that would show me life in Howa. The animals, made in Britain, were splendid-—anatomically correct, each perfectly scaled, durable, and neatly colored—I loved them as much as the children did. Before the "geodramas" began I asked each child to identify the animals, just to make sure everyone knew what they were playing with as they enacted their dramas. Without fail, every child identified the cows, bulls, goats, chickens, and camels. But they all stumbled on the sheep. Those plump wooly British sheep were a world apart. Who knows what pastures they traveled, and what sparks might be provoked by encountering them?

5. Disrupted Landscapes of Production and Reproduction

When the aim of labor is not a particular product, standing in a particular relation to the particular needs of the individual, but money, wealth in its general form, then firstly, the individual's industriousness knows no bounds, it is indifferent to its particularity and takes on every form which serves its purpose.

—Karl Marx, *Grundrisse*

Maybe it was the lorries. Maybe it was something else—the plumpness of those wooly sheep, the disappearance of the doleibs, something in the air. But virtually every child—girl or boy, rich or poor, student or not—went to market in the course of their "geodramas."[1] No matter what the plot or how long its duration, at one point or another each child put a miniature sheep, goat, or even a cow in a toy truck and went to town to sell it. Getting and spending were already a big part of the game in Howa, and selling off animal wealth was one way to "play." To paraphrase Marx (1973), money had entered the community and then it became the community. Marx was describing the erosive and constitutive effects of the money form associated with ascendent capitalism. These effects were readily apparent in Howa.

In the wake of the Suki Project, money was fast becoming the "generalized representative of wealth" and the medium of all social exchange, dissolving old means and intentions of production and becoming the connective tissue that bound people to one another and the broader society. The children in Howa were keenly aware of the dissolution and reconstitution underway in their community as they engaged in reproducing—remaking—it in their own ways. Their games, their conversations, their desires, as much as their daily routines at school or work, were all a part of the process.

This much I hope has been clear from the foregoing chapters, but things were changing dramatically as these children came of age. What had Howa become as a community? What was its relationship to Sudan and the rest of the world? What were the relationships between children's everyday practices and the terrain of production; between their learning and knowledge and the social relations of their community; and between disruptions in the production of space and nature at different scales and the material social practices through which children constructed their identities and negotiated the conditions of their everyday lives then and as they grew older?

To begin to answer these questions, this chapter will focus on disruptions and reconfigurations in the production of space, nature, and social life in the household, the village, the nation, and more generally. I will address displacements in the relationship between production and social reproduction, focusing on the production and exchange of knowledge to examine evidence of, prospects for, and responses to deskilling in Howa, particularly among young people. Finally, I will explore responses to these sweeping changes in Howa, and the ways these changes may lead to new constructions of identity and rework the geographies of everyday life.

Altered Relations of Production and Reproduction

Children in Howa, like children everywhere, produced their identities as they made their way through their everyday lives. Absorbing and making their own the cultural forms and practices of their families and community, children acquired the knowledge and skills shared locally in connection with production and reproduction. While these practices and their social matrix are always fluid and potentially unstable, in most historical geographies everyday life is more constant than precarious. By the 1980s this was not the case in Howa; earlier practices, expectations, and assurances of social life, however hard won and fragile, were no longer so secure. The productions of space, nature, and social life associated with the Suki Agricultural Project were most directly responsible for these changes in everyday life, but it is important to remember that they were only the most obvious local manifestation of much broader changes afoot in Sudan and elsewhere. As money becomes the community, the process dissolves older community forms by ratcheting apart, disrupting, and rewiring preexisting social relations of production and reproduction.

Suki Agricultural Project

Money became the metric of social life in Howa as insistently as the Suki Project redefined the local political economy and ecology. As detailed in previous chapters, the project, begun in 1971, absorbed most of the peasant agriculturalists living in Howa and engaged them in contract farming as tenants in the scheme. Tenants were required to cultivate cotton and groundnuts in 100 percent rotation as cash crops and were simultaneously prevented from planting sorghum, the staple food crop, anywhere on project lands. Most existing farm plots and their surrounds were leveled and graded as part of the project, pushing the cultivation of other crops and nontenant agriculture to lesser and more distant areas, along with various complementary economic activities, such as grazing or forestry. These shifts made it much more difficult for farmers to work outside of the cash nexus, in essence gearing their production toward exchange value rather than goods, such as sorghum, for their households' consumption. Tenant households, meanwhile, had higher needs for cash than was customary before the project because a greater number of farm inputs were required and had to be purchased. Finally, the political-economic and political-ecologic changes brought about by the Suki Project transformed many formerly free, self-produced, or commonly available goods into commodities, including, for instance, sorghum and fuelwood, thereby exacerbating the need for cash across the board. In these ways and others, the Suki Project was the definitive impulse propelling Howa into the capitalist money economy in its relations of production and reproduction.

Money Becomes the Community

In a chapter on money in the *Grundrisse,* Marx vividly explains the social relations brought about and represented by money as a general form. He notes that when money enters a community as a "generalized representative of wealth and as individual exchange value," it alters the social relations and object of labor such that labor is commodified and becomes wage labor. The object of wage labor is not a particular product (or use value) but money (exchange value), and money in turn purchases commodities produced through social labor. This situation "is the elementary precondition of bourgeois society." The transformation from subsistence to bourgeois society is often provoked by the introduction of commodities that encourage new needs and desires among a particular population and draw growing numbers into relations of monetized exchange. Money itself becomes the "*real community*" because "it is the general substance of survival for all" and the integument that joins everyone (Marx 1973, 225, emphasis in the original). This process was heightened in Howa by the shifts produced by the agricultural project and its entailments. In each of my visits to the village over a period of fifteen years, money, rather than particular products or other forms of wealth, such as grain or animals, increasingly became the object of labor. As the need for money expanded incessantly, so, too, did the range of tasks people undertook to get it. This was also anticipated by Marx, who noted that when the aim of labor is money rather than a particular product, "the individual's industriousness knows no bounds" (224). He could have been describing Howa.

Disruptions

As money became the community, the changes fueled a number of disruptions in the village. While most of these disruptions had been entrain prior to the incursions brought about by the agricultural project, all of them were accelerated by the shifts associated with the Suki Project and the larger social relations of production and reproduction with which it was associated. Among the most important of these disruptions in Howa were commodification, the monetization of the local economy, socioeconomic differentiation, labor migration, the expansion of education, and the separation of work and play. Each of these represents an incursion of money into social relations and the commodification of such things as labor, knowledge, and time.

Commodification

Many goods that had been freely available or commonly held in Howa were fast becoming commodities within the first decades of the project. Sorghum, formerly self-produced, was fully commoditized in Howa by its exclusion from the Suki Project. Its price zoomed up 2000 percent during the first decade that most local agriculturalists had stopped growing it.[2] The appropriation of land by the project also limited and ultimately led to the degradation of pastures in the vicinity. The devegetation and shrinkage of grazing lands stressed the local livestock population, which suffered periodic losses associated with poor dry-season grazing and drought. The trend exacerbated a tendency toward the commodification of meat that had been underway since the establishment of two butcher stalls in the village during the 1960s. Prior to their establishment, which effectively commodified meat locally, meat was less readily available in Howa, though animals were relatively abundant. Likewise, the appropriation of so much forested area into project lands seriously curtailed the availability of wood in the vicinity. As demand for woodfuel remained unaltered and even increased with local population growth while forestry practices remained largely the same, wood, too, was gradually commodified in Howa. While those who could afford to purchase wood and charcoal occasionally did, the shift enabled others—often young people—to make money on the sale of fuelwood. Finally, as some households had more disposable cash and others a more acute need for it, water became a bit of a commodity as well. About fifteen children and teens routinely sold water in the village to supplement their households' earnings. The dollar or so they made each day made a difference to their families' budgets.

On another front, as some residents accumulated wealth and diversified their economic activities, an increasing number of small shops were opened in the village and a growing number of trucks began plying trade routes in the region. Several trucks went daily from the village to nearby market towns taking local residents to sell, buy, or trade various goods, and returning with an expanded range of commodities, such as fresh fruits and vegetables, to sell. The dozen or so general merchandise shops that did business in Howa all had approximately the same limited inventories, including tinned tomatoes, flip-flops, cigarettes, batteries, school supplies, and a range of dry goods. People still went to the market towns of Dinder, Sennar, or even Suki to buy most other merchandise, such as cloth, dishes, pots and pans, or furniture, but the local shops were increasing in number and each stocked a broader range of consumer goods than village shops had sold only a decade before. The fact that Howa was able to support a dozen or so shops and that their inventories were growing in size and variety suggests not only the enhanced significance of commodities of various sorts in everyday life, but the increased monetization of the local economy.

Between the commodification of goods, such as sorghum, wood, meat, and to a lesser extent, water, and wider access to enlarged realms of trade, the importance of money grew. Its power made the effects of socioeconomic differentiation more apparent as certain people began to consume at new levels, while others found staple goods like sorghum less affordable everyday. But, wherever one stood in the economic spectrum, money had become a strong lure, and there was a fairly general desire to have more of it.

Monetization

With commodification and the production demands of the agricultural project, which placed a serious burden on tenants to come up with cash in order to procure agricultural inputs, the monetization of the local economy galloped ahead. As Marx (1973) anticipated, labor—itself commodified with the expansion of capitalist relations of production and reproduction—was directed increasingly toward exchange rather than a particular use value or accomplishment, and money came to define a growing number of relationships and exchanges, including those within families. But the process by which money became the community was as intensely international as it was local. The "invisible hand" was everywhere. As capitalist relations of production expanded in the village, the broader economy of Sudan began to seriously founder, along with many others in Africa and elsewhere in the "third world." These problems, associated with global economic restructuring as well as with clientelism, corruption, and the persistence of the structural inequalities of colonialism and its "developmentalist" descendants, had local repercussions.

The various strategies for postcolonial "development," which in Sudan continued to be led by the expansion of cash crops for export, had not produced sufficient income at the national scale to begin to repay a broad and growing array of bilateral and multilateral debts. Sudan's "debt trap" deepened and grew as its economy stalled and foundered. During the first decade of the Suki Project (between 1970 and 1981), for instance, Sudan's external public debt went from .3 billion to 4.8 billion dollars, increasing from 15.8 to an astonishing 59.3 percent of the GNP (Walton and Seddon 1994, 184). To help ensure repayment to a range of northern financial institutions and states, the International Monetary Fund (IMF) instituted Sudan's first structural adjustment program (SAP) in 1978. As is by now well known, SAPs are generally predicated on the removal of food subsidies, the emphasis of export-based agriculture, currency devaluations, and broad decreases in public spending. In Sudan these measures provoked the first of several "austerity" or IMF riots by the beginning of 1982 (Walton and Seddon 1994). The riots, which capped a year of sporadic protests, took place in many parts of the country, including rural areas, which were, of course, hard hit by the SAPs through measures that removed subsidies on staples, such as sugar, and altered production relations in many irrigation schemes. The latter was accomplished in part through the introduction of the "individual account system," which had been pioneered by the Suki Project (see Ali 1985a, b; Bernal 1991). Part of the increased price of sorghum, but by no means all, can also be traced to structural adjustment. In the absence of price controls, sorghum prices increased dramatically after each devaluation imposed by the IMF. But sorghum prices were also seriously affected by price gouging on the part of the mechanized farmers of eastern Sudan, who controlled an increasingly large share of its production and frequently chose to market it to the oil-rich states or smuggle it to neighboring countries such as Chad and Ethiopia, where it commanded a much higher price than it did domestically (Ali 1985a).[3]

The debilitating effects of the expansion of capitalist relations of production in Howa were thus worsened by the fact that as the local economy was more fully monetized, the economy of Sudan was entering a deeper and deeper crisis. The effects of the crisis distorted the normalized trajectory of monetization and threw a monkey wrench into the path of capital accumulation across geographic scales, but more to the point, they also compounded the squeeze experienced by people in Howa in the face of commodification and the monetization of so many forms of exchange.

Differentiation

These changes, together with those associated more directly with the Suki Project, exacerbated already existing socioeconomic distinctions between households as they instigated new and more ferocious patterns of differentiation. The agricultural project underscored old and created new forms of inequality in Howa in three key ways. First, from the outset there were fewer tenancies to distribute than there were households. Some householders—whether by their own choice or not—did not receive tenancies and were thereby cut out of a key and ascendant economic activity in the village. Second, and along the same lines, because there was a fixed number of tenancies available to residents of Howa, when new households were formed they could rarely acquire one. Tenancies tended to be kept within a family, but even then they were not frequently available to change hands for demographic reasons. Parents of adult children were often quite young and thus remained economically active themselves for many years; at the same time most households included several sons who would eventually vie for a tenancy (see O'Brien 1984). Third, not all tenancies were created equal. Because of the vagaries of location and the subtle distinctions in the land allocated, some fields were more productive than others, and these differences were self-reinforcing. Where success enabled some farmers to avail themselves of additional means to boost their productivity, such as mechanizing certain operations or hiring labor during periods of intensive demand, failure pushed other farmers into debt, either to the project for advances on the costs of production or to local merchants and moneylenders, some of whom engaged in illegal crop-mortgaging activities. In these ways social differentiation begot further differentiation.[4]

These social divisions were often built on longstanding ones of more modest size. Some families had accumulated wealth long before the Suki Project through building large herds, participating in private cotton schemes along the Blue Nile, and/or engaging in trade or money lending, and this gave them an advantage in all subsequent economic activities, including tenant farming. Those who had tenancies in private pump schemes along the Blue Nile, for instance, were given priority in the allocation of Suki tenancies. Several of them, and others with *wasta* (social connections) not only managed to get more than one tenancy—in some cases registering them to wives or infant sons—but they appeared to have gotten the best ones as well. More privileged residents seemed to have received a disproportionate share of the tenancies closest to the village. At the very least, these fields were the most convenient, but they were also closest to the major irrigation canals and this made them first in line to receive water. Shortfalls or problems along the canals, which were frequent (see Euroconsult 1988; Suki Agricultural Corporation 1997), were other tenants' problems. Apart from reinforcing old socioeconomic disparities, the project fostered new ones through controlling access to land and other productive resources and the peculiarities of its accounting and other systems of operation.

Finally, socioeconomic differentiation was exacerbated by the availability of labor or other forms of support from members of the extended family and household, counterbalanced by the nature of their dependencies and needs. Despite the resourcefulness and often exhausting hard work done by so many in Howa, growing impoverishment was the lot of most village households. Income from the tenancies was inadequate for most households, but very few tenants (6 percent) supplemented it with regular, permanent, wage labor. Rather, people worked as independent woodcutters, charcoal makers, crafts people, petty entrepreneurs, and the like, either in the interstices of their agricultural work or in the off-seasons (67 percent of all tenants supplemented their incomes in this way). Only 37 household heads (11 percent of all households), tenants and not, were regular wage workers, while 144 men and women in the village reported working at least occasionally as agricultural laborers. Over 54 percent of these day laborers were women who, with adolescent girls and children of both genders, predominated in all harvest work, especially cotton picking. In most village households, this mixture of economic strategies enabled survival but not much gain, especially in the face of an increasingly commodified life. Within a decade of the project's inception, there was common agreement among adults in Howa that local socioeconomic disparities had not only become more widespread, but they had become heightened as well.

Commodification of Labor Power

As these shifts in household labor strategies suggest, the commodification of labor power was both an outcome of and a catalyst for money becoming the community.

One of the early effects of the production relations and seasonal labor demands of the project, for instance, was the diminished importance of communal work parties, or nefir. While in the past, villagers cooperated to accomplish various agricultural tasks, the Suki Project was predicated on household self-sufficiency, mechanization, and hiring field hands as necessary. While I never heard anything from project authorities that specifically discouraged nefir, and indeed they persisted in Howa albeit with less frequency, the compressed time and intensity of certain tasks were not conducive to work sharing among tenant households because everyone was under pressure to accomplish appointed tasks according to a tight schedule. In addition, those strapped for cash, tenants and not, scrambled to find remunerative work in and outside the project. In this way everyday forms of labor were commodified as people increasingly bought and sold labor power among neighbors and friends.

Labor dynamics were reworked within the family as well. With almost all tenancies allocated to men in the village, the project administration assumed the availability of household labor and the ability of men to mobilize the labor of their wives and children. They were not wrong. Nevertheless, the agricultural labor of women and children in the cotton and groundnut fields represented a marked shift from the labor dynamics that had prevailed previously. While villagers indicated that children had helped their fathers in the cultivation of sorghum and sesame, these crops were substantially less labor-intensive than either cotton or groundnuts, and this difference was reflected in children's everyday lives. Children and adolescent boys helped to take up the slack on several of the tasks that were new to the project or had been attenuated on account of it. Among these were the maintenance of the irrigation ditches, furrowing and sowing (sesame was broadcast), and the mandatory four weedings of both cotton and groundnuts. Perhaps even more striking, while women had had little to do with the cultivation of sorghum and sesame, they played a significant role in the agricultural project.

The cotton and groundnut harvests were accomplished almost entirely by women, teenaged girls, and children. Cotton picking was the main agricultural task for which labor was hired in Howa, and most of this work was done by local residents. Women, teens, and children worked almost constantly during the cotton and groundnut harvests, earning between US$.75 and $1.11 a day on a piece-rate basis.[5] However minimal the compensation, this income was crucial to many households. Girls' contributions were particularly important in this regard. More than twice as many girls (111) as boys (48) worked as paid field hands in Howa. Most of the women working the harvest were past their prime childbearing years, but some younger women picked cotton with their families. Some even moved their entire households out to their tenancies, staying in temporary field dwellings to maximize their collective labor time. This practice was more prevalent among those whose tenancies were relatively far from the village.

The harvest was the most labor-intensive aspect of cotton (and groundnut) cultivation; over 208 estimated person-days were required to harvest a five-feddan cotton tenancy (Bernal 1988). Given the importance of women's and children's roles in the harvest, it is clear that a substantial proportion of the increased labor associated with the agricultural project was carried out by them. Without the relatively cheap labor power of local women and children—including those from their own households—tenants would be hard-pressed to harvest their crops on time. While the success, such as it was, of the agricultural project depended on the ready availability of this labor, the harvest was a two-way street for women; the money they earned in most cases was their own to keep. In this way the commodification of labor associated with the project was contradictory—it simultaneously tapped into patriarchal relations as a means of securing a labor force for the harvest and it loosened the hold on women as they secured another relatively autonomous source of personal income.[6]

While as the foregoing suggests, there was a ready and often tapped labor market in Howa, with the number of available laborers growing as more young men came of age without access to land, this market was increasingly saturated and was in any event casual (see Kevane 1994; O'Brien 1983). The commodification of labor also took place outside of agriculture. Young men without access to tenancies, for instance, occasionally found work in the project offices and workshops. More commonly, young men, including some who had tenancies, worked as day laborers in the nearby market towns of Sennar, Suki, and Dinder. Most of them found work as cargo loaders and carriers on a sporadic basis. Except for the few men in Howa who found employment in the project headquarters in Wad Tuk Tuk, most engagements with the labor market outside of Howa were partial and casual. They suggest a transitional phase in the commodification of labor in Howa.

Despite the growing importance of money in the local economy and the increasing importance of labor "commuting," there was little labor migration. Only eighteen households (5.4 percent) reported members working elsewhere, almost all in urban areas of Sudan, although larger numbers migrated seasonally for agricultural and other work and a growing number found casual employment in the nearby towns, which they could commute to as necessary. There was virtually no foreign labor migration. In the early years after the first oil shocks, when the expanded wealth of the oil-exporting states made them a magnet for labor migration, most of the Sudanese who migrated to Saudi Arabia and the Gulf States were from urban areas and tended to be more educated than the average population. By the 1980s, as Sudan's economy continued to sink, its government was overthrown, and the civil war resumed, a growing number of emigrants hailed from more rural areas, particularly from villages along the Nile (see Bernal 1991; Galal el Din 1978). Still, Howa seemed immune. The relatively minimal role of labor migration there suggests both its relative insulation from the larger cash economy and the continued ability of its population to provide for themselves locally, despite the pace of commodification there. The erosive local effects of monetization and the kinds of desire commodification engendered seemed to ensure that it would not be long before Howa produced its own crop of *mughteribiin* (labor emigrants). Labor migration was in certain ways just the extreme edge of more mundane processes associated with the ascendence of capitalist relations of production in Howa: the commodification of labor power and the proletarianization of the local population. But the process of labor migration exacerbates many of the trends that engender it because it ups the ante on desire and opens up new standards of consumption and wealth.

Education and the Commodification of Knowledge

The effects of children's increased labor played out in other arenas of their everyday lives. The expectation of "development" is that "modernization" and infrastructural improvements will liberate children and others from various forms of drudgery so that, among other things, child labor will decrease while school attendance and "free" time will increase (see Rodgers and Standing 1981; Cain 1977; Nag, White, and Peet 1978; Tienda 1979; Middleton 1970; but cf. Porter 1996; Levine 1996). I thought as much myself before I lived in Howa. But these sorts of changes are not among the guarantees of "development"—quite the opposite, it seemed. As Marx (1967) made clear in the first volume of *Capital*, the early stages of capital accumulation in any particular place have historically depended on the conscription of child labor. Neither history, nor geography seems to have altered this situation. While the continued importance of child labor in urban and industrial areas of the "third world" is well recognized, my research indicated that capitalist "development" brought about an intensification and expansion of children's work in the countryside as well. Thanks to new cultivation strategies and requirements, environmental degradation, and heightened monetization, the Suki Agricultural Development Project and its entailments led to increases in children's labor, measured both in time spent and in the range of tasks undertaken. Much of this work was undertaken within and for the household. Indeed, children's labor was often a bulwark against hiring labor and thus simultaneously conserved household financial resources and provided a valve on the local labor market that helped keep wage rates down (see O'Brien 1984). In poorer households without the resources to hire labor, children's labor enabled the timely completion of tasks such as clearing, planting, weeding, and harvesting.

The effects of these shifts were uneven and exceeded the realm of agricultural labor. They were more acute for children from the poorest and most marginalized households in Howa, especially nontenants. These children not only added to their households' income, but in providing the means of existence under conditions of increasing commodification, their work enabled their families to avoid cash expenditures. But the nature of the changes underway in Howa tended to increase the labor time of children from wealthier households as well, particularly those headed by tenant-merchants. These children often had broader work responsibilities than others because of their households' economic diversification, which required that work be doled out along particular lines of specialization. Wealthier families tended to groom certain children for particular tasks so that all arenas of the household's work and economic activity—present and future—would be covered "in house."

These conditions curtailed school enrollment and attendance in Howa at the same time that a greater premium was placed on school learning in the larger society.

While the changes brought about by the project seemed to make it ever more difficult for children in Howa to attend school, the need for formal education as a means to success was felt more sharply there and elsewhere in Sudan. Nevertheless, the significance of schooling in children's lives, as well as its impending importance in future children's lives, felt very much up for grabs. As I've indicated before, only a minority of school-aged boys and almost no girls attended school in Howa as these contradictions emerged. The majority of those who did attend left early because of economic necessity, and very few continued past the sixth grade in the best of circumstances. According to my survey, only 42 percent of those who ever attended school in Howa reached sixth grade, the final year of primary school. While people commonly expressed an appreciation for the alternate futures possible for educated people and for the kinds of knowledge and skills that might be acquired in school, the reality of the pressures of production and reproduction in the everyday lives of most households made school a luxury.[7]

Even among the wealthy in Howa, the relationship to school was ambiguous. While boys from wealthier households commonly attended school, many of them left prior to graduation. The others, like most boys in Howa, did not continue their education in secondary school. In wealthier households, adults seemed to view schooling within the larger strategy of household diversification. School was a way to provide literacy and numeracy skills to selected sons, while others learned how to market livestock, run the family business, manage a truck, oversee agricultural production and the like. Sons groomed in these directions either never attended school or left it after a few years. For these families, more than others in the village, formal education neither functioned, nor was perceived as a means to economic success or status. It was one strategy among many for maintaining and expanding wealth and power.

Although the increased demand for children's labor and earnings in so many households in the decade following Howa's inclusion in the Suki Project apparently led to decreases in the ratio of students to nonenrolled children, it seemed that school enrollment would eventually increase in Howa precisely because of the social and economic changes associated with the project (see O'Brien 1984). But this was only likely to occur when the viability of other forms of learning began to erode. The "glamour" of education was certainly not enough to draw most people into the system, and the appreciation people commonly expressed for formal education seemed more ideal than real. Almost everyone spoke of schooling with high regard, responding to my interview and casual questions as if they had every intent of sending their children to school or wished they could do so, but what they actually did was often a dramatic departure because of necessity or deep ambivalence about the government schools. When I first got to Howa in 1980, the only person from the village ever to go to university tended to walk around like a self-appointed prince. When I would sing songs in praise of him, naively expecting collective pride in this unusual native son, many retorted with thinly disguised contempt that he wasn't much good on the farm or with any other kinds of work, really.

As more people become disenfranchised and landless, however, the vocational preparation offered by the school was seen more widely as worthwhile—whether the case or not—and was increasingly likely to edge out the various forms and practices of socialization and learning outside it. Added to that, the deepening cultural integration of Howa with the larger social formation, through such things as the proliferation of radios and a few televisions, more travel and improved communications, the social extension service of the agricultural project, and proximity to the project headquarters, would no doubt encourage greater school attendance because that was the position of the urban and professional elite, whose views were increasingly influential in the area. Finally, and intimately connected with the preceding, the cultural forms and practices associated historically with ascending capitalism tend to encourage school enrollment over the long term because of workplace demands for a prepared (and disciplined) labor force, the use of "standards" to screen potential workers, and technological changes that eventually reduce the need for children's work. My expectation that the role of formal education would increase in Howa was borne out when I returned there in subsequent years. These changes will be discussed in chapters 7 and 8.

School, of course, was not the only way to develop alternate vocational skills and acquire new kinds of knowledge. Young men who came of age and found themselves with few viable work options in the village by the early 1980s most commonly looked in nearby towns and sometimes further afield for employment opportunities. Most of them were unqualified for most forms of employment and found work as day laborers, usually stevedores, picking up what skills were required as they went along. Truck driving was perhaps the most alluring off-farm job for young men and boys in Howa. It was well compensated, the opportunity for independent trade and getting bargains on various commodities was ever present, and the romance of the road was compelling. The way to secure a position as a driver was to serve an apprenticeship as a driver's assistant. Within a decade of the project's establishment, several adolescent boys and young men had begun coveted apprenticeships on the dozen or so trucks in Howa. Acquiring new skills and occupations, such as driving or day work in the towns, was of growing importance to young people in Howa excluded from agriculture by the land tenure relations of the project, and from other forms of work by their lack of preparation and the stunted nature of Sudan's economy.

The shifting role of formal education and the heightened importance of various apprenticeships in people's everyday lives were among the many disruptions and realignments brought about by the agricultural project and its broader social relations. They represented a commodification of knowledge in several ways. Schooling offered a more specialized body of knowledge whose contours and purveyors were credentialized by the state. Such knowledge has a tendency to be fetishized as a thing in itself, concealing the social relations that simultaneously produce it as such and make it salient as something to be exchanged. Apprenticeships, on the other hand, represented a twinning of both on-the-job training and indentured labor. While the latter offered a form of situated learning, school learning worked largely in a different register. What was learned in a situated manner in schools was not the formal curriculum, but a particular relationship to learning and knowledge (Lave and Wenger 1991). School knowledge was useful for different ends than the "local knowledge" exchanged between elders and children or among the peer group. School knowledge was tested more formally than the knowledge exchanged in the give-and-take of everyday life, and the formal tests tempered the flow of those deemed "qualified." The learning associated with practice had no such valve on it, but as its forms and practices were made more superfluous by the changes associated with "development," commodification, and the degradation of the local environment, the "qualifications" of children in Howa began to seem more perversion than preparation. Yet the outcomes of children's learning—in school and out—were up for grabs in Howa as the social relations and practices of production and reproduction were unhinged from their previous moorings in the wake of the Suki Project and its attendant shifts. If in ceding ground to the school, parents thought they were better preparing their children for the altered future, their goal was not always achieved. Apprentices to truck drivers and in the towns were better off, but their numbers remained quite small. Most young people coming of age in Howa during the 1980s seemed well prepared for futures that were likely to elude them, and underprepared for what most likely lay ahead.

Commodification of Time

If the commodification of knowledge was one aspect of the rise in formal education and the eroding viability of other forms of learning, the commodification of time accompanied the production relations associated with the Suki Project. The commodification of time is one of the hallmarks of the ascendence of capitalism (Thompson 1967). While most people in Howa still organized their daily rounds of work without recourse to clock time, its seasonal tempo was metered to some extent by the project authorities, who distributed particular inputs at set times and scheduled other operations according to the availability of personnel, supplies, and machinery, or the timetables of either the project as a whole or the government marketing boards. Unlike the situation prior to the project, when farmers responded to the arrival of the rains and other seasonal shifts, the scheduling of events in the project often missed or clashed with environmental cues or conditions. This situation notwithstanding, most tenants and others still had relative autonomy in scheduling their work and leisure, at least on a day-to-day basis.

Children were more constrained in this autonomy, but that was nothing new. Parents set children's work schedules according to their own convenience and children by and large complied, though not always happily. Nevertheless, as the previous chapter laid out, with increases in children's work time and changes in the kinds of work they were responsible for doing, there was a growing separation between the activities of work and play in their everyday lives. School attendance hardened these divisions and added new ones, and over the long term these shifts contributed to the commodification of time and the consignment of play or leisure outside of what "counts." This change, which was underway during the years I worked in Howa, marks a significant alteration of everyday life there, and suggests the breadth of disruptions in the social relations of production and reproduction that were set in motion most significantly by the Suki Project and the ways "money was becoming the community." Each of the disruptions detailed here fueled these political-economic changes as much as they were set in motion by them.

Consequences of Disruptions for Children's Everyday Lives

The processes of socioeconomic differentiation, commodification, and environmental deterioration were interconnected and had strong effects—individually and collectively—on production and reproduction in Howa. These effects were likely to have serious repercussions both on the children as they came of age and on the larger social formations within which they lived their lives, contemporaneously and in the future. The shifting ground of that future was far broader than Howa—indeed the disruptions there were connected intricately with changes in the national, regional, and global arenas.

Given these disruptions across geographic scale, along with the more immediately felt constellation of practices and social relations of production and reproduction associated with the Suki Project, it appeared that many of the skills and much of the knowledge acquired by the children were unlikely to be of much use in their futures. The very sociosymbolic, political-ecologic, and political-economic relations that created the conditions in which children acquired and used their formidable environmental knowledge were creating conditions that would undermine any possibility that young people could use this knowledge effectively as they came of age. What children learned about work and the environment, and how they learned it, seemed, paradoxically, to be a form of deskilling. Young people in Howa were learning how to work a system that was under erosion, if not complete erasure. While paradoxical spaces or moments, like play or mimesis, encompass possibilities of disruption and transformation, they also reflect painful contradictions (see Rose 1993; Desbiens 1999), and these are important to understand.

Changes in the Production and Exchange of Knowledge and Skills

One of the signal areas of change was in the cultural forms and practices associated with children's environmental learning and knowledge. The changing nature of their everyday lives alone suggests altered opportunities and practices for the acquisition and use of environmental knowledge. But the broader shifts that were taking place in Howa, affecting, among other things, the relationships among the household, peer group, state, market, and workplace as arenas of social reproduction, along with the practices of reproduction associated with each setting, also had profound effects on what children learned, how they learned it, and what the knowledge meant over the long term.

Children's everyday environmental interactions were altered by the disruptions in the local political ecology and political economy. They spent an increasing amount of time working in activities that produced an income or saved household expenditures for newly commodified goods. Among the most important activities here were agricultural work, fuelwood provision, selling water, and odd jobs, such as food hawking. Other tasks had long consumed children's time, but environmental problems had made them more time consuming. Most significantly affected by environmental degradation were herding, providing fuelwood, and gathering wild foods and other resources from the local environs. Finally, gendered household labor dynamics persistently elicited a substantial work contribution from children because keeping the ideals of purdah placed a relatively large burden on children, who did tasks that tended to be women's responsibilities in other parts of Africa, such as water and fuelwood provision, agriculture, and petty trading. The disruptions engendered by commodification and the heightened monetization of the local economy also increased children's work across the board in Howa by simultaneously introducing new tasks and prodding a greater orientation toward cash. The problems created by these shifts during a time of deepening economic crisis at the national level and sharpening socioeconomic differentiation at the local scale resulted in unequal increases in children's work and widening differences among children in the sorts of responsibilities they had.

The other disruptions in the social relations of production and reproduction were more specific to children: the changing valence of formal schooling and the growing separation between work and play. Children's play, alone or among their friends, for example, was an important means of environmental learning in Howa, and despite the pace and scale of the changes taking place there, the peer group remained a fairly stable setting for learning about and using environmental knowledge. Among their peers, children's work and play frequently remained bound—temporally, conceptually, and metaphorically—and their learning seemed vitally reinforced by this association. However, as I have noted, the thick ties between work and play in Howa showed signs of fraying. Most centrally, the increased time children spent in tasks related to income generation and capital accumulation often left them little time for play in general and removed them from the company of their friends. This, of course, was not uniformly the case, as the experience of shepherds attests. But many times when I observed children assisting their parents in the fields, the pressure to get a particular task done was palpable, and I occasionally saw parents impatient with children "wasting time" trapping birds, snacking, or otherwise "goofing off." This attitude reflected the ways that time itself was taking on a new meaning with, among other things, the extralocal scheduling of tasks and other work rules associated with the project. If work and play are separated and children's peer groups become settings for play alone, they are gradually isolated from the larger society caught up with work. With these changes, the balance between work and play as activities of environmental learning and interaction shifts as well.

If these conditions isolate the peer group, so, too, do they trivialize play as a "childish" activity in the eyes of adults. The conceptualization of play as a trivial and inessential activity consigned to inferior symbolic status because of its separation from work is surely part of the deracination of everyday life that capitalist "modernization" brings (see Aronowitz 1973, 59 ff). Discrete from work, play remains important as a means of socialization and learning—and may even become more important. Play divorced from work, however, is less grounded in the general experience of the community, and in this way often is viewed as inconsequential—a minor practice. Of course, with great difficulty and unsure results, minor practices are able to rework "major" ones from within, and this is precisely the immanent power of children's play (see Katz 1996). This understanding of play dovetails with my analysis of it as a mimetic practice.

Contemporary and Future Consequences of Deskilling

All of these changes prompted inequalities in skills acquisition among children along various axes, including fathers' occupation, household socioeconomic status, and gender. At the same time the consequences of having acquired various skills or learned particular kinds of knowledge were up for grabs and uncertain at best. Children learning to be farmers—all the better for the increased labor demands of irrigated cultivation— would lack the land resources to employ their skills and knowledge as adults. On the other hand, those who were in school and learning material at a remove from the environmental conditions of Howa were likely to find themselves both ill-prepared for the kinds of work available locally and inadequately educated for other vocations. Because men's work roles were changing more rapidly than women's, these concerns were likely to be more serious for boys. However, the implications of girls not acquiring a basic environmental education may prove to be more important for the village over time.

The consequences of these inequalities and differences in the ways children acquired and had a chance to use environmental knowledge were serious. If children in Howa learned most about the environment by participating in the work of agriculture and animal husbandry, and this pattern of learning favored boys and the children of tenants in particular, then the changes taking place in Howa were likely to have multiple and uneven effects. First, if, as appeared likely, men increasingly left the village in search of work, then women would be left to provide for their families' subsistence on a daily basis. Under these circumstances, women's relative inexperience with farming and their lack of training in the sequencing and coordination of agricultural practices may hinder their ability to provide for their families' reproduction on a sustained basis and lead, at least temporarily, to declines in rural productivity. This eventuality, however, could radically transform women's "place" in Howa and lead, among other things, to purdah unraveling a bit as women engage in agricultural or other forms of production outside the home.[8] As women changed their positions in the relations of production and reproduction and gained experience in other realms of work, they were likely not only to turn shortfalls in productivity around, but to alter the social relations of power in the village as certain of the gendered labor dynamics of their households were reworked.

Second, if male labor migration leaves women to bring up their families largely on their own, as has been the case in many parts of Africa and increasingly so in Sudan, women's lack of environmental learning and inexperience in agriculture, combined with the intensity of the work itself, may limit their ability to teach this knowledge and its associated skills to their children. In this way, previous educational gaps as a result of gender, earlier instances of deskilling, and the results of differentiation further break down the general structure, content, and exchange of environmental knowledge, and may lead to yet greater differentiation and the marginalization of much of the remaining population. By these means, the household becomes thwarted as a site for reproducing the kinds of local knowledge and social actors that ensured survival previously, and increasingly becomes the locus for reproducing capitalism, both intentionally and unintentionally. Herein lies another paradoxical moment, for while household practices may indeed begin to reproduce capitalism, they are also treasure troves of resilience, especially when the survival of household members is at stake. The agile responses of households in Howa facing the vagaries of the agricultural project promised as much. Even more to the point perhaps, the experience of female-headed households in other parts of the world—similar and not—suggests that the women in Howa will find in themselves and their community a reservoir of dormant knowledge and other strengths to make something work out of their changed circumstances. Some of the sting of deskilling is undone as reskilling takes place, even if its individual toll is often enormous.

Nevertheless, rural productivity may decline as the changing relations of production and reproduction, along with the ensuing redefinition of vocational skill, dislocate the household as the center of production and reproduction. These dual dislocations have resulted historically in the depopulation of the household as waged work is found outside of the home and as children leave in growing numbers to attend school. As a result, less labor is available to the rural household to maintain previous levels of agricultural productivity, and the household is relegated to a secondary "domestic" status. As waged work increases in relative importance, unremunerated segments of the population, predominantly women, children, and old people, lose power in relation to waged workers (see Dalla Costa 1972, 21–22).

These changed conditions and the altered material social practices accompanying them were likely to be of serious consequence for the children as they came of age and tried to find their own footing on this new and shifting ground. Most boys, I have argued, were not likely to have access to land because of the constricted land tenure relations of the Suki Project. The agricultural project not only dominated the production landscape, but its structure sharply limited the number of tenancies available for new registrants. Both circumstances, coupled with household and village demographics, effectively proletarianized the population and were likely to drive young men to leave the village in growing numbers. While casual employment in the fields was not enough to sustain them, these young men were an important source of agricultural labor in Howa, and their absence was likely to be felt in the fields, especially during periods of peak labor demand. These seasonal demands were likely to affect patterns of migration and the contours of proletarianization. In the long run, the broad changes underway in Howa and Sudan might lead to an adult population unable or unwilling to undertake the work associated with the Suki Project, at least on its old terms. As the primary arena of work shifts from agriculture to nonfarm employment, environmental knowledge—along with the ecologies of its acquisition and use—was likely to become less important and more piecemeal in Howa. If dislocation or deskilling alone would no doubt lead to declines in agricultural productivity, the two together were sure to.

In sum, the changes underway in Howa, connected broadly to incorporation in the agricultural project and other shifts in the material social practices of everyday life, were leading to the destabilization of the household as a site of production and reproduction, possibly spiraling declines in rural productivity, an intensification of local impoverishment and with it socioeconomic differentiation, and an erosive process of deskilling that promised to exacerbate all of the other problems. These effects were made worse by the grueling inhospitableness of the Sudanese national economy, as well as global economic restructuring. Ground to a pulp by transnational political economics and domestic self-destruction, the national economy was incapable of absorbing more than a handful of the thousands it was driving from the countryside. At the same time, time-space compression spurred by the increasing monetization of the local economy and the commodifications associated with it, folded young people ever more tightly into an economy of desire, made more acute by their distance from what that economy offered and more poignant by the sense that they were jettisoned just as they were engaged by this broader realm of desire and exchange. The issues associated with the simultaneity of the compression and expansion of the experienced economy will be taken up in the concluding chapters. What was clear in the midst of all this was that just a decade into the Suki Project, young people in Howa were being catapulted out of their community into an intensely uncertain future.

A Conclusion or Thoughts toward "Displacements"?

I initially chose to examine children's learning and knowledge because I thought the production and exchange of knowledge would be an arena rife with the evidence of resistance. I thought I might find resistance by examining closely what and how parents consciously taught their children, the kinds of knowledge children shared among themselves, and the diverse relationships people had with schooling. While this remains a good supposition, the situation, not surprisingly, was more complicated. The cultural forms and practices of children's learning and knowledge form one of the fault lines that traverse social reproduction and transformation. This line, perhaps more than others, is fissured by the distances between intention and actuality, between hope and achievement, and between effort and circumstance. Thus, while parents in Howa wanted their children to be well prepared for the future that lay ahead, the forward motion of this imagining was constantly subjected to the undertow of historical circumstances.

In this paradoxical time-space that propels people forward and pulls them backward at the same time, anything can happen. Gardening along fault lines is risky business, but they make for fertile grounds, where people can sow what they know. What will grow and how it gets harvested is anybody's guess. What I have tried to get at here is that people's responses to almost overwhelming changes in the political economy, political ecology, and sociosymbolic forms and practices in and around Howa have not just been those of immiseration and capitulation, but extraordinary resilience and reformulation as well. These practices—which I prefer to distinguish as resilience, reworking, and resistance, rather than presume that quite varied responses are all resistance or homogenize their distinct qualities—are interconnected (see chapter 9). Their boundaries are blurred and passages between them can be almost imperceptible. They are rooted in and help produce what James Scott (1985) calls "dignity" among people facing grueling conditions in their everyday lives that are not of their own choosing or creation. If Scott, who does not distinguish between what I am calling resilience, reworking, and resistance, is careful to define the limits of such counterhegemonic practices, he is more intent on how critical they are for undergirding subsequent broader oppositional practices. Beyond their socially reinforcing and fortifying role, these practices also act in and on the world, sometimes changing it. In Howa—where changed patterns of household labor enabled sustenance, and incipient social forms, such as new attitudes toward schooling, anticipated new conditions of production—the amalgam of people's responses to the disruptions of their everyday lives worked as a bulwark against the changing productions of space, nature, and social life heralded most decisively by the Suki Project, and made their progress a struggle far from won.

PART III
DISPLACEMENTS

6. New York Parallax; or, You Can't Drive a Chevy through a Post-Fordist Landscape

It is in the desert that seditious thought ferments, but it is in the city that such thought erupts.
—Louis Gabriel Gauny, *Le Philosophe Plébian*

Metaphors of displacement became commonplace by the end of the twentieth century. This is not surprising in a century characterized by physical dislocations—forced and chosen—in numbers, at scales, and across distances heretofore unprecedented. At the start of the twenty-first century, the metaphors of displacement riddling the language suggest something other than "simple" physical dislocation—something spatial, but not physical at all. Postmodern discourse, for instance, heralds the displacement of received notions of progress, while globalization is touted as a "space of flows" and simultaneity is celebrated as the spatialization of time (see Soja 1989; Castells 1996). As Castells and Soja both know, that simultaneity is wildly uneven. In the space of flows of global capitalism, some places are ever more tightly bound to one another, while others are marooned (Trouillot 1996; Dematteis 2001). Marooned and effaced, people in these places are ever more aware of what they are missing thanks to "globalization."

Such spatial referents intrigue me both as a geographer and as someone who works with children. For some groups of "marooned" young people, the displacement of received notions of progress is experienced viscerally and bitterly. In the thwarted trajectories of their everyday lives, time is indeed reconfigured. When a sense of the future is foreclosed, development's "next stage" does not necessarily follow in time. For many the future is displaced and/or occluded; it is there, of course, and its simultaneity with other futures can be imagined spatially as a derailed "zone" to which certain people by virtue of class, race, gender, sexuality, or nation are consigned. Parallels between young

155

people's development and economic development are apt; their "derailed zones" only differ by scale. However, it is important not to lose sight of the physicality of these spatial relations and the ways that metaphoric and material space are intertwined. To this end, it is salutary to remember and take seriously John Berger's (1974, 40) admonition that in late modernity, "it is space not time that hides consequences from us."

This chapter turns on a couple of displacements to make good on this insight. The most central is across geographies, from Sudan to the United States, to expose the derailing of children's futures in disparate places as common and simultaneous consequences of, among other things, particular and linked global economic processes. In "unhiding" these consequences and developing the connections between them, I also want to insist on their physicality, to show the ways that the material social practices associated with displacement work on the bodies and spaces of children in locales as different as New York City and rural Sudan. If New York City is at the margins of the known world from Howa—in "Nimrica, just before Fez"—then Howa is at the margins in the view from New York City, not even part of the jumbled terra incognita across the Hudson River in Saul Steinberg's well-known map for *The New Yorker*. Yet young people in both places suffer, endure, cope with, and are tantalized by the effects of capitalist-driven globalization in startlingly similar, albeit predictably different ways.

And so, from the banks of the Hudson, in an unclear relation to Fez, I look at Howa. This chapter offers a parallax view of Howa through a lens focused on New York City to reveal how the modernities associated with globalizing capitalism in both places have parallel, common, and intersecting bases and outcomes. My intent is not only to deexoticize Howa by examining its problems and possibilities within the rubric of capitalist social relations of production and reproduction that obtain in localities worldwide, but to link it analytically to other places experiencing analogous problems and possibilities, including New York City, which might seem at first glance to have little in common with a place like Howa. Drawing specific connections between such places can reveal particular "global" effects of the material social practices associated with capitalism in very different locales.

These often counterintuitive connections call for a spatialized politics capable of developing a translocal response to the destructive effects of processes such as global economic restructuring, disruptions in social reproduction, or deskilling. In this effort, I want to be clear that I am drawing a *structural* comparison between Howa and New York City, and by implication to many other places as well. My project is not comparative, strictly speaking, but analytical, focused on drawing out the structural similarities in children's lives in both places. The daily routines of children in New York are of less interest here than are the effects of global economic restructuring and other political-economic and cultural processes on particular aspects of social reproduction, most centrally those associated with the public grounds wherein knowledge is produced and exchanged among children: schooling and public space. My intent here is to reimagine the "topographies of global capitalism" and thus to gesture toward a different spatial and political consciousness that might counter them.

"Global" Economic Restructuring

While Howa reeled and responded to disruptions in its landscape and social relations of production and reproduction in the 1970s and after, New York City suffered
a few disruptions of its own. A surfeit of capital, following the post–World War II
boom that had produced the suburbs and the interstate highway system in the
United States and reconstructed Western Europe and Japan, was funneled increasingly into "development" projects in South America, Asia, and Africa. With the
decolonization of Africa, a "market" grab was well underway as relative newcomers
to transnational plunder, most notably the United States, vied with former colonial
powers to establish markets and investments there and elsewhere in what has become
known as the "third world." This is, of course, an old and well-known story. I
rehearse it here only to show that the deteriorating fortunes of U.S. and Sudanese
children—not yet born when these patterns of international investment were put in
place—share some common foundations. What is too glibly called the globalization
of capital is not just about free trade, the IMF, or megacorporations that evade traditional modes of national regulation. The globalization of capital, which reworks
the scale and temporality of uneven development, has serious and often deleterious
local and embodied effects. The complexity of investments at a transnational scale is
often mirrored and sustained by a narrowing of investments, and thus productive
activities, in particular "locals." The struggle for viability in these narrowed landscapes of production and reproduction takes a serious toll on children coming of age:
their bodies and their fortunes riddled with, as much as riddles of, global, national,
and local effects and processes.

The Suki Project was a direct effect of these reworked transnational relations of
production and reproduction. In the planning stages by the early 1960s, Suki was one
of the first state-sponsored agricultural projects in Sudan to be funded by a consortium
of international interests, including the United States, Japan, and Kuwait. It was representative of a new era of "development" projects delinked from traditional bilateral
relationships and thus it reflected both the internationalization of capitalist interests
and the spreading of risk associated with investments in newly sovereign states. Postcolonial Sudan was touted as the potential "breadbasket" of the "third world," Africa,
or the Middle East, depending on who was talking. Many of Sudan's "development"
projects were geared to expanding the mechanized cultivation of basic foodstuffs—particularly sorghum—on large holdings for sale domestically and abroad, and to simultaneously reducing subsistence farming through the widespread introduction of
cash-cropping schemes. While the allocation of leaseholds for mechanized sorghum
cultivation was riddled by patronage and the program eventually dovetailed with IMF
structural adjustments emphasizing the production of export crops, the more abstract
thrust of much of Sudan's development strategy was that food be commoditized, while
subsistence cultivators were proletarianized. How this turn of events played out in
Howa has been the focus of this book. The question here is what this turn of events
might have had to do with growing up in New York City.

The development industry fits within a web of financial, political-economic, and strategic enterprises with an increasingly global—as opposed to bilateral or even multinational—ambition. Apart from its initial ambit of incorporating underdeveloped countries within a broader system of global exchange and the strategic nature of many "development" relationships during the cold war, the work of development in capitalist countries had a Keynesian inspiration and effect. In underwriting development projects in Sudan and elsewhere, northern financial institutions, many of them based in New York, hoped to realize a higher return than seemed possible in more fully capitalized areas of investment at home.[1] By the late twentieth century, the national capitalisms of the old industrialized countries had reneged on their Fordist promises at home, and a reworked and truly transnational capitalism had emerged. While, like all capitalisms, transnational capitalism was directed toward the accumulation of capital, its reworked form encouraged and was sustained by a global strategy of investment less and less hindered by national loyalties or regulation. As the realm of capitalist production was increasingly globalized, capital was drawn away from the older industrialized areas of the United States and Europe toward areas of higher return—some of them in "underdeveloped" parts of the world, some of them at vastly different scales, such as the cellular or genomic—eventually producing a landscape specialized at a finer scale. From the perspective of capital, less redundancy at local and regional scales simultaneously streamlined accumulation on a world scale and widened the purview of investment sites. From the perspectives of the workers of the world, the possibilities for employment were seriously constrained by capital's mobility, which tended to produce more homogenized and narrow work landscapes locally.

The decline of manufacturing in older industrialized areas such as New York was one of the effects of globalizing capitalism. As the Suki Project was getting off the ground at the end of the 1960s, New York City was losing the manufacturing base of its economy. In 1966, 22 percent of the city's job base was in manufacturing, but by 1993 (when children born around 1971, like those with whom I worked in Howa, would be young adults) that figure had dwindled to 9 percent (Ehrenhalt 1993, 43). This process continued through the turn of the century so that by 2001, only 6 percent of the city's job base was in manufacturing (http://stats.bls.gov/eag/eag.nyc.htm). Between 1970 and 1980 alone the city lost almost 294,000 jobs, including a third of its manufacturing jobs. As manufacturing declines continued and accelerated, the number of "knowledge-based" and service jobs increased, many of them in the finance, insurance, and real estate industries (FIRE) as well as in services, particularly health services (Ehrenhalt 1993; Fitch 1993). If the former were reasonably well paid, the latter were anything but. Although these industries have suffered ups and downs over the decades, the general trend has been their growth—sometimes stupendous—while the role of manufacturing has continued to recede. This state of affairs has severely circumscribed the palette of possible work futures for working-class children in New York City. The prospects were all the more serious for young people with limited educations, the likes of whom had been able to find secure and relatively well-paying manufacturing and industrial employment in earlier periods (Wilson 1996).

The derailment of New York children's futures, along with the shaky conditions of their present, struck me as startlingly similar to what was happening to children in Howa and elsewhere in Sudan as a result of agricultural "development." With obvious differences, children in both settings were being displaced from futures that had been reasonably secure just a generation earlier. This displacement is signaled in the chapter's ironic subtitle, which points metaphorically to a preparation for one life—producing "chevies"(Chevrolet automobiles) and all that went with it in a realm, a "post-Fordist" landscape, that was no longer set up for or interested in such forms of production.[2] This localized hollowing-out of children's prospects is traceable, at least in part, to global economic restructuring and the globalization of capitalist production. My argument here is that global economic restructuring transforms the scale of uneven development, producing common effects in disparate local settings. The displacement of certain young people from secure employment, along with their reconstitution as "deskilled," is one of these effects, as is a recalibration of the relationship between production and social reproduction.

The material consequences of this recalibration for children's everyday lives in New York City are the focus of this chapter. Focusing on these issues in New York offers a parallax perspective on Howa as a place encountering and grappling with the global maneuvers of capitalist production and their consequences for social reproduction. The parallax perspective provides the groundwork for developing a translocal political response that takes that globalization and its altered spatialities seriously (see Katz 2001b).

Urban Disinvestment and Geographies of Children's Everyday Lives

Children growing up in New York since the 1970s, particularly working-class children, have been caught increasingly between a present that had all but abandoned them and a received image of the future they weren't likely to get. By the 1990s, the process appeared complete—poor and working-class children in New York, particularly those who were black or Latino, increasingly survived a present that *had* abandoned them and struggled toward a future that was ever receding and implausible. These conditions were not experienced as metaphor, but were played out on their bodies, on their homes, on their neighborhoods. Poor and working-class children could see their declining "value" in the dilapidated conditions of the city's public schools, in the city's litter, which was strewn in poorly maintained neighborhood parks and playgrounds, and in the unsafe and decaying public spaces of the residential city. City, state, and federal budgets for housing, health, and education since the 1970s testify not only to the ever-deteriorating conditions in the everyday life of so many urban children, but to the broken promise of a better life that undergirded American aspirations (and mythology) for most of the twentieth century.[3] The economic boom of the 1990s hardly changed this picture, even though the city was awash in money. In fact, the staggering levels of wealth associated with the booming stock markets, coupled with extensive cutbacks in all aspects of the social wage and the new limits on local, state, and federal social welfare imposed in the mid-1990s, made the gap between rich and poor that much starker by century's end.

What was going on? As the world became the "oyster" of a transnationalized capitalism and space was less of a barrier to various investments, New York City was strengthened as a financial center and began to decline as a manufacturing center. Finance and its supporting services—increasingly dependent on electronic communication—became the key to the New York economy beginning in the late 1960s, while manufacturing and its supporting services began to retreat from the city and other parts of the long-industrialized northeastern United States to areas with lower input costs that had been made newly economical by the construction of the interstate highway system and the possibilities offered by advances in telecommunications. The number of manufacturing jobs in New York City went from a high of nearly one million in 1950 to 368,000 by 1990. This loss was compounded by the elimination of most port-related employment in the city. The jobs that were added during that period were generally high-end, finance-related, and "knowledge-based" jobs or low-skill, poorly compensated, and often irregular service jobs.

The employment pattern that resulted for men shows a concentration of unemployment and temporary or part-time work among those who had dropped out of high school, were poorly educated, and were members of racialized minority groups (Wilson 1996, 26). The shifts have been dramatic. In the 1970s, fully two-thirds of men of prime working age who *did not* complete high school were employed full time in eight out of ten years, while by the 1980s only half were. The drop was even sharper among black men (Wilson 1996, 26). The situation was worse in disinvested urban neighborhoods that suffer enduringly high dropout rates. In New York City, the annual dropout rate remained above 16 percent a year throughout most of the 1990s, with Latino and African American students almost twice as likely to drop out than white or Asian students (Citizens' Committee for Children of New York 1999). Moreover, available data indicate that in New York State almost 12 percent of all children live in neighborhoods where the majority of men over sixteen worked less than half the year. The New York figures are 50 percent higher than those for the rest of the country (Annie E. Casey Foundation 1995, 96). Unemployment not only results in poverty, but in enduring and systemic joblessness, producing a social environment in which children get used to the idea that paid work is uncommon. This perspective—particularly destructive during a period of sustained economic growth elsewhere in the city and nation—compounded with incessant victim-blaming rhetoric surely lowers children's expectations for themselves in the future.

For poor and working-class people, even the city's overheated 1990s boom was less than it appeared. These groups suffered drastic retrenchments after the late 1980s, when New York's previous boom imploded. In the four years between early 1989 and the end of 1992, for example, New York City lost more than a third of a million jobs (Ehren-halt 1993, 42). Evidence suggests that the 1989–92 recession gouged deeper and lasted longer in the New York region than elsewhere in the United States (see Regional Plan Association 1996). As late as March 1996 the *New York Times* chronicled the waves of job losses that were crashing routinely on middle-class clerical, managerial, and pro-fessional workers who, by turns, were becoming increasingly shell-shocked, bitter, fear-ful, and mean spirited. While that recessionary period has been eclipsed by the record boom that followed, it remains that New York State has the most unequal income dis-tribution in the country and is the only state that has both one of the ten highest poverty rates *and* one of the ten highest per capita income levels (Fiscal Policy Insti-tute n.d.). Moreover, the gap in wages and other forms of compensation for workers defined as skilled and unskilled widened considerably during this period as the com-pensation for skilled workers and professionals rose, while it sank for "unskilled" work-ers (Passell 1998). Neither did the boom change the fortunes of those living in conditions of entrenched poverty, whose situation was made worse by the welfare cuts of the mid-1990s, which limited and denied to many of them the basic assistance they once relied on, including food subsidies, housing subsidies, and access to health care. Many of these cuts fell the hardest on children.

Indeed, the number of children born into and living in poverty reached extraor-dinary heights during the boom years of the 1990s. As former U.S. Senator Bill Bradley graphically put it at the 2000 Democratic National Convention, the swelling number of poor children in the United States could compose an enormous city. In the richest country in the world, 13.5 million children—a fifth of all children—lived in families earning less than $13,000 a year, below the federal poverty threshold for a family of three (*New York Times* 2000). And this in the midst of the longest sustained boom since World War II. In New York City the situation was even worse. The per-centage of children born into poverty in New York City reached its highest levels dur-ing the late 1990s boom, just as various "safety net" welfare provisions were being reduced and eliminated (Ramirez 1999). At the same time poverty rates also rose sharply among those families considered "safe." Households with two parents, at least one of whom was employed and had more than a high school diploma, faced higher rates of poverty in New York City during the 1990s boom than during the boom of the 1980s (Levitan 2000).

The city of poor children is an apt metaphor. In the last quarter of the twentieth cen-tury, poverty became more concentrated among children and young people in the United States while decreasing dramatically among those over sixty-five. Between 1970 and 1995, poverty among older people declined by 50 percent while it increased 37 percent among children (Finnegan 1998; Males 1996). Poverty reduction among those over sixty-five still had a ways to go, and these declines reflect progressive social policy as much as the secu-rity offered by corporate and state-sponsored pension plans and federal Social Security, both of which were jeopardized for current and future generations coming of age. But part of the gains made by older Americans were the fruit of tax revolts, whose costs were disproportionately meted out on young people (see Finnegan 1998). The Bush adminis-tration's 2001 US$1.2 trillion tax cut represents a similar mortgaging of young people's prospects in favor of the contemporary gain of adults, particularly wealthy ones.

Those coming of age with few skills and stunted educations faced increasingly bleak employment prospects as New York's economy was transformed in fits and starts during the waning years of the twentieth century. Many have noted that despite the drop in unemployment rates to near record lows in New York and more broadly in the United States during the last few years of the 1990s, certain parts of the population remained persistently jobless or employed only as temporary or contract workers (see Levitan 2000; Fiscal Policy Institute 1999; Passell 1998; Wilson 1996). Unemployment among teens sixteen to nineteen, for instance, increased from 18 percent to over 36 per-cent between 1988 and 1993, decreasing to 29 percent by 1996. While there has long been a gap in the unemployment rates of African American, Latino, and white youths, by the 1990s it was closing—at the high end—as all teens faced narrower employment prospects (Citizens' Committee for Children 1999, 112). At the same time, there were serious declines in the real earnings of many of those who did work. The annual income for all males between the ages of twenty-five and thirty-four fell 26 percent in real dol-lars between 1972 and 1992. The earnings of black men in their twenties who did not complete high school fell 50 percent during roughly the same time period, while among white high-school dropouts they fell 33 percent (Annie E. Casey Foundation 1995, 6).

Untimely Presents/Displaced Futures

Under these increasingly mean conditions, those growing up in poor neighborhoods suffer not only the direct effects of their households' poverty (made worse by welfare "reform"), but the broader social effects of poorly equipped schools, inadequately trained teachers, degraded public spaces, and the like. As with the "compression" and "expansion" in Howa, which brought people in greater touch with expanding horizons of consumption and the effects of global capitalism while marooning them on its out-skirts, poor children in late-twentieth-century New York City grew up in a city of great and growing wealth that likewise seemed to maroon them increasingly on its margins. The jarring simultaneity of the processes of embrace and exclusion made the enthusi-asm for college expressed by the elementary school children in East Harlem with whom I worked during the early 1990s seem particularly fragile, their families' support and dedication notwithstanding. Indeed the strong weave of community on their block and in their households made the obstacles of class, race, and urban inequality that much more apparent in the face of the children's unquestioning and much supported sense that they would go to college and even beyond.

Employment figures, coupled with enduring disinvestments in public higher educa-tion in New York, suggest that many poor and working-class children, particularly those in black and Latino families, will continue to face futures with diminished possibilities for finding stable and reasonably compensated work. In the face of these displaced futures, young people experienced untimely presents suffused with measurable and non-coincidental decreases in the level of social investments in them and their everyday environments. Just as manufacturing "has been New York's *forgotten* economic sector," so have those who might have worked in manufacturing become the city's "forgotten" children (Ehrenhalt 1993, 43, my emphasis). It has not been benign neglect.

The spaces of consequence in children's everyday lives tend to be extraordinarily local.[4] In contemporary U.S. cities, for instance, children under twelve spend almost all of their time within a few kilometers of where they live: in the homes of family members or friends, in schools, and in the open spaces of their neighborhoods (see, e.g., Boocock 1981; Medrich et al. 1982; Van Vliet 1983; R. Hart 1986; Katz 1994; Gaster 1991; Valentine 1997; Wridt 2000). Given the intensely local nature of children's lives, the disintegration of public funding for housing, schools, and neighborhood open spaces hits them harder than other urban dwellers—there's just so far one can vote with little feet, or even bikes, and children have no rights to even the veneer of public accountability that comes with "citizenship." Being "grounded" in the disinvested neighborhoods of places like New York City gives new meaning to this term, long associated with punishment. Yet young people in such places try to manage their situation and negotiate the grounds of their everyday lives as best they can. As Damon, a seventh-grade boy working with Caitlin Cahill (2000, 262) said, "Here on the Lower East Side it's pretty nice but there is drugs, violence, and racism therefore it's not very nice. But people are nice. And if you want to come here you have to know what to wear and where to go." Rehearsing this ambivalence, other students participating in Cahill's project imagined the future of the Lower East Side as "hell" or a "junkyard," while others thought it would be "nicer," though distressingly some of their more positive images included the possibility of their own displacement through higher rents and gentrification (Cahill 2000, 259–60). The questions of gentrification, of visibility and invisibility, are quite material. Cahill notes that while the young people with whom she worked on the Lower East Side were keenly aware of gentrification, they did not include a single gentrified establishment or block on maps that she asked them to make of their neighborhood use, and indeed they found those places threatening. Meanwhile, as the visible city flourished, the problems of neighborhood poverty persisted and even worsened in New York, exposing children to unsafe and inappropriate outdoor environments, poor schools, and limited services and amenities that were taken for granted in other parts of the city. With "economic restructuring," the relative decline in investments in the social reproduction of certain parts of the population has been marked. These declines have taken a visceral toll on New York's poor and working-class children.

Historical Geographies of Children's Learning in New York City

Schools

New York City public schools were transformed in many ways between 1950 and the end of the century. Most notable in terms of their impacts on children's education

Figure 29. Schoolyards in New York City, particularly in poor neighborhoods such as this in Harlem, were frequently in disrepair, had little play equipment, were unsafe, and were not appealing to children of any age.

were the shift from the centralized administration of elementary education to so-called community control in 1969 (largely reversed in 2002); the institution of a vast array of federally mandated special education programs that have absorbed an increasing proportion of the budget and the not-coincidental growing number of children determined to have "special needs"; the development of "magnet schools" that offer specialized or enriched curricula largely at the junior and senior high school level; and most recently, the "charter schools" movement. During this period, public school enrollment shifted dramatically from a profile that more or less reflected the demographics of New York City to one completely skewed toward poor and working-class black and Latino students.[5]

The most telling story for children lies in the area of programming. It is not enough to look at dollars allocated and spent, for even when these have increased, the increases have not kept up with those in surrounding suburbs. For teacher salaries, the gap had become particularly acute by the late 1990s. Moreover, as a look at the distribution of funds for programming reveals, certain federal mandates for education resulted in deep and growing inequalities in the support available for programming in what became an unworkable zero-sum game. A focus on the distribution of funds for special programs in the New York public schools reveals where some of the erosions in education have come. Since the middle of the 1970s there has been an enormous increase in expenditures for "special education" in compliance with Title XX, a federal bill that mandated equal access to education for all children. According to the staff of the Citizens' Committee for Children of New York, by the 1990s Title XX programs received approximately 25 percent of the education budget (including teacher and other salaries), but served only 13 percent of the total number of students enrolled.[6] Apart from these programs, bilingual and English as a Second Language (ESL) programs have burgeoned in recent years in response to growing numbers of non-English–speaking students and legal mandates that they receive appropriate language instruction. The funding for such programs, too, has increased dramatically since the 1970s, though it has never been clear that these monies are spent effectively (see Willner and Amlung 1985).[7] While Willner and Amlung indicate the many ways that funding allocations for so-called limited English proficient students have not reflected the enormous inputs for these programs—notably the discrepancies in the numbers of qualified bilingual faculty versus the growing number of limited English proficient students—it nevertheless seems clear that the mere earmarking of these funds has limited and even reduced funding available for other education programs.

It is a deeply problematic political calculus that pits these sorts of special programs against one another. In the climate of retrenchment that began in the 1990s and the "revanchism" that has succeeded it, many so-called enrichment and after-school programs probably would not have survived anyway (see Smith 1996). But because schools were mandated to provide programs for "special needs," "at risk," and non-English–speaking students, politicians had a screen and an excuse for defunding and eliminating crucial activities such as after-school programs and the curricula offered by various "resource room" teachers, including specialized instruction in the arts, sciences, and languages. Young people working with my students, colleagues, and me frequently bemoaned their lack of options for gathering after school and the narrow palette of resources—physical and educational—available to them during the school day. Xavier, a child from one of the schools participating in a schoolyard improvement project I codirected, was invited to speak at a citywide schoolyards conference. He told the assembled—without irony—that he hoped his schoolyard would be improved by the time he graduated high school more than six years hence. The audience, which included administrators of his upper Manhattan school district, the director of the Board of Education's Office of School Facilities and her staff, policymakers, funders, designers, and educators, was amused at his "realistic" time frame, while I naively thought he was too pessimistic given our participatory process and the commitment to schoolyard change expressed at all levels of the school administration. As it turns out Xavier was not "realistic" enough. By the time he graduated, only a small part of the work anticipated had been undertaken. Years later the schoolyards remained largely unimproved, but were compromised by some of the work in progress. The perennial excuse was lack of funds, although during the period in question, another school in the district—in a more privileged neighborhood—completed a major schoolyard renovation.

Likewise, after-school and summer programs suffered throughout much of the 1990s. As a young woman growing up on New York's Lower East Side during that time told me, "I don't want to learn anything about this neighborhood. I just want to be out. . . . [I want] more things for teenagers. I want my children to have more than I did, more than my brothers and I have to do." Starting in 1998, however, spending for

Figure 30. A program for redesigning this Harlem community schoolyard came out of a participatory process that included the school's students, staff, and administration; community leaders; residents of neighboring buildings; and young people who hung out there. The program was the basis for an international design competition that resulted in a number of terrific and feasible designs. Despite this community effort facilitated by our university research group, New York City and Board of Education politics ensured that progress on the redesign flagged for years. During the same period in the 1990s, we witnessed several other schools in more privileged neighborhoods in the district and beyond receive major overhauls, without benefit of a community-inspired participatory design process.

"after-school and summer program instruction and administration" not only was reinstated, but was increased several hundredfold in New York City. This increase was largely for summer schools necessitated by the thousands of children who failed once the public school system was forced to do away with its embarrassing and bankrupt policy of "social promotion." That large numbers of children were failing was not surprising given the cuts in outlays for basic classroom education that were reflected in such things as increasing class size, chronic shortages of supplies, including books, the growing reliance on "per diem" teachers (particularly in poor school districts), the hemorrhaging of experienced and highly qualified teachers to higher-paying districts outside the city, and the elimination of many forms of classroom assistance that enabled children to have more individualized instruction. Such basic educational supports as school libraries were also gradually disappearing in New York City.[8] This situation was made worse by the curtailed operations of neighborhood libraries.

Another realm of decline was the deteriorated physical infrastructure and space of many if not most New York public schools. Funding for maintenance decreased dramatically after the city's fiscal crisis in the mid-1970s, leaving increasing numbers of public school children to attend aging schools in desperate need of repair. Many maintenance and minor repair problems were deferred indefinitely, even when they posed hazards to children. The situation did not abate with the city's economic recovery and eventual booms. By 1999, nine out of ten schools in the city were said to be in need of repair or renovation with a backlog of maintenance work orders numbering in the tens of thousands. Still, the city spent less per pupil on maintenance than any other major region in New York State (New York City Board of Education 1995).

While the cost of redressing years of neglect was estimated at $6.4 billion, the Board of Education only allocated about half that amount in its 1999 five-year capital plan, ensuring the Sisyphean problems would endure (Citizens Budget Commission 1999). Given the age of many of the school buildings in New York City—more than 50 percent were built before 1940, a third still burned coal in the 1990s—the issues of physical plant have been particularly problematic. As work orders languish, minor repairs become major and inconveniences become hazards. For instance, in 1998, 69 percent of the city's schools needed extensive roof work to make them watertight, while 86 percent needed plumbing work, 91 percent needed their electrical systems upgraded (three-quarters of them needed completely new systems), and nearly 80 percent had heating and ventilation problems (New York City Board of Education 1998b). The 1994 asbestos crisis, which required extensive school closings to remove long-neglected friable and flaking asbestos, became emblematic of the schools' physical deterioration but produced little real change in expenditures. By 1999 maintenance spending in the schools was estimated to be about 29 percent of what was needed to maintain them properly (Citizens Budget Commission 1999). These issues of physical repair completely sidestep improvements such as air conditioning, which is not a luxury if a suitable work environment is to be created. This problem became especially serious as more children were required to attend summer school, and will get worse if space shortages are resolved with schools running on a twelve-month calendar, as many policymakers wish.

"That's not a gym; that's old classrooms!" (Jim, Lower East Side high-school student quoted in Krenichyn 1999, 47). If the budget was shrinking, enrollments were not. By 1995 enrollment, at its highest level since 1977–78, exceeded capacity at over half of the city's schools and has continued to grow (New York City Board of Education 1995; Citizens Budget Commission 1997). Space shortages led to the use of lavatories, showers, gymnasiums, and closets for classrooms and offices in some schools. Indeed, the "old classrooms" referred to by Jim served as a cramped (thirty-by-five meters) gym for a Lower East Side high school and were then were put into service at lunch time to provide recreational space for all 430 of the school's students in a thirty-minute period (Krenichyn 1999, 47). While such problems of overcrowding and shortages of appropriate facilities had become routine in some areas, they were making news headlines by the start of school in September 1996, not only because they were so severe, but because they were projected to last and even worsen over the next decade. The Board of Education blamed the city, the city blamed the state, the state blamed the federal government, and everyone pointed a finger at the burgeoning population of foreign-born children. But despite the hand wringing and finger pointing, little was done. By the 1999–2000 school year, 59 percent of New York's students were in public schools filled beyond their capacity. While this figure had declined slightly over the previous two years, the rate at which the board progressed in alleviating school crowding would have required more than a decade to solve the problem (Citizens Budget Commission 1999). The disinvestment, lack of planning, and class and race politics that were at the heart of the matter were routinely sidestepped by politicians, policymakers, administrators, and journalists intent on making the crisis appear as if it had sprung on them unawares. It would have been hard not to have anticipated the problem, given that fewer than a hundred new schools had been built in the decade between the early 1980s, when enrollments started picking up again, and the early 1990s.[9] Little improved during the 1990s. According to the most recent figures, schools in thirteen of thirty-one community school districts in New York City were operating at over 105 percent of capacity (Citizens' Committee for Children 1999).

Crowded conditions, of course, compromise the education that children receive. Overcrowded classrooms make it difficult, if not impossible, for teachers to reach all students. These conditions are particularly difficult for children who require special attention, and with the relative proportion of foreign-born and poor children increasing, the future does not look better. While enrollment increased steadily from its low point in 1982, the school budget remained static through the mid-1990s. In the face of the substantial growth in enrollments and increases in costs during that period, stagnation amounted to a serious and self-reinforcing squeeze. Not only did the city's contribution to the school budget not grow as fast as its available resources, but beginning in the early 1970s and afterward, the budget share put into education by both the city and the federal governments declined. While the state had previously made up for many of these declines, it remains that even where the numbers suggest growth or at least stability in expenditures, the level of so-called mandated expenditures had become so great that very little went to program improvements by the 1980s.

According to then Chancellor Joseph A. Fernandez, funding for program improvement from any source had become essentially nil by 1991 (New York City Board of Education 1991, 1993).[10] The *Chancellor's Budget Requests* since the 1980s have routinely noted that New York City is shortchanged by the state—educating a greater percentage of New York State's children than it receives "education dollars" for. Equally troubling is the significant and widening gap between the amount of state aid per pupil received by the city and the rest of New York State, even though "New York City's educational tax effort exceeds the State average" (New York City Board of Education 1989). By 1991–92, the average allocation for the city was $3,140 per pupil, while for the rest of the state it was more than 10 percent higher (Scheuer 1993). Similar differences are reflected in disparities in student expenditures. In 1995–96, while New York State spent an average of $9,255 per student, New York City spent $8,213. Just north of the city, in wealthy Westchester County, expenditures averaged $12,701 per student. The disparities with other metropolitan area counties were only slightly less stark (Citizens' Committee for Children 1999).[11]

These contrasts in expenditure express clear educational advantage and disadvantage, geographically marked. They can be read in various woeful markers of academic achievement. For instance, in 1990 only 66 percent of New York City children in third grade read at the "state reference point" for their year (which means reading at or better than one year *behind* the one tested), while by sixth grade the figure was 71 percent. In math the showing was better, but the trend was reversed: 87 percent of third graders were at the reference point, but only 80 percent were by sixth grade. The rest of the state's children routinely scored eight to fifteen percentage points higher than the city's public school children, and the gap between city and other students' scores grew along with the gap in per student funding (Citizens Budget Commission 1997).

In a similar vein, as late as 1998, city schools averaged only one computer for eleven children, while in the rest of New York State there were six pupils for each computer. Even at that, only 41 percent of the computers in the New York City schools were "new generation," with a 486 microprocessor or better. City schools were said to trail the state by five years in this increasingly crucial measure of educational opportunity (Citizens Budget Commission 1999). They were unlikely to catch up any time soon. By the Board of Education's own estimates, it would require about $2 billion to reach their computerization goals, but because of the pressing needs engendered by overcrowding and the system's crumbling infrastructure, they were forced to allocate their capital budget to construction, leaving only $300 million over the five years from 1999 to 2004 for technology (Citizens Budget Commission 1999). One proposal was to give a laptop to all public school students in grades four through twelve, at an estimated cost of $900 million dollars over ten years from 2000 to 2010, to be paid for through advertising—available to children who can "click and order" things—on the Board of Education's Web sites. As if this were not craven enough, it took parental outcry following the Board's initial proposal to ensure that at least these commercial Web sites would not be the same sites as those used for educational purposes. Advertising revenues were anticipated to exceed the costs of getting more than 750,000 students and teachers online, and a portion of all sales made through their sites would go to the board (Wyatt 2000). Public disinvestment breeds ethical bankruptcy.

While it is important to remember that urban disinvestment preceded and precipitated a (middle) class exodus from New York and other cities beginning in the late 1950s, and this exodus was as racialized as it was class based, it is also the case that after the racially charged fights over decentralizing the New York City school administration at the end of the 1960s, those who could afford to, particularly middle-class white parents, increasingly sent their children to private schools, where expenditures per student were on par with those of the affluent suburbs around the city. Not only did the racial composition of New York City's public schools change markedly during this period, but within twenty years—by the 1990s—more than 20 percent of the elementary and secondary school population in New York City was in private schools. The racialized class composition of this distribution is stark. The deterioration of public education in New York City thus reflects not only the diminished tax base of the city—both corporate and residential—but also the absence of pressure from more privileged sectors of the city's population, who, especially since the 1970s, increasingly opted out of the problems with the school system to deal with their educational ambitions privately. Indeed, according to Michael Powell (1995) writing in *New York Newsday*, politicians and policymakers increasingly speak of education not as "a middle-class service," but, in the dreaded parlance reserved for welfare and foster care, as an "entitlement program."

Individual private solutions to the problems of education in New York City are only the tip of the iceberg. More problematic is the public sector's increasing recourse to privatized means to resolve, ameliorate, or sidestep public problems. Among these strategies are school and business partnerships, school "adoptions," voucher programs, expanded employee-training programs intended to pick up where the schools have failed, corporate advertising, and even the wholesale private management of schools and school districts. With the exception of voucher programs, which are intended to subsidize private decisions to "buy out" of the public schools, and private management schemes, which are intended to turn a profit, it can be argued that the rest of these programs reflect corporate commitments to education and the "community," however loosely imagined. But this is only part of the story. The insistent recourse to public–private partnerships as a matter of policy (by the 1990s there were hundreds of so-called partnerships operating within the New York City school system as a whole) is at best contradictory and at worst a bankrupt abdication of the state's responsibility to educate all children equally, however inadequately this was ever accomplished.

Public–private partnerships represent a different—a more self-interested and contingent—sort of corporate support for education. Unlike taxation, which ensures at least some measure of "interest-blind" distribution of wealth and services, "partnerships" enable businesses to pick and choose what they will and will not support as they succeed in reducing their share of the general tax base. By 1996 only 6.9 percent of general tax funds in New York City were generated by corporate taxes.[12] Ironically, or perhaps not, private support for education is "written off" their taxes by businesses, further reducing the tax levy funds available to the city and state. While employee training and remediation programs directly acknowledge and compensate for the failings of the public education system, public–private partnerships often do the same thing less explicitly. With both strategies corporate clout is directed inward to provide business with what it needs in terms of "human resources," while representing themselves as generous patrons of education. All the while, not only has the corporate tax burden been reduced by these and many other strategies, leaving schools further strapped, but by developing programs that address their own needs, corporate leaders are that much less likely to bring pressure to bear on the schools to educate all children well.

The extent of the cuts in public education is staggering. Through the first half of the 1990s, the New York City public schools absorbed more than $2.25 billion in budget cuts and this did not turn around until 1997 (Powell 1995). After years of serious reductions, the initial increases seemed to disappear down great wells of need, including, as detailed above, dilapidated schools, overcrowding, the almost criminal neglect or outright annexation of play spaces such as schoolyards, the near elimination of after-school athletics and cultural programs and their drastic diminution within the school curriculum, the unyieldingly low number of students who completed high school in four years (only 42 percent in 1992, it remained 48 percent in 1997), and students' persistent underachievement on increasingly important standardized tests (Citizens' Committee for Children 1995, 1999).

At the same time, the consequences of "failing" have become more devastating, with lifelong repercussions. The "school-to-work transition," as it is called, has become increasingly rocky: employment for people with basic skills has diminished in New York as elsewhere in the United States. High school graduates, to say nothing of dropouts, are hard pressed to find stable employment that offers a living wage in the restructured political economy of New York City. While previous generations who did not complete high school were able to find work in New York's numerous factories or its thriving port, for example, such possibilities for secure and largely unionized employment have been drastically reduced in the contemporary economy. While this reality is assumed in contemporary political discourse, it remains that young people's limited prospects are routinely laid on their shoulders: their inadequate training, their poor work attitudes, their lack of skills, and so on. The persistence of this victim-blaming ideology works to mystify, if not authorize, policies of neglect. Worse, it directs attention, willfully or not, to epiphenomena of the problems, rather than to their structural heart. This situation has more in common with the one in Sudan and elsewhere in the "third world" than most people would like to admit. Before I draw out their common threads, I want to look at another arena in which the withering of public support for social reproduction in New York City is palpable.

Open Space

Funding for the New York City Department of Parks and Recreation, which has a minuscule budget compared with the Board of Education, suffered even more draconian cuts than the schools in the last decades of the twentieth century. In times of economic contraction, and especially during periods of fiscal crisis—both of which had become chronic conditions in New York, the boom of the late 1990s notwithstanding—funds for open space and recreation quickly get constructed as a luxury. While in the first half of the twentieth century New York City's parks and recreation programs were a well-funded model for much of the United States, the Department of Parks and Recreation received a decreasing proportion of the city budget beginning in 1945. Nevertheless, because overall spending continued to increase citywide, funding for parks, open spaces, and recreation grew steadily for three decades following World War II, even if their share of the overall budget shrank. The retrenchment that followed the fiscal crisis of the mid-1970s was so severe, however, that twenty years later the department had not recovered, and advocates such as the Parks Council were predicting that it would never recoup what had been lost in capital development, maintenance, and staffing, to say nothing of the gutting and devastation of recreational and other programs (Citizens Budget Commission 1991).

Since the 1960s, when the "vestpocket" park made its appearance, virtually no significant parklands have been acquired by New York City. Indeed, beginning in the 1970s, the city shed responsibility for substantial areas because of limited funds for their maintenance and operations. In 1974, for instance, 13,000 acres were transferred to the National Parks Service, while later in the decade, all land adjacent to the city's highways and parkways was ceded to the Department of Transportation. "Load-shedding" management policies were instituted in 1978 to help rationalize scarce maintenance funds by turning over various park facilities to private concessionaires. At the same time maintenance crews dedicated to particular sites gave way to roving crews, leading to the erosion of routine maintenance and ultimately serious physical deterioration. As in the schools, deferred maintenance became a way of life in the Parks Department and much slipped between the cracks—literally. By 1980 the Parks and Recreation workforce was less than half of what it had been in 1965. Moreover, it was impossible to rebuild the staff at all until New York City reentered the bond market in 1981 (Carr 2000). Likewise, capital projects were stymied repeatedly following the mid-1970s fiscal crisis, with no reinvestment until after 1981. Even at that, the number of capital projects undertaken without the infusion of private funds diminished. The share of New York City's capital projects fund allocated to the Department of Parks and Recreation has also eroded since 1945, when 7.5 percent of the city's capital expenditures went toward parks (Citizens Budget Commission 1991). By the mid-1990s, less than 4 percent of city capital funds and less than .6 percent of its operating budget was spent on parks. The political, economic, and fiscal climate of late-twentieth-century New York made it unlikely that these figures would increase in the foreseeable future.

As this situation might suggest, staffing was one of the most hard-hit areas in the Parks Department, especially staffing for programming and recreation, which was cut to the bone in the 1970s, with little recuperation since. The cuts remained apparent through the 1990s despite the creation in the middle of the decade of a jack-of-all-trades position known as a "playground associate," who, among other things, was to coordinate recreational activities, engage in community outreach, *and* take care of routine operations and cleanup. As the department instituted its own policing in the late 1970s, it cut recreation staffing, making clear its new priorities. The Park Enforcement Patrol, as it was known, was complemented by urban park rangers beginning in 1979. The rangers taught conservation and led educational tours, but also patrolled the parks. From 1979 to 1990 the recreation staff, already small, was more than halved (from 602 to 271), while the patrol and ranger staff grew from virtually nothing to 151 (Citizens Budget Commission 1991). These shifts suggest changed priorities within the Department of Parks and Recreation—less play leadership, limited though that was, and more policing. Indeed, by 1993 there were only 129 full-time recreation employees, while the patrol staff had grown to 244 (New York City Mayor's Office 1994). But during this period of steep cuts in maintenance and ongoing cuts in recreation, horticultural, forestry, and even administrative staff, one area of employment grew. Staffing for capital projects—architects, designers, and engineers—increased by more than 100 percent. The emphasis on capital improvement was fueled largely by the phenomena of public–private partnerships for park "enhancement" that burgeoned in the 1990s following the successes of the Central Park Conservancy.[13]

There is, of course, a geography to these investments and disinvestments, and it is one that insistently favors the "flagship" parks—such as Central Park in Manhattan, Prospect Park in Brooklyn, and to a lesser extent Van Cortlandt Park in the Bronx and Flushing Meadows Park in Queens—at the expense of less visible and less prestigious neighborhood parks and playgrounds throughout the city. While the flagship parks offer recreation facilities, they are intended more for the "passive" enjoyment of a cross-section of the population. Flagship parks compose nearly a third of the parkland in the city, but hold only 5 percent of the playgrounds. Playgrounds and other recreational facilities tend to be freestanding and thus do not benefit from expenditures earmarked for New York's larger parks. This might not be so bad if these flagship parks were more accessible to young people, because each of them offers fantastic opportunities for play in fields, forests, glens, ravines, and wetlands. However, because of the large and growing concern for children's physical and social safety in the public environment, most parents do not allow their children to visit these incredibly rich settings unaccompanied until adolescence at the very earliest. In the Harlem neighborhood where I worked on a schoolyard improvement project during the 1990s, most parents did not allow unaccompanied children to visit Central Park, only two city blocks away, until they were at least twelve years old. It was almost as if this extraordinary play environment, literally at their doorsteps, did not exist—a waste made worse by the limitations and poor quality of the open spaces available to these children in their apartment complexes and at their school. These problems are remarkably stubborn in poor neighborhoods lacking clout with the Board of Education and City Hall. After a decade of attempts at schoolyard improvement at two adjoining community schools in Harlem, almost nothing had changed in the material environment despite parental initiative; despite our research group's orchestrating a participatory design project culminating in an international student design competition and involving the schools' students, faculty, administration, staff, parents, and neighbors, along with other potential users of the space; and despite the support of the local school district (Katz and Hart 1990). In a similar situation, an African American mother told Julia Nevarez de Jesus,

> In Riverside Park on 97th Street, they have dinosaurs and the kids interact better there. The design reflects the atmosphere of a politically correct neighborhood, empowered parents, they take care of things. That playground has a parkman, police presence, and vendors. Here is not the same; power without economics, it's a mere symbol. The problem with the sunken playground (at the 110th Street entrance to Central Park) is that it is so isolated and out of the way. In order for the community

to take advantage, it has to be available for all and not just for a few. (Quoted in Nevarez de Jesus 1999, 224.)

Were staffing available more widely in New York's parks, flagship and neighborhood, the everyday lives of city children, especially working and middle-class children, would change markedly. But it is precisely in such arenas that public disinvestment in social reproduction is most apparent, the advent of "playground associates" notwithstanding. Unlike Howa, New York City children's opportunities for autonomous, culture-building play are severely restricted by these circumstances, as many children have little choice but to remain home alone each day after school or be subjected to a completely regimented schedule of after-school activities or supervised play. These prospects also limit their chances for the gross-motor, cognitive, and skills development that are associated with freer forms of outdoor play. The consequences of these losses and limits are not trivial, and comprise the grist of profound forms of deskilling.

These lost opportunities for social, intellectual, and physical development are not the only costs of the disinvestment in public space in New York City. There are pronounced and measurable consequences on children's bodies and minds, too, witnessed in such things as the high rates of childhood injury that result from the absence of safe and attractive play environments or the erosive effects of the fear that so many children consider "normal." A Harlem Hospital study found higher child mortality rates in central Harlem than in Bangladesh (McCord and Freeman 1990), and, apropos of the concern with open space, Harlem Hospital's Injury Prevention Program linked the incidence of childhood injury in Harlem (among the highest levels in the city) to the deterioration of playgrounds, parks, and schoolyards in the vicinity. An extensive study by them indicated that the most common cause of childhood injury in Harlem, following falls, was from motor vehicles, encountered largely in the course of play and other activities on the street (Davidson et al. 1994). While the study found that gunshot wounds were tragically the cause of 14 percent of fatal injuries to children in Harlem, it remains that headlines scream with stories about cross fire or intentional shootings, while less dramatic injuries resulting from the systematic inattention to children's space and play needs are more injurious to those under twelve years old in both absolute and proportional terms (see Davidson et al. 1994; Citizens' Committee for Children 1999).

In tandem with their epidemiological studies, the Injury Prevention Program also surveyed over five hundred parents whose children were seen at the Harlem Hospital pediatric emergency room about their perceptions of playground safety in the neighborhood. Parents identified numerous environmental hazards in the play spaces of their community, but indicated that they nevertheless visited these environments with their children for lack of other options. As my colleagues and I quickly discovered in our work in Harlem, parents were keenly aware of the discrepancies between their children's play spaces and those elsewhere in the city. As a Latino mother remarked to Julia Nevarez de Jesus,

There is little hygiene, that's why I barely visit that one [a playground at the 110th Street entrance to Central Park]. Different from the one that is on 59th and Columbus Circle, there is someone cleaning all the time, very often a truck passes by and picks up the garbage, very often somebody is sweeping, if someone throws garbage to the ground you get a summons, if you are drinking beer beverages they give you a summons, in other words you can see that [it] is more hygienic there, they are more concerned with hygiene there. (Quoted in Nevarez de Jesus 1999, 216.)

The Harlem Hospital program also conducted a survey of the neighborhood's 113 playgrounds (including schoolyards), and the written and photographic documentation of their hazardous conditions garnered institutional, political, and community support for tackling these conditions more systematically (Laraque et al. 1994; Nevarez de Jesus 1999).

Since their pivotal study of childhood injury began in 1988, Harlem Hospital staff have joined with neighborhood groups to provide supervision and safe open spaces for children's play in the area as part of their broader children's injury prevention program. Their efforts to reclaim these sites—cleaning, refurbishing, maintaining, and staffing various play spaces in collaboration with other organizations, as well as with children, teens, and adults from the neighborhoods where they worked—resulted in immediate and measurable reductions in childhood injury. In 1988, for example, 31 percent of all childhood injury admissions to Harlem Hospital were the result of motor vehicles, while in 1989, the first year of their program, this figure declined to 22 percent. According to Dr. Barbara Barlow and Aissatou Bey-Grecia of the Harlem Hospital Injury Prevention Program, there was a 25 percent reduction in emergency room admissions stemming from schoolyard injuries and a 12 percent decline in emergency admissions resulting from playground injuries overall between 1988 and 1989. It seems safe to conclude that these were largely the result of the program's interventions and community mobilization in staffing and improving playgrounds and schoolyards in central Harlem (see Laraque et al. 1994). Injury rates continued to decline in subsequent years. Within ten years of the program's inception there was a 50 percent reduction in major trauma admissions and injury rates in Harlem Hospital's catchment area (Davidson et al. 1994; Injuryfree.org/harlem.htm 2000).

The program's work suggests the importance not only of safe public spaces for children, but of community mobilizations on their behalf. Here, too, the ground is uneven. While the Harlem Hospital Injury Prevention Program under Dr. Barbara Barlow spawned a series of similar programs in other cities under its umbrella (with major funding from the Robert Wood Johnson Foundation among others), Dr. Barlow told me that the program still had difficulty securing funds for their projects in Harlem, despite their measurable successes in reducing childhood injury. In my own work on a participatory project to improve a couple of schoolyards in Harlem that lasted throughout the 1990s, we experienced similar difficulties in securing funding for modest, but much needed, improvements in these neighborhood spaces. Yet at the same time, our project spawned a foundation-funded program through the Division of School Facilities to make minor improvements to schoolyards citywide through small-scale participatory projects. Meanwhile, the schoolyards at the Harlem schools where we worked continued to languish until one of the principals managed to wrangle funding from the Manhattan Borough President's office. While she raised $300,000, it was well under the budget necessary to complete the overhaul we had collectively worked out years earlier (see Katz and Hart 1990).

These experiences suggest some of the problematic presumptions that undergird the growing reliance on public–private partnerships to compensate for various shortfalls in public funding for public space and other arenas of social reproduction. While some of the efforts of the public–private partnerships so highly touted by the New York City Parks Department have focused on recreation and the improvement of some neighborhood parks and playgrounds, it is important to remember the broader context of their work and the insistence of their focus on the more visible aspects of the city. Most of the community-based partnerships that have sprung up in New York since the late 1990s can tap only limited funds and rely entirely on volunteer efforts to get things done. Advocates of park-enhancement partnerships such as the former Parks Commissioner, Henry Stern, and the former Chairman of the Central Park Conservancy, Ira Millstein, present partnerships as an example of how disparate communities can improve public open spaces of all types and sizes. But their representations are at best wishful and at worst highly cynical.

Suggesting, as Millstein (1995) did, that neighborhoods outside of midtown Manhattan have access to "revenue streams" to improve or staff their parks and playgrounds adequately is not only predicated on flawed logic, it can paradoxically serve to authorize further public disinvestment in open space. By compensating for shortfalls in public expenditures for parks that matter to wealthy and powerful constituencies, partnerships can inadvertently foster further erosions in governmental funding for public space. By touting their own example as a way to cope with such shortfalls, they reinforce inequalities in access to safe, stimulating, and attractive public spaces. It remains, for instance, that the exemplar of park enhancement partnerships, the Central Park Conservancy, had an endowment of $96 million for fiscal year 1999, while the next most prestigious partnership, the venerable Prospect Park Alliance in Brooklyn, had an endowment of "only" $2 million. While this gap speaks volumes, it says nothing of flagship parks in other boroughs whose partnerships did not even have endowments, but which rather raised funds to support specific projects and operations. The Friends of Van Cortlandt Park in the Bronx, for example, had a total budget of $100,000 for fiscal year 1999. If the budget gap between the Central Park Conservancy and other flagship partnerships is this extreme, it suggests the limits of this strategy for all but the wealthiest constituencies dealing with prime real estate. Neighborhood parks and playgrounds almost everywhere else are destined to languish without necessary funds, public or private.

The preceding is not to argue against the importance of community-based partnerships and volunteer efforts, but only to make clear that the means to cope with the toll of government disinvestment in the public environment are highly uneven. Indeed, one of the areas of intensive community effort in open space has been in the establishment and tending of community gardens. In New York City, community gardens are often located in poor and working-class neighborhoods characterized by disinvestment, landlord abandonment, vacant lots, and a dearth of public open space. More than 850 gardens have been created and cared for largely through volunteer neighborhood efforts with the assistance of various community and citywide organizations. The results, whether flowers or vegetables in shared or individual plots, have been widely appreciated by residents as gathering places, oases, destinations for children, and focal points for community organizing and activities. Indeed, a community garden featuring primarily vegetables was all of these things to the residents of an East Harlem block where I worked in the early 1990s.

Such possibilities notwithstanding, in spring 1998 the city under then Mayor Rudolph Giuliani ordered the transfer of 741 gardens from the aegis of "Project Green Thumb" to the city's development agency (Housing Preservation and Development), and ultimately the auction block. While the auction was disrupted, the mayor's office was aggressive in moving in on some gardens, perhaps most egregiously, bulldozing the Children's Garden of Love in Harlem as school children watched from their classroom windows in November 1998. Giuliani then scheduled an auction for 119 of the gardens in May 1999. While this move led to widespread struggles against the mayor's initiative and the auction was blocked, it was only through the last-minute intervention of singer Bette Midler, who garnered private funds and subsidized the purchase of the gardens by the Trust for Public Land and the New York Preservation Project. Giuliani's successor, Mayor Michael Bloomberg, has been far less aggressive in this regard. In September 2002 his administration authorized means to preserve about 400 community gardens (in addition to the 100 or so gardens preserved in the earlier agreement with the Trust for Public Land and Midler's Preservation Project), and to transfer more than 150 plots to private developers for the construction of low-income housing. The agreement was much appreciated by scores of community groups and residents who had worked and played in the gardens over the years. For the many who lost their gardens, some of the sting was removed by the promise that the plots would be used for low-income housing, though many were skeptical in that regard.

The picture I have drawn concerning New York children's access to safe public space suggests the stark material consequences of urban disinvestment at the heart of transnational capitalism. These problems and their cascading effects are recognized widely by adults in the city. However, as with the problems of schooling, many residents resort to private means to resolve them. Middle-class parents who are not able to stay at home with their children, for instance, often pay a baby-sitter to accompany them to after-school activities, including visits to places like Central Park. Likewise, higher-income households are able to afford and arrange for a greater range of after-school, weekend, and summer programs for their children. While these strategies reduce their children's dislocation from the public environment more readily and safely than the often isolating options available to poorer households, middle-class families increasingly have resorted to securing private spaces for their children's play, either within their housing developments, in gated communities, on the property of private schools or clubs, or through various pay-for-play programs. As has proven to be the case with schools, when the middle class tends to its children's needs privately, its members bring less pressure to bear on government and other institutions to provide for the needs of all children. The upsurge in private–public partnerships focused on "park improvement districts" or "adopt a park" schemes has produced the same effect, in many cases dividing the already uneven landscape of childhood in New York even more sharply.

These increasingly stark boundaries mark, among other things, different opportunities for children's learning and other experiences along class, race, and gender lines. The loss of these learning, recreational, and leisure opportunities among certain groups of children in New York as a result of public disinvestment, privatization, and shifts in outlays for social reproduction can lead to their deskilling. The consequences of deskilling in New York, as in Sudan, are made worse in the face of a rapidly changing and unpromising work landscape. Deskilling is provoked not only by the poor quality of the education children so often receive in the city's public schools; its sources can also be found, as I have suggested, in the loss of various social and cultural skills once acquired in the public spaces of the city in the course of autonomous "free" play as much as in supervised recreational activities. At stake are both gross-motor and cognitive skills, cooperative and adjudicative skills, the development of self-regulation and mutual respect among peers, and all manner of serendipitous discovery from other kids, their joint activities, or the city itself.

At the same time that children have lost access to so much of the richness offered by the urban milieu, they face a work horizon at once flattened and more demanding. Rather than confront the structural underpinnings of the shrinking job base and the unemployment it engenders, it has been more common to blame young people's joblessness on their lack of skills, preparation, and appropriate work attitudes. Yet in a very real sense, working-class young people have been *deskilled* by the circumstances in which they come of age. This argument is made not to blame young people for their sporadic work histories or unemployment, but quite the opposite—to note that, during a period in which flexibility and the ability to learn in a range of contexts may have become young people's most valuable skills, many of the key avenues through which this suppleness has been traditionally acquired have been foreclosed in the everyday lives of many working-class children and others. On the other hand, for many poor and working-class people coming of age in places like New York, even these questions are moot. Most of the jobs available to them have no such demands for flexibility and learning agility. But neither do they offer job security, living wages, or the benefits packages that similarly tedious jobs offered in the past.

Harlem Meets Howa

By the late twentieth century, children in New York as much as in Howa were growing up in the crosshairs of global economic restructuring. These crosshairs—the increasingly transnational nature of capital investment and disinvestment, and the local deformations engendered by it—not only targeted children in both places, but their very intersection provokes the urgent question: Who bears the costs of social reproduction in a "globalized" political economy? As the flexibility and spatial fluidity of capital have become more pronounced, the rooted nature of many aspects of social reproduction has become more problematic. This problem is temporal as well as spatial. Not only does the relegation of so many workers and potential workers outside the shrinking zone of regular employment reduce capitalists' concern with the future considerably—why should they pay to develop or sustain "resources" that are unnecessary?—but the geographic suppleness of transnational capitalism severs the relation between place and profit in ways that limit or make fleeting capital's commitments to any one of its locales of operation. Social reproduction suffers in consequence.

This chapter has addressed some of the more pernicious effects of this process for children in New York City. In displacing my analysis to New York I wanted to demonstrate how a very different population of young people from those growing up in Howa were similarly challenged, deskilled, and sidelined by political-economic and cultural processes associated with and propelled by global economic restructuring, and the ways they, too, were being ill prepared for the futures they were likely to face. Doing so disturbs the presumed geography of "globalization" and makes clear the structural similarities between vastly different places such as New York City and Howa. Analysis of these similarities—here focused around children's lives and therefore social reproduction—provides a means for imagining and constructing a political project around what I call countertopographies of globalization. This project will be taken up in chapter 9. Rather than holding fast onto the creaky categories of "first" and "third" worlds or theorizing global flows in bulk, looking at the common effects of restructuring in vastly different locales makes viscerally clear not only what Michel-Rolph Trouillot (1996) would call the "fragmented globality" of being marooned by the transformations in the scale of uneven development associated with "globalization," but makes good on a broader project of "unhiding" the consequences of globalized capitalist production by showing people "throughout the whole world in their inequality" (Berger 1974, 40).

That inequality is made and maintained in the course of social reproduction. Looking closely at the different means and mechanisms by which particular people in disparate settings are pressed and "excessed" by globalization's effects on the material social practices of social reproduction, and finding at their heart strking similarities amid a welter of obvious and not inconsequential differences, calls for a response to globalizing capitalist production that similarly crosses the normalized boundaries produced by it. My research in Howa and New York offers an account of growing up as certain territories and social formations latch onto global networks while others drift further away, albeit with enhanced awareness of the very global networks and flows that strand them (see Dematteis 2001; Katz 2001a, 2001b; Trouillot 1996). Large numbers of poor and working-class children in New York City, as well as the bulk of those coming of age in underdeveloped rural Sudan, are among the stranded. Among the common antecedents of their stranding are the altered material social practices of social reproduction as capitalist production is increasingly made global, and particular localities and/or populations within them are written out of the equation that determines the future. This situation is not greeted passively, of course, but it is much more difficult to compete for the future from the netherworld "beyond Fez," to say nothing of what sort of political response might be effective in the face of being marooned from the promises of a future that one has been encouraged to want.

The costs of social reproduction in capitalist social formations are borne largely by the household, the state, civil society, and capital through the workplace. The balance among the four varies historically and geographically, and is the outcome of ongoing struggles between particularly positioned social actors and the structuring forces of society. Under contemporary conditions of global economic restructuring, a century of gains in both expanding what is defined as "socially necessary" to reproduce the society and getting capital and the state to absorb an increasing share of its costs has begun to be reversed transnationally. From labor "givebacks" in industrialized countries to the reapportionment of burden that underlies structural adjustment programs imposed by the International Monetary Fund on "third world" countries unable to meet international debt payments, capitalists have begun to renege on their commitments to share the costs of reproducing the labor force, to say nothing of the conditions of production associated with, say, the physical environment. Inasmuch as transnational and other capitalists have become adept at reducing their tax burdens through a variety of means, governments—internationally and at all scales—have been hard pressed and increasingly unwilling to maintain former levels of support for social reproduction and the social wage (whether high or low). As a result, the costs of social reproduction have shifted increasingly to the institutions of civil society and more pointedly to individual households, which may tend to the work of social reproduction themselves, draw on the support of their extended social networks (which may intersect with those of civil society), and/or accomplish it with recourse to the market.

This shift was set entrain transnationally during the last two decades of the twentieth century, a period when household resources were being stretched to the limit for many, and it has contributed to widening the gap between wealthy and poor households as much as between wealthy and poor nations. In Sudan, for instance, IMF-mandated devaluations, tax increases, and eliminations of price controls, along with a host of other "stabilization" and "structural adjustment" measures that began in 1978 had particularly sharp effects on poor households throughout the country. Moreover, the insistent, even dogged, focus of the IMF and World Bank on the largely export-oriented agro-industry sector of the economy (despite its abysmal fail-ures to generate significant earnings or contribute substantially to the GDP and its utter meaninglessness to the sustenance of most rural households) was equally per-nicious. Rain-fed nonmechanized agriculture was virtually ignored by the invest-ment strategies of the IMF and its affiliates, even though three-quarters of Sudan's population earned its living from dryland cultivation (see Hassan 1994).

Families in Howa were hard hit by these transnational and domestic policies and practices. The end of food subsidies—an "adjustment" strategy that shifted the burden of part of Sudan's staggering foreign debt to its citizens—subjected households in Howa, most of which had been self-sufficient in grain production prior to the agricul-tural project, to even greater vulnerability as they attempted to procure their dietary basics in what became an even more volatile market. It is likely that children's nutri-tional well-being suffered in consequence. But even more generally, "austerity meas-ures" of the sort required by the IMF and other institutions, and the nature of the investment strategies pursued by these multilateral institutions—which in Sudan have consistently favored cash crops at the expense of food production—impede children's survival and compromise their well-being because, among other things, they diminish the number of calories consumed per capita, stimulate "overurbanization," and under-mine economic growth. These problems, in turn, curtail funds for health workers, crip-ple immunization programs, and reduce other forms of social spending that benefit children (Bradshaw et al. 1993).

Likewise, children and families in New York City and elsewhere in the United States have been made to cover an increasing proportion of the costs of social repro-duction—monetary and otherwise—as a result of the steady erosion of the social wage and steep cuts in social welfare and expenditures on child care and health care at the city, state, and federal levels over roughly the same time period as structural adjustment has affected Sudan. Indeed, New York's ruling class–inspired public–private partner-ship known as the Municipal Assistance Corporation issued bonds to bail the city out of its 1975–76 fiscal crisis, instating in return stringent neoliberal restrictions on New York City's budget that had much in common with, and might be seen as a homegrown trial balloon for, the sorts of structural adjustments insisted on by the IMF for debtor nations just a couple of years later.

The costs of neoliberal strategies such as these are often felt most sharply at the interface between production and social reproduction. Cuts in social welfare through-out the 1980s and beyond, for instance, came at a time of increased and enduring unemployment. As the number of children on public assistance rose citywide each year during the early 1990s, the monthly welfare grant remained stagnant after 1989, and well below the basic costs of social reproduction. Not only were the amounts inade-quate to secure the basic means of existence, as witnessed, among other things, in the shocking numbers of evicted-made-homeless people in New York and the burgeoning numbers relying on soup kitchens and the like,[14] but there was also intense pressure at the local, state, and federal levels (finally achieved in mid-1996) to limit the time that an individual could receive public assistance and to require recipients to participate in a work program. The welfare-to-work transition was systematically impeded, however, by the lack of support structures, such as child care, education allowances, health insurance, or transportation subsidies, that might have facilitated welfare recipients' participation in the paid labor force. Worse still, the first wave of people hit the five-year limit on public assistance imposed by the 1996 welfare reforms just as the financial boom of the 1990s imploded. Puncturing the "security" concerns generated in the wake of September 11, for which no expense has been spared in New York City, are the humble security concerns of a growing number of visible homeless and hungry people, about 40 percent of whom are families with children, focused on securing a meal, shelter, and other means of daily existence.

Children, particularly poor children, are increasingly made to bear the costs of social reproduction under global capitalism, whether in New York or Howa. The "end of welfare" in the United States and the mean-spirited rhetoric that has accompanied it, coming on the heels of the massive taxpayer-financed bailout of the savings and loan industry, calls to mind former Tanzania President Julius Nyerere's outraged question, "Must we starve our children to pay our debts?" His sentiments—in reaction to the structural adjustments imposed by the IMF—are in danger of becoming as apposite in the United States as in Tanzania or Sudan.

The metaphor of crosshairs has multiple entailments. I might just as easily have said that contemporary children grow up in the crosshairs of the increasingly transnational tenor of capital investment and disinvestment and the globalization of desire, with its attendant consumption practices. Targeted this way, the circumstances of children are that much more troubling. As capital reneges on its Fordist promises in the global north, and the promissory note of "development" is recognized as bankrupt in the south, children in both places have nevertheless been drawn into the swirl of increased consumption that makes poor children's lack of money and their limited prospects for its acquisition even more acute. The alienation, anger, and despair that ensue pock the face of social life transnationally. The disfigurement is often blamed on young people rather than on the global (and local) marketeering strategies that engender it, despite the obvious and growing vigor of those strategies (see Chin 2001; Kapur 1999; Seiter 1993).

These circumstances call for and create a range of responses. As the bulk of this chapter has detailed, the political-economic practices associated with global economic restructuring during the last two decades of the twentieth century—itself a response to the various shocks experienced by multinational capitalism in the late 1960s and early 1970s—have reflected, among other things, a reduced willingness on the part of capital to sustain social reproduction when its commitments to production in any single locale have proven increasingly ephemeral. The combination of this capital mobility, together with the Taylorist techno-rationalism and disdainful, almost taunting, tax rebellion[15] that accompanies it, has provoked the scarring disinvestments, "austerity measures," and privatization schemes that have so seriously undermined everyday life and compromised visions of the future in both Howa and New York.[16] Drawing analytic connections between these dissimilar sites reveals not only ties between and similarities in local forms and manifestations of global economic processes, but in tracing the chilling semblances in consequences for New York and Howa it becomes clear that any effective response to the continuing globalization of capitalist production must redress its serious costs to social reproduction transnationally. These common grounds and struggles are taken up in chapter 9.

Figure 31. Collaborators in work, play, and learning.

7. Howa at the End of the Millennium

Small Displacements, the Return

Why, I wondered, had I assumed that getting to Howa would be just like before? As I stood on the eastern side of the Sennar Dam Bridge early in the summer of 1995 looking in vain for a truck or four-wheel-drive vehicle going my way—I'd already given up on finding a familiar face—I began to feel like a total idiot for not imagining that everything would have changed. All I had done the last decade was imagine change, but when it came to "real life" rather than rhetoric, I seemed to be stuck on the bridge with all my "junk"—the "junk" a long-standing joke between me and my family in Howa—looking for transport that was nowhere to be found. I had imagined endless security searches of the bus between Khartoum and Sennar (there had been only one) but never thought that the market in Sennar might have changed or that communication across the bridge (the only crossing over the Blue Nile for forty kilometers) would be hung up. I had been lulled into the imaginary of timelessness when I saw that the buses from Khartoum to Sennar were the same exact ones I had always ridden, more than a bit worse for wear, and the truck stops were the same. The tea sellers, a decade of searing inflation later, still refused to charge me for tea without sugar. All the more shocking, then, to find the Sennar bus depot in a new place, and not a truck in the market heading to the eastern side of the Nile. This part of "the schlep" was always the trickiest, and now it was to have a new twist. My fantasy of return had never ended with my being stranded—even for a night—in Sennar or in some other village along the way "home."

Getting to the east bank was merely expensive; the rest required perseverence in high-cajole mode and a nervous canvassing of the dwindling number of vehicles leaving for points east. Definitely back in "the field," I was so hot and exhausted by the time I secured a ride that I had to struggle to stay awake as the familiar swirl of dust, heat, and diesel pummeled my face the whole journey.

We reached the outskirts of the village just before sunset, and people were returning from the fields. My heart was jumping out of my skin, my eyes were out on stalks. It still does not seem possible that the first person I really saw was Ismail, and I would never want to untangle the simultaneous compression and explosion of time, space, and emotion that occurred as our eyes met. I was already crying as I tried to bolt from the still-moving truck, while Ismail, also in tears, ran toward it. Even after a few days' separation, Sudanese greetings are like incantations. After years of absence, of remembering, of forgetting, of death, and of change, it seemed as if we would never break off our ritualized but emotional greeting. In the midst of this mix of tears, dirt, and sweat, my "junk" was assembled on the ground around me, the truck driver was waiting to be paid, and Entisar, the graduate student from Khartoum University who had accompanied me as a research assistant, had disembarked and needed to be introduced. Ismail and I stopped our greeting, or at least paused for a few moments, while I took care of business, and in a moving purring huddle of dust, emotion, and luggage, we all made our way to the gate of his family's courtyard a few meters away. After eleven years of being away, but not absent, I was back in Howa.

> We fear a big disaster is coming. People who used to have animals lost their income, people who used to cut trees to make charcoal, have lost their [source of] income. The Suki Scheme, on the other hand, has its own problems that increase year after year, and people who depended on it to earn a living lost their income. People who depend on bildat [rain-fed farms] lost their income. This is a huge disaster and we are all afraid of it. . . . [M]any people have left the village to go to other places where they can find jobs. (Interview with Rashid, 6 July 1995)

Following the line of change from Howa to New York and back again, there are lessons to be learned, both sobering and inspiring. If nothing else, returning to Howa in 1995 dispelled any sense that there is linearity or a clear plot line in development narratives. Taking stock of the conditions in Howa in 1995 made the Manichaean dance between "good" and "bad" outcomes that much harder to do. Upon first glance Howa was sturdier and wealthier and had more amenities. Just driving in I could see hand pumps, a new school, and a rather grand mosque under construction. I was amazed that many of the people I saw returning from the fields were on Chinese bicycles rather than on foot or donkey. I quickly, and happily, discovered that thanks to an initiative by UNICEF, many families had installed pit latrines within their houseyards; the hand pumps were likewise courtesy of UNICEF. Perhaps even more surprising was "Souk Libya," a nightly market named after a popular market in Khartoum. The name, along with the profusion of Chinese bicycles, Toyota pick-up trucks and Land Cruisers, among other things, were signs of invigorated cosmopolitanism, heightened commodification, and more money circulating in Howa by the mid-1990s than had been the case in previous visits.

The cosmopolitanism was fueled by the expansion and intensification of labor migration. A dozen years earlier it had been unusual to find anyone from the village engaged in labor migration, except those working within the region, such as those who produced charcoal seasonally in area woodlands or commuted to work as casual day laborers in nearby towns. While in 1981 fewer than 6 percent of village households reported a permanent labor migrant among their members, by 1995 that percentage had increased to almost 30 percent as labor migration had become a routine feature of life in Howa. Not only was it common to find labor emigres traveling to more distant points, including Libya, Saudi Arabia, Iraq, and the Gulf States, but I came to realize that the entire geography of Howa's sustenance had been reconfigured to encompass distant places, among them the regional towns, the capital city of Khartoum, the forests around al-Renk in southern Sudan, and overseas.

This reconfigured space was in part an outcome of the deterioration of the local landscape, but at the same time—and somewhat paradoxically—it enabled the continuance of older patterns of land use and social exchange. The expanded geography of everyday life allowed the survival of Howa as a political economy and a working landscape in a form that remained tethered to—and recognizable from—its past. In many parts of rural Africa it is common to find economies kept afloat by the remittances of migrant laborers. Elsewhere in Sudan, particularly in the riverine north, international labor migration had long been a fact of life. Howa, however, was almost completely outside of these national and international circuits until the late 1980s, when after a decade of grueling political and economic transformation in Sudan, the pace and extent of labor migration picked up there as well. What was perhaps most interesting, and certainly most politically repercussive, was how these new political-economic relationships did *not* undermine earlier political ecologies, but rather enabled their endurance, despite myriad contradictions and problems. The expanded field of material social practice that I found in Howa in 1995 tells the twisted tale of "development" and its disintegrations.

Excavating a Historical Geography of the Intervening Years

If at first glance, Howa appeared sturdier and in better shape by 1995 than before, a longer look, behind the brick houses and mud-walled streets, revealed otherwise. The local political ecology had been decimated in the twenty-five years since the Suki Project had been established. Each of the environmental problems I had documented in the earlier phases of my project had intensified since my last visit, more than a decade earlier. The surrounding woodlands had thinned considerably since the early 1980s, when they were already sparse. The extent and quality of pasture around the village had deteriorated so much that relatively few animals were kept in Howa by 1995 compared to 1981. The devastating drought/famine of 1984 had killed off or forced the sale of many animals across semiarid Sudan, and herd numbers had never recovered. Villagers spoke frequently of livestock dying of starvation or illnesses brought about by poor grazing in the years since then. Indeed, one of the most shocking things traded in Howa's new Souk Libya was milk. Milk had never been considered a commodity in Howa. Farmers retained close ties with their pastoralist roots and relatives, while every household kept at least a couple of goats for milk, ensuring that milk was abundant and freely shared. Its commodification by the 1990s was marked by virtually everyone as a drastic and mournful change of fortunes for them and their village.

The intervening years for the agricultural project had been nothing if not uneven. As I have indicated, the Suki Project was predicated on an intensive plan wherein tenants cultivated half cotton and half groundnuts in 100 percent rotation on tenancies of 10 feddans (4.2 hectares) each. The project from its inception took land and labor time away from what had been the prevailing pattern of cultivation—sorghum for subsistence and sesame for exchange. After the Suki Tenants Union won the right to cultivate sorghum within their groundnut fields, almost all of them supplanted this lucrative crop to ensure food security during the periods of rapid inflation and political instability that characterized the 1980s. According to local residents, groundnuts were entirely displaced by sorghum in and around Howa by 1987. The shift was spurred in part by rocketing prices for sorghum and sagging prices for cotton and groundnuts following the 1984 drought/famine and in part by the not-unrelated resentment of the local population at having been required to forsake sorghum—the basis of their diet and the central crop of their existence prior to the project—for an agricultural agenda dictated to meet the needs of the central government and its wealthy supporters. As I have noted, the bargain struck by the tenants and project administration required tenants to continue to cultivate cotton, which was still seen as one of the cornerstones of Sudan's economy. Despite extensive turmoil during the 1980s,[1] the government of Sudan, through the Suki Project administration, ensured that tenants continued to cultivate cotton.

But after the fundamentalist Islamic government of Lt. General 'Umar Hasan Ahmad al-Bashir came into power following a coup in 1989, the ensuing struggle to consolidate power so preoccupied them that they neglected the agricultural sector almost entirely.[2] Not only did the military government virtually ignore the previous government's commitments to agricultural development in central Sudan, but no agricultural inputs—including seed—were supplied to the Suki Project (and others) after 1989, and irrigation pumps, canals, and other infrastructural elements were left to deteriorate. In the void, farmers and community leaders in Howa created a renegade landscape where anyone who could diverted irrigation ditches toward their own tenancies and whatever other fields they could commandeer, including some outside the project area. At the same time, the new government made a virtue of adversity and in a single gesture bought agrarian peace and tried to ensure nutritional self-sufficiency through a 1990 resolution that opened all project lands to sorghum cultivation. In Howa, the farmers, almost to a one, reverted to the cultivation of sorghum on all available land. In a single move, they pursued household food security and removed themselves from the contractual strictures of production for the world market.

Except for a smattering of horticultural crops and the occasional patch of sesame, nothing but sorghum was grown in the area between 1990 and 1993. By the end of this period, yields suffered dramatic declines thanks to compromised soil quality and severe pest infestations. By this time, the National Islamic Front government, now stabilized if no less reactionary, was reassuming control over Sudan's numerous agricultural projects. The government began to restore the irrigation system of the Suki Project and set up a system for distributing agricultural inputs so that tenants would once again grow cotton as a cash crop.

A newly elected Tenants Union Committee, ostensibly sympathetic to the government, initiated the reinstatement of cotton cultivation in the project area. They began slowly; in 1994 cotton was cultivated, with modest success, on 15,000 feddans (6,300 hectares), about 18 percent of the total project land. In the new formulation, all operations were to be paid for or done by the tenants themselves without any help from the Ministry of Agriculture or the project administration. According to a member of the committee living in Howa, the transition was successful. Over 11,000 feddans were productive, yielding a respectable 33,000 qantars of cotton total (a qantar is equal to 100 pounds [45 kilograms] of ginned cotton).[3] While yields of 3 qantars per feddan are considerably lower than the 4.5 estimated in the original feasibility study for the Suki Project under good conditions (MacDonald et al. 1964, 92), they were higher than average yields during several years in the 1970s and 1980s. The cotton grown during the 1994 season, moreover, was produced under less than ideal conditions wherein, among other things, irrigation canals were silted and obstructed, and frequent power outages impaired the main pumping station, suggesting more promising yields as problems were ironed out by the reinvigorated project management.

The Suki Project, from its inception, was predicated on tenants absorbing most of the risks of crop cultivation and failure. As I have suggested, the project ushered in a form of accounting with striking parallels to what in other realms is known as post-Fordism. Unlike any other agricultural project in Sudan at that time, the Suki Project pioneered the "individual account system," which placed almost all of the risk and expenses onto the individual tenant, rather than the tenants as a group or the state. It was intended to encourage harder work. But, as I think I have made clear, despite the tenants' extraordinarily hard work, the project and its accounting system resulted in more pronounced differentiation among individual tenants in and around Howa, reflecting success and stability amid struggle and widespread impoverishment.

The accounting system of the project was even more onerous for tenants after 1993 because they received absolutely no inputs from the project administration. While tenants in the past had been responsible for paying for various inputs such as land, water, pesticides, fertilizers, and ginning, these costs were deducted from their accounts. In essence, these inputs or the funds to purchase them were advanced to tenants by the project, if only because the project administration was itself under pressure from the Ministry of Agriculture to produce. Nor did tenants in the past pay for their cotton seed, which was distributed by the project. But in 1994 tenants were required to pay up front for all inputs including seed, even though most lacked the money to do so. The executive committee appealed to various government agencies for assistance, with only modest success. By 1995, in keeping with a worldwide trend toward privatization, they managed to secure a loan from the Farmers' Bank. Their efforts by then were supported by the new administration of the Suki Project, which, it seems, had also become better established by 1995.

Nevertheless, the original individual account system had come home to roost; tenants and the project as a whole faced debts that hitherto had been treated laxly. According to a Tenants Committee member, the outstanding debt of the Suki Agricultural Corporation was approximately £S70 million (US$140,000 at the greatly devalued 1995 exchange rates). While the debt had been largely a paper debt since the project began in 1971, the efficient (and cash-strapped) al-Bashir government was keen to collect in 1991. Most of the money owed was for the basic elements of cultivation, notably land rent, water, and services, such as plowing and canal maintenance over the years. Thanks to the individual account system, the debt was owed by the cash-poor farmers themselves, rather than by the project as a whole. The amount owed per tenant was relatively modest—just over £S9,200 or approximately US$18.50—given an average of 7,600 tenants in the project over the years, but this was not necessarily easy to come by. The equivalent of just a bit more than the price of two 50 kilogram sacks of sorghum in 1995, each tenant's debt represented about ten days of work for the average adult male in 1995. To put this figure in further perspective, it was more than a month and half's salary for poorly paid teachers and other lower-rank civil servants, roughly equal to women's income on the sale of decorative prayer and sitting mats after sixty days of (part-time) work, and nearly twice the average monthly remittance of £S5000 sent by household members working in the towns, as reported in my 1995 household survey. That an additional £S5,000 a month made a difference to so many households' earnings suggests that the burden represented by an even share of the outstanding debt to the project and the Ministry of Agriculture was not inconsequential for most households. Few tenants had disposable income of that kind, and fewer still would be keen to accrue it in order to pay past debts to a project about which many of the poorer tenants still felt bitter. Indeed, a tenant representative indicated that even among those who did have the wherewithal, debt repayment was uneven at best.

Tenants also owed money to the bank. During the few years that the local population cultivated sorghum on their own, they were advanced money from the Farmers' Bank, which purchased sorghum futures with a 30 percent latitude in either direction. If the price of sorghum at harvest was more than 30 percent less than the bank advanced them, the tenants were obliged to pay the bank the difference so that the bank's loss did not exceed 30 percent. Likewise, if the harvest price was 30 percent greater than the bank had advanced, it was obliged to compensate the tenants accordingly. In the course of this arrangement over the years, tenants came to owe money to the bank. As sorghum prices increased again in 1994, the tenants reached a new agreement with the bank that gave them a choice: either they gave the bank 60 percent of their yields or they repaid 60 percent of their debts. Those tenants who had the means but did not repay their loans had their tenancies taken away by the Tenants Executive Committee. While this plan reduced local agricultural debt considerably, it also demonstrates the blurred lines among the Tenants Union, the project administration, the Ministry of Agriculture, and the Farmers' Bank under the Bashir government. Tenants' well-being and solvency consistently took second place to the broader ambitions of productivity and capital accumulation in these arrangements.

Apart from this type of financing from the Farmers' Bank, which was known as *salamm*, banks also offered farmers short-term loans—a system known as *mogawala*—to cover various agricultural inputs such as fertilizer, pesticides, or seeds. While interest was forbidden in Islamic Sudan, the banks collected a "profit" of between 2 and 5 percent a month for the duration of the loans, which were generally repaid within a year. Finally, crop mortgaging or *shayl*—long illegal but never fully suppressed in Sudan—had again reared its head in Howa, this time with a new name, *al bai al agil*, which literally means deferred sales. As ever, merchants or banks would purchase a farmer's crop, or a portion of it, at a fixed price at the start of the season, to be repaid in kind or money during the harvest, when the farmers could almost always expect a much lower price for their crop. Thus the risk is borne by the farmer, while the gains of increased productivity are enjoyed by the money lender.[4]

The focus on productivity seemed to have led to some relaxation of the regulations around work practices and economic arrangements within the project. In the past, tenants were obliged to cultivate their own fields with family or hired labor, but there appeared to be a bit more latitude in 1995 concerning how fields were farmed, as long as they were farmed. Partnership arrangements and rentals of tenancies were permitted, and several people surveyed mentioned that they had "bought" a tenancy. These practices may all still be forbidden technically, but according to Mohamed Ahmed, a member of the Tenants Executive Committee, the committee will not stand in the way of any farmer trying to grow cotton, sorghum, or groundnuts through any tenure arrangement. As he said in an interview, "We [the Executive Committee] decide what is to be cultivated, but who is going to cultivate it? We don't ask about that." Indeed, there was also a bit more license in what was cultivated. Long gone was the 100 percent rotation between cotton and groundnuts. While sorghum had been legitimated as a third crop in the Suki Project in 1981, project authorities approved the cultivation of legumes as a fallow crop when the project was reestablished in 1993. Perhaps in recognition of how disaffected farmers had become during the early years of the Suki Project, when sorghum cultivation was prohibited and work practices were ordained from above, the administration and executive committee of the reconfigured scheme did not stipulate the variety of sorghum to be sown,[5] leaving the choice to individual tenants, many of whom, after all, had cultivated sorghum for decades.

Given the importance of sorghum to the local diet, and farmers' long-term familiarity with its cultivation, producers could be counted on to get good yields if at all possible. Ironically, the reintroduction of cotton cultivation in 1994 appeared to have improved sorghum yields following a season of poor harvests. Production had been compromised by severe insect infestation that may have been the result of having cultivated sorghum intensively in a single area without rotation for several years. In the old rain-fed system (bildat), farmers cultivated sorghum in single plots for upward of twenty years, but their fields were dispersed, so insect infestations were less likely to ravage an entire crop. When cotton was reintroduced in Suki, not only did it impede the spread of insects because it was interspersed among the sorghum fields, but farmers said that the insecticides used on the cotton had beneficial effects on the nearby sorghum crop without compromising it by direct application. Except for the bad year in 1993, most farmers in Howa produced more sorghum than their households consumed throughout the first half of the 1990s. The surplus was marketed by individual producers.

At the same time, I noticed that bildat cultivation had made a bit of a comeback around the margins of the village. Several people mentioned that since the 1980s they had resumed growing sorghum outside the irrigated areas, and indeed there were more rain-fed fields than before at the boundaries of the village and its outskirts. Reestablishing the dry-land cultivation of sorghum in the vicinity of Howa improved local food security, especially among nontenants, and reduced dependence on the Suki Project, which never had promised much to subsequent generations and which had proven particularly fickle during the late 1980s. Perhaps even more surprising, I learned that there had been a small resurgence in the dry-land cultivation of sesame as a cash crop among local farmers. While the two sesame oil presses that had operated in Howa in the past were defunct by 1981, there were no fewer than four camel-driven oil presses in the village when I returned in 1995. Moreover, rain-fed sesame had held its own as a cash crop for export. In part these (renewed) cultivations took place on project land that was laxly controlled for the first part of the 1990s, but in part it reflects an expansion of farming into areas that had been disregarded a decade earlier, whether because of soil quality, the labor involved to make them cultivable, distance from the village, or the lack of need.

In another realm, I saw that several people had cultivated gardens along the banks of the Dinder just outside the village. While only a few old-timers still cultivated these *juruf* in the early 1980s when I first worked in the village, horticulture was more widely practiced on my return in the mid-1990s. Vegetable cultivation was a means toward securing subsistence for those outside the agricultural project, and for making ends meet for those within it. But the increase in vegetable cultivation also reflected the changing food tastes and aspirations of the local population. Informants suggested that it was exposure to the dietary practices of the towns that led more people in Howa to want to grow and eat certain vegetables. The shift reflected not only new forms of embodied consumption, but the commodification of everyday life, wherein the increased circulation of money cultivated and enabled particular tastes, simultaneously encouraging development of the wherewithal to satisfy them.

If the terms, conditions, and effectiveness of cultivation had varied over the rough times between 1983 and 1993, the conditions of animal husbandry seemed only to have deteriorated. As previous chapters have documented, the environmental effects of the project's land-tenure arrangement, which removed 1,050 hectares in the vicinity of the village from mixed land use to intensive irrigated cultivation, contributed to the deterioration of pastures and the decline of woodlands. From early on people complained plenty that the reduction and decline in grazing areas made it harder and harder for animals to make it through the dry season, and they noted repeatedly that they were losing livestock as a result of poor and reduced grazing opportunities. The drought/famine of the mid-1980s hit under these conditions. Herds were decimated and many in Howa were never able to restock afterward. Those who did restock tended to find alternate means of grazing for them, especially during the dry season. By 1995, most large holders had given up grazing their animals exclusively near the village. Instead they renewed relations with pastoralist relatives who took their animals seasonally, hired shepherds to graze the animals further afield for extended periods during the dry season, or enlisted family members, generally young men in their late teens or early twenties, to take the flock to distant pastures for several weeks at a time. Apart from households with less than twenty-five animals, few relied on local grazing areas year-round. Even at that, the number of people with modest animal holdings seemed to have dropped quite a bit over the decade, largely as a result of the drought/famine.

By 1995, then, there seemed to be fewer households in the village with sizeable flocks—upward of fifty small animals—and a sharp reduction in those with modest holdings of between ten and fifty small animals. The socioeconomic differentiation among households was heightened as many lost their animal wealth. It seemed that most households that kept animals at all had fewer than ten by the middle of the 1990s. Large holdings were more hidden from view than ever, with animals out of the area for longer stretches. The much-bemoaned commodification of milk—traded anonymously in the nightly Souk Libya—was a sign of this change.

The declines in pastures were accompanied by severe reductions in wooded areas as well. Local woodlands deteriorated following the clearances of the late 1960s that made room for the Suki Project. Nevertheless, for at least fifteen years after the inception of the project, during which woodlands grew progressively sparser by all accounts, the local population remained able to procure adequate wood for household fuel and construction needs, as well as to engage in small-scale commercial charcoal production from local woodlands, even if they had to use lesser species and take more time to accomplish the necessary tasks. By 1995 these open-canopy forests were no longer adequate for anything other than basic subsistence requirements. Even at that, fewer species were available, their quality as fuel, fodder, or construction material had diminished, and the average size of trees to be cut or lopped had been reduced. Moreover, while charcoal production was more important than ever in the constellation of income-producing activities, it required a vastly expanded radius to accomplish. The men who engaged in charcoal production as a seasonal means of income during the hot dry months between harvest and planting routinely went to the area around al-Renk, on the White Nile over two hundred kilometers away. This area of southern

Sudan was literally "off the map" during the time of my original stay in Howa. I never heard of a single person from Howa going there between 1980 and 1984 when I lived in or regularly visited the village, but my research suggests that by 1995 at least a quarter of the men in Howa between the ages of eighteen and fifty went to al-Renk regularly to cut wood, burn charcoal, or otherwise participate in the charcoal trade.[6] This altered geography of everyday life helped sustain Howa's viability. This stability was purchased on the increased mobility of a large and growing number of its residents, a contradictory arrangement that will be discussed in the concluding chapters. Here I want to look at some of the specificities of the shifts outlined above, refracted through the original children's lives as they came of age.

Live to Tell—The "Children" Grown Up

In the altered geographies of sustenance in and around Howa, the children with whom I had worked came of age. The global issues of Sudan's debt, its international isolation and pariah status, the national crises of its civil war and faltering economy, and the regional problems of environmental degradation and infrastructural disintegration impinged on their everyday lives palpably. Most of them—by then in their early twenties—were scrambling to make a living in and around Howa, its deteriorated landscape and depressed economic horizons notwithstanding. For most, this necessitated seasonal labor migration for themselves or their husbands, or working out the familiar triad of agriculture, animal husbandry, and forestry within a vastly expanded field. Several of them had gone further in school than most of their generation, only to find their diplomas or even college education counting for little in terms of employment. Most of the young men were forced to attend the government's "Popular Defense Forces" (PDF) or "People's Militia" training, which was initiated in Howa in 1995, and there was a low-level buzz in the village about some young men joining the war against Southern Sudan for lack of other opportunities or as a means to secure either entrance into the civil service or a visa to work abroad. In the eroded ecologies of their everyday lives, Sudan's debt-ridden war economy ate away at these young people's futures and made joining a war against other Sudanese seem a viable option. Despite, and quite apart from, this horrific calculus, there was somehow great resilience among these young people. Here again, the simple binaries of good and bad or positive and negative collapse under the weight of development's unfolding, this time personal rather than economic.

When I returned to Howa in 1995, I found and interviewed fifteen of the sixteen surviving and now grown children from the original study.[7] The sixteenth, Merwan, was working as a farm laborer a few hours' drive south of the village. His family got word to him that I was around and wanted to talk with him. He tried to visit, but the rains made travel difficult and he was not able to reach Howa before I left. I did speak with members of his family and others concerning his life during the intervening years. My discussions with each young person focused on what they were doing now in their lives, encompassing their family and work lives, how they thought life in the village and the village itself had changed, what changes they saw in Sudan and what they thought about these, whether and how they used or left aside the knowledge they had learned as children, what aspirations they had for themselves and their children, what they wished they had learned as children, and how childhood itself had changed in the time since they had been children.

The stories they told were remarkable and mundane, inspirational and sobering, sad and optimistic, and usually all of these at once. No one was complacent. Education had proven no guarantee of anything; the most educated were the most dejected, but those with little or no formal education and no family assets were pushed to the limits of their resourcefulness. Perhaps most remarkable was that, except for two women who had married men from outside the village (though neither more than twenty-five kilometers away), only one of the group had left Howa permanently. These young people were from a pivotal generation. Born roughly the same year the project was established, which permanently altered the course of Howa's history and the contours of its geography, the children had grown up in the broad sweep of "development" amid the still strong—in some cases vital—residues of what came before. Their unfolding futures reflected and often replicated this liminal state. These young people straddled both worlds—if they can be so neatly divided—but the ways they were stuck or at a disadvantage in the world of their parents were made more poignant by their knowing more intimately than those who came before the promises of modernity. Their desire to partake of—and contribute to—those (nebulous) promises formed a critical tension in their lives, and for some, was its defining characteristic.

The still unfolding fates of these young men and women were typical of their generation, although it seemed that they were slightly more likely to have stayed in school than others of their cohort (admittedly, girls in school had been purposely overrepresented in my original sample [two of the seven girls were students]). A quarter of the grown participants had finished or were still finishing higher secondary school in 1995, and this was a substantially higher percentage than what had prevailed previously. In 1981, for example, fewer than 2 percent of those in school even reached the final year of higher secondary school. The generation with whom I worked—born with the Suki scheme and thus under the sign of Howa's propulsion into a much broader and less predictable set of social relations of production and reproduction—may well have been an early wave in the changing tide of school attendance. As more people came of age under the difficult-to-negotiate circumstances produced in part by the political ecology associated with the agricultural project and in part by the broader political-economic conditions that prevailed in Sudan, school attendance came to be seen as holding more of a promise for the future than it had before.

In other regards these young people were typical of their generation. More than half of the women were married, but only two of the nine men were. It does not seem insignificant that the married men were the only two tenants in the group or that the two never-married women were the two who had gone to school, though obviously the numbers are too small to be conclusive. All of those who were married had or were expecting children. The lives of the married women were focused on their work as homemakers and mothers, whereas the women who were not married worked in their parents' households, both at domestic chores within the hosh and also outside doing harvest work, collecting wood, fetching water, and in the case of Layla, who had completed higher secondary school, working in an office job in Wad Tuk Tuk, where she lived. The young men worked at a variety of jobs including agriculture, animal husbandry, forestry, and charcoal production, as well as various nonagricultural trades and professions. Many young men had more than one job, varying by season and straddling different arenas of work and income. Almost all of the young people lived in Howa for at least part of the year, and the five who did not lived relatively close by. The specific turns in the young people's lives reflect three important shifts in Howa associated with what I call time-space expansion (see chapter 8), notably the extended field of work, the expanded culture of education, and the heightened monetization of everyday life. These shifts are mutually constitutive and each to some degree reconfigured the familiar constellations of work and residence in Howa.

Expanded Fields of Work

> I do a little bit of everything. I was working in Kassala in a bakery making bread. I also worked as a construction laborer, as a shoveler and plasterer. They paid me a monthly salary. I spend some time away and then I come to stay with my family. I'll stay here now until the end of the season. . . . I go after December, after we harvest the sorghum. I'll go anywhere to find a job so I can make money. Sometimes I work as a trader, sometimes in construction, any kind of work, I just want to work. I'll go to Kassala, before that I worked in Khartoum, mainly in Omdurman. Really! I was also working in a bakery there. But then, I didn't go back to Omdurman, I went to Kassala. I headed east to try my luck there, hoping I might get something more out of it. It's also a nice place. . . . Very beautiful! The views are beautiful too, it's full of orchards. There's fruit everywhere, my God! . . . They're all good people there. . . . There's not one person from Howa there. . . . I'm the first one to see it. (Interview with Idris, 7 July 1995)

The expanded field of work was palpable in the trajectories of several of the young people with whom I had worked. For some, like Idris, the broadened terrain of work was experienced through a seasonal migratory pattern that might include a few months of wage labor or itinerant work in a town in addition to the usual round of agricultural work in and around Howa. For others, like Sami and El Amin, it involved going further afield to do what had previously been done closer to home. Still others, among them Merwan, Muna, Mohamed, and Sofia, lived and worked elsewhere, though none more than fifty or so kilometers from the village. Finally, some, like Talal, extended the repertoire of familiar work routines to take advantage of new opportunities around Howa.

Idris was remarkably resourceful. For the previous six years or so—since he was eighteen—Idris had worked all around central Sudan as a baker, petty trader, agricultural day laborer, charcoal maker, restauranteur, and construction worker. It was his habit to seek work through the dry months and return to Howa in time to help his father during the agricultural season. Indeed, he had just returned from Kassala to be on hand to help clear and plant his family's fields. During the rainy season Idris also worked as an agricultural day laborer in Howa, and like many others in the village, including Sami, he went south to harvest sorghum in the weeks leading up to the local crop's maturation, when he would return and work locally.

In his years as a seasonal itinerant laborer, Idris had lived or stayed in a number of places including Omdurman, Kassala, Shima (a town near Kosti on the White Nile), and Wad al-Nayal on the Blue Nile, about a hundred kilometers south. He had learned a number of trades in his travels, including baking, building, and restaurant work, and was an agricultural laborer in various orchards southward along the Blue Nile and in the Rahad Project to the northeast. While, like many others in Howa, Idris had once gone to al-Renk and further south to make charcoal, he said he found work in the towns more appealing and abandoned charcoal making after one year. From the sound of it, he was game for almost anything and seemed to take great pleasure in the places he had been, the people he had met, and the various kinds of work he had mastered.

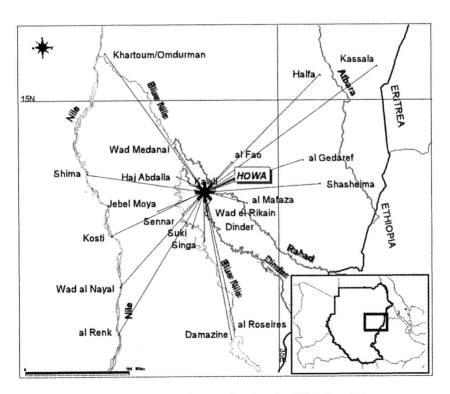

Figure 32. A baker, a poet, a merchant, an adventurer: the trajectories of Idris's itinerant labors.

Like his older brother, who was a medical assistant working near Rahad about forty kilometers away, Idris learned his work on the job, and it sounded as if he thrived at whatever he tried. Of course some things required more than know-how. In the early 1990s, Idris opened his own restaurant in Shima, near the White Nile town of Kosti. While in Sudan restaurants tend to be outdoor eateries or food stands that do not require large infrastructural investments, they do require some initial capital to invest and money to purchase supplies and raw materials on a regular basis. Idris did not have the money to make a successful go of the restaurant on his own. The following year he went to Omdurman and then next to Kassala, working as a baker. Given how enamored he was with the beauty and verdancy of the northeastern town, it was no surprise that he planned to return to Kassala after the harvest to resume working as a baker, even though he said the work was so hot it made him break out.

Idris was the most flexible and adventurous of all of the now-grown children with whom I had worked from the outset. The fortunes of his family—never that great— had deteriorated as he came of age, and his work had become crucial to helping them out. Having lost their tenancy, Idris's father cultivated a small bildat and worked as an agricultural laborer during the rainy season and a charcoal producer during the dry months. Apart from the economic problems faced generally in Howa during that period, Idris's parents were getting older and less productive, and had few children around who could assist them. Idris was the fifth of eleven children, and the second son. The only other boys in the family were still adolescents in 1995. Most of their sisters had married and gone to live with and contribute to their husbands' families. Thus it fell to Idris and his older brother, who by then had his own household in the Rahad area, to help provide for their family. Both young men sent small remittances (between £S15,000 and £S30,000 [US$27–54] a year) as well as clothing to their family. Idris painted a picture of living hand-to-mouth and working nonstop to help support his family:

> Now children also help their parents [farming], but more than before. Then people had animals, they had things. They'd go to the fields and come back refreshed, not tired. They'd go from here, having eaten something, and then come back and eat. But now, people go early in the morning without eating anything, they go and come without eating anything. They have to go and work for people to get money to buy something to eat. When they come back they buy food to make something to eat.

His worry was buffered somewhat by his clear delight in the maverick ways in which he took care of his responsibilities. And that was not all. Apart from being a jack-of-all-trades, Idris was an accomplished poet and seemed to relish exercising his creative skills in his travels.

For others, the expanded field of work was perhaps less adventurous and poetic. El Amin, for instance, worked as a hired shepherd for three families in a nearby village. He spent most of his time away from Howa, either in the nearby village where he was employed or out in the grazing areas relatively close to it. He tended about 180 animals at a piece rate of £S50 per animal a month, earning £S9000 a month (about US$16 at then current rates). He was the main source of support for his aging parents and two sisters. His father, who had never had a tenancy, cultivated a small rain-fed field and worked as an occasional petty trader at an extremely modest scale, while his mother made and sold simple woven grass mats to help support the household. El Amin had worked as a herder for more than twelve years, initially for families in Howa and eventually in the village nearby. While he seemed to enjoy the work—and as a shy and retiring young man it suited him well—El Amin's earnings were inadequate to ensure the sustenance of his family. Moreover, he complained that herding was becoming more difficult all the time, especially during the dry season, thanks to substantial devegetation in the local environs. "The pastures are gone," he said. "Shepherding is hot [difficult]. . . . I have to go far, really far . . . to find good grazing." As in his childhood, El Amin's family lived hand to mouth, and given their lack of resources and their children's lack of schooling, there were few prospects for changing these conditions. It is no small irony that it was the very conditions of environmental deterioration that created the possibility of El Amin's employment as a professional shepherd. When access to adequate grazing was more secure, there was little need for hired shepherds to go to more distant pastures.

Sami, another of the children whose household had few resources of any kind, was also scraping by and drawing on an expanded terrain to do so. Living with his widowed mother and younger brother, he continued his father's work as a charcoal maker, but like most men in Howa without a tenancy (and many with) he had to depend on his daily labor for income. Like many others, Sami worked not only in Howa and the Suki Project, but as an itinerant agricultural laborer elsewhere in the region during the planting, weeding, and harvesting periods of both sorghum and sesame. Sometimes he was picked up in Howa or a nearby town as part of a work gang taken for a couple of weeks to harvest in the moister areas toward the south. Other times he spent a couple of months away during the autumn (from mid-September to November), picking up harvest and other agricultural work in areas such as Jebel Moya west of Sennar, the Rahad Agricultural Project to the northeast, and points south. In the village he found day work on his own, and when nothing was available he might help his mother and younger brother in their small rain-fed field.

While Sami's work strategies depended on an expanded geography, there were ways that these were necessitated by a localized shrinkage of his space of work. For instance, unlike his old-timer father, Sami did not tend a garden along the river, although these gardens were more prevalent in 1995 than when Sami had been a child. This option was not available to Sami because his father had been evicted from his jeref a few years earlier by the local landowner, who had leased him the plot on the banks of the Dinder for years for what must have been a nominal amount.[8] As interest in garden cultivation increased in Howa, the jeref land along the river became more valuable. By evicting Sami's elderly father, the owner was free to sell or rent the land to someone else or put it to otherwise more profitable use. The family had fought the eviction all the way to Dinder town, but had lost. As Sami pointedly noted,

They only care about those with money—if you don't have money, they'll get you. . . .
Everything works by money, if you don't have any, nothing in the government goes
your way. If you don't have money, they'll take what you have.

This local manipulation of wealth and power not only deprived his father of a source
of income and household nutrition during the last years of his life, but foreclosed any
chance of Sami's cultivating a garden as he came of age.

Sami remarked that he would have liked to cultivate a tenancy because the water
was reliable and there was a chance to profit from the various crops again, but without
reserves of cash he had no chance to acquire or establish one. He meanwhile resisted
cultivating a bildat, noting that it was too risky for someone with no resources. He
detailed all of the possible problems of rain-fed cultivation, noting, for instance, that
crop pests or late, early, inadequate, or excessive rains could ruin a harvest. He made
it clear that it was not just that these eventualities would take the product, but that
they would waste the seed and labor time he would have put into the effort. This risk—
which is intrinsic to dry-land agriculture—was too much for men like Sami, who not
only lived hand-to-mouth themselves, but had families dependent on them. Of course
these were precisely the circumstances that prevailed for most households in Howa
prior to 1971, when the agricultural project was introduced, but at that time commodification had made few local inroads, so earning cash was not a critical issue for most
farmers though clearly crop shortfalls undermined food security and household subsistence in some years.

As it turned out, Sami's mother cultivated a small bildat with occasional assistance
from her sons. According to her, in a good year, their one-and-a-half-feddan field,
rented within the project area, provided five to six sacks of sorghum, of which they
could sell about half. The economics of this activity were fairly straightforward. In 1995
land within the project could be rented for about £S4000 (about US$7.50) a feddan
for the season, while a sack of sorghum sold for the same amount or slightly more
(£S5000). If things went well, the sale of sorghum would more than cover the land rent
paid by the family, while at the same time they produced enough grain for their own
subsistence. If things did not go well, however, they would be better able to absorb the
loss with Sami's mother doing the work than if he had spent the time on it. While rent-
ing a field within the project gave the family a more certain water and food supply,
they nevertheless were not able to forego the cash Sami earned from his daily agricultural work.

Family losses ricocheted into others' lives, too. Merwan's family, for instance, had
lost most of their considerable animal wealth over the years, especially during the mid-
1980s drought, and these circumstances seemed to have forced him to work outside of
the village. The family told me that Merwan worked to the south as a farmhand during
the rainy season and as a petty trader during the rest of the year, but others whispered
something else. According to them, Merwan had become a thief. Having reportedly
stolen animals and other goods from people in the village, he was apparently driven away
to find work elsewhere when he reached adulthood. Be that as it may, it sounded as if

he had left off stealing, and was making his way as a farm laborer by 1995, but his situation demonstrates that people in Howa were, of course, not impervious to the lure of crime when other remunerative options seemed foreclosed. Indeed, while Merwan's petty thieving may have ruffled local feathers, some of these same people spoke admiringly of those who had managed to get jobs in government and used their office for personal gain. In Howa as elsewhere, "white-collar" crime, even in its earliest iterations, was held to a different standard and marked by a different sensibility.

If Merwan was in some sense pushed from the village, others were pulled. Among them were Muna and Sofia, who had married young men from outside Howa, and Ahmed, who lived in Dinder with his brother's family while he by turns worked and attended secondary school. Muna's move—a dozen kilometers up the Dinder to a village not unlike Howa, albeit a bit larger and much closer to Dinder town—was less dramatic than Sofia's. Sofia had married a cousin who grew up in Dinder town and she had moved there in 1992 when their first child was about four years old.[9] Her husband was in the military working as a park ranger in Dinder National Park, about a hundred and fifty kilometers southeast of the town. Like most young women living with their husbands' families, Sofia helped with the cooking and household chores for the extended family, in addition to tending to her own household and taking care of her children. Her husband's work, which included keeping nomads from grazing their animals in parklands and otherwise protecting wildlife in the little-visited national park, kept him away for months at a time. According to Sofia, he returned to Dinder town for a brief visit every couple of months.

Sofia had been somewhat cosmopolitanized in her married life. She appeared very "modern" in her concerns and outlook, and expressed a greater consumerist zeal than most of the people with whom I spoke. Among other things, she was the most outspoken of all the grown children regarding what I might have brought as gifts from the United States. In the course of our conversations she mentioned that she wanted clothes, shoes, jewelry, a modern house, a car, and other things. Most startling—as an indicator of change—was that, in response to a question concerning what she wanted for her children's futures, Sofia referred to a Toyota Land Cruiser as a "Layla Owli." Layla Owli is a well-known Egyptian actress, whose name, by dint of her full face, seemed to have become synonymous with Land Cruisers. I never heard anyone else refer to them as such in Howa, and it seemed an artifact of Sofia's mediated urban life.

About changes in Howa she enthused, "People want to build high-rises now, they want education, they want to go to Saudi Arabia or go to the towns. They want to go to America, Italy, Port Sudan, Kassala, Nyala. People have started to realize that there are other good places. They're more open-minded to other parts of the world. We have these aspirations because we've grown up, we've learned and we want a better life. Farming is only making a living, and we want more than that." As her unusual place names might suggest, Sofia had traveled further (Khartoum and Omdurman) than any of the women in the original group, and her eyes for the future were most definitely turned away from Howa. She mentioned approvingly that people in the village had become "more open," looking to work in towns and "outside'"in Saudi Arabia and Iraq. She was intent on providing an urban life for her children, insisting that they get educated and then work as they pleased. This stance was reinforced within her family. Not only was Sofia alone among all the children with whom I had originally worked in pursuing a solely urban life—such as it was in low-key Dinder town just twenty-five kilometers away—but her younger brother had moved to Khartoum, where he had opened a "big" store.

The inroads that capitalism had made in the area were clear from the insistent way Sofia wove together her consumerist desires and her educational ambitions for her children. Like so many with whom I spoke in 1995, she used the term *arab* to describe perspectives once widely shared in the village. In one generation, people in Howa had come to see themselves as having been "arabs" in the past. While locally, and through much of central and northern Sudan, arab referred particularly to nomads, it had come to signify, as it does in many areas of Sudan, a lack of sophistication and worldliness. Just a dozen years earlier, people almost never referred to themselves—past or present—as "arab," and at times they took pains to distinguish themselves from arab relations or express bemusement at their folksy ways. By 1995, however, people in Howa constantly referred to their past selves as "arabs." The term was invoked particularly around questions of education. When I would remark on the burgeoning school population or the nearly completed secondary school in the village and ask why people thought enrollment had increased so much, especially for girls, most would say, "We were 'arabs'" in a way that conveyed, "What did we know?"

Such self-reflexivity, interlarded with self-derision, comes from a kind of "other-worlding"—seeing oneself as others do and internalizing that sense of difference—that arises in the course of travel and social interaction that straddle multiple worlds. The shift was absolutely shocking for me, given a frame of reference stretching back to my first night living in Howa not fifteen years earlier, when dozens of women visited and not one asked me anything about my life or where I'd come from. Part of their reticence was surely shyness and the awkwardness of my limited Arabic, but part of it seemed to rest on the presumption that my life was fairly similar to theirs, despite my having been catapulted alone into their midst. As my strangeness grew apparent over the ensuing weeks, the questions came in a torrent and never let up. But the sort of self-referentiality I found by 1995 was utterly different from anything that had come before, especially in the way it revealed the Janus face of self-denigration and newfound sophistication provoked by the seductions of capitalism and modernity.

While these kinds of cosmopolitanizing experiences had intensified in Howa during the previous decade, they almost always cut both ways. Many in Howa, as elsewhere, made not assimilating to the social patterns associated with the urban middle classes, colonial or postcolonial, almost a point of honor, and took pride in their identities as farmers, as herders, or as followers of highly spiritual Sufi paths.[10] Merwan's derisive mocking of schoolboys when he was a child was typical. But in the fourteen years since Merwan shared his contempt for schoolboys with me, Howa had been battered by the encroachments of new social relations of production and reproduction and the machinations of the broader economy, experienced most forcefully, perhaps, in the displacements suffered by those coming of age, who found few opportunities in the traditional mix of economic activities likely to sustain them under contemporary conditions. For these reasons more than others, school attendance had been revalued among the local population. Rescripting their past selves and perspectives as "arab" while reworking their contemporary ones were part of the process, done in the hopes of giving themselves and their children more of a leg up in the difficult conditions they encountered. Cosmopolitanism was nothing if not pragmatic.

Expanded Culture of Education

> Now people understand more—look at the school—in the past girls didn't go to school, only boys. You found very few girls—three or four—in school, because people in the village said girls should not study with boys. There was no school for girls so girls studied with boys, but their parents and others in the village didn't like that. . . . But now there are many girls who study with boys in school. It's a big difference from before. [Q: Why did this happen?] Before people didn't know things. They hadn't been to cities and seen how girls live in towns. Now they've seen it can work and have become convinced that girls should be allowed to study with boys. The coeducational schools in towns were an example to them. It's because of the contact between urban and rural centers. They realized that if girls and boys studied together it would not create problems between them or for their parents. (Interview with Awatif, 4 July 1995)

Such pragmatic reworkings were long in coming, but were quite palpable by the 1990s. Several of the original group with whom I worked had gone to secondary school, classrooms had been constructed and women teachers had been recruited to teach girls separately in the primary grades, a secondary school was under construction within the village, and the local discourse concerning education had shifted in both obvious and subtle ways. Among those with whom I had worked, Ismail had received his secondary school certificate, Rashid was on leave from Khartoum University, Ahmed had recently returned to secondary school in Dinder town to complete his certificate, and Layla, who had moved to the project headquarters in Wad Tuk Tuk as a child, had completed secondary school, but had not yet passed the exam to receive her certificate.

Both Ahmed and Layla had been stymied by family crises. Ahmed had had to interrupt his education for a couple of years between intermediate and secondary school when he ran out of money for school expenses following the death of his father. As he told me, "I worked in the Dinder market to make some money and go back to school. At that time we didn't have any money. My father died and there was no one taking care of us or helping us after he died, to give us money to buy books or supplies. So I had to leave school for a short period. I was selling bread in the market. After I made school expenses, I came back to school. . . . I really wanted to study."

Intertwining new local tendencies toward both expanding the terrain of work and a heightened regard for education, Ahmed was living with his elder brother in town while working and attending school. Both young men sent money back to their mother and younger siblings in Howa. While in school, Ahmed supported himself with a job in the "General Security" forces in town. He told me that he planned to sit for the Sudan School Certificate the next year, and hoped to gain a place at one of Sudan's universities. Layla's education had also foundered after her father had had a disabling automobile accident just as she was completing her studies at the higher secondary school in the nearby town of Singa. Though she completed her studies, she had not been able to pass her exam in the aftermath of her father's accident. She intended to sit the exam again, but in the meantime she was living with her family in Wad Tuk Tuk and working an office job there.

Awatif was one of the only girls in her generation to have attended several years of primary school in the village, but she elected to leave school after her fifth year for a couple of reasons: first was the social pressure she felt as one of the only girls in school, and second was her desire to earn money by participating in the harvest along with her friends, sisters, and mother. Unlike most other girls in Howa during that time, she did not leave school as a result of parental pressure exerted either because her labor was needed or because they found it shameful for girls to study with boys. As she told me, "When I left school I left by my own choice. My father didn't ask me to quit. [When I was younger] I thought I would want to continue my education, but when I saw others picking cotton and getting paid for it while I'm studying alone, I changed my mind and quit school. We were only a few girls in school at that time [five]; the majority of girls didn't go to school. They were picking cotton and so I joined them." Awatif's father was unusual in Howa at that time, not only because he allowed his daughter to attend the coeducational school beyond the second year, but because he approved of her older sisters attending the women's classes sponsored by the project's social extension program. At the time he was virtually unique in advocating that Awatif continue in school, suggesting to me that she might grow up to be a social worker, teacher, or health practitioner. But in the end she left school earlier than she might have, thanks to a combination of peer pressure and the discomfort she experienced as a nonconforming preadolescent girl, expressed partially as a desire to earn money along with her friends.

It was not clear that completing one's education would bring solace in any event. The frustration levels of Ismail and Rashid—the two who had completed their higher secondary schooling and received a certificate—were among the highest of all the young adults I encountered. Having gone the distance in school, they expected some sort of reward or at least acknowledgment for their efforts—not necessarily an easy life, but something "better" than farming. Instead, Ismail endured an elementary teaching position in a nearby village that paid him only £S10,500 a month (US$19 at then current exchange rates). This lowly sum even included a supplement (da'am al gharya, literally "support of the village") from the village where he worked that almost doubled the pay of their teachers; otherwise his base salary from the government including allowances was a paltry £S5,500. As he put it,

> I shouldn't work as a teacher, but I have been forced to work in this profession. . . . The money is bad, but also no one wants this work. Nobody wants this; only if you can't find work outside would you take this. I searched everywhere! The banks, offices—when I couldn't find anything, I took the teaching job. I searched in Singa, in al Dinder, in Suki, you see? I looked in Sennar, I went to Khartoum and I worked there in a shop, but it wasn't much work. That's all, just a store. . . . and the work is minimal, one can't eat off what he makes in a month in a shop. So I came back and I checked out the teaching jobs. I applied for this bad teaching job and I got it.

Rashid languished bitterly in the village, on leave from Khartoum University and his position in the Khartoum offices of the National Fund for Students. He had left the university after one term because he could not afford his studies and was tormented over both not going to the university and going. In the interview he was unqualified about his desire to return to his studies (and unambiguous about how disastrous things had become in Howa and in the country more broadly). Yet in other discussions, Rashid baited me to prove that there was any advantage to completing a university degree given the dire state of the economic situation in Sudan at the time. As it was, he earned only £S12,000 a month (less than US$22) in his government position, which was not enough to make ends meet, especially in Khartoum. More than returning to the university, he was eager to go abroad to work and earn some real money, but to do so legally he had to participate in the Popular Defense Forces training, which he was doing that summer along with about sixty-five other conscripts from the village. Following the training, Rashid would be forced to serve two years in the army—the compulsory tour for those with higher secondary educations. He did not relish the prospect, but he was desperate to get an exit visa to work abroad and this seemed to him the only sure way:

> I must be a soldier! [And go] to the war or anywhere the government wants me to go. Whether I like it or not, I have to finish the two-year period. I must be . . . I must be . . . I must go, I must go to it. There's no choice. . . . Everyone must be a soldier! Every Sudanese must be a soldier. . . . university graduates spend one year, those with higher secondary educations must spend two years, and anyone below that level should spend three years in the People's Defense. [Q: So they will take teachers from rural areas and put them in war?] Yes. . . . They take doctors!

Ismail was also in militia training, but he had other things on his mind. He was eager to marry Nowal, his father's brother's daughter, herself a recent high school graduate, but was thwarted by the difficulty of coming up with the funds to purchase the furniture and housewares considered necessary to start a new household, as well as to pay a modest bridewealth (*mahr*) to her father, and to assemble the trousseau of clothing, shoes, jewelry, perfumes, and cosmetics that people in Howa referred to as the *shunta,* for the suitcase in which it was presented to brides.[11] He lovingly showed me the *angareb* (rope bed) and other items he had already purchased and stored in the corner of his family's house, but he was far short of the £S220,000 (US$400 at 1995 exchange rates) necessary to procure the goods required for marriage according to Howa's prevailing standards for moderately prosperous families such as his, to say nothing of the wedding party, which was also paid for by the groom. At his £S10,500 monthly salary, Ismail was a long way off from marriage, even with assistance from his parents and other relatives, none of whom had yet promised any. He participated in the Popular Defense Forces training in the hopes that it would facilitate entrance into the civil service or provide the means to an exit visa so that he could temporarily work abroad. But he also toyed with the idea of emigrating illegally—as so many did—so that he could avoid military service and make some money.

Young men from other parts of Sudan commonly emigrated to the Gulf States or Saudi Arabia in order to amass the wealth necessary to start their own households (see Boddy 1989), but that was not the case in Howa until the 1990s. As Ismail's experience suggests, labor migration was likely to become the predominant route to marriage for all but the poorest young men in Howa. His financial difficulties and the suspension in which he and Nowal lived suggest the cynical effect of the nubile promises of martyrdom on offer daily in Howa at the Popular Defense Forces training sessions. With Sudan's civil war declared a *jihad* by the Islamicist government, anyone who died for the cause would be a martyr and gain entry into Paradise. Paradise was presented by the militia and more widely as a lush garden with beautiful young women available to serve young men's every need. A young man living in the hot dust of Howa, single for lack of resources, could understandably be drawn to the militia as a way out.

Another means to an exit was *wasta,* or connections. Ismail told me that it was impossible to get any kind of office work in the towns without "strong wasta." When we spoke, he was banking on the eventual connections of his cousin Muna's husband, who, eight months earlier, had begun working for the Department of Taxation in Dinder, collecting taxes on agricultural products. Ismail assumed that in time his cousin-in-law would be able to get him in, too. Indeed, wasta has been a major propellent and emollient in Sudan for as long as I have been going there, and young people from Howa suffered for their lack of this kind of "cultural capital." While this much is obvious from an abstract perspective, it sometimes hit me in the guts:

> After Ismail told me his lack of "strong connections" (*wasta gowiya*) prevented him from getting a job outside the village, I deluded myself into thinking that I could provide some wasta for him. It happened accidentally. When [my research assistant] Entisar and I left Howa we stopped to visit her relatives in Sennar. Her uncle was the director of the parastatal power company there, and he and his family lived comfortably in government housing. For a variety of reasons, Ismail came to Entisar's family's home while we were there. It was late in the day by then, and in typical Sudanese fashion, the family pressed him to spend the night. Ismail and Entisar's uncle stayed in

the men's quarters of the house, conversing most of the evening. When I went to visit them and say goodnight, I sang Ismail's praises, telling our host that he was looking for a job. It seemed a great wasta opportunity, but almost as I said it, I could see Ismail through the middle-class urban eyes of Entisar's uncle and realized excruciatingly that Ismail probably looked "traditional" or naive to him. As I recoiled from the injuries of class (obviously at a remove), I had a sharpened sense of how hard Ismail's road out of Howa would be. The director of the power company no doubt reserved his "strong connections" for the children of his relatives and friends, and could offer nothing to Ismail my naive interjection not withstanding. (Field notes 1995)

One day when Ismail was telling me about his experience in completing higher secondary school and sitting for the exam, he used a proverb that translates roughly as "winds blow against the sailor's wish." He was very proud to have passed the Sudan School Certificate examination, but clearly disappointed that his scores were not adequate to get into any of Sudan's universities. Ismail was as sharp and hard working as they come. I was always certain if anyone would "make it," it would be him. The national examination system was, of course, designed to cull students at each level. As more and more children attended primary school without equivalent expansion at the higher levels, especially the postsecondary, larger numbers were jettisoned at every stage. The scores for passing through were becoming astronomical, even during the 1980s. The disadvantage for young people like Ismail or Rashid was clear. They competed against urban children whose lives generally offered infrastructural and social capacities, such as electricity and homes with books and literate parents, that supported schoolwork in ways not found in Howa. When I returned in 1995 and heard my university friends fretting about whether their children—in elite schools, well read, media savvy—would get into any universities, and reflected on what this concern might mean for young people in Howa, the increased starkness of the disparity was brought home.

Of course, some students from Howa have competed successfully. A total of fourteen young people from the village had gotten into university between 1981 and 1995. (Prior to 1981 only one person from Howa had ever attended university.) Nevertheless, the examination system performs the lie of democracy (see Bourdieu and Passeron 1977), producing subjects like Ismail, who rued the winds against him rather than the gross unfairness of the way the system was stacked. Like "tracking" in New York City, the steep pyramidal structure of the examination system in Sudan ensured that children from poor and powerless families were, for the most part, kept that way, while the few who succeeded made the whole system plausible.[12]

Altered Familiarities

In terms of water—it became available through hand pumps. There is also greater access to grain mills than in the past. And the people themselves have changed. Now they want education more than before. . . . There have been changes in children's lives.

Now they know more about life. We were more naive. They're different in their thinking and behavior. In some ways they are similar to us, in others different. (Interview
with Layla, 11 July 1995)

In many ways, those who had left school or never even attended were at an advantage
in the production landscape of Howa and its surrounds. These young people did not
suffer as much from dashed expectations. They seemed better able to live in their own
bodies and be at home in Howa pursuing some version of an agricultural life, albeit on
a reconfigured terrain. For most of them, new activities were added to the mix of agriculture, animal husbandry, and forestry, which helped them to make a go of living off
of some version of the traditional combination. Not surprisingly, some measure of family wealth or assets helped tremendously in these pursuits.

Saddiq, for instance, was thriving when I returned in 1995. Never having completed a year of school, Saddiq had worked as a herdboy for his family's flocks throughout his childhood. As an adult, he was a tenant farmer and shared in his family's
considerable animal wealth and other assets, which included at various times a Toyota
Land Cruiser, a shop, storehouses, and a market truck. In the rainy season Saddiq
worked as a farmer and in the dry season he worked as a trader, largely in villages
nearby, though he occasionally went to markets further afield. At times he attended to
the affairs of, and sometimes even tended, the family's animals, but this usually was left
to his slightly older brother, Mohamed, or a hired shepherd.

This scenario was not all that different from the situation that had prevailed in the
family when Saddiq was a child. Then as later the family—of six daughters and three
sons—held diverse assets collectively, and their father, El Haj, seemed to have a strategic approach to how he educated and drew upon his children, particularly the boys.
Saddiq's oldest brother, Babiker, was sent to school, while Saddiq, from the age of
seven, was designated the family herdboy. Their middle but less savvy brother,
Mohamed, was displaced by Saddiq early on for the crucial task of herding, but he was
not sent to school either; instead he assisted with agricultural tasks and occasionally
spelled his younger brother herding. While all the children were grown by 1995, the
family still worked as an economic unit guided by El Haj. As was customarily the case,
his married daughters contributed to the families of their husbands, who provided for
them, while his adult sons and their growing families lived within El Haj's hosh. The
various households within the hosh worked as an ensemble. Babiker and Saddiq, along
with their father, handled the family's business dealings and took care of farming their
tenancies. Mohamed did not participate in the business, but he worked their tenancies and occasionally tended the livestock, which by 1995 were routinely grazed some
distance from Howa.

The extended family was well set up by actions taken by El Haj years earlier. When
the Suki Project was established, for instance, he managed to obtain several tenancies
by registering them in the names of his wife and young sons. Later on they were able
to register for still other tenancies so that within their extended family of four men they

held six tenancies by 1995. When Saddiq was a child, his father and elder brother worked as tenant farmers. The family owned a general store near their compound and kept over a hundred animals as well. In cooperation with El Haj's brother, who owned a truck, they were involved in widespread trade networks during certain times of the year. They had a storage house in their hosh that facilitated their holding onto goods, such as grain and charcoal, that they purchased relatively cheaply to sell when prices were dear. The family enterprises had continued along these lines during the intervening years. They had clearly been able to ride out various economic and political-ecological crises better than most in Howa, and they had parleyed their assets so as to invest in new enterprises, such as their Land Cruiser. When Saddiq came of age he assumed the tenancy held in his name, and took a more active role in managing various parts of the family businesses with his father and brothers. In our discussions he laughed at his fortune, noting pointedly that what he did to make money did not require book knowledge. "I heard an adult literacy class was coming to the village. If it comes, that's great, but if not that's no problem either. If I don't study, I still make money." While he insisted that he wanted his children to be different from him and go to school, he also said that he thought the nation benefited more from successful farmers than from the surfeit of (frustrated) educated people it had. It was no wonder that, quite the opposite of Rashid, Saddiq told me he thought all of the changes in Howa since his childhood had been positive.

But he and his family were more the exception than the rule. Their situation revealed the importance of household assets to the course of individual trajectories. Sami and El Amin, whose families were almost completely lacking in assets during their childhoods, seemed to have fallen even further behind as they reached adulthood. Neither young man had attended school, neither came from a tenant household, and neither could afford to acquire a tenancy through any means: partnership, rental, or "purchase." On the other hand, Talal, who was the son of a resourceful, though by no means wealthy, tenant, was faring reasonably well in the village, pursuing an amalgam of the familiar work routines. Talal, recall, had left school after third grade because his family needed both his assistance and the income he made as a water seller. Not only had Talal's father managed to do well with his tenancy during the intervening years, but Talal had purchased one in his own right and was cultivating cotton, groundnuts, and sorghum in the recently rejuvenated Suki Project. Unlike most young men his age, Talal was set up well enough to have gotten married and start his own family. His father, who also cultivated a five-acre bildat most years, had established a general store to complement his farm tenancy, and recently married a second wife—a clear sign of economic stability.

While Talal's life bore much similarity to his father's and he and his brother assisted their father in his various economic activities, he had moved outward as well. During the dry season Talal traveled to daily markets in villages around Howa—themselves a new phenomenon in the area—to sell vegetables. "I buy sacks of onions, vegetables, or tomatoes in the market and sell them piecemeal in the local markets," he said. "It's okay, it's not bad—it's just for the off-season—but it's better than staying home and doing nothing. Trading gives me something a little different to do." However small his profit, Talal's trading enabled him to work near the village, even during the dry season when others went further afield. Notably, he had never done charcoal-related work, and he was unusual among men his age in having never been to al-Renk. In years when the rains were late, however, Talal would take his family's small flock of animals further south to graze for a couple of weeks or so until the rains came or the agricultural season began. He had a remarkably different perspective than Idris or Sami, who noted more than a few times how they had to work each day in order to eat. It was not that Talal was floating free, or that he had the assets of someone like Saddiq at his disposal, but his existence seemed much less precarious than that of some of the others.

Why things had worked out this way for him but not for others was not totally clear, but certain things were telling. While having a tenancy was no guarantee of economic well-being (it was often quite the opposite), those without tenancies or any assets except their own labor power who continued to pursue livelihoods connected to the more traditional agricultural sector or involving irregular day labor were likely to have become more impoverished than either those who were tenants or those nontenants who engaged in activities involving capital accumulation or that were connected more directly with the broader (often nonagricultural) economy. This much may be obvious: the rich get richer. But it bears noting because it makes clear that the area's incorporation into the national and global economies was in no way an "equalizer," but neither was there any neat tendency toward proletarianization among the local population. There were several reasons for this. For one, many people in Howa, old and young, actively resisted the shift that nudged (or shoved) them away from the constellation of economic activities that had sustained people in the village for more than a century. For another, there was a reconfiguration of the intimate and distant that enabled people to stay afloat in some semblance of the familiar. And finally, the economy of Sudan did not provide many opportunities for those who were evicted from the countryside or who might, under more hospitable circumstances, be tempted to leave. The three are integrally related, and raise questions—similar to those called forth in restructured economies of the global north—about the ways people's resilience and strategies of reformulation can be turned against them, and about what form "resistance" might take in a political economy as eviscerated as it is eviscerating. These questions are taken up in chapter 8.

The girls now grown were at the heart of those intimate reconfigurations that enabled the village to stay afloat, that altered consumption practices, that formulated new values, and that began to produce new subjects for the altered conditions that simultaneously called forth these reconfigurations. All of this notwithstanding, women tended to encounter the altered familiarities of life in Howa in a mediated fashion, through their husbands' or fathers' situations. Despite, or perhaps because of, this buffered position, married women often seemed at the vanguard of new consumption practices and their centrality to social reproduction made them acutely aware of the monetization of everyday life in Howa. These interests—and their role in furthering the advance of capitalist relations of production and reproduction in and around Howa—were perhaps most acutely expressed by Miriam and Sofia, but they infiltrated the practices and concerns of some of the other women as well, and were crucial to the production of new values and different kinds of subjects (see Joseph 1998). As Nowal lamented,

> [My husband] is poor, he's poor, he doesn't have anything. . . . Everything is becom-
> ing expensive. Things were cheap before. Life is getting hard. . . . For people who have
> things, things here have changed for the better, but for those without, things have got-
> ten a little worse. Since there is a lack of everything, people have to work hard [in
> farming]. Those who can't do that, have to go outside, to Saudi Arabia, to work. But
> only those who can afford to, leave Sudan. Those who can't afford it, have to stay.

Miriam's marriage, by contrast, had elevated her economic status considerably. She had grown up in a tenant household of average means that had accumulated a bit of wealth in the years since she was a child, and in recent years had opened a bread bak-ery that was thriving.[13] Their oldest son, Miriam's younger brother Mustafa, was work-ing in Khartoum in what she and her family referred to as a "supermarket" (a neologism and innovation both). He helped his family out by sending them about £S5000 (less than $10) a month, as well as clothing on occasion. Miriam's husband's family was among the wealthiest in the village; they were successful farmers, had considerable ani-mal wealth, and had carried out diversified economic activities for years, not unlike Saddiq's family, to whom they were related. Within this constellation of activities, Miriam's husband owned a truck that he drove as a wholesaler, plying a route between Khartoum and al-Damazin, a town on the Blue Nile about two hundred kilometers south of Howa. He transported and sold charcoal from the south and returned with clothing and other goods from the capital to sell in al-Damazin. He was routinely away from home for two to three weeks at a time, coming back to the village for a night or two before returning to his trade.

Miriam, with their three children, lived on the edge of town among her husband's large family. In addition to taking care of her children, she cooked, cleaned, laundered, and otherwise tended house as part of this extended family. Among her duties were cooking for and otherwise seeing to the needs of guests, a responsibility she shared with the other women of her husband's family. She also made grass mats for sale. She had learned this craft as a young child working alongside her mother and older sister, Fatima. Her sister, now divorced with two children, still made mats as well, but living back with her parents she also helped with their bakery business, as did their other adult sister and brother, still unmarried and living at home. When I asked Miriam if she, too, helped out, she said no, but noted that when she visited she sat with them when they took breaks as the bread was baking.

Miriam's life was relatively less burdened than those of her sisters and many other young women in the village. Like many young women in Howa and elsewhere, Miriam was interested in fashion and she said she spent time making perfumes and other cosmetics to enhance her beauty and care for her body. Muna and Sofia, who were also relatively comfortable in their marriages, also mentioned personal care activities, such as decorating their hands and feet with henna and taking sandalwood smoke baths, and noted their interests in clothing styles when they were telling me about their lives. These activities, which were pleasurable to them, were also intended to arouse their husbands. While all young married women engaged in these activities, often communally, those with more time and disposable income obviously had a greater chance to enjoy these simple embodied pleasures. Miriam seemed to have the leisure time and wherewithal to indulge more often than many other women in Howa. She also seemed to want to keep it that way.

After telling me that she wanted her children to attend school and not to have to do chores, such as fetching water and collecting wood, that she had done as a child, she asked me if I could help her get contraceptives. While in the past women often told me they were interested in controlling their family size, noting generally that their husbands were not, Miriam was particularly well informed and assertive. She told me that the easiest kind of birth control to obtain was through injection (Depo Provera), but because of its harsh side effects, she wanted pills instead. She was insistent that she did not want any more children, but it was not clear if she would have the means to obtain pills or other contraceptives through the national health-care system without the agreement of her husband, although women in Sudan occasionally obtained contraceptives secretly. Miriam's views and knowledge suggested both that a wider base of information was now available to nonliterate women and that there was a more definitive interest in controlling family size than there had been in the past. Her interests and practices at the very least intimate the performance of a new kind of gendered subject in Howa. Reconfiguring Howa and remaking values at the site of the body are intertwined, of course. They suggest not only the centrality of social reproduction in making social life and thus social change, but the multiple scales at which this occurs (see Joseph 1998; Marston 2000; Jakobsen 2002).

At a more quotidian level, Miriam seemed to be opting to focus the work and other resources associated with rearing a family on her three children, rather than pursuing the time-honored strategy of building a power base for herself by bearing many children. Indeed she may have been taking another tack for strengthening her position through maintaining her "bridelike" qualities to keep her traveling husband's interests piqued (see Boddy 1989, 183, for a discussion of both strategies in northern riverine Sudan). Of course, all of Miriam's comments may well have been the result of her having three children five years and younger. Nevertheless her expressed desire not to have any more children than the three she already had was unusual, though it was congruent with her equally unusual adamance that her children would not do any manual labor:

> I want them to go to school, I want one of them to be a doctor, the other a judge. They will be learned. . . . I don't want my children to work in farming. They don't need to learn anything about it. When they get a little older, I'll take them to school.

They should study only, not go to the fields, not collect wood. We can buy everything without taking their time by asking them to collect wood or work in the fields. These are hard jobs and there is nothing gained from them. They're just tiring, but they're no use. . . . Education will help my children. With it they can go anywhere.

Muna, who had been married since she was about fifteen, offered a different perspective. She seemed to delight in her ever-growing family, which by 1995 included four children. Muna was the daughter of a tenant of modest means and a mother from a prosperous and powerful family in Howa. A few years after her mother's death in 1981, Muna had married and gone to live with a young man from a village about twelve kilometers up the Dinder River. Her husband, Omer, was a tenant farmer who also grew sesame on rain-fed fields and worked as a tax collector out of Dinder town. He was responsible for collecting the tax on sorghum from local farmers. In addition to taking care of their children and keeping house, Muna helped out with the housework, laundry, and hospitality work of her husband's family. Like many women in Howa and elsewhere in the countryside, she made mats to sell and kept the income for herself. Like Miriam, she enjoyed smoke baths and hennaing herself, and had the time to pursue these activities, which were geared to maintaining an active sex life as much as being a pleasurable way for women to spend time in some solitude or to socialize with friends.

Her husband seemed to have attained a cushion of support for them by working abroad for two years between 1987 and 1989. He spent a year in Iraq and another in Saudi Arabia working in construction and retail. Omer was there with his friend Mustafa, Muna's maternal uncle. By the time of my visit, Muna's cousin Ismail was counting on Omer's position at the tax department to help him get a job there as well. Ismail saw the family connection as a means of accessible wasta, and he wanted secure employment so that he could marry Mustafa's daughter. This web of relationships suggests the close weave of social networks in the area, even on the rare occasions such as this, when people married outside of their families and the village. At the same time, the nature and form of these relationships reveal the ways that geographical extension was anchored close to home while simultaneously enabling the tight weave that sustained it to persist in altered local circumstances.

While Muna had not traveled particularly far from the village—like almost all young women in Howa the farthest she had gone was to the nearby towns of Sennar, Dinder, and Suki, a radius of about forty kilometers from home—she had been somewhat cosmopolitanized: first by having moved away from Howa, even if to a village much like it, but also through hearing about her husband's travels and the experiences of her two elder brothers, one a truck assistant and seasonal farmer and the other a teacher now back in Howa. Living away from Howa meant that Muna had a greater level of mobility than most young women in the village. She would travel back with her children now and again to visit her family, and living that much closer to Dinder town, she also went there on her own without difficulty. Nevertheless, Muna, like

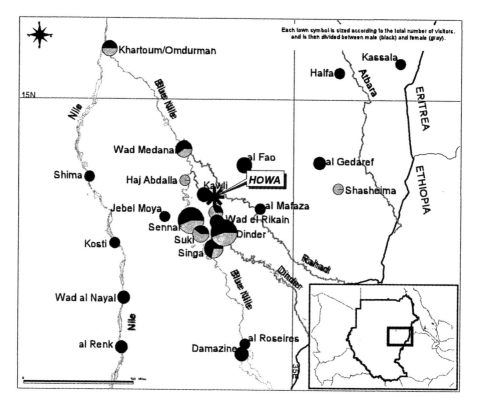

Figure 33. Young people's journeys: as of 1995, the sixteen surviving young people with whom I had originally worked had collectively traveled widely throughout central Sudan. Not unexpectedly, the young men had traveled further and more frequently than the women. Most of their journeys were in search of employment. These travels represented a sea change in the everyday life and expectations of young people in Howa and were a major precipitant of the rural cosmopolitanism that percolated in Howa by the mid-1990s. Each town symbol here is sized according to the total number of visitors, and is then divided between male (black) and female (gray).

most young women in Howa, still had much in common with women of their mother's generation.

Muna's liminal outlook was reflected in her desires for her children. She wanted them to be educated in school, but unlike Miriam, she also wanted them to know how to do the tasks associated with a rural life. She made a point of saying that she had taught her children those things she had learned during her own childhood. In our discussions, she mentioned that mothers like herself had a perspective on bringing up children that was different from the prevailing wisdom when she had been a child. She said that young mothers talked, played, joked, and laughed with their children much more than mothers had done in the past. When I suggested that her mother had done that with her, she insisted that it was different now because there was more openness between parents and children. To illustrate that there were now no barriers preventing children from communicating with their parents, she noted that her children were able to tell her things about their aspirations, even as simple as wanting to be like her when they grew up. She said they told her they wanted to have smoke baths and henna as she did, and maintained that she would have never been able to tell her mother the same. While I could accept that a shift in parenting practices had taken place, and Muna, like Miriam, had embraced ideas she considered more forward looking and modern than their mothers had, I balked at her suggestion that children now were "devils," while in her day they had been "easy" and "obedient." I had known this mom as a child, and while I would not have called her a "devil," she certainly had been no angel. Nevertheless, it was interesting to hear explicitly new norms for child rearing being expressed, just as it had been to hear Miriam's desire for effective and safe birth control. Both reflected a new kind of self-awareness, agency, and reflexivity than I'd heard previously, which marked the (re)production of new values and new kinds of subjects. As Muna put it,

> People here have changed for the better. They are becoming more sophisticated, civilized, and educated. They have new hopes. In the past they weren't quite polished. Just like "arabs" (nomads). Now people understand things more, they're more sophisticated. Before you'd just sit in the hosh. You wouldn't want to go out or do anything. That was women's lot. Now you feel that you would like to meet with people most of the time. You feel eager to talk with them, to see this one and that. You even go seek them out for a visit or a chat. But in the past women just stayed inside. Now I go visit people to talk.

Figure 34. Angels, devils, remembered childhoods: as a mom, Muna tried to convince me that—unlike her children—she had always been a well-behaved child. My memory (and photographic evidence) suggested otherwise. The mischief of memory is intergenerational. Many fathers took pleasure in tales of how, as children, they played while tending their families' flocks, while insisting that their sons never engaged in such antics.

If married women were a sort of vanguard of altered consumption practices, unmarried and divorced women were enacting new subjectivities in the realms of work outside the home. Suad, another of the girls with whom I had worked, had had a more difficult adulthood than Muna or Sofia. She had been married briefly, had had no children, and was now divorced. Like virtually all divorced women in Howa, Suad was back living with her family. She contributed to their household in various ways, including doing domestic chores such as cooking, cleaning, laundry, and fetching water, although the latter, along with collecting wood, generally was done by her never-married younger sister, Baha. Suad earned money by making mats, embroidering sheets, tablecloths, and napkins, and working during the harvest picking cotton and pulling groundnuts. Her father was still a tenant but his eyesight was failing, and the bulk of the work was done by his sons, one who was working as a truck loader during the dry season and the other who was still a student. A third son, a high school graduate, worked as an inspector in the government-run Asalaya sugar factory along the White Nile. All of the women in the family—Suad, her mother, and her sister— were piece workers during the harvest period.

Suad's means of income reveal certain features of the local political economy. Her participation in the harvest was in keeping with the gender division of agricultural labor that had long obtained in Howa, as in much of northern Sudan. Men, assisted by children, did the clearing, planting, and weeding, and harvested crops that had to be cut, such as sorghum and other grains, while women and children, mostly girls, worked the harvest, picking cotton, pulling groundnuts, and harvesting vegetables and legumes. Young married women rarely participated in any of these tasks because of the customs of seclusion that were followed in Howa. The preference was for "brides" and as far as possible all married women under thirty-five or so to stay within the hosh of their extended family—natal and affinal—during daylight hours, except to get water nearby, visit relatives, attend social functions, and seek medical attention. While certain parts of seclusion began gradually upon puberty, and marriage often followed within a few years, many never-married girls and young women, as well as divorced women without children such as Suad, worked alongside their mothers and older female relatives in the fields during the harvest or collected firewood in the vicinity. The abstract rules of purdah were fairly loose in Howa and economic necessity often bent them still further. Because Suad had greater spatial autonomy than many other young women, she was able to use more of the knowledge she had acquired as a child.

Suad drew not only on her knowledge of agriculture and local environmental resources, but also on what she had learned as an adolescent participating in the social extension classes offered to women through the project. It turns out that these classes taught women marketable skills in previously unfamiliar crafts. While plaiting grass and palm prayer and sitting mats was common among women in Howa, embroidery was fairly new. Suad had learned embroidery and other needle crafts from the "women guides" who had been sent to the village under the aegis of the agricultural project in the early 1980s. At the time I naively thought of the extension program craft classes as some sort of "ladies auxiliary" activity, a sweetener to the literacy classes offered. But their intent, as I quickly realized on my return, was to teach women skills that enabled them to contribute to their households' earnings with the sale of handicrafts. This intent, I recalled, had been made quite explicit when the classes were introduced, but somehow I had ignored this. My scripting of it as auxiliary felt all the more misguided when I returned to find that the skills acquired in the social extension classes actually did enable some women, including Suad, to maintain an autonomous source of funds under the radically changing economic conditions brought about by the very project offering the classes. The classes at once anticipated and helped propel the turn toward a more all-encompassing cash economy. By teaching marketable skills that were traditionally gendered feminine, the intent of the "women guides" was to encourage and enable women to contribute to household earnings without substantially altering the existing gendered division of labor.

Reframings

The unfolding of these young people's fates suggests the indeterminacy and unevenness of capitalism's peculiar embrace of the village. Their stories reveal the ways that the encroachment of the broader economy underscored previous inequalities but erased others, all the while producing an uneven landscape of production and reproduction where yet new inequalities were created as old socioeconomic patterns were reworked. Having and successfully holding onto a tenancy seemed crucial to the economic fates of most of the families, notwithstanding all of the upheavals associated with the project over the years. Of course, holding onto a tenancy successfully over a number of extremely difficult years itself required some measure of economic resources, such as animal wealth, other kinds of investments, economically active children, as well as a fair degree of luck and savvy.

Nevertheless, none of their fortunes could be simply attributed to any one thing—least of all anything that might be cast as an "entrepreneurial spirit." Members of virtually all the households with whom I worked were entrepreneurial and resourceful, but that spirit did not necessarily forestall economic ruin or guarantee success. Part of the equation went all the way back to what resources a family had when the village was first incorporated in the Suki Project. Quite a few had been tenants in private pump schemes along the Blue Nile, for instance, and this seemed to stand them in better stead as farm tenants in the Suki Project, while others owned sizeable herds that protected them against agricultural failure and economic crisis. But apart from these fairly obvious things, there were more arbitrary contingencies at work. The location of a household's tenancy within the agricultural project, for instance, could have a significant bearing on yields—some fields never received adequate water while others were routinely flooded—and over the years the effects of this situation were compounded. Of course, those with advantageous locations did not necessarily chalk up their success to that. Neither did they see others' failures as stemming perhaps from their poorly situated fields or from some other contingent circumstance.

The mystifications of capitalism are among its earliest crops, and in Howa it was no different. People in Howa, especially those who benefited and profited from the economic and other changes associated with the project, tended to attribute their success to their own "hard work" and ability. The implication—sometimes stated—was that those who failed to thrive within this new production landscape did so because they lacked skill, ability, or diligence. While naturally these qualities were not uniformly distributed, it was clear that even within the small group with whom I worked, success or failure was not simply an artifact of their possession. What became clear in retrospect was that household diversification—a sort of "flexible specialization"—was crucial to economic survival and well-being, whatever the socioeconomic level. The generation coming of age in the 1980s and 1990s (among them the young people with whom I had worked) was often at the heart of this diversification. The ways they negotiated the economic landscape produced under conditions beyond their control required, by 1995, an insistently further reach, both in geographic and individual terms, to make any difference at all. Even then, under the desperate political-economic conditions that obtained in Sudan at that time, most households and individuals worked harder and wider just to stay in place.

"Just staying in place," of course, involved not only new forms and geographies of production, but also the (re)formulations of subjectivity that are the grist of social reproduction. Women figured centrally in these material social practices, which collapse distinctions between public and private realms. When I interviewed the now grown girls, they tended to answer my questions concerning their work by saying initially that they did not work, because (apart from Layla) they were not engaged in steady remunerative labor. Like many homemakers in the industrialized north, the women did not construct the tasks of social reproduction as work. Of course when I started listing the chores of everyday life, they all chimed in about the extent and nature of their participation in these chores, acknowledging that they were indeed work. But the construction was symptomatic. In the course of the interviews, and even more so in listening to them repeatedly as I have been writing, I found myself getting annoyed, first at the narrow purview of most of the young women's focus, and then at myself for finding their responses boring or their lives less interesting to report than the men's.

A lot of what I found boring was the insistent focus of the young women on the domestic sphere, as if the larger world did not matter. When I asked how life in the village had changed, they almost uniformly told me what had changed for them personally, with little attention to broader cultural, political, economic, or environmental issues. Almost everyone, men and women, described various physical changes in the village and its environs—more houses, new water pumps, fewer trees—but the women tended to filter broader changes through the sieve of their own experience. Muna, who was recounting all the ways life had changed for the better, barely skipped a beat when I mentioned that a lot of people had told me they faced economic hardship. Yes, she agreed, but then noted that impoverishment was a problem "in their families, but not the village." Yet this sort of response may be the trick of capitalism, rather than necessarily the result of having a narrow or personalized vision of change. Indeed, Muna's statement mirrored one by her grandfather years earlier when he suggested that people who had not done well with the project had only themselves to blame. Still, something else was going on apart from a justification of economic differentiation and the individualization of social problems. Women's lives had *not* changed as much as men's had.

Women coming of age in the 1990s were by and large staying in Howa and pursuing lives not wildly unlike their mothers'. A small number had moved to Dinder or other nearby towns and a few to other villages in the vicinity. But whether in Howa or a short way away, young women from the village were for the most part homemakers rearing several children while living among their husbands' families. Like their mothers, they took care of their children, prepared food, cooked, cleaned, laundered, ironed, tended guests, and on occasion fetched water. As before, the women's intersections with the ever-broadening cash economy were several. Those who were married negotiated with their husbands for small amounts of cash to pay for daily provisions like coffee, tea, and onions. While men went themselves to purchase many of their household necessities, they and their wives also sent their children or nieces and nephews to local shops to purchase supplies as needed. Most women, including those with whom I worked, produced goods for the market. In addition to the needlework learned through the social extension program, or sometimes from mothers or older sisters, they wove grass and palm mats for sale in towns. As was the case for their mothers, the money earned was theirs to spend, and not for household maintenance, which was still considered a man's responsibility. In impoverished or female-headed households, women's earnings provided more of a mainstay of support, of course. Before marriage and after the prime child-bearing years, women also earned money during the harvest when they picked cotton, pulled groundnuts, and harvested vegetables, some of which, such as beans and okra, were considered women's crops.

If this relationship with money was perhaps more extensive than it had been in earlier periods, its contours were not that different from what had come before. Nevertheless the relations and practices of social reproduction were changing as "money increasingly became the community." Women's negotiations of new consumption patterns, of differentiation, of the horizons of their children's employment, began to alter their subjectivities, to change the work of social reproduction, and to produce other kinds of subjects. These material social practices of their everyday lives (re)made the social relations of their households and extended families, but also the village itself. If this stability was purchased through the geographic and educational extensions I have been discussing, it also made the forays of that extensivity—largely by men—possible. The gradual creep of the new and the possible took hold and was performed not just in the routine tasks of everyday life, but in the quiet, the playful, the slip.

Women's leisure time, such as it was with children always nearby and the time-consuming work of processing food and cooking three meals a day over a three-stone fire, was spent talking with one another over late-morning coffee or late-afternoon tea. These conversations—which filled the time after meals were prepared, eaten, and cleaned up after, or while women were engaged in tasks such as laundering or mat-making—were often intermeshed with the tossing of cowrie shells, which certain women read for the others, telling fortunes, illuminating problems, prying apart relationships, and drawing various issues out in the air, opening new terrains for conversation. These were also occasions for gossip, advice, and stories. Such stories and exchanges charted, produced, reworked, and translated the world, fusing and infusing worlds of the past, present, and future; the distant and proximate; the imagined, remembered, and wished for. These "worldings" did not so much stage a parallel universe to the men's comings and goings, but created a simultaneous one that infused and was infused by them. They were as vital a part of reproducing Howa at the end of the millennium as the men's journeys were. If the physical world of men's work in Howa had expanded dramatically over the past decade, this extension was reflected and seeded in a reframing of the world that I am calling rural cosmopolitanism. It came in many forms, and was sown in many places. One languid afternoon, the matriarch of the family with whom I lived told us of her remarkable journey to Mecca:

> Nafissa, who was well into her sixties, had never been further than the regional towns before she and her youngest son made the Hajj in the early 1990s.[14] Always a wonderful storyteller, Nafissa told tales of Mecca that were as mesmerizing as her stories of Howa during her childhood. The utter strangeness of air travel was made manifest in her hands. She lavished detail on the shape of the seats and the comfort of their cushioning—making me see them through her desert eyes and feel them as a body accustomed to sitting hunched forward on a plain rope bed might. No detail escaped her; the rows of paired seats, the curvature of the walls, the oddity of seatbelts, the plastic in the windows, and the coolness of the conditioned air were rendered gloriously as providing the greatest of comforts. The gravitational force of taking off exhilarated her, and the nature of the receding ground was described vividly, her excited delight in the ascent and the miniaturization of the world still palpable. And then there was the service. While as Nafissa aged she garnered considerable attention and assistance from the members of her large extended family, she was also someone whose entire existence had been enmeshed in caring for others, especially after her only daughter died in 1981, leaving seven children in greater need of her care. She absolutely basked in the utterly unanticipated service she received from the flight attendants, and marveled at the compartmentalized food and perhaps most astonishing, clean cool water in "a paper."

Since that day, I have found "water in a paper" pretty marvelous myself. It reenacts the rush when something in the taken-for-granted world is ratcheted out of whack. Turning the very notion of "travel as metaphor" on its head, Nafissa's storytelling was able to make my familiar strange and to "other world" air travel. At the same time, her airplane stories made the strange familiar to her family and friends with the same gusto

Figure 35. Nafissa, a grandmother many times over, never sat in a chair with a back. Such chairs, of vinyl strung over metal, were rare and implicitly reserved for men. Her ease, like almost everyone's, was found on a rope or leather strung bed. She found the airplane seats on her Hajj flights amazingly comfortable.

as the stories of her childhood made the trampling of elephants and the calls of nearby wild animals so vivid that her grandchildren momentarily would be afraid to go out in the fields, even though the animals were long gone.

After writing this I realized that Hajj stories are a genre of oral narrative unto themselves. This is not surprising, given that the Hajj stages an encounter between so many rural people and modernity, including unfamiliar technologies, urban life, varied forms of wealth, and engagements with people from all over the world in a foreign country (see Cooper 1999). At the same time "grandmother tales" are central to *hajwa*, a varied genre in Sudan that includes folk tales, songs, riddles, and stories that convey customs, beliefs, values, social histories, environmental knowledge, cautionary tales, and a wealth of encounters with the novel, the strange, and the possible. Nafissa's stories of past, present, and future worlds, which held everyone in thrall whatever their topic, were of a piece with all those stories—stories told lying down under the stars, over sweet coffee or milky tea, in mid-laundry, walking to the fields, whiling away the sweatiest part of midday, preparing *kisra*, engaging children. I told my share—of washing machines and satellites, of my family and friends, of snow, wooden houses, universities and elevators, of wounded popes and presidents, of air travel, time zones, dogs, and how much our cows weighed. The rush of tales—everyone's—at once domesticated novel horizons and experiences and let people imagine themselves in their possibilities or in the eventualities of their collapse.

8. The Strange Familiar

If you have a pen like that, you eat. If you have an ax, you don't.
　　　　　　　　　　　　　　　　　　　—Zeineb Dafalla

Endurance of Rural Life

The perseverance of Howa's rural assemblage may be counted as a victory in the small wars of attrition that proletarianization sparks. Local residents were not driven from the countryside in the numbers witnessed in other places experiencing similar political-economic and political-ecological disruptions of enduring (but not unchanging) social relations of production and reproduction. The seismic displacements I had imagined and predicted after my earlier field research mercifully had not occurred. Nevertheless, some of the familiar had been rendered strange and some of the hitherto strange had grown increasingly familiar. The sociospatial form in which people in Howa were able to continue their work there was not what it once had been, but neither was it utterly new. Nor was it "residual" in the stilted and teleological framework associated with theories of articulated modes of production. Its endurance and evolving contours reflected and revealed the vitality of the material social practices of people in Howa, among them the young people with whom I worked, as they confronted—and created—conditions of existence that sometimes sent them reeling, but which were often unremarkable, if difficult. But it was the spatiality of these practices that was vital to the continued durability of the patterns and processes of production that had long prevailed in Howa. Making ends meet in Howa was increasingly built on an exploded geography of everyday life. And this "reworlding" was one of the most amazing stories of all.

Time-Space Expansion

This exploded geography, which I call "time-space expansion" (*pace* David Harvey [1989]), existed with and enabled a particular reformulation of the local. It was also reflected in and propelled by a rejigging of people's understandings of themselves and the world that I call rural cosmopolitanism. Harvey suggests that one of the signal effects of contemporary capitalism is "time-space compression" brought about by productions of space and technological changes that make it possible for communication to be further flung and cheapened, so that "the time horizons" of decision making shrink, while the effects of these decisions ricochet across an ever widening and differentiated space (147). While from the perspective of transnational capitalists and those living directly in their midst the world may indeed be shrinking, on the grounds of places like Howa—ever more marooned by these processes—it seemed to be getting bigger all the time. The two processes are of a piece. The sorts of transnational investments and disinvestments associated with time-space compression are, of course, part of what spurred the reordering of the social relations of production and reproduction in Howa. Modest versions of the advances in communications that foster time-space compression in the global north likewise facilitate a broader reach for many of Howa's residents in the search for work and income. But beyond this parallel, if wide gauge, experience of enhanced mobility, time-space compression and expansion are more profoundly intertwined.

Time-space expansion is the local fallout of time-space compression at a higher scale. If at the global and supranational scales capital, information, people, and things are moving faster and with greater intensity, the wake this motion creates across scale has required, as much as produced, expanded grounds of production and reproduction in Howa. People in Howa were able to continue to live in the village and work some combination of agriculture, animal husbandry, and forestry *only* by drawing on a terrain *1,600 times larger* than what had sufficed for these activities only ten years earlier.[1] And this spatial strategy only allowed them to stay in place, both literally and figuratively. Given the nature and costs of displacement—from home or secure and familiar work—just staying in place was an achievement.

The expanded field of everyday life was witnessed, then, in the performance of "old" economic activities, such as grazing, charcoal production, and agriculture in new, broader, and more distant terrains; in newer modes of economic engagement, such as petty trading and casual day labor that brought villagers to nearby towns; and in more enduring activities that took place elsewhere, including entrepreneurial ventures or regular service, clerical, and industrial employment. While these expanded terrains of work and everyday life were of course the result of improvements in communication and transportation, and so were associated with the "annihilation of space by time," the notion of compression obscures not only the nature and lived experience of the spatiality of everyday life in Howa, but the double displacement that gave it its character. If one of the hallmarks of people's spatial experience by 1995 was its extensivity but continued rootedness in Howa, the other was that Howa itself was simultaneously becoming more distant from the centers of finance capital and the enhanced capacities of communication associated with them. In other words, time-space expansion is a way of theorizing first, the expanded field within which people engaged in the material social practices of production and social reproduction, and second, the growing distance of places like Howa, and Sudan more broadly, from global centers whose concentration and interconnections have been intensified through the practices and processes associated with time-space compression. A third aspect of this shift is that, thanks to time-space compression, people in Howa were much more aware of being marooned in this reconfigured global space than they had been in earlier periods, and the greater awareness of what is to be had not only increased desire, but made not having more apparent and painful than before. Thus there is a contradictory dialectic to the relationship between time-space compression and expansion in that the compression, which heightens the connections between various centers in noncontiguous space (what Michel-Rolph Trouillot [1996] calls "fragmented globality"), makes exclusion from this globality much more apparent to those it renders "outside," while at the same time it necessitates the expansion as a means of staying afloat in those ignored and excluded places.

Africa, and Sudan in particular, have not simply been "redlined" or written off as locations for serious capital investment, but they have suffered steep withdrawals of finance capital and direct investment in production and infrastructure on top of more than two decades of structural adjustment. Far from experiencing time-space compression, Sudan appeared to be hurtling further and further from most centers of power and capital, and Howa even more so.[2] In part because of Sudan's pariah status in the west thanks to its brutal and intractable civil war, but also because of Sudan's enduring (in many ways internationally imposed and reinforced) poverty, the distance between people in Howa and those in the global north or in other sites of cultural production (with the possible exception of those in Arab nations) grew in the last decades of the twentieth century. This distance was all the more apparent due to the sensation of "compression" elsewhere, but also because of historical and geographical circumstances in Sudan. Since 1956 the direct hand of colonialism was of course gone from Sudan, but that welcome absence was not filled by a marked increase of autonomous political-economic and cultural interaction with former colonial powers on anything approximating fair or equal footing, as Africa's redlining and the vicissitudes of years of structural adjustment policy made clear daily. To use Tim Brennan's (1997) compelling construction, the "shadow" of colonialism seemed to foreclose just as much as its direct "penetration" had, but without the minimal attention that a penetrating power might pay to a territorialized workforce. This, of course, is not to venerate colonialism in any way, but only to mark the sobering fact that its formal demise has not been as liberating or fruitful as imagined in Sudan or elsewhere. Capitalism's wily ability to recreate itself continually in the face of all manner of crises is mirrored (and abetted) by imperialism's equally stunning resilience.

Under contemporary conditions of "globalization," places like Howa remained "disconnected" from both hegemonic cultural forms and the possibilities associated with enhanced communication technologies, while their populations were, at best, forced to scramble to survive on the detritus of increasingly globalized finance and production capital, and, at worst, jettisoned entirely.[3] To the extent that that scrambling was eased it was because of (slender) connections to several Arab countries and a sense of solidarity with Islamic institutions and organizations. These, of course, were unavailable to the similarly "marooned" villages in southern Sudan, whose situations, in any event, were made far worse by the war. Of course, the local population was not powerless in the face of these circumstances, nor did they see themselves in such stark world historical terms (who does?). They were, as ever, struggling not only to get by, but to produce viable worlds for themselves and their families to inhabit, which of course they did, as I hope the previous chapter made clear. It is these contradictory worlds, which were simultaneously fragile and suffused with possibilities, that I want to explore.

I have suggested that time-space expansion is one of the key means through which people in Howa made their lives workable. But the boundaries of this reformulated geography were not infinitely expandable. The local and expanded fields of everyday life were bound to one another in a tense, contradictory, and delicate relationship. There were several aspects to this expanded field and its localizations. Among them were the expanded geography of sustenance and labor; the expanded culture of education; the expanded reach of the monetization of everyday life and with it broadened consumption practices; and the articulations between local Sufism and Islam, both in terms of the fundamentalism of the Sudanese state and the upheavals in Islam transnationally following the oil shocks of the 1970s. These "expansions" had intertwined and overlapped with one another and with the phenomena of "rural cosmopolitanism" I found in Howa by the mid-1990s. Rural cosmopolitanism was in many ways how both time-space compression and expansion came home to roost.

The three iterations of time-space expansion that I will look at are the expanded field of work and its propping up of what I will gloss as "rural life"; the heightened monetization of local social life in the crosshairs of unabating national debt and inflation; and the expanded culture of education and its effects on the landscape of Howa and the prospects of its residents. The three are interlinked, were associated with variants of what I am calling rural cosmopolitanism, and gave form to the reworked geography of everyday life, whose broadened compass enabled Howa's survival. Yet if the distinctly spatial strategies that people in Howa adopted by 1995 permitted the endurance of village life, the whole thing was hinged precariously on a set of social relations whose contradictions threatened to grow increasingly taut as time went by.

Rural Cosmopolitanism

Expanded Field of Work

The expanded geographies of sustenance and labor both enabled people to continue working largely as previous generations had and transformed the very grounds of that work. One of the seeds of Howa's burgeoning cosmopolitanism was men's travels. Yet it was these same travels that, somewhat paradoxically, sustained rural life. Men, whose different domestic responsibilities from women freed—and more and more frequently required—them to travel, increasingly worked in nearby towns and rural areas, in urban centers further afield, and more recently, in other countries. This travel, which was both necessary to, and the result of, the continuation of familiar agricultural livelihood strategies in Howa, also marked the cutting edge of new forms of production and earning there. As recently as twenty years earlier, it was rare for men in Howa to have been to Khartoum or any place further than the regional market towns, except under unusual circumstances. Not two decades before that, most of what infrequent trips there were to Dinder town (about twenty-five kilometers away) were made by camel. Yet by 1995, leaving Howa in search of work or business had become routine, and several young men virtually commuted to Dinder.

While it is common for rural people to seek work in towns when their home grounds have been undermined or disturbed by political-economic or political-ecological circumstances, or for them to stay in place and struggle along to make something out of so much less, it is less common to find people managing to do their old work with roughly similar returns by broadening its spatial compass. Yet what I found in Howa on my return was that even those who continued to cultivate, herd, and produce charcoal—to say nothing of those who took on new forms of work—did so in an ever-expanding field. The political-ecological conditions proximate to the village mandated this expansion of the terrain of traditional work practices. The compass of work was extraordinary. Charcoal was produced and marketed from forests more than two hundred kilometers away, either near al-Renk on the White Nile or al-Damazin on the Blue Nile; animals were grazed in distant pastures, some more than a hundred kilometers away, with pastoralist relatives, family members, or hired herders, who took flocks away to graze for weeks at a time; and young men worked as agricultural laborers or tenants in areas fifty or more kilometers distant. In other words, through a spatial strategy of extension, the familiar mix of agriculture, animal husbandry, and forestry that had been the mainstay of Howa since its settlement in the 1870s continued to sustain its population in the 1990s, albeit with obvious and probably fast approaching limits on the practical range of such "extensification." In this way and not coincidentally, time-space expansion offered a direct counterpoint to the "throw away values, lifestyles, stable relationships, and attachments to things, buildings, places, people, and received ways of doing and being" that David Harvey associates with contemporary time-space compression (1989, 286). It is not that residents were not "adaptable" to the new and "volatile" circumstances in which they found themselves, but that their adaptability reconfigured space more than their relations to "received ways of doing and being" (see Harvey 1989, 286–87).

Nevertheless, bigger changes were afoot. A growing number of young men in Howa, particularly those with little education and no access to a farm tenancy or other land, worked as day laborers in the regional towns of Dinder and Sennar. These men, who essentially commuted from Howa several times a week, worked most commonly loading trucks in these market towns. Despite their removal from the troika of agriculture, animal husbandry, and forestry, many of these young men participated in the ever-reliable charcoal trade and still worked some of the rainy season as casual agricultural laborers or assisting in their families' tenancies. Thus they straddled the realms of work traditional to Howa *and* those associated with the towns, often across quite truncated intervals (see Berry 1993, 62–63, on "straddling" realms of work as a strategy for ensuring economic security). By the mid-1990s, however, more and more men were either lengthening the interval at one or the other employment activity or dropping this pattern of straddled employment altogether. Men continued to work seasonally, but often stayed more permanently at various jobs in regional towns and urban areas further away, including the capital cities of Khartoum and Omdurman. Finally, a small but growing number of men from Howa had worked, were working, or were seeking work in the Gulf States, Saudi Arabia, Iraq, or Libya. They often emigrated illegally and spent two or more years working abroad, most commonly in service jobs. Leaving during the Hajj period often provided cover for illegal migrations to Saudi Arabia.

While men's activities brought them to new places and put them in contact with a wealth of less familiar practices, women in Howa, including the young women with whom I worked, lived in a highly circumscribed world. Their home ranges—the distances any of them routinely traveled away from home—did not exceed a radius of fifty kilometers, if that. Only one of the seven young women I interviewed—Sofia, who by then lived in Dinder town—had ever been to Khartoum or Omdurman, and this was typical for the village as a whole. Trips abroad, such as Nafissa's pilgrimage, were almost unheard of among women. Moreover, the vast majority of women in Howa were not literate, which limited the sorts and sources of information to which they were privy, although oral recountings such as Nafissa's of her airplane trip suggest how "traditional" forms of exchange carried novel content when local residents were exposed to new experiences and surroundings. This narrowed purview was compounded by the lack of electricity and telecommunications in Howa. Each of these factors hardened the contours of familiarity and kept encounters with difference—particularly among women and children—mediated by others or at somewhat of a remove.

Of course the village was riddled routinely by outside information, such as that brought by men, radios, visitors, or the rare car battery–generated television show, but it does no good to exaggerate or romanticize these flows of information. First, it is a given that no place—however remote, and Howa in the global scheme of things was not that remote—is outside the world of flows or impervious to outside influences, and indeed, even distinguishing what constitutes "outside" information is difficult. Second, the people in Howa, like many northern Sudanese, were descended from, related to, and still identified with pastoralists. Travel and the casual drift of information were integral to their lives and those of their still nomadic relatives,[4] and they did not seem overwhelmed or particularly entranced by new things and experiences. But third, the "world" encountered and assimilated in Howa, especially among women, was still fairly small, and easy romances with hybridity or globality do not alter that. People in Howa, especially women, were, if anything, struggling to be "modern" and partake of the promises of modernity more so than they were interconnected consciously with any sort of globalizing cultural hegemony or the patter of postmodernity (see Mitchell 1997).

While the spatiality of women's everyday lives did not constitute them or others in the village as outside of globalized spaces or "marginalized" in some generic sense,[5] these larger, more urbanized spaces were not the predominant domains that women in Howa negotiated or traveled. They did not seem to experience this situation as a lack. The women with whom I worked were accustomed to their location in various fields of power and meaning wherein their reach and formal influence were limited geographically, economically, culturally, and technologically. This is not to say that they endured "their place" timidly. Indeed, in many ways that was precisely what was being reworked by the effects of time-space expansion. If time-space expansion was embodied in men's travels, its reflection in rural cosmopolitanism equally transformed the terrain of women's lived experiences. The twinned practices and their associated experiences reveal the gendered nature of time-space expansion. For men, time-space expansion involved their own extension in space, but for women it brought about a complementary expansion of their interior world. Women's space, already oriented to the interior (see Boddy 1989), expanded internally—in the cultural forms and practices of social reproduction and in their imagined horizons for their children and the future. The forms of these expansions were key expressions of rural cosmopolitanism. If wanderlust did not figure much in women's aspirations for themselves, it was perhaps because their notion of travel was temporal, rather than spatial. Children were their vehicles to an expanded field, and the generation of young women with whom I worked imagined their children, boys and girls, moving into other kinds of (nonagricultural) work and living further afield in pursuit of these futures. In my earlier interviews, their own mothers had not conveyed such aspirations or altered geographies for them during their childhoods.

As Janice Boddy (1989) and others working in Sudan have found (see Vågenes 1998), the very interiority of women's lives and "place" in the world was understood by them as their particular source of strength. Understanding the house and hosh as the spaces within which they exercised power, the different groups of northern Sudanese women with whom Boddy and Vågenes worked exercised power in these "interior" spaces that was expressed most directly in the material social practices of social reproduction. From this position of power, the women understood themselves as embodying village life and protecting it from external threats that they scripted as a form of disorderliness. Men's more liminal exteriority—their ongoing transactions with "the outside"—enabled them to mediate and filter these influences within the hosh (Boddy 1989, 114–16).

In Howa men often played this mediating role, but the nature of their mediations was shifting in the 1990s as a result of the difficulties posed by the local manifestations of Sudan's deteriorating economy. These difficulties forced growing numbers of residents to seek work elsewhere, at once intensifying the flux in the boundaries of the village and scraping away the material social forms of its boundedness. As a result, the cultural practices of everyday life, within which women figured centrally, were taking on new forms. Not only were there numerous expressions of rural cosmopolitanism in Howa, but one of its aspects was seen in changes to the very spaces within which social reproduction took place. There was a growing number of fired mud-brick houses and more solid brick hosh walls replacing the previously ubiquitous mud-and-dung-houses and grass-enclosed houseyard spaces. These simultaneously solidified the boundaries between interior (private) and exterior (public) spaces in Howa and gave the village a more rectilinear feel. But other key sites of social reproduction had also been altered. The elementary school had grown and been complemented by a secondary school; there was a mud-brick men's "club" offering a battery-powered television that worked on occasion; and a new mosque was under construction that was by far the most impressive and ornate building in Howa, with its second story and sculpted facade. These physical changes in the village landscape conveyed as much as embodied broader social transformations underway there, many of which had to do with distinguishing private and more public realms of social reproduction.

Figure 36. Howa had always had a modest mud house as a mosque. With no minaret and almost everyone conducting their prayers at home, even on Fridays, it was not at all a focal point. By 1995 this elaborate two-story mosque was under construction with funds provided by national and international Islamic organizations.

New Consumption Practices

If men's and others' travels were one route to cosmopolitanism at home, another trajectory was through commodities and altered consumption practices that both reflected and increased the monetization of everyday village life. Like all travelers, men working outside the village brought newfound knowledge home as stories—stories that changed things. They also brought home things: gadgets, clothing, utensils, supplies, and various indulgences. This was nothing new. Urban fashion seepage, influencing both clothing and home decor, had long been a fact of life in Howa, but with more men on the road, fashion seepage and commodification had both intensified. One of the shifts was seen on the borders of women's clothing. The decorative embroidery and crocheting that women had learned in the extension classes years earlier were not just a means of income generation, but were also markers of the infiltration of a new fashion consciousness among many of the younger women in Howa, whose decorated *toubs,* sheets, and crocheted articles represented their embrace of what they saw as a more sophisticated style. These questions of style were mentioned by some of the women in their interviews and are a reminder that the "expanding world" also enters the community through things that are quickly domesticated. Those commodities and cultural practices that filtered through and were embraced most obviously by women in Howa were those that were easily incorporated into the interior spaces that were their domains—their toubs (which Boddy [1989] likens to portable enclosures) and their homes—and were associated especially with the material grounds and practices of reproduction: bed, food, and children. Nevertheless, as my interview with the more urbanized Sofia suggested, the desire for commodities—in her case a Land Cruiser, clothing, and jewelry from the United States—was beginning to exceed the domestic realm for both women and men by 1995.

But what of this? Here, too, the expansion of desire—which I take as a marker of rural cosmopolitanism—was taking place against the backdrop of Sudan's increasing debt and the punishments of structural adjustment, all of which made the expanded field of commodities and the monetization of everyday life fold in on themselves. Consumption has long been a way of incorporating people into the capitalist fold, and certainly the desire for things—new things—appeared to be on the rise during each of my visits to Howa beginning in 1980. But in the dire economic circumstances of 1995, this desire foundered on limits more severe than in other places and times. Indeed, one of the things I initially found amusing in 1995 was that people who had worked abroad brought home electronic equipment, such as videocassette recorders (VCRs) and televisions, as well as pickup trucks, generators, and other "useful" things. I initially misread the electronics as trophy purchases—what else could a VCR be but ostentation in a place without electricity and no prospects for it for a long time to come? But rather than desire folding in on itself as farce, these unopened boxes of equipment were, I came to realize, new-age goats. A perfect "breed" for a devegetated environment, these goats required little care, and, like traditional wealth on the hoof, were available to be sold as the need arose. In other words, one of the key forms of savings and investment

Figure 37. Old goat/new goat: Wealth has long been stored on the hoof in Howa, but by the 1990s, as grazing lands disappeared and people increasingly worked outside of Sudan, a new form of congealed wealth appeared—the VCR and other electronic products. In a village without electricity (and few prospects for it in the coming years) I had imagined VCRs as trophy purchases or wild indulgences in optimism, but I quickly realized that they were a new kind of goat, ready to sell as required and far easier to maintain than more fleshy variety.

Why not cash?

historically in Howa was livestock, but with enduring devegetation, especially after the 1983–84 drought/famine, livestock, severely diminished in number, began to be more of a liability or burden than a relatively secure investment. At the same time, as people began to straddle non-rural lives they veered away from pastoralism, while simultaneously encountering a wealth of new products. While most of those who accumulated substantial assets invested them in things like trucks, four-wheel drives, pickups, or small businesses, and some continued to invest in livestock, they and others with smaller sums also invested in particular commodities as a form of congealed savings, much as they might have done with animals. I came to see small "flocks" of VCRs as assets that could be sold piecemeal when the need for cash arose. In the mean time there was always the dream of electricity, and the use of generators (another form of congealed wealth) seemed to loom on the horizon.

Expanded Culture of Education

Things smuggle ideas and vice versa. I have noted that women's (and others') illiteracy was world-shrinking in its manifestations. In 1995 people in Howa were rescripting their relationships in and to their everyday world, and embracing education in ways they had not in earlier times. This embrace, which began more than a decade earlier, was another manifestation of rural cosmopolitanism in Howa. As they adopted an expanding culture of education, people began to identify themselves as distinct from "arabs" in the sense of nomadic rubes. While this new and shifting identity was invoked in a variety of situations, it was most commonly expressed concerning education. The new regard for education was witnessed, among other things, in the establishment of a lower secondary school, the hiring of several women teachers, and the construction of a higher secondary school. Whereas in 1981 42 percent of the boys and 4 percent of the girls between the ages of seven and twelve attended school in Howa, not fifteen years later, 69 percent of the boys and 43 percent of the girls in this age group attended. These increases, of 75 percent and 1,000 percent respectively, were nothing short of astonishing. While my 1981 survey found that only 1.6 percent of those ever enrolled in school reached grade twelve, by 1995, 9.3 percent had and with the higher secondary school soon to be completed, this figure was likely to soar. More than simply an increase in urban influence on people in Howa, the heightened attention to education reflected their conscious and quite active scramble to keep up with changes they experienced as limiting their own and particularly their children's horizons.

The new views on education had begun to take root during the 1980s, with the first generation to come of age under the agricultural project. The shifting attitudes toward education were enmeshed with shifting ideas about girls' schooling. Not only had there been the 1983 self-help effort to install standpipes throughout the village, in part to free girls to attend school, but within a few years, women teachers were engaged to teach girls in classes separate from boys. The availability of single-sex education broke down yet another barrier to girls' education frequently expressed by parents in the earlier phase of the study. All of these activities—which were village initiatives—point clearly to the vigorousness and creativity of the local population in the face of change. Development was not simply washing over them, leaving them dispossessed and ragged, but was a set of material social practices with which they contended in specific material ways that suggested great flexibility. Nevertheless, even educated, their children faced enormous obstacles, as the cases of Ismail and Rashid so poignantly reveal.

Contradictions of Time-Space Expansion

Each of these instances and expressions of time-space expansion in Howa—which were connected to work, exchange, and cultural production (notably formal education)— embodied a contradiction that may over time continue to be held in tension or may become untenable and disrupt hitherto viable strategies for coping with the political-economic and political-ecological problems that were part of Howa's encounter with "development." The expanded geography of everyday life for those still based in Howa, for instance, was likely to reach serious physical limits in the next few years. For one, Howa was not the only village in the area that had expanded its reach in agriculture, animal husbandry, and most importantly, forestry. With growing numbers of disenfranchised young men in the region and a dearth of nonagricultural employment, even the expanded field of work would be under pressure within a few years without serious reforestation efforts or more effective range management. Beyond that, the edges of this expanded field already stretched more than two hundred kilometers by 1995, and it was not clear how much further the field of work could extend without breaking the tether back to Howa. It seemed likely that men would begin to replace space with time and simply move further afield on a more permanent basis, substantially and perhaps irrevocably altering the social relations of production and reproduction in Howa, whether or not women migrated as well.

The second expression of time-space expansion intertwined with rural cosmopolitanism was manifest in the expanded monetization of the local economy. Monetization worked hand-in-hand with commodification. In the 1980s the commodification of formerly free or commonly held goods was well under way and an increasing number and variety of fairly modest consumer goods were making their appearance in the local market. By 1995, the painful effects of money's erosive effects were apparent everywhere in Howa. Money had "become the community" (see Marx 1973, 225). The commodification of milk was perhaps the most painful marker of this shift, wherein the metric of social life became disembodied abstracted exchange, rather than a weave of more diverse and multiply connected social interactions and mutual obligations. As Nowal lamented, "Now even your *uncle* will sell his vegetables to you." But another potent marker was the decline and alteration, though not the disappearance, of nefir—communal work parties that would work in the field of a relative or neighbor one day in exchange for a meal or the meat shared from a *karama* along with the promise that a similar group would work in their fields another day. With money increasingly mediating all exchanges, karamas had all but disappeared in Howa, except for ceremonial occasions. And what people called nefirs in the 1990s were usually paid work parties, rather than mutual exchanges of labor and food. While milk was the last to go, it was commodified completely after the devastation of local herds in the famine-drought of the mid-1980s.

This is obviously an old story, as capitalism's sweeping-up of communities worldwide into the pleasures and dangers of abstract exchange attests. Historically it has been a progressive story for the most part, even if it has been painful for the many who most immediately experience its disjunctures. But, as Marx made clear, money's ascendence presupposes the full development of exchange values and therefore a corresponding organization of society, and it is here that the contradiction lies. One of the aspects of underdevelopment rooted in early colonialism but continuing through the structural adjustment programs of the late twentieth century was that the sources of finance and production capital, and the decisions made about it, were almost entirely extralocal. Having the control of capital centered so far away placed serious impediments on the full development of exchange values. The social infrastructure and capital to purchase the newly available labor power simply were not there. Money dissolved the community without sponging it up elsewhere, leaving only an ooze of raw desire and increasing frustration. By 1995 the ooze was rising as the village was woven tighter to capitalist exchange while its relative distance from the centers of capital grew. The quickening outmigration of young men from the village in search of work and their desperate consideration of the People's Defense Forces as a way out were only the first fruits of the jarring contradictions brought about by money becoming the community under conditions of "time-space expansion." Stockpiles of VCRs would not protect Howa's struggling households for long.

Finally, the expanding culture of education, which was a means of reworking the displacements experienced by many in the village because of the agricultural project and its broader entailments, had its contradictions as well. The shift within a single generation from one poorly attended six-year primary school staffed solely by men to an eight-year primary-secondary school with a staff of men and women, and eventually a new higher secondary school for local students, attests to the increasing value the local population placed on education. The idea that education might provide a way for children to succeed in a rapidly changing world was widely shared in Howa. Everyone I interviewed in 1995 mentioned the importance of their children's education, not just for the children's sakes, but so that Sudan might benefit from and "make use of" them. Young people who stayed in school dreamed of attending universities or working at jobs that were considered less taxing, what they referred to as "easy," "soft," or the ultimate, "cold" work. But their expanding horizons and ambitions were foreshortened almost as fast as they came into being by Sudan's political-economic circumstances. The efforts of village residents to alter their circumstances through education were working. The generation coming of age in Howa in 1995 was markedly different from their predecessors and were likely to be just the leading edge of a more educated rural population. Yet it was not clear where they might go in Sudan with their educations and this was its signal contradiction. Even among the first group of educated young men like Rashid and Ismail, most found themselves at odds: unable to find work that compensated adequately to support themselves or start a family, and falling frustratingly short of the broadened expectations encouraged by schooling.

The expansion of rural education has long been associated with broadened ambitions and the acceleration of outmigration, but here again those who might leave had few places to go. Rashid could barely survive on his salary from the Ministry of Culture and could not afford to continue at Khartoum University, despite earning a coveted place there, while Ismail's compensation as a teacher in a nearby village, even with a bonus from the village, was not enough to allow him to get married, even after several years of saving. Expansion continually rubbed against disintegration. Formal education was widely seen as key to expanding the known and knowable world and thus was given increasing pride of place in the village. Yet as this occurred, Howa appeared to be producing a population that was no longer at home in its world, but was not welcomed by any other, despite the country's obvious need for them and the local population's sense that they were producing something of value.

As the international managers of capital debilitated Sudan with structural adjustment programs and the withdrawal of most investment and assistance funds, and the government of Sudan wasted its resouces—human, "natural," and financial—on an unending war, the people of Howa kept themselves afloat by reworking the spaces of their everyday labor, expanding the opportunities for their children's schooling, and entering into an increasing number of social exchanges, of both production and consumption, inflected by capitalism. In framing these relationships as "time-space expansion," I have tried to point to the exacerbation and intensification of capitalism's uneven development and its explicit spatialization. Global capitalism is not homogenous capitalism, and its weak and receding outposts like Sudan seem all the more so as global networks increase and intensify elsewhere. Much of what is understood as globalization is imperialism by another (anemic and depoliticized) name, and part of the way places like Sudan are treated by those in charge of global capitalism is of a piece with the "revanchism" that characterized many urban areas of the global north at the same time (see Smith 1996). Sudan's treatment at the hands of the IMF or the United States government, for instance, was punishing and mean-spirited; the 1998 bombing of a pharmaceutical plant in Khartoum North as revenge for the bombings of U.S. embassies elsewhere in Africa was perhaps the most outrageous expression of pervasive revanchism. The destruction revealed not just a spirit of revenge, but the ignorant tendency of the United States to construct all African countries as interchangeably problematic.[6] As the latter suggests, part of the problem was less vengefulness than utter apathy and indifference: a cordoning off of Sudan and places like it as somehow not worth the effort, the investment, or the incorporation into globalized capitalism, except as abject debtors.

In the face of these conditions, coupled with the civil war, Sudan disintegrated as it struggled to "develop." In rural areas like Howa people scratched out a living from the available stuff of their everyday life. Their resilience was staggering. But it was constantly used against them, and it was not clear how long the contradictions embedded in time-space expansion and the various forms of rural cosmopolitanism I witnessed could be sustained before they, too, came apart. Neither was it clear what the shape of that coming apart would be—would Howa become increasingly depopulated as its younger residents departed in larger numbers for urban areas nationally and abroad? Would the money earned overseas be reinvested—as some of it had been already by 1995—in rural industries, such as seed oil and flour mills, brickworks, or food-processing plants? Would men continue to migrate—further and for longer periods—but women stay in the village and take over agricultural production? Would the government's fundamentalism undermine or chafe against local followings of Sufi paths to such an extent that it sowed the seeds of its undoing? These scenarios are just a few of the more imaginable possibilities for the future, and suggest the open-endedness and vitality of the ways that people produce the historical geographies of their everyday lives, even in the face of rather harsh changes.

It would be too easy to chalk up these responses as "resistance," as has become all too fashionable in contemporary analyses of social change. Such one-dimensional categorizations occlude the variety of responses to the shifts underway and their different effects on the material social life of Howa. These variations must be more carefully pulled apart so that their forms and broader consequences not only are better understood, but might be connected to other settings and material social practices. The next chapter takes up these concerns with reference to both New York and Howa. In both settings, as the troubling but redolent new rubs up against the disrupted old, it becomes all the more urgent to find (and create) the conditions in which old and new can be reworked to take on new (and even fantastic) meaning (see Benjamin 1978b). It happens all the time.

9. Negotiating the Recent Future

In the dark times will there be singing? Yes, there will be singing about the dark times.
—Berthold Brecht, 1936

If the shape and circumstances of the strange familiar associated with time-space expansion and rural cosmopolitanism call forth and reflect material social practices that interlace old with new and enable people to get by, reconfigure themselves, and reimagine if not reconstruct their worlds, then it is important to look at how these practices intersect with and alter the arc of capitalism's engagements with their community. In this vein I don't have anything that compelling or comforting to say. The process of transformation is uneven, slippery, and shot through with as many derailments as possibilities. The cultural forms and practices of everyday life in Howa described throughout this work give a sense of the constancy of reinvention and promise at least the possibility of interruption, but they also make clear that "interruption" was not on everybody's agenda. Indeed, many could not scramble up capitalism's arc fast enough. If time-space expansion expressed a kind of resilient accommodation to altered circumstances of production, it also—in certain of the permutations of rural cosmopolitanism—reworked the texture of everyday life in Howa in ways both problematic and fortifying. For instance, while the insistent commodification of social life was one of the most problematic entailments of rural cosmopolitanism, the broad expansion of education was one of its more stabilizing aspects. But given the political-economic circumstances of Sudan at century's end, the dissolving effects of the former appeared stronger than the reconstructive effects of the latter.

There were, of course, some creative acts of consumption that helped to mitigate some of the ways that money "dissolved the community," as Marx would have it, but

239

I do not want to exaggerate these. Consumption is at best a partial means of incorporation into the social relations of production and reproduction associated with capitalism, and alternative practices of consumption are not resistance. A VCR is not a goat, and deploying it as such is not so much resistance as a survival tactic. A VCR that is a goat is not a VCR. And while acquiring a VCR is not evidence of globalism triumphant or incorporation into consumerist bliss, neither is it a form of heady reinscription or recuperative self-construction. Celebrating such acts as resistance is a cheap thrill, usually voyeuristic, a balm to critics in the global north that may be no less exoticizing than earlier renditions of Orientalism and constructions of the self-possessed "other." Likewise, the other side of rural cosmopolitanism, witnessed in an energetic broadening of local access to education, did not constitute resistance either, however much it represented a formidable reworking in less than a generation of local material social practices and shared beliefs. Such creative reworkings of everyday life, whether through inventive consumption practices, altered work geographies, new commitments to schooling, or otherwise, suggest great possibilities for the reformulation and fluid stability of social life in the face of great changes (see Boddy 1989). In their very depth, breadth, and specificity these reworkings also suggest what might be gained by unpacking not only the categories of people's responses to capitalism's uneven developments, but the category of "resistance" as well.

The people with whom I worked, in Sudan as much as in New York over a period of some fifteen years, did what they could and a lot of it was creative. They worked the borders and confluences between their old ways of life and the new, but their acts—big and small—were almost all contradictory, with immense potential fallout. Just as many people in Howa straddled the old and new realms of work and social practice routinely in their everyday lives, there was an "interior" and perhaps less visible form of straddling reflected and projected in the practices of social reproduction. In these practices—wherein people produced and reproduced themselves as social, political, and economic subjects—the edges of the contradictions and fault lines created between and exceeding these two realms were engaged as a matter of course: obviously a tricky business. And while, as I have argued about children's playful practices of social reproduction, there lies coiled in these reproductive engagements (with their excesses and slippages) the mimetic possibility that something new will be created that is discontinuous, the social power to make good on such "flashes" of possibility and insight as Benjamin (1978a) would have it, is generally expended otherwise. In these scrambling engagements they were not alone. Indeed, all over the world "development" driven by global economic restructuring produces similar contradictions between resources available and possibilities engendered, leaving people scrambling to make themselves viable in the face of the relentless, uneven development that is the hallmark of capitalism (see Smith 1984).

These circumstances call for and create a range of responses. Just as there are ties and similarities in the local forms and manifestations of global economic processes in Harlem and Howa, so, too, are there in the nature, style, and effects of the responses at both sites. These fall loosely into three fluid and overlapping categories that I've come to call the 3 Rs: *resilience, reworking,* and *resistance,* each carried out at a range of scales and by a number of differently situated actors. These practices work off of and in response to one another, as much as in reaction to the changes imposed and engendered by "global economic restructuring" and its local manifestations. Throughout the 1990s but starting earlier, the conditions produced by "restructuring" were associated with, and commonly expressed a fourth "R": *revanchism,* the vengeful social, cultural, and political-economic policies and practices of ruling groups and nations who in the 1960s and 1970s faced a number of "others" who questioned and sometimes threatened their power and authority (Smith 1996). The widespread anticolonial and anti-imperial wars and rebellions, broad-based civil rights movements, women's liberation struggles, student uprisings and other social movements—only just curbed, disciplined, and in some instances broken by the late 1970s—seem to have provoked a shaken international ruling class and its allies to unleash a range of vengeful strategies, such as "welfare reform" in the global north and structural adjustment in the south, not only to reinstate their power and the proper order of things, but to discipline those who fought or fight for it to be otherwise. The discursive and material fallout of these strategies— inflicted for over two decades transnationally and across geographic scale—has been devastating for untold numbers of communities and debilitating to many forms and practices of organizing and response.

By the 1990s the ethos of revanchism was widely taken for granted in both the global north and south, so much so that its neoliberal essence was distilled in the unapologetic hegemonic claim that "there is no alternative." The broad practices associated with revanchism created many of the conditions of everyday life in Howa and Harlem at the time of my work and they continue to be the ether of everyday life today. While money often "becomes the community" because its power is seductive, the means through which capitalism and ongoing capital accumulation have been insinuated in the routine practices of everyday life historically have been disruptive if not violent. When they take root, capitalist developments engender an array of responses ranging from unalloyed acceptance through almost magical reconfiguration to outright resistance. Given the social and other costs of neoliberal capitalism conveyed by global economic restructuring and various "development" initiatives, I have focused not only on how people make sense of these processes and incorporate themselves into their fold and vice versa, but have also looked intently for instances of their resistance to these processes. Indeed, that was my initial motivation for focusing this project on children's learning and their use of knowledge. But these oppositional responses, as I have suggested, can be unpacked to refine conceptualizations of resistance that have come to seem too broad and too uncomplicated to be of much use in the face of the erosive conditions associated with contemporary capitalism.

My intent in teasing apart different categories of response and effects, then, is to diffuse, if not burst, the romance with "resistance" (see Abu-Lughod 1990; Moore 1998). Not that I hadn't fallen for it myself. Like many critical scholars of my generation, my project was driven in part by a search for resistance to the depredations of capitalism and other sources of exploitation and oppression among the "subaltern" peoples with whom I worked. Like many of my Marxist, feminist, and poststructuralist colleagues—especially those working in cultural studies—I was intent on finding instances of what Gramsci called "independent initiative" in the welter of wildly uneven and rapidly shifting fields of power. Locating and working through the oppositional possibilities for these "independent" and even counterhegemonic actions and practices and the multiple arenas of their effect, work in this vein succeeded in simultaneously complicating capitalism and making it less monolithic and all-embracing. Not incidentally, these endeavors helped to loosen the depressing yoke of the Frankfurt School's reading of cultural practice and the possibilities of opposition. But it is time for a corrective. We cannot understand oppositional practice or its possible effects if we consider every autonomous act to be an instance of resistance.

Those who champion all such acts as resistance, most notably James Scott (1985; 1990), but also Paul Willis (1977), Aihwa Ong (1987), and Jean Comaroff (1985), to name a few of the most considered, tout their counterhegemonic nature and note that they draw on and fuel an oppositional consciousness checked by realistic appraisals of success of more grandiose or visible gestures. I agree. Indeed, I consider my work akin to theirs. But finding "resistance" in each discursive or other cultural practice that might be construed as autonomous has become an industry, especially since Foucault, in which it seems an independent reading—of anything—is enough to challenge prevailing matrices of power and dominance (see, e.g., Ortner [1995] and Brown [1996], who both raise similar concerns). When almost anything can be constructed as an "oppositional practice," I find myself bored and unconvinced. In what ways do such practices respond effectively to the massive disruptions in productions of space, nature, and social life that pierce people's everyday lives in the course of capitalist development? When it comes down to it, feeling good, even when it is called something as fancy as "reconstituting one's subjectivity in the face of power," through all manner of discursive practices and independent readings is simply not enough to transform the social relations of oppression and exploitation that are the cornerstone of so many people's daily lives. Autonomous, even "counterhegemonic" agency is just the beginning. Yet it is so often presented as an end.

To make more fruitful ends of such beginnings, I have tried to delineate between the admittedly overlapping material social practices that are loosely considered "resistance" to distinguish those whose primary effect is autonomous initiative, recuperation, or *resilience;* those that are attempts to *rework* oppressive and unequal circumstances; and those that are intended to *resist,* subvert, or disrupt these conditions of exploitation and oppression. The way I have laid out these overlapping responses is obviously toward stronger forms of oppositional practice, but they are interwoven and mutually sustaining. Acts of resilience and instances of reworking often provide the groundwork for stronger responses, but so, too, can an organized oppositional movement, for instance, create the political space or opportunity for various autonomous initiatives—the restorative and strengthening acts of what I am calling resilience. While each of these responses is necessarily situated, it is possible, and indeed important, to build upon and across them so as to oppose the mutable structures and forces of oppression and exploitation in ways that both transcend the particularities of location and "jump" geographic scale, both of which are necessary to match the fluidity and reach of globalized capitalism. As capitalist production relations and various discursive practices from the global emporia alter the grounds of everyday life, the practices associated with resilience, reworking, and resistance make their struggles harder, their progress uneven, and their outcomes indeterminate. If capitalism is the death wish of modernity, these practices are the best hope we have that it won't succeed.

One Plus Three Rs: Revanchism, Resilience, Reworking, Resistance

Revanchism

At the end of the twentieth century, globalized capitalism was producing effects in multiple and quite different locales that were particularly venal. Income and wealth disparities between rich and poor—whether countries or classes within countries—were enormous and growing, even as "safety nets" at all levels were shrunk, retracted, or shredded. While the northern industrialized countries experienced the longest period of sustained growth in their economies since World War II and unprecedented numbers of people became investors in domestic and international stock markets, there was simultaneously a diminution of real wages transnationally, widespread defunding of state welfare programs, a reduction in "development assistance," and an unwillingness to forgive national debts in the so-called third world (except insofar as it bailed out investment banks in the global north), coupled with structural adjustment measures both newly imposed and enduring to help secure repayment. These strategies support and are undergirded by a set of social, cultural, and political-economic practices that Neil Smith (1996) has dubbed "revanchism." Revanchism encompasses the material social practices of meanness and revenge. Smith (1996, 211) suggests that revanchism is the manifestation of class, gender, sexuality, race, and nation terror experienced by those in power who sense they are facing an "other" out of (their) control. These sentiments were at a fever pitch by the late 1980s, when the children with whom I worked were coming of age. In the United States, for instance, revanchism was witnessed in, among other things, the vicious antiurbanism that demonizes powerless people in ways that foster and feed a diabolical assortment of social and economic practices arrayed against them. The discursive production of cities as out of control, "gang youth" as unredeemably violent, or teen mothers as delinquent reprobates,[1] for instance, enables as much as it springs from a set of social policies that support policing over parks, prisons over schools, and strict limits on welfare rather than an expansion of child-care and jobs programs.

But revanchism is apparent in the global south as well. Not only are third world countries and their leaders routinely demonized in the press and government circles of the north, but these areas have been systematically constructed as scenes of unremitting violence, disaster, and despair that seem to spring from a kind of naturalized inadequacy of both blood and soil. This discourse—from which the history of north-south exploitation and oppression has been omitted—enables the north to enforce a range of destructive policies, including punishing "structural adjustments" that drive up prices for staple foods, callous population programs predicated on the notion that famine is a natural rather than a social problem, exclusionary immigration policies, and, in Africa at least, a retreat from any sort of investment, including the extension of credit, repeating on a larger scale the urban policy of "redlining," which has been responsible for destroying so much of the property and infrastructure of the neighborhoods where it has been practiced.

While the visceral nastiness of revanchism may be rooted in the terror it expresses and the revenge it exacts around destabilized privileged identities, it is important to remember that along with its explicit ties to pernicious and problematic social policy and practice, revanchism is a recuperative response on the part of dominant groups to the enactments of resistance and other forms of opposition by oppressed peoples. Indeed, the notion of revanchism first evolved in the wake of the Paris Commune and exacted its toll on those who had struggled to realign privilege and redistribute wealth. Recalling this reminds one of the deep and enduring links between the material social practices of variously situated actors operating on a range of levels transnationally, and in their sometimes wild oscillations, the possibilities for recalibrating power relations. As this dialectical framing might suggest, revanchism has provoked some responses of its own, and these can be traced in multiple locales, as well as historically.

Resilience

In Howa, as in Harlem, just getting by in the face of the oppressive and increasingly mean-spirited circumstances I am associating with revanchism was often predicated on innumerable small acts of *resilience,* which themselves fostered yet other ways to get by each day. As I argued in part 1, the changes associated with the Suki Project so altered the grounds and relations of production in Howa that rural impoverishment and socioeconomic differentiation increased, new kinds of work cropped up in the local environment, the domestic division of labor was altered, and notions of "qualification" were recast, precipitating as much as precipitated by signs of widespread deskilling. Each of these processes was fraught; the practices they called forth negotiated the very edges of the contradictions between new and old formulations of everyday life that I traced above. Under these circumstances, young men coming of age were increasingly likely to migrate in search of work, leaving women and older men in charge of household production and reproduction. At the same time it seemed likely that this situation would lead to declining agricultural productivity and further deskilling in the area. And this was precisely the terrain of the resilience I found in Howa. One of the profound shifts I witnessed over the two decades I have been going to Howa was the time-space expansion discussed in the previous chapter. This extraordinary reformulation of the very grounds and compass of everyday life was a remarkable instance of "resilience" on the part of the people in Howa. In and of itself, the spatial extension of older economic practices precluded the intense rural depopulation and deskilling that so commonly have followed in the wake of agricultural "development" projects elsewhere.

Not only did time-space expansion enable people to remain rooted in Howa while acquiring experience and employment elsewhere, thereby keeping the village more or less afloat, but it drew on the broad sweep of shared local knowledge. People's dormant knowledge was brought into play with the return of rain-fed sorghum cultivation, the expansion of riverbank gardens, and the growing participation of local men in sesame cultivation elsewhere. But dormant knowledge—both idiosyncratic and shared— might be tapped in other ways as well, such as among women left to tend the fields in their husbands' and brothers' absences. While the agricultural learning of girls was neither as systematic nor as detailed as that of their brothers, women who found themselves having to cultivate, such as Sami's mother, would be able to draw on the considerable environmental knowledge they had gained as children but had not actively used in their adulthoods. These circumstances would no doubt alter the typical practices of female seclusion and might even lead to the development of new divisions of household labor and power, among other eventualities, making clear the multiple valences of power and resistance in everyday life. Whether in the men's negotiations of their new work geographies or women's renewed engagements in agriculture, tapping dormant knowledge was the way that people were inventive in the face of finding themselves constituted as "deskilled" or "unqualified." Time-space expansion provided grounds in which their accumulated knowledge remained relevant.

These practices also reveal the intricate ties between landscape and knowledge. Not only is knowledge embedded in place and practice, but particular landscapes make certain kinds of knowing (and practice) possible (or not). This much may be obvious, but it often goes unrecognized. The loss of forests or the elimination of rain-fed fields, for instance, renders moot many aspects of forestry work and particular cultivation and water management strategies. Without their requisite geography, there is no gum collection, fruit picking, or charcoaling. As landscapes are lost or reconfigured, one of the casualties is a viscerally situated knowledge and the embodied ways of learning and knowing associated with it. But if the loss of specific landscapes results in the loss of particular kinds of knowledge along with the means of its acquisition, the strategies of spatial extension I found in Howa open an arena in which dormant knowledge comes into play. By extending the compass of their everyday lives, people in Howa found ways to recover and reconnect to landscapes wherein their knowledge remained relevant. In enabling the endurance and extension of particular geographies of production and reproduction that helped to sustain the local population, time-space expansion represented a politics of resilience.

Such outcomes are, of course, contradictory. As the members of rural households remade themselves in the face of new circumstances, they also helped to advance and sustain capitalist accumulation elsewhere. Remaining in the countryside, they subsidized the family wage and enabled the emigration of lone male workers, who then could work for longer hours and lower wages. If their acts of resilience sustained them, they also supported the general trajectory of the developments that necessitated these acts in the first place. This double edge notwithstanding, resilient acts are self-reinforcing, and inasmuch as they are fortifying, they offer the possibility of fostering something beyond recuperation. In many historical geographies, recuperation itself is an achievement.

Small acts of resilience also helped sustain people in the New York communities where I worked. I think of the block in East Harlem where I did some research in the early 1990s. One man, a former heroin addict who had lost his wife to HIV-AIDS, was bringing up their two adolescent sons alone, working in a needle-exchange program doing HIV-AIDS education, and managing to be part of the web of care that characterized and held together the block. His neighbor, one of the key weavers of this web, was an Oberlin graduate with four children between the ages of two and seventeen. She worked in the day-care center on their corner and was a powerful neighborhood activist. Her power worked "up" and "down"—she took on the schools, the landlords, the city, and the drug dealers with zest and without intimidation. At the same time she treated the block like an extension of her household (where she kept careful tabs of what was going on), offering guidance, encouragement, and reprobation in measured turns. She exercised enormous influence that was rooted in local affinities and was deployed both through establishing and nurturing matrices of care and mutual aid, and through more conscious forms of care taking and opposition. The social relations of care and concern that Jane Jacobs (1961) marveled at among the petit bourgeoisie, professional, and working-class neighbors on the Lower West Side of Manhattan in the late 1950s were in abundance on this long disinvested but deeply resilient East Harlem block.

The everyday acts of neighboring—the mutual relations of care giving, the sights on the future that help both young and old people keep hope, stay alive, and even thrive—that I identified on one block in East Harlem and in my work with a group of parents, teachers, and school administrators in Central Harlem determined to rehabilitate two schoolyards in their neighborhood (Katz and Hart 1990) were myriad, as they often are in poor communities (see, e.g., Hernandez 2000; Williams and Kornblum 1994; Sachs 1993; Stack 1975). These practices, along with other cultural forms and practices such as gang membership, community self-help organizations, and religious affiliations, not only enable material and spiritual survival, but also the recuperation of dignity in a range of small transactions (see Vigil 2002; Bourgois 1995). This dignity, what James Scott (1985) calls the "minimal cultural decencies that serve to define what full citizenship in local society means," enables people to get by, to enter reciprocal relations, and to shore up their resources, all of which are crucial underpinnings of projects to rework or resist the oppressive circumstances that call them forth. Nevertheless, it was sometimes staggering how people's resilience got used against them in the small and large indignities of everyday life in revanchist New York and structurally adjusted Sudan.

Reworking

As the name suggests, the practices of *reworking* are those that alter the conditions of people's existence to enable more workable lives and create more viable terrains of practice (see Pred and Watts 1992). Reworking deploys a different kind of consciousness than the acts of resilience that sustain people facing difficult circumstances or the rituals that authors such as the Comaroffs (1993, xvi) suggest help to "make and remake social facts and collective identities." Projects of reworking tend to be driven by explicit recognition of problematic conditions and to offer focused, often pragmatic, responses to them. They generally operate on the same plane and scale that a problem is experienced, although their effects—both in terms of practical outcomes and for producing consciousness—are often much broader. Projects of reworking are enfolded into hegemonic social relations because rather than attempt to undo these relations or call them into question, they attempt to recalibrate power relations and/or redistribute resources. This is not to say that those engaged in the politics of reworking accept or support the hegemony of the ruling classes and dominant social groups, but that in undertaking such politics, their interests are not so much in challenging hegemonic power as in attempting to undermine its inequities on the very grounds on which they are cast. There are two interconnected aspects to the material social practices of reworking: one is associated with redirecting and in some cases reconstituting available resources, and the other is associated with people's retooling themselves as political subjects and social actors.

In my New York research I found both sorts of reworking going on. Among the instances of reworking focused on reconstituting available resources were projects addressing children's everyday lives in the public environment. Responding to the racialized class pattern of disinvestments in public space (discussed in chapter 6) were, first, an association of parents and school staff at a pair of community schools in Harlem that had organized to transform the barren and poorly maintained concrete spaces that passed for schoolyards, and, second, and in a similar vein, the participants in a community effort inspired and led by Dr. Barbara Barlow of Harlem Hospital that was dedicated to the reconstruction of children's outdoor play environments in central Harlem. Both groups were committed to reducing childhood injury and, not incidently, to providing safe and attractive neighborhood spaces. A third instance of reworking, which focused on people remaking themselves as social actors, was seen in the ongoing work of the Center for Popular Education in East Harlem. The Center was documented at the behest of community-based researchers participating in the CAMEO Project, in which I was also a participant during the early 1990s. The scope of the project was described by its acronym, CAMEO, which stood for the Community Autobiography Memory Ethnography Organization. As the name suggests, the project was an attempt by community residents and people from the university to fuse research, documentation, and organizing to produce broad grounds of action through, among other things, collectively defining what was to be done and then doing it.

The schoolyards project was initiated by a parent-school playground committee with whom a group of us at the City University of New York collaborated with. The parent-school group was responding to the complete dearth of safe and interesting play environments in south-central Harlem, where a pair of community schools were located. They were especially concerned about the lack of early childhood play spaces. Given that community schools were mandated by New York State to serve the broader needs of the community—through such features as longer hours, after-school and adult programs, and extracurricular cultural and social events—the two adjoining elementary schools selected by the parent committee seemed an ideal place to develop age-appropriate play environments that also included gardens, quiet places for local residents to sit, and recreation facilities for children, teens, and others in the neighborhood to use during nonschool hours. To this end, we developed a successful funding proposal and a participatory design process for the complete renovation of the two schoolyards so that they might serve as open space resources for the neighborhood in general and provide more stimulating and safer play environments for the schools' children.

The school district's playground committee; an additional group of parents; the schools' staff, administration, and students; and on occasion, groups made up of tenants, merchants, residents, and others from the surrounding neighborhood worked together for over five years against the vicissitudes of Board of Education neglect, neighborhood disinvestment, and a recalcitrant director of School Facilities (who played an incessant game of bait and switch with the schools over funding the schoolyards) to see to it that the changes we envisioned together for those schoolyards were realized on the ground. The struggle, hampered by the relative undervaluation of play environments by various public authorities and would-be funders and by the financial constraints facing the city and private foundations following the 1987 stock market crash, was an example of *reworking* an interlocking set of problematic and even debilitating circumstances, including neighborhood disinvestment, the deterioration of public school environments, and the widespread unease parents felt about risks to their children in the public environment, to create new built environments that better served the needs expressed by neighborhood groups and individuals. After more than five years of planning, pleading, and plowing ahead, construction finally began on the schoolyards in 1995. But it took several more years and one of the principals managing to secure $300,000 from the Manhattan borough president's discretionary budget for it to happen, and even then, only part of the design was ever realized. The playgrounds project initiated by the Harlem Hospital's Injury Prevention Project, discussed in chapter 6, was likewise part of an effort to rework the conditions that compromise poor children's play safety and access to the outdoor environment.

Other projects of reworking that cropped up in my New York work included the everyday practices of *El Centro por Educación Popular* in East Harlem, which was documented in video by the CAMEO project. The Center for Popular Education was established by a group of women to provide bilingual education—especially Freire-inspired literacy education—to members of the East Harlem community (see Benmayor et al. 1992). Their self-help initiative was a powerful force in reworking some of the structural and individual obstacles faced by women and others in East Harlem attempting to secure jobs, housing, schooling, welfare, legal residency, and other rights, goods, and services. *El Centro* has also been a site for organizing more collective responses to the conditions that create and sustain these obstacles in the first place. Of course, in choosing to document the work of el Centro, CAMEO participants— residents of East Harlem themselves—were building on and supporting its work assisting people to redress the structural inequalities and injustices they faced. Like- wise, community-based CAMEO participants elected to produce a visual and oral history of a moribund but once thriving neighborhood market, *la marqueta.* At first I thought this video project was a bit of salvage nostalgia, but I quickly realized that it, too, was part of a politics of reworking. In tracing the hulk of what was in a damp cav- ernous space under the railroad tracks, the video producers were projecting a vision of what could be—a thriving market at the core of their community. As this endeavor reminds, projects of reworking were not so much counterhegemonic as they were a recognition of what was privileged by hegemonic social forces. While these projects can be seen as attempts to partake in or join that privileged space more fully, there are mimetic possibilities as well. Tracing and retracing the spaces of the old, somewhat ghostly neighborhood market, the producers hailed viewers to experience its evacuated ghostliness, to imagine it as again bustling, to visit and walk it, and in their reflective/prospective presence to remake a thriving neighborhood market.

Projects of reworking were likewise common in Howa. Steeling children for the future was at the core of various determined projects of reworking there. If seeking new forms and sources of knowledge, as well as conserving and finding new grounds for the expression of existing skills and knowledge, were among the responses to deskilling that might be considered resilient, the more conscious, collective, and active response of expanded schooling was a strategy of reworking. In Howa during the 1980s schooling functioned more as a luxury than as a necessity for the local population. While most of the village population professed to value formal education, it remained that less than a quarter of all primary school–age children attended the school that had been there since the beginning of the 1960s.[2] This gap, I have suggested, was rooted in the (appar- ently intensifying) need for children's labor across a range of productive and reproduc- tive activities in Howa; in the widely held view that formal schooling was unnecessary, and possibly counterproductive, for success in farming and animal husbandry; and in the waning but widespread perspective that education for girls—especially alongside boys—was inappropriate, and for the most part unnecessary.

The first boys to come of age after the agricultural project was established found work without too much trouble in the offices, workshops, and fields of the agricul- tural project. By the 1980s, within a dozen years of the establishment of the project, however, this local labor market was pretty much saturated, and subsequent genera- tions of young men were having a harder time finding steady work anywhere in the vicinity of Howa. As the proportion of landless households relative to those with ten- ancies grew, older patterns of learning and training no longer seemed so appropriate.

Traditional assurances about the future were coming undone by the 1980s and the local population seemed well aware of it. In 1983–84, village leaders took action through two related strategies: providing standpipes throughout the village that, intentionally or not, freed children's, especially girls,' labor time (see Mascarenhas 1977), and planning the construction of a girls' school.

I took these acts by Howa's village council to be direct responses to conditions they understood to be rendering their children "deskilled" in the face of the future. Of course, this act of reformulation was predicated on many more things than just stemming the tide of deskilling. One of the most important of these was the growing influence of the discursive practices associated with the elites in Wad Tuk Tuk, the project headquarters a few kilometers away, who had been in their midst for over a decade, and with whom Howa's leaders had fairly steady contact. Not only did this population routinely educate their children and seem better off for it, but there was a girls' primary and middle school in the town that by its very existence demonstrated a viable way around the reticence concerning coeducation. A small number of families in Howa sent their daughters to these nearby schools, and within a decade several women teachers were hired to teach in the village so there could be separate classes for girls and boys.

Of course, as the original school in Howa attested, it is one thing to have a school and another to have high levels of school enrollment and attendance. But by the mid-1980s parents were clearly starting to weigh the benefits of having their children's assistance against what this might bode for the children's futures. At some level the village council was responding to these concerns in joining their provision of standpipes and classrooms for girls. These shifts suggest, though I have no hard data to support it, that by the mid-1980s school enrollment in Howa was starting to increase. Given the ongoing pressures of local impoverishment at that time, this trend was sure to be uneven, slow to evolve, and dicey in its course. But by the time I returned in 1995, enrollments were not only far higher than they had been previously, but the relatively large number of students who had either graduated or were in secondary school indicated a definite sea change regarding education during a relatively brief time. The pace and scope of reworking were clear in my survey responses. While in 1981 only 23 percent of village children seven to twelve years old were in school, by 1995, 56 percent were enrolled. There was a 75 percent increase in the enrollments of boys this age and a staggering 1000 percent leap in girls' enrollment, all in less than fifteen years. Because the expansion of formal education in Howa involved tremendous investments of self-help funds generated from the sale of state-provided sugar in the village cooperative, it intertwined both aspects I have identified as reworking: redirecting available resources as new ones were produced, and reformulating the social agency of young people while revamping what it means to be prepared for the future.

As with the practices associated with resilience, those of reworking, such as increases in formal education, had contradictory outcomes. While it is, of course, true that the forward trajectory of capitalism requires particular forms of training, sorting, and disciplining workers, one would have to be stupefyingly functionalist to argue that

that was all formal education was. Alphabetic and numeric skills are empowering and open new worlds to those who acquire them, but as the testimonials of Ismail and Rashid in chapter 7 made clear, formal education was not necessarily a passport to anything but frustration in Sudan's harrowed economy. While the fluidity and creativity of local projects of reworking were impressive, they could not always match the depths and extent of Sudan's economic stagnation and the drain of its devastating civil war. But there was another side to this, too. Sudan's economic and internal problems intensified international labor migration, particularly among young men, and because of this there were new and growing opportunities for educated women in the civil service and public sector, as well as elsewhere. While most of these positions were filled by urban, educated, middle-class women, it was conceivable that these opportunities might eventually reach places like Howa, drawing its newly educated daughters into social service, education, and health-care employment, as Awatif's father had imagined so many years before. While in the mid-1990s there was not yet a culture of women working outside of their homes in Howa, save the village midwives and teachers, all of whom were from outside, the extent and pace of the shift in attitudes and practices concerning female education in Howa presages just such a transformation. As these shifts and responses might suggest, the politics of reworking were iterative in the face of both the devastating changes in the local and larger economies and their more mundane manifestations (see Katz 2001b).

Equally important, as the work of Paolo Freire and those he has inspired makes clear, acquiring the skills of literacy can be a form of consciousness raising that enables oppressed and exploited populations to harness their insights into the causes of their oppression and build a critical collective response. Certainly that was the case in East Harlem's Center for Popular Education, and similar pedagogic projects were possible in Howa, although that was not the approach of either the schools or the women's literacy classes sponsored by the project. On this frontier, the politics of reworking blends with resistance.

Resistance

If reworking reorders and sometimes undermines the structural constraints that affect everyday life both to make it more livable and to create viable terrains of practice, resistance takes up that terrain with the invocation of an oppositional consciousness. Practices of resistance draw on and produce a critical consciousness to confront and redress historically and geographically specific conditions of oppression and exploitation at various scales. While it was easy to identify numerous instances of resilience and reworking from my work in New York and Howa, discerning resistance was more difficult. Acts of resistance are indeed rarer than the others, given the consciousness-building involved and their explicitly oppositional character.

While the groups and individuals with whom I worked directly in East and Central Harlem were not involved in an explicit politics of resistance when I was working there, the activist group West Harlem Environmental Action (WHE ACT), formed in 1988, was working at about that same time on building a broad but neighborhood-based political movement to oppose environmental racism.[3] Inspired by some of the same issues that drove the people I knew in East and Central Harlem—questions of children's (and others') health and well-being, the provision of safe open space, the neighborhood environment, and most specifically the construction of a huge noxious sewage treatment facility topped with a state-of-the-art park on the Hudson River abutting West Harlem—WHE ACT developed an intricate oppositional politics to redress not only the pollution and aesthetic problems caused by the plant, but to frame these within the broader and at the time still relatively novel framework of environmental racism.

WHE ACT, founded by three West Harlem activists out of a less oppositional coalition against the treatment plant, included many of the same sorts of concerned and active long-term neighborhood residents who were associated with the various activities of resilience and reworking that I documented in East and Central Harlem. But in constituting the North River Sewage Treatment Plant as the latest in a long line of noxious facilities sited in Harlem and thus as the outcome of enduring and structural environmental racism, WHE ACT built a broad oppositional politics that went well beyond the plant (Miller, Hollstein, and Quass 1996). While the group was composed largely of elderly women residents of the neighborhood and explicitly drew on their "local knowledge" to situate their campaign within the dense fabric of community-based politics and resonant issues such as neighborhood well-being and environmental illness, WHE ACT also rallied direct action campaigns, organized and mounted a legal case against the city for the damages caused by the facility, and connected with other organizations working within New York City and beyond on questions of environmental justice (Miller, Hollstein, and Quass 1996).

In their suit against New York City, for instance, WHE ACT collaborated with the powerful Natural Resources Defense Council (NRDC), which in turn secured the pro bono legal representation of a respected law firm to prosecute the case. The case was eventually settled out of court, awarding the West Harlem community a $1.1 million settlement fund to be administered by WHE ACT and NRDC, and through a consent decree empowering WHE ACT to determine whether the actions taken by state and city environmental agencies were adequate to solve the problems caused by the treatment plant, as well as to monitor the flow and capacity of the facility (Miller, Hollstein, and Quass 1996, 81). But the success of WHE ACT's politics of resistance went beyond this breathtaking victory. The organization drew on local gendered notions of "home-place" to encompass the neighborhood and raised various "quality of life" issues to redefine neighborhood politics as resolutely "environmental." At the same time their work across constituencies and concerns made clear that such environmental politics were inseparable from those of social justice (Miller, Hollstein, and Quass 1996).

In Howa there were several apparent avenues of resistance. Many of these, not surprisingly, were concerned directly with the regimes of production and work practices associated with the Suki Project, which had so obviously failed to deliver on its promises to the people of Howa. One of the great expectations of the project—and it is clearly one of the longest lived hallucinatory fantasies of Sudan—was that the local population would become wealthy or at least economically secure from cultivating cotton. Not only did this not come to pass, but the cultivation of cotton was almost uniformly a losing proposition for tenants. The cotton fields elicited all sorts of maverick forms of resistance. One of the most effective was the local predilection to allow and even encourage animals to graze on the ripening cotton. Not only did this act destroy the crop that benefited the project long before the individual tenant made a piaster, but it nourished animals stressed by the deterioration of local pastures brought on by the project itself. Inasmuch as the local population was able to hold onto its animal wealth—such as it was—it was able to retain some measure of economic autonomy from the agricultural project.

These renegade acts were also recuperative, because those who succeeded in fattening their (or even others') animals in their fields seemed to bask in the kind of satisfaction of "getting one over" on a superior. De Certeau (1984) calls such moves "tactics" because they engage in opposition without a space of their own, that is, they encroach upon—in a temporary, often stealthy way—the space of the dominating power in order to recuperate something. Scott (1985) defines all such moves as resistance because they redress—however fleetingly and even covertly—imbalances of power and resources. But I consider the illicit grazing to be resistance because people understood it as a means to redirect the flow of resources to them in a way that deliberately undermined the success of the agricultural project. Indeed, the project not only lost whatever crop was consumed, but incurred additional expenses in patrolling the fields against this form of "theft." Nevertheless, satisfying as it was, letting goats sneak into the cotton fields remains just a "tactic" of resistance. First of all, even thinking of it as "theft" already cedes ground—literally and figuratively—to the state laws and regulations that determine access to land. Prior to the project these were for all intents and purposes of no consequence locally except for the state forest reserves, which were routinely entered "illegally" (see Peluso 1992, 12). Thus the resistance embodied in "poaching" is one that necessarily "insinuates itself into the other's place" (de Certeau 1984, xix). But second, allowing grazing on cotton did not involve building something larger on the subversive consciousness that invoked it. Indeed, the consciousness that inspired illicit crop consumption might have been more resentful and angry—or even just more pragmatic—than "oppositional." And if resistance is to be more durable and broadly effective, something more than anger should drive it: a vision of what else could be.

One of the broader efforts at resistance in Howa that also—and not coincidentally—involved the agricultural project was the successful struggle on the part of the Tenants Union to cultivate their staple food crop, sorghum, on project lands. As was detailed in chapter 3, the price of sorghum had risen astronomically during the first decade of the project. Prevented by the project administration from cultivating sorghum, tenants were doubly hurt by these price increases. They were not only accustomed to the security of cultivating their own *aysh* (the name itself means "life"), but in good years they had the opportunity to store or sell surpluses. If they were scandalized by the gouging prices, so, too, were they frustrated at not being in on the bonanza. Local anger, built on increasing impoverishment, was palpable. Tenants, who generally made their money from groundnut sales, frequently diverted their labor from cotton cultivation to other field activities that would increase their groundnut yields or enhance their animals' well-being. These acts of resistance, like allowing the goats to graze on the cotton, "cheated" the project. But the Tenants Union wanted to recuperate some control over both what was cultivated and how their labor time was spent. To this end, the union organized and lobbied extensively at the Ministry of Agriculture in Khartoum for permission to cultivate sorghum within the project. Just before the start of the planting season in 1981, Suki tenants were granted permission to grow sorghum in a quarter of their ten-acre allotments. The catch, of course, was that the land devoted to sorghum had to be cut from their groundnut, and not their cotton, allocations. The union's success was, typically, double-edged; simultaneously saving tenants money on sorghum as it cut into their profits from groundnuts, it was in every way a "disintegrating development." Nevertheless, at the time of its implementation, the strategy benefited the tenants overall, and seemed to be an important symbolic victory for them as well.

There were other acts against the agricultural project over the years that might be understood as resistance, notably when farmers diverted the irrigation canals to better water or extend their own fields. But these practices took place during the period between the late 1980s and the early 1990s when a series of national governments were vying for and struggling to maintain power. The agricultural sector, at least around Howa, was largely ignored during these struggles, leaving people to fend for themselves. During this period, with little project supervision and few inputs, assistance, or supplies, local farmers returned to cultivating sorghum almost exclusively. But almost by definition, this resilient savvy was not set against any clear authority pressing a particular regime of control in the area, and so was not an instance of resistance. As often as not, the farmers' strategies worked against one another—diverting irrigation water is an obvious case—rather than against the project, the state, or another dominant group in the area. Not having been there during this time, I am reluctant to suggest that these practices were evidence of differentiated forms of resistance so much as they were scrappy acts of resilience that enabled some residents to expand control over what—at least temporarily—were common property resources at others' expense (see Peluso 1992, 16). Given the intensification of already quite steep socioeconomic differentiation in Howa between the mid-1980s and the mid-1990s, and listening to the reports of farmers afterward, it was clear that these local practices of renegade cultivation were more differentiated and unequal than collective.

But these same intervening years had also been associated with the disastrous return of civil war to Sudan, and the circumstances of war had also engendered a political response of resistance. Here the politics of resistance was in a different vein than that associated with the agricultural project and, not surprisingly, the social actors involved were different. Resistance in this instance turned more on questions of social reproduction than on production and thus involved women and those coming of age more directly, though most of this opposition was as yet outside of Howa in 1995. As the discussions in chapter 7 suggested, young men in Howa and elsewhere in Sudan often attempted to evade military service by emigrating to the Gulf States and Saudi Arabia (usually illegally) or keeping themselves outside the disciplinary circuits of the Sudanese state (though this was increasingly difficult). As ever, people in Howa tried to avoid taxation regardless of its association with the war, although they were keenly aware of the connection between their increasing and more vigilantly collected taxes and the war's escalating costs. But in a more concerted effort, women in Sudan were beginning to protest the war directly. Whereas in Howa I found mothers fretting about the war and the possibility that their sons would be drafted (their feelings exacerbated by the inauguration of militia training in the village during the summer of 1995) women in urban areas, where the war's presence had been felt more directly for a much longer time, had begun to take direct action.[4] One of the most poignant forms of resistance was that women had begun to keep their sons from attending their Sudan Certificate Examinations upon completion of secondary school because that was where conscription took place—no diploma, no draft notice. The certificate is necessary for graduates to continue their education or to secure any kind of employment requiring a secondary school education. These mothers were desperate enough to compromise their children's futures so as to possibly save their lives. The mothers' tragic bargains were widely recognized. But in perhaps the most startling development of all, women also took to the streets in protest. Public demonstrations against the National Islamic Front government were extremely risky and rare, and several women were arrested in Khartoum in December 1997 for publicly protesting the war.

The parallel with mothers' protests elsewhere, such as the Asociación Madres de Plaza de Mayo in Argentina, Mothers for Peace in Zagreb, or the international Women Strike for Peace founded in 1961 to protest nuclear testing and in particular its effects on children, should be obvious. But there is also a parallel—though in a different register—with a poignant contradiction at the heart of WHE ACT's protests around the North River Sewage Treatment Plant. In that case, WHE ACT insisted that the city close the large park built atop the facility until its safety could be assured. They argued that the toxic emissions produced by the plant posed unknown hazards to children and others using the park, and insisted on a testing and monitoring program (Miller, Hollstein, and Quass 1996). Their opposition to the park—which cost $128 million to construct—in a neighborhood desperate for open space for children and others to play in shares a common thread with the protests of the mothers in Sudan who kept their sons from graduating. If evidence were needed of the diabolical contradictions and constraints of resistance at the margins, these two cases, both involving quintessential issues of social reproduction, provide it.

In New York, as in Howa, various enactments of resilience, projects of reworking, and, to a lesser extent, acts of resistance were common, staged in moments and over time with repercussions both local and more wide ranging. These practices were overlapping. I have distinguished between them for practical reasons—not to create arbitrary categories of practice, but to better inform praxis. Clearly, much of the area between, and even within, these broad categories is gray but fertile. Children in both settings, for instance, resisted the identifications offered by the larger society by constructing identities outside the normative trajectory. In many cases their elders were approving if not complicit, but in others, children's oppositional subjectivities went against the household grain as well. The cultures of herdboys in Sudan and gang members in the United States both offered "outsider" identifications while providing a strong basis of solidarity and mutual support. I associate these sorts of practices with resilience. But these same social and economic relations also fostered and enabled practices that might skirt, if not undermine, some of the key circuits of capitalism in ways that could be associated with tactics of resistance. Like participation in the underground or informal economies in U.S. cities and elsewhere, some of the practices associated with gang membership or other "outsider" affiliations can siphon off income from so-called legitimate capital accumulation and simultaneously evade taxation.

These actions and their effects raise the question of consciousness in all *its* grayness. While the subversive, undermining, and even resistant practices of "outsider" groups and individuals can and do funnel money away from the circuits of capital accumulation, and may be driven by a consciousness of marginalization, oppression, or exploitation, they do not stand a chance of dismantling or substantially altering the conditions that create and maintain that marginalization, oppression, or exploitation. Indeed that is not their intent. Whatever the problems of traditional Marxist notions of consciousness and ideology, that tradition surely captured the importance of *coming to* consciousness: of being a class (or other kind of group) not simply *in* itself, but *for* itself through a recognition of the social relations of position. In this process of becoming—of consciousness raising—a nondominant group does not simply recognize the conditions and social relations producing them as such, but also the means through which these social relations are obscured or naturalized in their society. With this awareness can come a realization of the need for resistance, for undoing these uneven power relations and undermining the means through which they are set in motion and enforced. Coming to this sort of consciousness calls for something more than sabotage or even subversion and may provoke or release a vision of change, of utterly different social relations. That sort of consciousness can come from any quarter and historically has—the product of much hard work—but is likely to emerge in everyday acts of "resilience" and the processes of "reworking" as much as in the course of more targeted and conscious acts of resistance. If resistance draws on this sort of consciousness to work the difficult line from subversion to transformation, the question becomes how it might be brought to the fore in the course of the sorts of struggles around everyday life that are charted here. This is where the vitality of mimesis comes into play.

Mimesis and the Revolutionary Imagination

The mimetic faculty, I have suggested after Walter Benjamin (1978a), is a means to spark consciousness and provoke an alternative, oppositional, and even revolutionary imagination that can see in the same, something different. Like other thoroughly materialist ways of knowing, the mimetic faculty fuses apprehension with transformation through a visceral connection between knowing and doing. Tapping into or rejuvenating the mimetic faculty, then, can be a means of coming to historical consciousness. Historical consciousness for Marx and others stems from a recognition that what is is the result of a process of historical development, and thus is not immutable. Coming to consciousness at once denaturalizes that which appears given and exposes the enormous work involved in making the world of appearances seem permanent and natural. And so it is with mimesis, wherein that knowledge is bound with the everyday acts of making and remaking social life and things. Of course, the very routine nature of this work (and play) usually obscures this knowledge and its potential "release," as Benjamin might frame it, but it is there. As I argued in the discussion of children's play in chapter 3, immanent in making the everyday world is the knowledge that it *is* made, the tough sedimentations of uneven social relations within which this process occurs notwithstanding. It is on these grounds of embodied seeing, knowing, and doing that I imagine the fission between mimesis and the "three Rs": a fission potentially powerful enough to produce another "R," revolution, or at least a revolutionary imagination.

While it may be a stretch to go from children's play to revolution, I do so in the same spirit that others invoke utopian "spaces of hope" (Harvey 2000). If utopias allow us to imagine a different world, the mimetic faculty can provide the spark to fire its making. Rather than holding up a utopia—a place that is no place—I want to call forth the sort of playful imagination, openness to possibilities, and freshness of energy that we find in children's play, even in the face of limited horizons. This sort of imagination—a potentially revolutionary imagination—is in desperately short supply under the globalized conditions of capitalist production that have been the focus of this book. In the face of the sort of dismalism these conditions provoke, where neoliberal leaders feel emboldened enough to proclaim that "there is no alternative" to capitalism's rapacious trajectory, it becomes crucial to find ways to spark this imagination and then build upon it. If the kind of consciousness to do so can arise in the embodied knowing associated with the mimetic faculty, then, as Benjamin suggests, it may be found coiled within adults.

The knowledge that what is given is always made up and thus could be made different is perhaps unlearned, forgotten, or dulled by routine in most adults, but like the "dormant" environmental knowledge that I found among the now-grown children in Howa, this consciousness is there to be "released" under particular conditions (see

Buck-Morss 1989). These conditions may emerge in the course of endeavors to make something new out of existing conditions that I have associated with resilience, reworking, and resistance. Where scholars like Taussig (1993, 21) probe the mimetic faculty for the sensuous, almost magical, connection between "the body of the perceiver and perceived" as a means to release the power of knowing that the material world is a social product, I am more interested in the ways that consciousness might be "released" in the course of the mundane practices that engulf life's magic. And here the parallels Walter Benjamin saw between development—the coming to adulthood—and history—the making of the present—are instructive. In his writings Benjamin works against the teleological narrative of history as a linear chain of events, concerning himself instead with how history is "shot through" with the present. In interrupting the homogenizing temporal chain to the present, Benjamin "reclaims the debris of history from the matrix of systematicity in which historiography had embedded it" and thus disrupts received understandings of the past (Gregory 1994, 234). Reconceiving history this way, where the past is no longer "a fixed point" to be understood definitively in the present but rather "becomes the dialectical turnabout that inspires an awakened consciousness," enables the present to be understood as a "moment of revolutionary possibility," but only through what Benjamin called a "dialectical image," which draws the fragments of history in a particular direction (Buck-Morss 1989, 338, quoting Benjamin, *Gasemmelte Schriften* 5:490–91). In other words, the present as "now-time" guides the reassemblage of the past so that it is neither "infinite" nor "arbitrary," and its revolutionary possibility turns on this "dialectical image" (Buck-Morss 1989, 339). Likewise, Benjamin reframed child development to retrieve and reimagine what was discarded and "lost along the way" (Buck-Morss 1989, 263). In a direct parallel with his interest in finding the revolutionary present in history, Benjamin was fascinated with the child's consciousness, wherein a visceral "connection between perception and action" was produced and maintained through mimesis. Exhuming and reinvigorating this consciousness, he contended, was key to revolutionary consciousness in adults (Buck-Morss 1989, 263). Perhaps in this light it is not too much to suggest that if Benjamin's dialectical image "reclaims the debris of history" to reassemble its fragments in a new and radically different way, kids' play reclaims the debris of geography to do the same. The children in Howa took its refuse and detritus, literally its dirt, its debris, its shit, and made worlds in which they imagined they had a place.

Making a place for young people in danger of being excessed by the processes of capitalist globalism is not child's play of course, but if it is to be more far-reaching than making do with debris, it will require new sorts of political imaginations. And here I mean the political imagination borne of the mimetic faculty, as well as a political imagination whose geography might match that of capitalist globalism. If, on the one hand, I have traced a line from resilience to resistance, from subversion to transformation, and from mimetic play to a revolutionary imagination, I have also tried to trace a more geographical line that runs from Howa to Harlem and back again. Tracing it "unhides" the dispersed and seemingly discrete consequences of global economic restructuring and reveals some of the potent responses to it across localities.

To build on these dispersed instances of opposition that take place in different registers, lasting for different durations and focusing on different issues, requires the construction of vigorous social movements. While the nature, composition, and practices of such movements are beyond the scope of this book, it seems important to imagine their potential terrain, both literally and metaphorically. In focusing on Sudan with the insistent counterpoint of New York, I have tried to make clear that the increasingly globalized expression of capitalist relations of production, the tenor of neoliberal global economic restructuring, and the broad retreats from the social wage that have been associated with them have common local and regional effects, such as deskilling, community destabilization, and a reordered relationship between production and reproduction. Uncovering these similarities in locations as different as New York and Howa and tracing the connections between them through a "countertopography" suggests the importance of imagining and making change across scale, space, and setting. This countertopography is offered not only to make vivid the particular connections I found, but to inspire political and geographic imaginations vibrant enough to grapple with the myriad ways global capitalism and other large-scale processes ricochet through and between disparate places.

Doing a topographical analysis of Howa and Harlem, for instance, makes sense in a new more vitally spatialized register of the kinds of displacements children can suffer in the course of broad-scale political-economic change. Not only does this kind of analysis expose the simultaneity of particular disruptions associated with globalizing capitalist production—refusing to let geography hide consequences—but in drawing a "contour line" that links the fates of children in rural Sudan and the urban United States it is meant to insist on the connections between North and South, East and West, and to defy the localist and nationalist logics that have become the basis of so much political identification. This effort to reimagine our connections—especially the ones between disenfranchised young people in New York City and rural Sudan—is all the more vital in the wake of September 11, 2001, and the responses to it. Countertopographies can slice through the lethal binaries of "us" and "them," calling forth political projects that confront what it means to live—everywhere—in the shards of capitalist modernity, and make impossible the maneuvers of global capitalism and militarized adventurism that would use those shards as a weapon.

Table A.1. Children's Labor Contribution to the Work of the Village by Task

Activity/Duration	% Accomplished by Children*	Economic Significance
A. AGRICULTURE (May–February)		Central
1. Shelling Groundnuts	90	
2. Clearing	10	
3. Hoeing/Plowing	10	
4. Planting	60	
5. Irrigation	10	
6. Weeding	30	
7. Harvesting	40	
8. Threshing/Winnowing (Groundnuts, Sorghum)	##	
9. Marketing	10	
B. ANIMAL HUSBANDRY (Year-round)		Important
1. Herding (<50% of households)	90	
2. Feeding/Watering (Nursing Mothers, Donkeys, Cows, Fattening)	20	
3. Misc. (Birth Problems, Illnesses, Injuries, Cleaning)	20	
4. Marketing (Occasional)	0	
C. HOUSEHOLD (Year-round)		
1. Food Procurement		
a. Gathering (Seasonal–Sporadic)	90	Limited
b. Hunting (Rare)	20	Marginal
c. Fishing (Rare)	##	Marginal
d. Buying (Errands) (Daily)	70	Central

Table A.1. Children's Labor Contribution to the Work of the Village by Task *(continued)*

Activity/Duration	% Accomplished by Children*	Economic Significance
2. Food Preparation		Central
a. Cleaning (Daily)	20	
b. Pounding		
i. Major (Seasonal–<5 times/year)	10	
ii. Minor (Daily)	20	
c. Grinding (Only When Mill Closed–Rare)	30	
d. Cutting (Daily)	30	
e. Mixing (Daily)	10	
f. Cooking-Including Making Fire (Daily)	20	
g. Serving (Daily)	10	
3. Child Care (Year-round–Daily/Most Households)		Central
a. Feeding	40	
b. Minding	50	
c. Bathing	30	
d. Comforting	40	
e. Disciplining/Mediating Disputes	30	
4. Cleaning (Year-round–Daily)		Central
a. Dishes	30	
b. Sweeping	70	
c. Picking Up/Tidying	30	
5. Laundering/Mending/Sewing (Year-round)		Central
a. Washing (Weekly)	30	
b. Ironing (Weekly)	10	
c. Mending (Sporadic)	10	
d. Sewing New Clothes (Rare)	10	
D. WATER PROVISION (Year-round–Daily)		Central
a. Private	70	
b. Commercial	100	
E. FUEL PROVISION (Year–round)		
a. Firewood Collection (Regular/Not Daily)	60	Central
b. Firewood Chopping (Bi-Weekly to Weekly)	20	Central
c. Charcoal Production (Seasonal–Regular)	10	Important
d. Charcoal Scavenging (Seasonal–Occasional)	70	Marginal
e. Kerosene/Diesel Purchase (Lamps) (Daily)	70	Central

Source: After ECA, 1974 (Table of Women's Labor Contribution Per Task Per Unit of Participation).

* These figures represent my own best *estimates,* and are accurate to within ±20%. They are based on my structured and casual observations throughout the field period of children's work in particular and the work of the village in general.

No estimates.

Table A.2. Summary of Children's Participation in Environmental Work

Activity	Percent Participating at Least Sometimes N=17	Gender	Nature of Children's Contribution	Proportion of Total Effort Undertaken by Children[a]	Temporal Nature of Work	Importance of Task in Village Economy[b]
Agriculture						
Shell Groundnuts (seed preparation)	65	F/M	Independent	4	Seasonal	1
Clear	18	M	Auxiliary	1	Seasonal	1
Plant	41	M/F	Assist	3	Seasonal	1
Weed	47	M/F	Auxiliary	2	Seasonal	1
Pick Vegetables	24	F/M	Auxiliary	2	Seasonal	2
Pick Cotton/Groundnuts	29	F/M	Auxiliary	2	Seasonal	1
Bird Scaring	18	M/F	Independent	4	Seasonal	2
Animal Husbandry						
Feed/Water	18	M	Auxiliary	1	Regular	2
Animal Care	18	M	Auxiliary	1	Regular	2
Milk	6	M	Auxiliary	1	Regular	2
Shepherd	24	M	Independent	4	Regular	2
Water Provision						
Well	65	F/M	Independent	3	Regular	1
Riverbed	35	F/M	Independent	3	Occasional	1
Canal	18	M/F	Independent	3	Occasional	1

Table A.2. Summary of Children's Participation in Environmental Work *(continued)*

Activity	Percent Participating at Least Sometimes	Gender	Nature of Children's Contribution	Proportion of Total Effort Undertaken by Children[a]	Temporal Nature of Work	Importance of Task in Village Economy[b]
Fuel Provision						
Collect Fuelwood	53	F/M	Independent	3	Regular	1
Cut Fuelwood	12	M	Auxiliary	1	Regular	1
Charcoal Manufacture	12	M/F	Assist	1	Seasonal	2
Scavenge Charcoal	24	F/M	Independent	3	Seasonal	3
Retrieve Flotsam	12	M	Independent	3	Seasonal	3
Food Procurement						
Trap Birds	12	M/F	Assist	1	Seasonal	3
Pick Vegetables	24	F/M	Independent	4	Seasonal	2
Pick/Gather Fruit	35	F/M	Independent	4	Seasonal	2.5
Other	12	F	Independent	4	Seasonal	3

a. Approximations based on my observations.

1. ≤ ¼ total effort expended on task
2. > ¼ ≤ ½ total effort expended on task
3. > ½ ≤ ¾ total effort expended on task
4. > ¾ total effort expended on task

b. Importance to household maintenance or reproduction is subsumed under this head.

1. Central Significance
2. Medium Significance
3. Incidental Significance

Glossary
Colloquial Sudanese Arabic Terms

angareb	woodframe bed strung with rope or plaited with leather, used universally in Howa
aradeib	tamarind tree and its fruit
aysh	literally means "life," but is the local word for sorghum
bildat	rain-fed fields generally associated with subsistence cultivation
cambo	temporary shelters ("camps") built in the fields to facilitate a household's participation in long work hours, especially during the harvest
doleib	fan palm tree and its fruit (*Borassus aethiopicum*)
feddan	unit of land measurement equal to .42 hectares or approximately one acre
gena	seeds, children
gutiya	round building made of grass, stalks, and wood with conical thatched roof
hahiya	high wooden platform constructed in sorghum fields on which children stand to scare off birds
hakim	doctor, used in the village to refer to the local health practitioner
hawasha	farm tenancy (pl. hawashaat)
"hawashaat"	"tenancies"; children's farming game
hosh	houseyard
humbock	fruit of the *Capparis decidua*
jallabiya	caftan
jemmam	shallow well dug in sandy riverbed

jeref	riverbank garden (pl. juruf)
kakool	gum oozing from various acacia trees
karama	Slaughtering an animal with the intent of sharing the meat; from noble-minded, honor, generosity. Now usually to give thanks on a special occasion and/or to honor a special guest.
kedunka	short-handled hoe (mandated by the Suki Project administration)
kerrib	eroded land along riverbanks, riven by gullies, it is largely impermeable
khalwa	Quranic school
khudra	leafy green vegetable growing wild in the area
kisra	thin sorghum pancakes
lalob	fruit of the *Balanites aegyptiaca*
mahr	bridewealth
malod ga'ad	standing hoe (hoe used from a standing position)
malod wagif	sitting hoe (hoe used from a squatting position)
maya	shallow depression that fills with water during rains, a seasonal pool
molayta	leafy green vegetable growing wild in the area
muezzin	those who perform the call to prayer
mughterib	international labor emigre (pl. mughteribiin)
murshida	woman guide, instructor, or leader; refers to social extension teachers or leaders
nas	people, used to refer to family groups
nefir	communal work party convened to accomplish short-term intensive agricultural task
nubg	fruit of the *Zizaphus spinachristi*
purdah	seclusion of women from public observation
qantar	a measure of weight. In Sudan a qantar is usually 100 rotls, or about 100 pounds. A (large) qantar of cotton is 315 *rotls,* the amount needed to produce 100 pounds (44.93 kilograms) of ginned cotton lint, which is often referred to as a small qantar.
qoz	sand dunes
riba	interest (on money)
roda	child-care center, nursery school
Shari'a	Islamic law
shayl	a credit arrangement that involves crop mortgaging (technically illegal, it is widely practiced in Sudan)
shedduck	children's hopping game, played by teams trying to reach opposing goals
shemasha	derogatory term for street people, literally one who has been in the sun too long
suteb	edible root of a plant that grew in the seasonal pools, favored by shepherds

teganet	earthen ridges for impounding water in fields
toriya	short-handled hoe (mandated by the Suki Project adminstration)
tuhur	purity, cleanliness, circumcision
tukl	round building made of grass, stalks, and wood with conical thatched roof, often used as a kitchen
wasta	social connections
weka	undomesticated okra
wekab	starchy ash made from burning doleib palm branches, used to thicken stews
wilid	to give birth, to produce seeds or fruit
zimman	the past
zir	large clay container for storing water, found in every village household

Acknowledgments

The first time I went to Sudan, in 1977, I got stuck on a train in the Nubian Desert within hours of arriving by boat from Aswan, Egypt. The train lurched to a halt seven kilometers from its starting point in the northern outpost of Wadi Halfa, nearly spectral after the real thing was drowned by the Aswan High Dam in the 1960s. No one on the train had a clue what was going on, least of all us—a small group of travelers clustered in the "new third-class" or fourth-class cars in the rear. Within minutes, most of the Sudanese passengers had decamped into the desert to relieve themselves, pray, and speculate on what was going on. We wouldn't budge, afraid the train would resume its journey to Khartoum and leave us in the dust, literally. After some time—I can't remember how long—we relented, left the train, and learned from fellow passengers that the engine had ceased and a new one was to be dispatched from the railroad headquarters in Atbara, thirteen hours south along the single track. *Insha Allah* it would be there by the next day and *insha Allah* it would not. Without so much as an official whisper from the train crew, we stayed in the desert through the night and most of the next day, got pushed back to Wadi Halfa by the rescue engine, and departed exactly twenty-four hours later the following day. In those twenty-four hours I learned more about patience and the limits of control than ever before. The experience cut through my privileged Western industrialized upbringing and its fetishization of clock time like nothing else. For better or worse, I have never understood time, space, and agency in quite the same way since.

This project did not begin then, but its seeds were surely sown, not just because I fell in love with being in Sudan as an impossible pleasure and pleasurable impossibility, but because on that train (which took another forty-one hours to reach Khartoum, 965 kilometers away) I learned the delights and possibilities of fitful progress, of slow motion, and even of being marooned. I internalized that rhythm more than was probably good for me, or anyone who has worked or lived with me, but each time this book has been sidelined in the desert it has been transformed and the journey forward has been something different. The possibilities of getting stuck and moving forward with a different perspective are fundamental to my project. To this end, it is fitting that I concentrate on children, who almost always find intrinsic pleasure in the world, even when it's hard, and who made much of the joys of dawdling, reinforcing my tendency to get lost in the playfulness of work.

My deepest and most profound gratitude, then, goes to the seventeen children in Howa who made this book possible. They shared their time, space, thoughts, feelings, and knowledge with me over and over and over again, never becoming impatient and always leavening our interactions with playful generosity. It is tautological that this study would not exist without them, but the privilege of knowing and working with Abdullah Abdusaddiq, Abdullah el Amin, Abdullah Yusif, Ahmed Ali, Alouwiya Nour, Amna Ibrahim, Asma el Haj, Hassan el Tom, Ibrahim Beshir, Mohamed Yusif, Naim Mohamed, Nesim Taha, Omer Ahmed, Rashida Tulhah, Yusif Fudlullah, Zahara Ahmed, and Zihoor Mohamed has been one of the deepest and most sustained pleasures of my life. Listening to the tapes, looking at their images, and watching the films documenting their work and play still make me smile and teach me something new about their lives. Visiting them again as young adults and learning about their vibrant lives and aspirations—once more shared with great generosity—was an extraordinary experience.

I am grateful to the parents and families of these young people, who were, without exception, hospitable, informative, generous, and gracious, even when they were completely perplexed about my incessant comings and goings. I especially appreciated the turning point in each household when they stopped treating me as a guest (or as an adult) and accepted that I'd sooner run off to work or play with their children than sit and drink tea with them. I wish I could go back now and share all that tea and time. My deep appreciation to the village teachers who welcomed me into their classrooms and homes, who conducted a villagewide survey of their own to complement and corroborate mine, who were always ready and great informants, and who were generous with their time and knowledge. Likewise to the village health practitioner and midwife who were hospitable, informative, and generous at every turn. My most heartfelt thanks to Leila, the social extension worker, who came to Howa at the same time I did, and in whose shadow I was welcomed. Leila and I lived together for the first couple of months I was in Howa. In a gentle and subtle way, Leila taught me to cook using local ingredients and a charcoal stove, to manage our water supply, to keep clean, and to be a gracious host even under duress. My immersion in village life was immeasurably smoother thanks to Leila, and her humor made even the rough bits easier.

Leila worked as part of the social extension program of the Suki Agricultural Project, which was run by the judicious, dedicated, and sensitive Awatif Musa Idris and her colleagues, Suad and Sofia, whose warmth and intelligence I so appreciated. Awatif,

Suad, and Sofia generously hosted me when I first moved to the region, helped me with my Arabic lessons, and set me up in Howa with a strong and loving tether back to their home in the project headquarters a few kilometers away.

The family who hosted us, *Nas* Fegeda, was astonishing in their warmth, care, humor, sensitivity, and generosity. Without exception they patiently and lovingly gave of themselves, shared all that they had, were attentive to our needs and problems, overlooked our mistakes, and took amazing care of us. The many nights we spent lying out and talking under the stars were gifts that continue to feel magical. I can never repay their loving generosity, but I have the deepest gratitude to the late Sheikh Ahmed Abdullahi Fegeda and his wives Um al Hassan and Sitt Agil, and his brother Abdusaddiq Fegeda and his wife Sitt Agil, along with their many children, grandchildren, sisters, brothers, nieces, and nephews. You have honored me with your love, generosity, and kindness.

I am grateful to many people at Khartoum University. My thanks to the librarians at the Sudan Collection at the University Library, who were always completely helpful and knowledgeable about that extraordinary collection. My deepest gratitude and admiration to Ushari Ahmad Mahmud, whose friendship sustained me in the early years of this project and who provided assistance with all things linguistic—from translating my survey and interview questions into intelligible colloquial Arabic to figuring out appropriate ethnosemantic categories for dealing with the children's rich and detailed environmental knowledge. I am grateful to my colleagues and friends in the geography department at Khartoum University, who always welcomed me in their midst and worked closely with me over many years. Ahmed Abdullah Ahmed was instrumental in setting me up to work in the Suki area, and Salih el Arifi shared his vast knowledge of Sudan, agriculture, and environmental processes without pretense and with extraordinary humor. Mustafa Khogali taught me a great deal about environmental change in Sudan and welcomed me into his family innumerable times. Yagoub and Abu Sin were great friends and informative colleagues whose gentle humor I always appreciated. Mohamed Babiker has been a friend since those early days, but several years ago he moved to New York where he has been an extraordinarily generous colleague, assisting me with transcriptions, translations, and all sorts of odd things, from the Arabic names of plants and birds to the meanings of nursery rhymes and children's songs. I have appreciated his assistance and friendship enormously. Over time, space, chaos, and longing, my relationship with el Haj Bilal Omer has been pivotal to everything I have done in this project. Without his love, support, and always hilarious assistance, along with the sweet company of his family, this project would have been much more difficult and a lot less fun.

These colleagues, who go back to the ancient origins of this project when I was a student and a research assistant on projects dealing with environmental change in Eastern Africa, remind of my earliest intellectual debts. Enduring and profound thanks to my mentor and earliest inspiration, Robert Kates, and to Leonard Berry, whose early work in Sudan provided the groundwork for my being there and whose constant and affable support made all the difference on several occasions. Roger Hart helped to shape this project from the outset and remains my colleague and dear friend to this day. Kirsten Johnson, whose close friendship I hold dear, was a role model for me; her political commitments, critical intelligence, and ethnographic sensitivity set a standard that I still aspire to reach. Rattling around Clark University when I arrived (and still when I left) was the inspirational ghost of Jim Blaut, whose brilliance exceeded the outrage of his being denied tenure. I had the pleasure of learning from his students and then from him. His support of me and this project and his advice along the way were not only of enormous help but a comfort in times of doubt. I miss his huge enthusiasm for life and continue to be inspired by his commitments to social and political change.

But the wheel turns, and as I inch toward my own dotage I have been fortunate to have worked with a number of fabulous and energetic research assistants, none more so than Entisar el Haj, who came with me to Howa when I returned in 1995—with rusty Arabic and not enough time—and made everything work. Entisar understood the project, the nature of fieldwork, the rhythm and sensibilities of people in the village, and my long-term engagements with them. She did an extraordinary job of completing a follow-up village survey and of interviewing the families of the children, now grown, and selected village leaders. In the years since then, Entisar has returned to the area to gather additional data from the agricultural project headquarters and maintained ties with me and people from Howa. Without Entisar, the follow-up part of this study would have been a shadow of what it is and much more difficult to undertake. At the City University of New York a group of dedicated, hardworking, and talented graduate students has assisted me in coding data; making tables and maps; and tracking down references, images, and the answers to innumerable questions—most of which, inevitably perhaps, ended up outside the text but were integral to what it became. Thank you to Susan Bercaw, Katherine Brower, Eric Graig, Mara Heppen, Doug Plumer, Dusana Podlucka, and Ania Slowinska for all their assistance, especially Doug and Ania, who in the last crunch made maps, tables, and images with great speed and skill, never showing the impatience they must have felt with my increasingly maniacal demeanor.

I am grateful to the National Science Foundation, the American Association of University Women, Clark University, and the Professional Staff Congress of the City University of New York for their support of this work. Thanks as well to the Aaron Diamond Foundation, which funded the New York portions of this research through a series of collaborative projects.

Speaking of New York, thank you to the students, staff, administration, parents, and neighbors of a pair of community schools, P.S. 208 and 185, in New York City. I am especially grateful for the generous assistance, support, and interest of the then associate principal, Norma Genao, and the research assistance of Harouna Ba and Rosario Mora. My deep thanks to all of the participants in the CAMEO (Community Autobiography Memory Ethnography and Organization) project in East Harlem. I am particularly grateful to Mercedes and her family and neighbors, as well as to her CUNY collaborators, Carmen Medeiros and Betina Zolkower. Thanks as well to Stanley

Aronowitz, who inspired the project in the first place. My colleagues in the environmental psychology and women's studies programs at the Graduate Center of the City University of New York have made a pleasurable, productive, and engaging intellectual home for me for many years, and I appreciate working in their midst. Thanks especially to John Seley for his assistance with chapter 6. Many thanks to Bill Kelly for his friendship, his intellectual example, and his extraordinary work as provost, which has transformed the Graduate Center in ways that are all wonderful.

As this book took shape, it has benefited from the astute readings of a number of reviewers whose insights I have appreciated, learned from, and mostly addressed. Without question they have improved the work. I am particularly grateful to Bruce Braun and Dorothy Hodgson, whose generous and critical readings were pivotal to completing this book. Their comments, along with those of Peter Wissoker, and the much earlier encouragement of Bob Netting pushed me to deal with underlying issues, questions, and tediums in ways that have vastly improved the work. I deeply appreciate Peter's generosity and gentle patience over many years and his graciousness in all things.

I have been fortunate to work with Carrie Mullen and Jason Weidemann at the University of Minnesota Press. My deepest gratitude to Carrie for her patience, gentle persuasion, frankness, and serious engagement with this project for many years. Many thanks as well to Jason who has performed technological and editorial miracles with humor, patience, and kindness in the final stretch. My appreciation and continued admiration to the artist James Groleau, whose work I have loved for a number of years. James was extraordinarily generous about my possibly using a print from his mezzotint series, "The Flowers of Turbulence," for the cover image. While it did not come to pass, it was a pleasure corresponding with James and finding so much resonance in our concerns. Many thanks to my sister-in-law Maggie Magee and her colleagues at Superior Street, who copied all of the decaying videotapes of this work. Deep thanks to the artist-cum-cartographer Peter Beeton (and his coconspirator, Caitlin Cahill) for making a series of scratches into lovely maps with style, speed, and great kindness.

Many friends, family members, and colleagues have inspired me, shared their ideas with me, made me laugh, comforted me when I cried, talked away days and nights, and otherwise sustained me with love and knowledge. My love and thanks to Tim Brennan, Stephanie Browner, Dan Eisenberg, Keya Ganguly, Derek Gregory, Richard Hamlin, Gill Hart, David Harvey, Do Hodgson, Laurie Hudson, J. P. Jones, Kristin Koptiuch, Gregg LaPore, Liz Margolies, Nancy Miller, Katharyne Mitchell, Richa Nagar, Gerry Pratt, Allan Pred, Ellen Rothenberg, Sue Ruddick, Haydee Salmun, Rick Schroeder, Lois and Allan Schwartzman, Nancy Shaffran, Matt Sparke, and Karen Winkler. My deepest love and appreciation to Sallie Marston, whose love, intelligence, friendship, and understanding are everything, always. Thank you to the last-minute title collective of Gill Hart, Jean Lave, and David Szanton, whose poetic imaginations lifted me out of more than titular impasses. Warmest thanks and love to Mae Ngai, who actually came up with the title. A special thank you to Hibot Tulhah, whose extraordinary presence on the cover of this book conveys in a flash what it means to grow up global.

My parents, Arthur Katz and Phyllis Katz, to whom this book is lovingly dedicated, have given me the extraordinary gift of unconditional love throughout my life. Their love gave me confidence, humor, and optimism, all of which make me at home in the world. Theirs is an amazing and all too rare gift, made better by their sense that there is nothing extraordinary about how they love. Thanks, too, to my parents' partners, Susan Katz and Marshall Feigin, who have added to the swirl of fun, support, and love in our family. All my love to Gary Katz, Maggie Magee, and Maeve Magee-Katz, whose love, fierce wisdom, humor, and generosity are among the deepest and surest pleasures of my life. My former in-laws, the late Robert Walden and Dayle Walden, have been my family since I was a teenager. I have always appreciated their genuine curiosity about what my work is about, their love, their friendship, and their wisdom. Bob was my partner in comic crime, and I miss him everyday. Love and thanks to Ronald and Nancy Smith, whose interest in my work, love, wry humor, and friendship have been so important to me for many years.

My love and gratitude to Mark LaPore, former husband, collaborator, and partner in crime. Mark lived with me in Howa for six months, making films of the children's work and play as well as his own extraordinary films of life in the deepening shadows of capitalism. He shared what I saw, made me laugh every day, got sick as a dog, and didn't hold it against me even when I had him out filming two days after his surreal surgical experience. Most important, he saw what I couldn't see and made it all different.

My love and deep appreciation to Neil Smith, who not only read the first draft—and the primordial soup—of the book and gave me the best comments and suggestions anyone could hope for, but he lived with the book for longer than anyone should have. While he didn't have to forgo all the usual things that partners do, because I was always ready to jump ship, he endured the frustration of really wanting this book done more than I did. I will always be grateful to him for the ways he cared about me and took pride in this project. His loving passion, rampaging intelligence, and critical edge infuse every word here. I hope he knows that, always.

And finally—really finally—my deepest love to Eric Lott, who in the last minute made the whole future. In the year since this book was "finished," Eric has lived with all the ways it was not—figuring out the cover, the title, the ways to represent it; supporting my (failed) attempts to smuggle just a few more funny and personal things into the text; and getting through the routine but loaded tasks of copyediting and proofing—not only breaking down and kissing away the frustrations and last bits of angst that infiltrated these (pre)occupations, but takin pleasure in the text itself, which made all the difference. His brilliance, love, empathetic generosity, and wild imagination have remade my life and infuse every day with joy and every isotope with bliss. One heart, onsra, always.

Notes

Preface

1. The name of the village and its inhabitants have been changed to protect their privacy.

2. I developed the notion of *topographies* as a way of getting at this simultaneity through thick spatialized descriptions of particular processes in place; and the idea of *countertopographies* as a means of tracing common experiences of, or reponses to, social or political-economic processes across multiple locales.

1. A Child's Day in Howa

1. Reliable figures on herd size were difficult to obtain, but judging from my villagewide census, animal head counts, and general observations, approximately 30 percent of the households in Howa raised animals at more than a subsistence level in 1981. Among those with more than ten small animals, a flock of fifty was relatively large.

2. At 1981 exchange rates, one Sudanese piaster was worth 1.25 U.S. cents, or £S1.00 equaled US$1.25.

3. Only 4.15 percent of the girls between seven and twelve years old in Howa were enrolled in the village school.

4. See Dalla Costa 1972; Hall and Jefferson 1976; Samuel 1975; O'Laughlin 1977; Willis 1977; Steedman, Urwin, and Walkerdine 1985; and Steedman 1986. Since the time I began this project, there have been several significant publications on the everyday practices of resistance among those whose lives are reconfigured by processes associated with the expansion of capitalist production or more vigorous forms of capital accumulation in what is now called the global south. James Scott's (1985, 1990) sensitive work among peasants in Malaysia is among the most distinguished and influential, as is the edgier and more fluidly Gramscian work of Jean and John Comaroff (Comaroff 1985; Comaroff and Comaroff 1992). See also Ong 1987 and Pred and Watts 1992.

2. The Political Economy and Ecology of Howa Village

1. According to the *Second Population Census of Sudan*, conducted in 1973, the rate of population growth in Northern Sudan was 2.5 percent (Sudan, Ministry of National Planning n.d.). The estimated rate of growth has increased to about 3 percent in the decades since.

2. O'Brien (1978) found similar responses regarding cultivation and soil fertility in his study of traditional agriculture in Um Fila, a village in the Blue Nile region.

3. If we understand modes of production as abstractions that enable the theorization of predominate social relations of production and reproduction, and further, acknowledge the materiality of global capitalism, which has relegated nothing outside of itself for five centuries, the difficulty of naming "noncapitalist" or "not-fully-capitalist" social formations becomes apparent. The problematic is more aptly conceptualized as one of transnational class struggle. With this understanding, a protracted discussion of what type of mode of production characterized Howa is not in order. For my purposes here it is more fruitful simply to locate the village within a general and differentiated production system and outline those socioeconomic changes that have the most bearing on production and reproduction as material social practices there. Henry Bernstein's deployment of Marx's notion of "natural economy" in his analysis of capital and the peasantry provides a useful framework for establishing the socioeconomic conditions that defined this context in Howa, although, of course, there was nothing "natural" about this economic formation (Bernstein 1982). For Marx, the natural economy was one based in agriculture complemented by domestic handicraft and manufacturing. Its central characteristic is that "a very insignificant portion" of the product enters into the process of circulation (Marx 1967, 3:786–87). In other words, "that the conditions of the economy are either wholly or for the overwhelming part produced by the economy itself, directly replaced and reproduced out of its gross product" (795). Bernstein uses the construct as an abstraction to suggest a social formation in which the production of use-values predominates, although there is an exchange of surpluses at a basic level. Because he uses natural economy as an abstraction and not a historical observation, Bernstein cautions that the various potential forms of organizing the social relations of production are left undetermined in his discussion (1982, 161). Since my purpose is an analysis of the relationship between production and reproduction as material social practices in Howa, and not one of the historical transformation of the village as a socioeconomic system, an abstraction such as "natural economy" is useful as a means for locating the village theoretically, even if its use is somewhat overdetermined and schematic. Nevertheless, I find the term problematic because these social formations are anything but "natural," and the term suggests a primitiveness or timelessness that compromises the examination of coeval and complex social formations such as that of Howa. I use the term here as a useful abstraction for situating the village economy wherein my concern is to examine the experience of change, new forms of identification and differentiation, how certain groups of children come to have particular knowledges, and how this knowledge is used as young people develop strategies for making their way through the shifting terrain in which they come of age.

4. While the residences of Howa were relatively close to the irrigated fields, it did not matter much at first because there was no footbridge over the major canal. Many farmers and field workers were forced to walk an extra few kilometers just to get over the canal (Hummaida Abdalla Hummaida 1977). The oversight was eventually rectified.

5. My villagewide household survey brought the diversity in economic activities home to me forcefully at the outset of the research. I had prepared a one-page questionnaire (see Figure 13) that asked, among other things, the occupation of all household members. I was very pleased with myself for including lines for second wives, children, and elders—the trouble was that I only included one line per person! I made good use of the margins to compensate for my

unthinking lack of attention to seasonal variations in work, the extent of local participation in the informal economy, and the multiplicity of remunerative activities in which people engaged.

6. Tony Barnett (1975, 1977) analyzes *shayl* or crop-mortgaging at length in his work on the Gezira Scheme in Sudan. Most strikingly, Barnett shows that the expenses entailed in producing crops within the project exceeded the cash advances offered tenants by the Gezira Board. This annual shortfall forces most tenants to mortgage their crops to wealthier tenant-merchants in the area. My findings suggested a similar process was underway in Howa despite the illegality of shayl. Indeed, an independent evaluation of the Suki Project conducted in the late 1980s confirmed that the advances from the project were routinely less than expenses. The report also notes, however, that most farmers did not take their debts to the project seriously and so these piled up year after year, limiting the project's ability to function effectively (Euroconsult 1988).

7. As noted earlier, labor migration, whether regional, national, or international, was not of major significance when I first stayed in Howa in 1981. Fewer than 6 percent of the households had members who had emigrated, and migration to Saudi Arabia or the Gulf States was virtually unknown. (Only one household in the village reported having a member working in Saudi Arabia in my 1981 survey. This young married man without children was a teacher who was working as a fruit seller abroad.) Yet working abroad was so common at that time in urban Sudan and many other rural areas that remittances largely propped up the national economy and many local economies. My research suggested, however, that the socioeconomic and political-ecologic changes then underway in Howa were creating conditions that would necessitate widespread labor migration, and thereby incorporate Howa differently within the global and national economies. As I show in chapters 7 and 8, this situation has come to pass.

8. The World Bank (1984, 218) estimated that in 1982 Sudan's GNP per capita was US$440.

9. Residents in Wad al Abbas, another village in the Blue Nile Province, gave estimates between $900 and $1500 as the minimum on which a household could live in 1981 (Bernal 1991, 81). Given that Wad al Abbas appeared to be slightly more integrated with the cash economy than Howa was at the time of the research, the villagers' self-reports support my estimates for Howa. Moreover, if the cost of meat is added to my minimal budget, it brings the total budget per annum to approximately $964, within the range provided by Wad al Abbas residents. My schematic budget is also supported by the findings of a careful household budget survey of the Gezira-Managil area conducted by the Sudanese Department of Statistics during 1963. While the actual figures are, of course, out of date, their allocation remains apposite. With the exception of milk, which in Howa was largely self-provided, my distribution of expenditures for foodstuffs was similar to those found in a sample of villages in the Gezira Agricultural Project that at the time were articulated with the cash economy in similar ways as Howa was in 1981 (Sudan, Democratic Republic of, 1965).

10. There were other forms of resistance in Howa and elsewhere in Sudan, but I am not qualified to assess them. For example, the growth of *turuq* (literally, paths), the religious orders or brotherhoods frequently associated with Sufism, was significant in Sudan. These religious movements had the potential to become an increasingly potent form of ideological resistance to the logic of capitalism (cf. el Hassan 1980; Karrar 1992). Beginning in the late 1980s they seemed to be overshadowed by the phenomenal rise to power of religious fundamentalists in Sudan, and it was not clear to me whether the spiritualism offered by Sufism could or would counter the fundamentalist trend, though it seemed to me that it was doing so. Its practices were recuperative and otherworldly, quite the opposite of the rigid disciplining offered by fundamentalism, and they have continued to hold sway in Howa, where, perhaps not coincidentally, I found little evidence of support for the fundamentalism purveyed by the government.

Other forms of resistance had a more political-economic cast. For example, there were several episodes of food riots in Sudan in the early 1980s in response to the International Monetary Fund's enforced lifting of government food subsidies. These riots were reported in the urban areas and ultimately contributed to the downfall of President Nimeiri in April 1985, but their role in the countryside was less clear. Bernal (1991, 65–66) reports that schoolboys in the town of Wad al Abbas rioted in January 1982, shrewdly selecting as their targets a local dry goods store, the local government council, and the irrigation project offices. The potential oppositional role of rural producers is enormous, and represents a significant threat to the forces of capital accumulation, public and private. See, for example, Taisier Mohamed Ali's (1983) analysis of the violence of the Sudanese state response to the organized resistance of cotton farmers in private and government-sponsored schemes.

11. In addition to the money collected for the pipes, sugar cooperative funds went to purchase diesel for the wells, to maintain the wells, and to repair the school, the clinic, the mosque, and the midwife's house. By these accounts, the cooperative sold over 100,000 pounds of sugar between 1981 and 1983. This astonishing figure represents approximately twenty-six pounds of sugar purchased per year for each man, woman, and child in Howa. As high as that figure is, most households indicated that they could not satisfy their demand for sugar from the cooperative alone. The rest was procured at a much higher price from the black market through village shops.

12. When Wad Tuk Tuk was developed there was talk of areawide electrification. The village council of Howa was asked if it would be willing to make a heavy investment for electrification. They refused to raise the necessary funds through the sorts of self-help initiatives they had used to fund the wells, school, and standpipes. Several years later, in casual conversation, several people remarked that this had been shortsighted, because they could see the conveniences of electricity that had not seemed worth the investment before. Because of areawide disinterest in the investment, Wad Tuk Tuk was served by its own generator. The costs of electrification had increased dramatically in the years since, making it unlikely that Howa and its neighboring villages would soon have another opportunity to develop electrical power.

13. Female circumcision (*tuhur*) has been illegal in Sudan since 1946 (Fluehr-Lobban et al. 1992). Nevertheless, it is practiced widely. Unable to stop the practice, the government and Islamic jurists have tried to regulate and modify it by sanctioning a modified form that entails a partial or full cliterodectomy but proscribes infibulation ("pharonic" circumcision), which entails the removal of the entire external genitalia and the near closure of the vagina. As a government employee, the midwife was enjoined from performing all but the sanctioned *sunna* circumcisions, but the local population rejected these in favor of the more extreme infibulation. The midwife was left with the choice of having tuhur performed by traditional midwives or performing the infibulations herself.

3. Children's Work and Play

1. The "prime" childbearing years are obviously of limited duration, and thus it is important to remember that purdah notwithstanding, women made a significant contribution to the outside work of the village, as well as, of course, the work they did within the houseyard. In any case, economic necessity often led even nubile women to fetch water and gather fuelwood, or most commonly, to assist in agricultural tasks, particularly during the harvest. However, if women had children who could do these tasks, they would remain in the household compound and rely on the labor of their children. While children tended to replace women in the more routine and circumscribed tasks of fuel and water provision, in agricultural activities, where

there were severe time constraints and some economic incentive, it was otherwise. In the intensive work associated with the harvest, for example, children were more likely to supplement than to replace their mothers in the fields, regardless of their households' socioeconomic status (see Schildkrout 1981).

2. While the literature on domestic labor often mentions in passing the importance of children for providing water for their households, the paucity of data on children's labor in rural areas, particularly within the household or in nonremunerative activities, is almost startling. The lack of investigation of this aspect of everyday life suggests the stubborn use of metropolitan categories to analyze decidedly different settings. Even in the limited literature explicitly concerned with children's work, few authors discuss, let alone document systematically, the labor participation of children in such important tasks as drawing water or collecting fuelwood. Here again, the metropolitan concern with remuneration and the market inflects the research. Thus, despite the importance of children's contributions in procuring household water supplies in so many parts of the so-called third world, it is difficult to compare my findings to those of others working on household labor dynamics in different settings.

3. Even though most people in Howa were aware that canal water was unhealthy, those who lived closer to the canal tended to rely on it rather than the river or its subsurface wells when the well was closed. Because the canal was always in flow, canal water was easier to fetch than the water that filtered slowly into the shallow wells dug in the riverbed. Thus, it was often the source of choice by young people looking to save some labor time; this was especially so among children who sold water and had to make multiple journeys to draw it. When the canal water was turbid with silt, however, many did return to the riverbed for water despite the relative inconvenience of fetching. Given that schistosomiasis was introduced to the area through the irrigation canals of the project, the health consequences for children drawing water from the canal were serious. The consequences of drinking the water—full of agricultural runoff containing chemical fertilizers, pesticides, and herbicides, as well as the usual microbial suspects— were serious and potentially long lasting as well.

4. Because systematic labor budgets were not undertaken as part of the field research with children or adults, all time data are my own best estimates based on extensive observation, and they have been checked in comparison with time budgets undertaken in similar socioeconomic and ecologic settings. Thus, when comparing children's labor contribution to that of adults, it is best to think of it in terms of general units of participation, rather than in minutes or in other precise measurements of time (see Tables A.1 and A.2 in the Appendix).

5. Again, the provision of woodfuel is a task in which women generally predominate in non-Islamic parts of rural Africa. The extensive participation of children in Howa in procuring wood, then, may be relatively larger than that of children in non-Islamic areas. But fuel provision was also an area of obvious and ongoing change in household work patterns. As wood supplies in the area deteriorated, increasing numbers of women, especially from households that could not afford to purchase larger pieces of wood, went out to the surrounding woodlands—purdah notwithstanding—to cut and collect supplies adequate to meet their needs.

6. A closer look at these children's charcoal scavenging expeditions provides a telling insight into village and household economics. The children's grandmother was almost sixty years old and the senior wife of one of the wealthiest men in the village. Yet during the hottest part of the year, she spent hours each week under the midmorning sun in temperatures near 50°C (122°F), scavenging charcoal to sell. The proceeds of her sales after a two-month period of work totaled about ten dollars. Her efforts demonstrate the marginal value of relatively small amounts of additional income, even in families considered wealthy by village standards. Also, and most likely the real reason for her work, this money was for her discretionary use. In most

families, the money earned by men was used to support the household, i.e., to purchase those means of existence and everyday goods that were not self-produced. Money earned by women, however, was for their own use, and except under extreme financial conditions, it was not used for household subsistence. Most women had access to discretionary funds only by earning their own money. As indicated in chapter 2, women in Howa earned money in the cottage industries of mat making, ceramics, food preparation, and hairdressing; from the sale of certain crops, such as beans and okra, which were theirs by right of a combination of their labor, financial investment, and custom; and from activities such as charcoal scavenging, cotton picking, and groundnut harvesting.

7. Part of the rivalry was for my attention. I lived in the household compound of both of these children and when I was not in "mad dog" mode roaming about with or in search of other children, I spent most of each day with one or both of them. The two were close in age and tended to be competitive with one another. My presence and interests sometimes seemed to exacerbate this—an ethnographer does not come to town that often—so when Ismail heard that I'd gone out scavenging with Muna, he *had* to go on the next outing. I, of course, benefited from the children's competition to show and teach me everything. In the process I learned that much more from two of the most loving and interesting (and helpful) "informants" an "ethnographer" could have. The tinge of irony is intended to suggest that while our relationships went well beyond the ethnographic, that was a big part of what bound us.

8. Children's work in agriculture was common in many parts of Sudan. In the Gezira Scheme in 1974, for example, children were a large part of the paid cotton-picking labor force. According to a government survey, almost 22 percent of the total labor force involved in picking cotton was under fifteen and over 8 percent of the total number of paid cotton pickers was *under* ten years old (Sudan, Democratic Republic of, Ministry of National Planning, n.d.; and M. Galal el Din 1977). These figures say nothing of the considerable number of children who helped with cotton picking and other harvest activities as unpaid family farm workers (see, e.g., Bernal 1991; Tully 1988). With these children included, the 1974 estimates were that between 16 and 17 percent of the cotton pickers in Sudan were under ten years old (Sudan, Democratic Republic of, Ministry of National Planning, n.d.). Data from my research suggest that little had changed, and with the proliferation of agricultural development projects producing cotton, the absolute numbers of child workers no doubt increased over the decades. This in a country that simultaneously had the goal of universal primary education by 1990.

9. Zorial® (norflurazon) is an herbicide targeted largely at grasses. It is a preemergence herbicide, meant to be applied prior to planting (though it will not be effective if the soils are not moistened). Some recommendations call for it to be applied prior to cultivation and then again after the growth has begun. In the Suki Project it was sprayed in a water solution after the crops had emerged, and well after the fast-growing greens were up. Thus when the greens were picked by children they were commonly coated with the white crystals of norflurazon. Although toxicity tests indicate that the herbicide is not a skin irritant, some of the children who picked the greens got rashes on their arms. It is doubtful that the toxicity tests would have incorporated people—let alone children—picking norflurazon-treated "weeds" and carrying them with bare arms for time periods as long as an hour.

10. The hazards posed by herbicides were compounded by those associated with the insecticides sprayed regularly on the cotton by crop dusters hired by the project administration. Because cotton was not primarily for human consumption (although cottonseed oil is consumed widely both in and outside of Sudan), the insecticides may have been selected with little regard for the risks of ingestion. Here again, administrators' lack of consideration for such factors as local diet and land-use practices when selecting pesticides and herbicides may have presented a serious health hazard to the population of Howa. Not only were noncultivated

plants collected for human consumption from areas adjacent to the fields and irrigation ditches, but most families cultivated at least a few horticultural food crops in these affected areas as well. These, too, were often tended by children. In addition, sorghum stalks and other grasses doused routinely with pesticides were cut and gathered from the fields for house construction, fencing, and fodder. Finally, domestic animals grazed widely in the cotton fields after the harvest, and may have ingested high levels of the pesticides. In these ways, the herbicides and insecticides used by the Suki Agricultural Corporation may have been consumed and handled far more than those who authorized them knew. In this vein, it is sobering to note that crop dusters contracted from eastern Europe sprayed their Ciba-Geigy chemicals without advance warning and with little apparent regard for the many people at work in the fields. My complaints to project administrators about these issues were ignored. Thanks to unconsidered pesticide use, children were unnecessarily imperiled as they joined in the otherwise pleasurable seasonal activity of gathering wild vegetables, and one of the only sources of fresh food remaining in Howa may have been less healthy than it appeared.

11. This notion of "habit" as a kind of "tactile knowing" fervently in need of "bursting its prison-world asunder" is developed by Taussig (1993, 25, quoting Benjamin 1969, 236). Like Benjamin, Taussig argues that radical change is effected at the depth of habit, "where unconscious strata of culture are built into social routines as bodily disposition." The work-play-work connections in the lives of children in Howa seemed to make for fairly durable routines. Of course, this strength may increase the power of their "bursting."

4. Knowing Subjects/Abstracting Knowledge

1. The centers were not an entirely bad idea, of course. The intent was to mix a practical agriculturally oriented curriculum with a basic academic one for children and to offer adults academic courses as well as extension services. The thought was that this would slow the pace at which those who, after only a few years in government-sponsored schools, turned away from agricultural work, but found themselves frustrated in their ability to find much in the way of gainful employment outside of it. Integrated Rural Education Centres (IREC) were intended to help coordinate the pace of educational change with the availability of nonagricultural employment and at the same time to increase rural productivity. While the IREC program was virtually stillborn in the 1970s, it would have been unlikely to have succeeded on its own terms had it been deployed, given the broader constellation of social policies and political economic practices in Sudan that led to the disintegration of so many kinds of agricultural production and spurred rural depopulation. Moreover, the history of such educational efforts suggests that they concentrate on large-scale, capital-intensive, and mechanized cultivation, and ignore, if not systematically erase, local knowledge of even the most effective traditional land-use practices. Finally, the whole enterprise sidesteps the ways that institutionalizing learning—of any kind—in a formal school at once constitutes a particular context for knowledge and insinuates that knowledge can be abstracted from context (Lave and Wenger 1991, 40). This contradiction seems particularly apparent around such things as agricultural knowledge, which so completely imbued local communities of practice in Howa.

2. In Sudan, where primary education has expanded at a much greater rate than secondary and certainly postsecondary education have, the examination scores required to attain a place in the university had soared by the 1980s. By the 1990s they had reached absurd levels that were almost guaranteed to keep everyone in their place rather than expand opportunities. Given that it was a national system, the children of Howa competed with children of the literate urban elite for coveted secondary school and university places.

3. While descriptions of the pedagogy associated with Khalwa—in Howa and outside—did not suggest great attention to interpretation or critical engagement, it seems government schools may be even more rigid in their vision of Islam, especially since 1989, when the National Islamic Front gained control over the government. Changes in local practices reflecting more conservative interpretations of Islamic teachings were noted on return visits to their field sites by Janice Boddy (1989) and Victoria Bernal (1991). Informants in both settings had "learned" to dismiss their earlier practices as borne of ignorance. People in Howa, on the other hand, were more inclined to Sufism than fundamentalism in their religious practices, and I found this to be the case as much in 1995 as in 1981. There was no Khalwa in the village at either time, nor at any time in-between.

4. The Spengler quotation comes from Goody and Watt 1968, which was cited in White and Siegel 1984 (260).

5. Ethnosemantic interviews with five of the children likewise elicited mentions of dramatically more species—a 175 percent increase—than in earlier requests for exhaustive lists of plants. The number of fodder resources mentioned by children participating in the interviews, for example, increased by 100 to 533 percent over what they themselves had indicated in the course of other research methods. There is no reason to think these increases were exceptional rather than the artifact of a thorough, time-consuming, iterative, and extremely productive research strategy that focused on developing particular categories of phenomena mentioned by the children in the course of recounting their daily practices. Thus, for example, if a child mentioned picking fruit, I would pursue both the category of "fruit" and of things that are picked. If he or she mentioned "okra" in response to the latter line of questioning, I would follow up with a question about whether okra was a fruit. If that answer was negative then I'd ask what it was. If the child answered "vegetable," I would ask what other kinds of vegetables he or she picked, and so on. In this way broad and eventually deep taxonomies of plant knowledge were developed for each of the five children. The intent of these interviews was to elicit shared rather than idiosyncratic knowledge, though of course each child's knowledge reflected his or her particular practical engagements, and indeed each interview began with and continually circled back to the children's everyday practices and the bodies of knowledge associated with them.

6. Ethnosemantic interviews are a linguistic technique aimed at eliciting taxonomies of shared knowledge, and through them, an archive of shared understandings of relationships and processes. While they elicit information on the content and construction of knowledge in abstraction from the processes and physical settings in which knowledge is used, they are fundamentally rooted in practice. The interviews themselves were focused on everyday events—a delineation of the child's day and routine activities—from which I pulled out associations, relationships, and categories that centered on some aspect of the environment. The children's responses were richly detailed, and they patiently endured my dull and incessant questions geared at channeling these descriptions of everyday life and the local landscape into taxonomies of plant knowledge and place knowledge that revealed their understandings of environmental process and interrelationships, among other things (Spradley 1979).

7. The children often spoke of *zimman* (the past), which I came to realize was almost a mythical time in the past when things were better. Like "the good old days" in English, references to zimman are unspecific, do not require one's own presence as witness, and rehearse a nostalgia and longing that are more about what feels wrong with the present than what was right with the past. The children followed their elders in frequently invoking the past as a time when there were plenty of trees, ample grazing, lots of wild animals, and a simpler kind of ease. Their mental maps sometimes reflected these geographies of longing that were not part of their own lived experience.

5. Disrupted Landscapes of Production and Reproduction

1. "Geodrama" was the name I used for one of the methodologies I used to elicit the children's environmental knowledge in action. The children were individually asked to model the village on a large patch of ground near my house using everyday materials, including dirt, straw, water, sticks, and the like. Some children made quite elaborate three-dimensional models, including houses and local physical features, such as the river, the canals, and the fields, while others made sketch maps of the village in the dirt. At whatever point that each child determined their model was complete, I gave him or her a set of miniature toys, including farm animals, farm machinery, trucks, tractors, and people (miniature soldiers clad as Sudanese women and men). After they identified the animals (many stumbling over those wooly northern sheep) the children were asked to show me "life in the village." All of them engaged in extended "geodramatic" play, using their models as the "sets" for enactments of everyday and not-so-everyday life. As they played I involved them in a running commentary about what they were doing and why. The transcripts of these conversations provide information and insights about the children's social and environmental knowledge.

2. As indicated in chapter 2, the price of a sack of sorghum in Howa went from US$2.50 in 1971 to US$50 only ten years later. While prices fluctuated over the years, a price change of this magnitude—2000 percent during the initial decade of the project—was absolutely punishing for the local population. It was all the more painful because it came at the precise moment that most local households went from self-sufficiency to having to purchase sorghum. The anguish and resentment, to say nothing of the impoverishment, were palpable.

3. The intimate ties between the mechanized farmers and the government of Sudan were seen during the famine of 1983–84, when the government refused to declare a food crisis (required in order to receive international aid) because international relief organizations would then demand the halt of all grain exports as a condition to release food and other forms of assistance. The mechanized farmers did not want to relinquish selling their sorghum for a high price to Saudi Arabia. The ultimate travesty was that the Saudis used the sorghum for camel feed, while Sudanese in western Sudan and elsewhere were starving.

4. These interhousehold and generational differences in access to tenancies say nothing of gender differences. Except in rare circumstances, the regulations of the project precluded women's access to tenancies. These regulations dovetailed with and reinforced gendered relations of production and reproduction in Howa that made men responsible for the support of their wives, children, and, if necessary, parents.

5. Cotton picking was notoriously difficult and poorly compensated work in Howa. It was done almost entirely by women past their prime childbearing years and girls between eight and fifteen years old. A small number of migrant agricultural laborers from southern and western Sudan also participated. Contrary to the expectations of project planners, almost no one used mechanized means to harvest their cotton. The going piece rate during 1980–81 was £S.30 (US$.37) per fifteen-pound basket (*guffa*). Most girls said they picked two baskets a day, while women generally picked three. The harvest lasted upward of three months, and work was available constantly during this time. It is interesting (and somehow not surprising) that of all agricultural tasks, cotton picking became the work of women and girls in Howa. Apart from demonstrating how quickly the least rewarding farm work got associated with women, it shows the fluidity of work arrangements and the relative flexibility of rules governing women's seclusion when new needs and circumstances arise. See Bernal (1988), who discusses similar issues of women's labor in a village about fifty kilometers north of Howa.

6. The prevailing local norm was that men's earnings were used to support their households, whereas women's earnings were theirs to keep or spend as they wished. Children's

earnings, on the other hand, were added to the general household budget. In times of hardship or in extremely impoverished households, these norms were breached, but this was not a matter people spoke about readily.

7. In the villagewide census I asked parents about their children's school enrollment. Only 23 percent of all children between the ages of seven and twelve were enrolled in school, 92 percent of whom were boys. About 19 percent of those thirteen to eighteen were reported in school, 96 percent of whom were boys. Enrollment levels in the largely rural Blue Nile Province wherewhich Howa was located were higher than in Howa, particularly among girls. According to government figures for the province, 53 percent of the boys and 25 percent of the girls between the ages of seven and twelve were enrolled in school in 1979 (Sudan, Democratic Republic of, Ministry of Education and Guidance 1981). Attending school was one thing, completing it another. In my census, a total of 315 people were reported to have ever attended school. Of these, fewer than 2 percent reached the final year of secondary school.

8. Purdah is anything but a stable cultural form or practice in or across settings. Economic necessity, changing social conditions, and new discursive practices all influenced the norms of seclusion; at some times and in some places they got tighter, others not. Speaking with older adults in Howa, I gathered that purdah was less marked in earlier periods than it was when I first went to Howa in 1980. Even then, I found the norms of seclusion in Howa to be far less proscriptive and gender relations to be far more relaxed than they were among the middle-class urban elite living in the project headquarters a few kilometers away. Indeed, one of the hallmarks of modernity seemed to be a tightening of the lived norms associated with purdah.

Examples from elsewhere in Sudan suggest the same. In Wad el Abbas, a village not far away but integrated in a cotton project in the 1950s, Victoria Bernal (1991) found that the restriction of women increased with integration into the project. Notably, women were less likely to be active farmers in their own rights in the project than they had been before, although they did work during the cotton harvest, as was common among women in Howa. In another vein, both Bernal and Janice Boddy (1989) found that purdah and other urban Islamic norms were strengthened in the Nile villages where they worked following Sudan's move toward Islamic fundamentalism. I did not find the same in Howa. Each of these examples, however, suggests the mutability of purdah and the possibilities for its rather rapid and differentiated change. This sort of change might be provoked by male emigration from Howa, for instance.

6. New York Parallax

1. An interesting twist on these circuits of capital—one that directly connects New York and Sudan—followed September 11, 2001. According to Ahmed Zaki Yamani, former oil minister and one of the founders of OPEC, the Saudis withdrew about US$200 billion from U.S. banks in the wake of the U.S. response to the attacks on the World Trade Center and the Pentagon. Some of this formidable sum found its way to Sudan, where Saudi Arabia had plans to invest $18 billion in agricultural and commercial ventures, among other things.

2. "Fordism" (after Henry Ford) was not only a means of organizing production in a Taylorist, assembly-line manner that routinized tasks and drew on interchangeable parts, but was also a set of social relations geared to ensuring that workers could afford the fruits of their labor. If one part of this relationship required production costs to be kept down, another part required compensation or access to credit adequate to enable auto workers to purchase automobiles—a neat means of creating both an expanded economy and a more satisfied labor force. Workers in this regime tended to be long term, unionized, relatively well compensated, and pretty much anchored in place around sites of manufacturing. "Post-Fordism," which relies on more dispersed

production and distribution strategies, just-in-time deliveries rather than deep inventories, and a much more contingent workforce, makes no such promises to workers to ensure continued capital accumulation by manufacturers. It is associated with all manner of deteriorations in the social wage.

3. While my broader critique here is that there has been a gradual but systematic disinvestment in the reproduction of certain parts of the labor force that has resulted in deteriorating public spaces in poorer neighborhoods, underfunded schools, and declines in support for housing and health care for poor and working-class families, it should be noted that until the end of the 1990s, various government policies provided a "safety net" that protected millions of people from the worst effects of poverty. Some interesting work by the Center on Budget and Policy Priorities has demonstrated that government antipoverty programs actually were effective in reducing poverty, albeit more so among older people than children. Their work demonstrates (if only to make the argument about what was about to be lost) that state and federal antipoverty programs—including direct assistance and tax credits—actually did "lift" millions of people out of poverty during the period between 1979 and 1995. To make their point about what was to be lost with "welfare reform" the authors overstate what it means to be "lifted out of poverty," but it is clear that federal and state welfare and tax programs did offer poor people a "safety net" that provided the basic means of their existence (Primus et al. 1996).

This safety net was shredded by the changes in federal and state welfare laws during the mid-1990s, which turned antipoverty measures into antipoor ones through drastic reductions in, and time limits on, various forms of direct assistance, including food stamps, housing allowances, and welfare payments for dependents. The authors argue that these programs were reaching an all-time high number of recipients by 1995 when, in the midst of what most economists consider the longest sustained economic boom of the twentieth century, state-supported welfare was gutted. The reforms and their disciplining effects have much in common with the IMF-inspired structural adjustment programs imposed on Sudan (and elsewhere) beginning in the late 1970s.

4. This discussion draws on my own fieldwork among young people in Central and East Harlem carried out over short periods in 1989 and in the early 1990s. Because my own field engagements in New York City have been relatively brief, I also draw on the field research of a group of doctoral students at the City University of New York who worked with me through the 1990s on questions of childhood, social reproduction, and urban disinvestment. For their individual and collective projects on young people in New York, I thank Harouna Ba, Caitlin Cahill, Gretchen Susi, Kira Krenichyn, Julia Nevarez de Jesus, and Pamela Wridt. Their work has contributed to my thinking and the writing of this chapter.

5. A 1958 census of the school population in New York City reported an enrollment of 19 percent "Negro," 14.2 percent Puerto Rican, and 66.8 percent "others" (largely whites). Almost forty years later, the figures were 35.5 percent African American, 37.3 percent Latino, 16.3 percent white, and 10.8 percent Asian (New York City Board of Education 1958; New York City Board of Education 1998a). While the former numbers generally reflect the demographic profile of the city on the eve of the urban disinvestment and "white flight" that characterized the 1960s, the latter show the extent to which whites have evacuated the public-school system in New York City. The situation is even more stark than it seems because many schools have concentrations of one racialized group or another, reflecting in part the residential segregation that characterizes much of New York City and in part the not-unrelated uneven distribution of resources among and within school districts.

6. In the 1990s, a growing number of children, disproportionately from nonwhite and non-Anglo backgrounds, were referred to special education programs in the New York schools. Many of these children might not have met strict definitions of "special need," but rather, were

having trouble keeping up with their school work for a variety of reasons. Their transferral to "special education" programs may reflect the recognition that it was here that resources were still available more than it was a strategy to provide these particular programs for the children. The strategy not only rid regular classrooms of "problem" children, but by labeling growing numbers of children "special needs," schools were able to attract specially earmarked funds. By the 1995–96 school year, New York State spent $1.4 billion on so-called special education. Just ten years earlier, the state's special education budget was a little over a third of that ($527 million). New York City's rate of special education was three times the national average (see, e.g., Borra 1996; Citizens' Committee for Children 1995; R. Hernandez 1996).

7. It is too easy (and increasingly common) to blame the problems of schools and schooling on the increase in foreign-born children. Between the 1989–90 and 1991–92 school years alone, the number of foreign-born students in New York City public schools increased from 36,000 to 120,000, or from about 4 percent to 12 percent of total enrollees (New York City Board of Education 1993). Clearly these shifts, which continued through the 1990s, placed an enormous burden on the public schools. The burden, however, is nothing new in a "city of immigrants" like New York. What has changed is the willingness to commit public resources to programs designed to cope with it.

I am not questioning the need for appropriate language education, then, but rather pointing out the zero-sum game that has been played on children's backs. In a period of shrinking resources, the dollars spent on language education are at the expense of general educational expenditures. When certain government mandates require particular programs—without assuring adequate financial support—their costs necessarily cut into funds available for other programs. As resources decline and demands go up, as has been the case in New York City, the programs that are cut into and undermined are more and more often of the "nuts and bolts" variety. New York City public schools in the 1990s had very few "frills" left to cut. Witness the overcrowding fiasco at the start of the school year in 1996, when 91,000 children were forced to study in improper spaces—lavatories, hallways, and locker rooms, for instance—without appropriate equipment, such as desks and chairs, to say nothing of computers and the like, and without access to basic educational resources, such as books, libraries, or gymnasiums. The situation and the annual fall ritual of decrying it—without doing much to alter it—speak volumes about public disinvestment in social reproduction.

8. At the same time as the number of school libraries in New York City was being reduced (more than one hundred elementary schools had no libraries at all in 1996, another forty had no librarians), New York City spent only $4.68 per student annually on library programs. New York State managed a per student expenditure of $12.86 while the national average was $14.08 (Kershaw 1996; cf., Educational Priorities Panel 1985).

9. Enrollments in New York City rose steadily throughout the century until 1971, when they began to decline as a result of aging baby boomers and urban depopulation. Enrollments dropped precipitously, however, following the fiscal crisis in the middle of the 1970s. Between 1975 and 1978 the number of students in the city's schools was reduced by 100,000, a startling 9 percent of 1975 registrants. Enrollments continued to fall until 1982, when they dipped below 925,000. Since then, with a couple of aberrations, New York City school enrollments have been increasing steadily. By the 1993–94 school year, with an annual rate of increase exceeding 2 percent, school enrollment surpassed one million for the first time since 1977. Beginning in 1991 enrollments increased routinely by over 20,000 a year. Not only was the student body growing, but it was changing as well. The proportion of poor children was increasing dramatically, as were the numbers of black and Latino children relative to whites (New York City Board of Education 1995).

10. Even as federal mandates for such things as bilingual and special education have increased, federal funding for education has declined. In 1976, for instance, 13 percent of the

New York City's schools' budget came from the federal government, but by 1994 this share had dwindled to 10 percent (New York City Board of Education 1994).

11. These figures gloss over the effects of inflation and the fact that given steady and substantial increases in per pupil expenditures for special education, spending for children outside of special education programs actually decreased. According to the Citizens Budget Commission (1997), the inflation-adjusted expenditure per student in New York City decreased by 10 percent between 1990 and 1996. Likewise, in 1996, with expenditures for special education increasing by about 4 percent per pupil, the actual outlays for children in general education classes decreased by 11 percent systemwide.

12. According to Richard Carroll of the New York City Office of Tax Policy, of $17.5 billion in taxes collected in New York City for fiscal year 1995–96, only $1.2 billion were from corporate taxes. This state of affairs throws corporate "generosity"—witnessed in such things as public–private partnerships—in a different, less beneficent, light.

13. These staffing questions entirely avoid the heavy reliance on so-called WEP (Work Experience Program) workers within the Parks Department beginning in 1994. The Work Experience Program—a cornerstone of New York's welfare reform policy—required all welfare recipients who were able (and that was broadly defined) to work in order to receive their welfare payments. At the start of 1994 there were about 600 WEP workers in the Parks Department, but within two years that number had grown to 3,600 and eventually reached more than 5,000. These workers, who were paid about two dollars an hour, were replacing salaried Parks Department employees who had been laid off in droves during the early 1990s and before (Citizens Budget Commission 1991).

14. The number of homeless people and nature of homelessness have changed dramatically in New York and other cities since the 1970s. As the production of public and low-cost housing all but dried up, gentrification forced up rents in many working-class parts of the city, and single-room occupancy and low-cost hotels were converted to uses with higher returns, the number of homeless people—including families—increased drastically. A new category of homelessness took root and grew during this time, reorienting the meaning and consequences of homelessness away from those populations traditionally understood to compose the bulk of homeless people—substance abusers or mentally ill individuals—to those who were homeless for economic reasons. Beginning in the 1980s, as many poor households clung to inadequate housing or doubled up with friends and relatives (a concealed form of homelessness), an increasing number became homeless in New York and elsewhere as a result of various strategies of eviction, explicit and implicit. From January 1983 through December 1984, for instance, the number of homeless families in New York City shelters grew from 1,400 to 3,300, an increase of 67 percent a year (Erickson and Wilhelm 1986). This was just the beginning. An astonishing 900 families entered the city shelter system on average *each quarter* between 1989 and 1994 alone (Citizens' Committee for Children 1995). Between 1995 and 1998 the average decreased to just under 700 per quarter (Citizens' Committee for Children 1999), but by 2002 the numbers were again on the rise.

15. The venality of contemporary "tax rebellion" is witnessed on a number of levels. The United States's infamous delinquency in paying its United Nations dues—by 1999 totaling about $1.3 billion—is a case in point. The simultaneous demonization of various "third world" nations as, for example, "terrorist," and the characterization of their leaders as inimical to democracy, using terminology unused for northern politicians, such as "strongmen" or "war lords," is a vengeful form of politics in the United States that authorizes and justifies its scandalous evasion of international responsibility. These issues are linked, of course. In 1999 the United States agreed to pay its outstanding debts if the UN agreed to various conditions, making the first installment payment at that time. Although the U.S. Senate approved payment of

the second installment in February 2001, the House of Representatives could not agree to its release until October 2001. The payment was released on 5 October, the eve of President Bush's visit to the UN to make the case for the United States' "War on Terrorism," which began against Afghanistan just two days later. The U.S. Congress finally approved payment of the third installment of its arrears on September 30, 2002, perhaps not coincidentally as the UN lobbying for U.S. interests in "regime change" in Iraq intensified.

16. The globalization of capitalists' passion for privatization came home forcefully when I found a report from the Suki Agricultural Corporation touting the "liberalization" of the market and advocating privatization as a means to increase efficiency and productivity in the project. Although the project administration attempted privatization in 1992 through the sort of public–private partnership that had by then become so common in the fiscal landscape of New York City, they found no takers in the private sector (Suki Agricultural Corporation 1997). As my research assistant, Entisar Mohamed Mahmoud, scribbled on the report, "the private sector never gets into a venture that is not profitable." Indeed.

7. Howa at the End of the Millennium

1. During the initial periods of this research, Sudan was under the leadership of Ja'afar Mohamed al-Nimeiri and the Sudanese Socialist Union (SSU), which came into power following a military coup in May 1969. The Nimeiri administration, which embraced and was informed by a range of progressive constituencies, among them the well-organized and influential Communist Party, initially had widespread popular support. The "May Revolution," as it was known, initiated a series of ambitious political and economic changes, including nationalizing the banks and a number of major industries; securing significant investment in "development" initiatives (including the Suki Project) on the part of Arab, European, and North American sources, both public and private; attempting to decentralize political power; and achieving a peace agreement in 1972 that effectively ended Sudan's enduring and often vicious civil war. But these achievements were not to last—they were undermined by a combination of forces, many of which can be traced to Nimeiri himself, including clientalism, corruption, and a hypocritically lithe politics of convenience that made enemies of friends and friends of enemies in sometimes breathtaking succession (see Niblock 1987; Khalid 1990; Woodward 1990).

By 1983 Nimeiri's politics of convenience were colored by desperation. In that year he further accommodated himself to the political agenda of the fundamentalist Muslim Brotherhood, which pressured him to impose Shari'a law on Sudan in earnest—both the Islamic north as well as the Christian and animist south. By September 1983 Nimeiri instated the notorious "September Laws," which imposed and enforced Shari'a law throughout Sudan. He established the "Courts of Prompt Justice,"which meted out strong and swift, though not necessarily fair, sentences executing or amputating the limbs of over 150 people and creating a campaign of terror and repression throughout the country. Nimeiri's embrace of the Muslim Brothers precisely when significant oil reserves were discovered in Southern Sudan antagonized many secular, left-leaning, and Southern Sudanese, rekindled the civil war, and contributed to his downfall in April 1985.

The nonviolent military coup of 1985 led by General Suwar al-Dahab ushered in a brief period of what proved to be fairly rudderless democracy. Nevertheless, within a year Suwar al-Dahab delivered on his promise to return to civilian government, and multiparty elections were held for the first time since 1968. Dozens of parties sprang up during the transitional year, but perhaps not surprisingly, the traditional political power bases—the Umma and the National Unionist Parties—received the greatest numbers of votes in the 1986 elections. Representatives of the Ansar-supported Umma Party (associated with the nineteenth-century Mahdi and his descendants) were able to form a majority and with some difficulty eventually formed a coalition government, with Sadiq al-Mahdi elected as prime minister. That fragile coalition broke down and was reformulated on a couple of occasions in 1987, but according to Peter Woodward (1990, 209; cf. Salih 1991), so little policy was being made during the period in any event, that it was not always obvious whether or not the coalition was in place.

2. Various coalition configurations sputtered along through the 1980s but none dealt effectively with Sudan's woeful economic state or advanced a process that might bring a peaceful end to the intensifying civil war. In June 1989 a coup was staged by Brigadier 'Umar Hasan Ahmad al-Bashir with the apparent (but initially invisible) support of the National Islamic Front (NIF) and its leader, the cleric Dr. Hasan al-Turabi. Al-Turabi was a wily politician who had crafted the NIF's rise to power over the decades in a quite calculated and slippery way. He used Shari'a, for instance, as a blunt instrument to assert but not develop an Islamic society. To this end, al-Turabi fought alternately for the expansion and enforcement of Shari'a and for its limitations as it suited his ambitions and the larger political backdrop within which he was working (Sidahmed 1996).

The al-Bashir/al-Turabi government was born out of an antidemocratic impulse and stayed in power throughout the 1990s thanks to its extraordinary commandeering of the apparatus of repression, violently attempting to silence internal opposition and flouting every attempt at intervention on behalf of human rights by international groups (see Human Rights Watch/Africa 1996). Flowery Islamist rhetoric notwithstanding, Sudan became a police state fueled by honeycombed surveillance, heavy-handed police practices, the continued prosecution of the civil war, and a frenzied attention to the borders, where it appeared that one crisis after another fomented by pesky neighbors had to be averted. Each of these crises and the scores of internal enemies that were to be routed were, of course, intended to create a sense of vigilance about the nation and its prerogatives among the masses. They appeared to be having precisely that effect in Howa when I returned in 1995, where the largely nonliterate population was roused by daily radio harangues against Egypt concerning the Halayib triangle in northeastern Sudan and about the continued aggression of the SPLA (Sudan People's Liberation Army) in the person of John Garang.

In a power struggle that ended in May 2000, 'Umar al-Bashir split formally with al-Turabi by freezing his position as Secretary General of their ruling National Congress Party. Al-Turabi's large presence had guided the Islamicist government from the time it came to power in 1989 until his "defiance" presented too much of threat to al-Bashir's presidency. At the time, al-Bashir appeared to be considering reconciliation with other parties and portrayed al-Turabi as a hard-liner who presented an obstacle to any thaw. If there was anything to al-Bashir's interests in reconciliation other than getting rid of al-Turabi, nothing came of it in the ensuing years.

3. Interview with Mohamed Ahmed, member of the Executive Committee of the Suki Farm Tenants Union, 8 July 1995.

4. These credit arrangements seem to be variations on the old theme of shayl, inflected by the new forms of banking ushered in with the ascendence of Islamic banks in Sudan starting in the late 1970s. Islam, of course, forbids the collection of *riba* (interest). In its stead, Islamic bankers have devised several clever and highly profitable means of banking. Among these are *mudarabah*, whereby the bank supplies capital to a business or individual and shares in the profits at a preset ratio; *musharakah*, which entails more of a partnership between agents of the bank and the businesses in question—resources are pooled, the project is managed by both groups, and profits or losses are divided at a predetermined ratio; the highly lucrative and popular *murabahah*, which entails the bank purchasing goods on behalf of a business or individual entrepreneur, who repays them at a later date including an agreed-upon "mark up"; and finally, *qard hasan*, or interest-free loans (Sidahmed 1996, 208). The financial arrangement described as *mogawala* in Howa seems to be a local cross between mudarabah and murabahah.

5. The varieties of sorghum grown included *Gadam Hamam, Faterita, Wad Ahmad, Gasabi,* and *Benan.*

6. The government of Sudan actively encouraged northerners, such as the men in Howa, to cut wood in the south. Their reasons were manifold. First, the government represented the work as patriotic, slyly implying that each tree might hide a southern guerrilla, and thus suggesting that deforesting the area would help the war effort. Second, the Bashir government was strapped for cash. Several phases of charcoal production were taxed, and the government managed to collect their share quite effectively. Third, the high-quality charcoal was sold in the urban areas, notably in the Khartoum vicinity, and thus satisfied a burgeoning urban population, whose access to other forms of cooking fuels was severely limited, given Sudan's lack of foreign exchange. Finally, participation in charcoal production enabled a large number of rural people to eke out a living without migrating to the urban areas. For these and other reasons, the expanded terrain of charcoal production among people from Howa represents an extraordinarily productive *political* ecology (Katz 2000).

7. The seventeenth child, Mohamed, had drowned in 1982. He had fallen into the river while shepherding alone and had been unable to swim to shore in the swift current.

8. Until the Suki Project appropriated so much of the land around Howa for the project at the end of the 1960s, most land around the village had been communally held. Families had customary rights to various plots of land for indefinite periods, and new or abandoned patches were allocated to cultivators by the village sheikh. Parallel to this system, jeref land along the river was by tradition privately held.

9. Most young married women stayed in their natal homes until their firstborn was about three or four years old or their second child was born. Most newlyweds lived in small, round, mud-and-thatch houses in the compounds of the wife's family, moving to more solid housing among the husband's family after a few years. Such was the case with Sofia's move to Dinder town.

10. While Sufism and its various *turuq* (paths or orders) have not been a focus here, they were an important part of the lives of many people in Howa who followed particular regional and local sheikhs and were deeply involved in the practice of a mystical and ecstatic Islam. While in many ways these practices, and the often charismatic sheikhs who were associated with them, were quite accommodating to the worldly intrusions of capitalism—many of the sharpest farm tenant-merchants were Sufi followers and most sheikhs appeared prosperous, in part from the sale of their services as counselors and their writing *hujab* (amulets) and other spiritual passages intended to protect, cure, heal, and otherwise assist petitioners—Sufism also provided an alternative consciousness and produced a liminal space of daily practice for people in the village that was quite separate from the political and economic concerns of advancing capitalism. These practices were also antagonistic to the fundamentalist versions of Islam purveyed by the government of Sudan beginning in 1989.

11. It is interesting to note that animal wealth was almost always a part of the bridewealth in the past, but when I asked about what marriage required in 1995, animal gifts did not come up. This omission, which surely was not uniform, reflects a diminution of the role of livestock in the local economy that was unthinkable only ten years before.

12. Other forms of power were made manifest in university attendance. The startlingly low numbers of southern students enrolled in Sudanese universities, including Juba University in the south, was testimony to the extent of entrenched inequality in the provision of educational resources. With the intensification of the civil war, Juba University was moved to Khartoum and thus made even more inaccessible to southerners.

13. The fact that a bakery would be thriving in Howa is itself testimony to the changing tastes associated with geographical extension and the ongoing monetization of the local economy. Just ten years earlier, bakeries could only operate successfully on a seasonal basis. The sole

bakery in Howa at that time worked during the harvest period, when women's work in the fields made them less available to make the sorghum porridge and pancakes that were the basis for almost all meals. Bread in any case was an acquired (urban) taste that was almost uniformly less preferable (except in my house) to the staple sorghum. While that remained the case in the 1990s, exposure to life in the towns had made wheat bread more palatable to many in Howa.

14. The Hajj, or pilgrimage to Mecca, is one of the five pillars of Islam (the others are the declaration of faith that there is no God but God, the five daily prayers, *zakat* or the sharing of wealth, and the observance of Ramadan, a month-long period of fasting). Accomplishing the Hajj requires substantial wealth, the subsidized flights and accommodations during the pilgrimage notwithstanding. Very few people from Howa, almost none of them women, had completed the Hajj when Nafissa went at the beginning of the 1990s. I can recall talk of only one person in the village making the Hajj during and prior to my earlier visits. Nafissa's pilgrimage was thus socially extraordinary as well as a great spiritual fulfillment to her and her family, most of whom followed a Sufi *tariq*. She was a devout Muslim, as was her husband, who had died a few years earlier without performing the Hajj. Surely, had Nafissa's husband lived, he would have made the Hajj rather than she, but I suspect that their sons supported Nafissa's Hajj not only out of respect for her, but in honor of their father, who was considered a holy man.

8. The Strange Familiar

1. Until the mid-1980s, people in Howa farmed, raised animals, and procured forest resources largely within a radius of 5 kilometers from the village, i.e, drawing on an area of 78.5 square kilometers. By 1995, however, the same work was only possible if it encompassed a radius of 200 kilometers or more, covering an astonishing 125,600 square kilometers just to stay "in place."

2. Of course my emphasis on global capitalism, and in particular its centers in the global north and largely western industrialized countries, may overstate the case of Howa's and Sudan's isolation by restricting what is understood as "globalization." As the story of the Hajj at the close of chapter 7 made clear, "globalization" comes in many forms, and people's encounters with "the global" or various manifestations of globalized modernity in Howa were more likely to be through Islam than through direct engagement with capitalist institutions. This is true likewise at the national scale in contemporary Sudan. Were it not for the assistance of several Arab states and Islamicist governments and institutions, for instance, Sudan's economy would be in even greater disarray. Indeed, as indicated earlier, the Saudis reportedly planned to invest some US$18 billion in Sudan's agricultural and animal husbandry sectors as part of the dispersal of the US$200 billion they withdrew from U.S. financial institutions following September 11, 2001.

3. The comparisons with Harlem are direct here. While, of course, Harlem's location in the United States enables access to all kinds of communications as yet unavailable in rural Sudan, the relative isolation of poor children in New York City compared to their wealthier peers in the city and elsewhere has become more manifest and consequential to their futures as electronic communication has become more central to economic life. Many of these working-class and poor children of color on the wrong side of the "digital divide" face similar dim prospects for sustainable, to say nothing of meaningful, work in their futures as the young people in Howa.

4. Janice Boddy notes that the people in the northern Sudanese village where she worked were rather flexible in the face of change, easily adopting new practices and sifting through others to produce a kind of fluid stability in their village life. I was struck by a similar fluid stability in Howa; time-space expansion is a case in point. It seemed that some part of this means of negotiating change and novelty must be attributable to their close historical and contemporary

relationship with pastoral nomadism, which creates its own kind of "rural cosmopolitanism" wherein difference is encountered routinely and changing circumstances are taken in stride. Interestingly, the cosmopolitanism identified by Boddy, in which new things and ideas are taken on (or not) in ways that reinforce cultural practices and identifications, was inflected by some of the same attributes as the cosmopolitanism I found flowering in Howa—a kind of spatial extensivity that propped up and stabilized a changing but sturdy and integral local (see Boddy 1989, 47).

5. The whole question of "marginalization" centers a certain set of often unnamed places and practices, smuggling in a spatialized hegemony and covertly fixing it as if there were not multiple and shifting centers and margins. The case of Islam as a form of modern globality or global modernity is a case in point often overlooked by Western and northern theorists and writers.

6. While Osama bin Laden had lived in Sudan for a number of years with the blessing of its Islamist government, they had forced him to leave a couple of years earlier at the behest of the U.S. government, with whom they wanted to reestablish better relations. The Clinton government was well aware of this when they bombed the pharmaceutical plant.

9. Negotiating the Recent Future

1. The interchangeability of the adjectives is as telling about the strategic uses of revanchism as it is revealing about the social policies to which it is tied.

2. Of course, they were professing this to me, an exemplar of someone who was nothing if not educated, and, being too polite to treat me like nothing, they claimed to value education more than they probably did. Nevertheless, the gap between their expressed ideals and their realities vis à vis education had little to do with pleasing or being polite to me, but was rooted in the impossibility of ensuring household reproduction without children's assistance and labor.

3. The material for this discussion of WHE ACT is taken largely from the excellent history of the group provided by one of its founders, Vernice Miller, in a chapter written collaboratively with Maya Hollstein and Susan Quass (Miller, Hollstein, and Quass 1996).

4. I want to be clear that the experience of the civil war in the north was nothing compared to the devastation and destruction in the south. The war, as ever, was fought almost entirely on southern grounds and thus people of the north were spared the direct devastation of their homes, villages, towns, livelihoods, wealth, and any semblance of order in everyday life that has been the lot of southerners since the middle of the last century, with only a decade of respite. The losses suffered by people of the north were largely financial, although with two million people killed since the war resumed in 1983 and untold property damage and displacement, the social and psychological toll of the war on all Sudanese is impossible to imagine. Apart from the enormous inequality between southern and northern loss of life, it remains that virtually all northerners who have died in the war were serving in the armed forces or the People's Defense Forces, whereas in the south, civilians—among them women, children, and the aged and infirm—have sustained heavy losses. Indeed it is civilians, including whole villages or pastoralist groups, who have been the target of much of the government's war against the south (see, e.g., Human Rights Watch/Africa 1996; Hutchinson 1996; Lesch 1998).

Works Cited

Abu-Lughod, L. 1990. The Romance of Resistance. *American Ethnologist* 17:41–55.

Ahmad, A. M. 1974. *Shaykhs and Followers: Political Struggle in the Rufa'a al-Hoi Nazirate in the Sudan.* Khartoum: Khartoum University Press.

Ali, A. A., ed. 1985a. *The Sudan Economy in Disarray: Essays on the Crisis.* Khartoum: Ali Abdel Gadir Ali. Distributed by Ithaca Press, London.

———. 1985b. The Sudan Economy and the IMF: A Background. In *The Sudan Economy in Disarray: Essays on the Crisis,* ed. A. A. Ali, 1–23. Khartoum: Ali Abdel Gadiir Ali. Distributed by Ithaca Press, London.

Ali, T. M. 1983. The Road to Jouda. *Review of African Political Economy* 26:4–14.

Ali, T. M., and J. O'Brien. n.d. Tenants, Peasants, and Seasonal Workers in Sudanese Agriculture. Unpublished (mimeographed) manuscript.

Ammar, H. 1966. *Growing Up in an Egyptian Village.* London: Routledge and Kegan Paul.

Annie E. Casey Foundation. 1995. *Kids Count Data Book.* Baltimore, Md.: Annie E. Casey Foundation.

Aronowitz, S. 1973. *False Promises: The Shaping of American Working-Class Consciousness.* New York: McGraw-Hill.

Barbour, K. M. 1961. *The Republic of the Sudan: A Regional Geography.* London: University of London Press.

Barnett, T. 1975. The Gezira Scheme: Production of Cotton and Reproduction of Underdevelopment. In *Beyond the Sociology of Development: Economy and Society in Latin America and Africa,* ed. I. Oxaal, T. Barnett, and D. Booth, 183–207. London: Routledge and Kegan Paul.

———. 1977. *The Gezira Scheme: An Illusion of Development.* London: Frank Cass.

Bateson, G. 1956. The Message "This Is Play." In *Group Processes,* ed. B. Schaffner, 145–51. New York: Josiah Macy Foundation.

Benjamin, W. 1969. The Work of Art in the Age of Mechanical Reproduction. In *Illuminations,* ed. H. Arendt, trans. H. Zohn, 217–51. New York: Schocken Books.

———. 1978a. On the Mimetic Faculty. In *Reflections,* ed. P. Demetz, trans. E. Jephcott, 333–36. New York: Harcourt Brace Jovanovich.

———. 1978b. One-Way Street. In *Reflections,* ed. P. Demetz, trans. E. Jephcott, 61–94. New York: Harcourt Brace Jovanovich.

Benmayor, R., R. M. Torruellas, and A. L. Juarbe. 1992. *Responses to Poverty among Puerto Rican Women: Identity, Community, and Cultural Citizenship.* New York: Centro de Estudios Puertorriquenos, Hunter College.

Berger, J. 1974. *The Look of Things.* New York: Viking.

Bernal, V. 1988. Coercion and Incentives in African Agriculture: Insights from the Sudanese Experience. *African Studies Review* 31, no. 2:89–108.

———. 1991. *Cultivating Workers: Peasants and Capitalism in a Sudanese Village.* New York: Columbia University Press.

Bernstein, H. 1982. Notes on Capital and the Peasantry. In *Rural Development,* ed. J. Harriss, 160–77. London: Hutchinson University Library.

Berry, S. 1993. *No Condition Is Permanent: The Social Dynamics of Agrarian Change in Sub-Saharan Africa.* Madison: University of Wisconsin Press.

Boddy, J. 1989. *Wombs and Alien Spirits: Women, Men, and the Zar Cult in Northern Sudan.* Madison: University of Wisconsin Press.

Boocock, S. S. 1981. The Life Space of Children. In *Building for Women,* ed. S. Keller, 93–116. Lexington, Mass.: Lexington Books.

Borra, J. 1996. Savage Inequalities? *Village Voice Educational Supplement,* 16 April, 6.

Bourdieu, P. 1977. *Outline of a Theory of Practice.* Trans. Richard Nice. Cambridge: Cambridge University Press.

Bourdieu, P., and J.-C. Passeron. 1977. *Reproduction in Education, Society, and Culture.* Trans. Richard Nice. London and Beverly Hills, Calif.: Sage Publications.

Bourgois, P. 1995. *In Search of Respect: Selling Crack in El Barrio.* Cambridge: Cambridge University Press.

Bradshaw, Y. W., R. Noonan, L. Gash, and C. B. Sershen. 1993. Borrowing against the Future: Children and Third World Indebtedness. *Social Forces* 71, no. 3:629–56.

Brennan, T. 1997. *At Home in the World: Cosmopolitanism Now.* Cambridge and London: Harvard University Press.

Brown, M. F. 1996. On Resisting Resistance. *American Anthropologist* 98, no. 4:729–35.

Buck-Morss, S. 1989. *The Dialectics of Seeing: Walter Benjamin and the Arcades Project.* Cambridge, Mass.: MIT Press.

Cahill, C. 2000. Street Literacy: Urban Teenagers' Strategies for Negotiating Their Neighbourhood. *Journal of Youth Studies* 3, no. 3:251–77.

Cain, M. 1977. The Economic Activities of Children in a Village in Bangladesh. *Population and Development Review* 3:201–27.

Carr, E. 2000. "Rediscovery and Restoration." New York City Parks and Recreation Department: http://nycparks.completeinet.net/sub_about/parks_history/history _rediscovery_restoration.html.

Castells, M. 1996. *The Rise of the Network Society.* Oxford: Blackwell Publishers.

Chin, E. 2001. *Purchasing Power: Black Kids and American Consumer Culture.* Minneapolis: University of Minnesota Press.

Citizens Budget Commission. 1991. *Managing the Department of Parks and Recreation in a Period of Fiscal Stress.* New York: Citizens Budget Commission.

———. 1997. *The State of Municipal Services in the 1990s: Crowding, Building Conditions and Staffing in New York City Public Schools.* New York: Citizens Budget Commission.

———. 1999. *The Three Cs: Crowding, Crumbling, and Computers: Background on Priority Concerns for the 1999–2000 School Year in New York City*. New York: Citizens Budget Commission.

Citizens' Committee for Children of New York. 1995. *Keeping Track of New York's Children*. New York: Citizens' Committee for Children of New York, Inc.

———. 1999. *Keeping Track of New York City's Children*. New York: Citizens' Committee for Children of New York, Inc.

Comaroff, Jean. 1985. *Body of Power, Spirit of Resistance: The Culture and History of a South African People*. Chicago: University of Chicago Press.

Comaroff, J., and J. L. Comaroff, eds. 1993. *Modernity and Its Malcontents: Ritual and Power in Postcolonial Africa*. Chicago: University of Chicago Press.

Comaroff, J. L., and J. Comaroff. 1992. *Ethnography and the Historical Imagination*. Boulder, Colo.: Westview Press.

Connell, Noreen. 1995. Better Security Comes with Better Schools. *New York Newsday*, A24, A26.

Cooper, B. M. 1999. The Strength in the Song: Muslim Personhood, Audible Capital, and Hausa Women's Performance of the Hajj. *Social Text* 60:87–109.

Dalla Costa, M. 1972. Women and the Subversion of the Community. In *The Power of Women and the Subversion of the Community*, ed. M. Dalla Costa and S. James, 19–54. Bristol: Falling Wall Press.

Davidson, L. L., M. S. Durkin, L. Kuhn, P. O'Connor, B. Barlow, and M. C. Heagarty. 1994. The Impact of the Safe Kids/Healthy Neighborhoods Injury Prevention Program in Harlem 1988 through 1991. *American Journal of Public Health* 84, no. 4:580–86.

De Certeau, M. 1984. *The Practice of Everyday Life*. Trans. S. Rendall. Berkeley and Los Angeles: University of California Press.

Dematteis, G. 2001. Shifting Cities. In *Postmodern Geography: Theory and Praxis*, ed. C. Minca, 113–28. Oxford: Blackwell.

Desbiens, C. 1999. Feminism "in" Geography: Elsewhere, Beyond, and the Politics of Paradoxical Space. *Gender, Place and Culture* 6, no. 2:179–85.

Duffield, M. R. 1981. *Maiurno: Capitalism and Rural Life in Sudan*. London: Ithaca Press.

Ebrahim, M. H. S. 1983. Irrigation Projects in Sudan: The Promise and the Reality. *Journal of African Studies* 10, no. 1:2–11.

Educational Priorities Panel. 1985. *School Libraries . . . No Reading Allowed*. New York: Educational Priorities Panel.

Ehrenhalt, S. M. 1993. Economic and Demographic Change: The Case of New York City. *Monthly Labor Review*, February, 40–50.

Erickson, J., and C. Wilhelm, eds. 1986. *Housing the Homeless*. New Brunswick, N.J.: Center for Urban Policy Research.

Euroconsult. 1988. *Rehabilitation of Es Suki Agricultural Project, Volume 1: Main Report*. Khartoum: Republic of Sudan Ministry of Finance and Economic Planning Project Preparation Unit.

Ferguson, H. n.d. *Food Crops of the Sudan and Their Relationship to the Environment*. n.p. Available in the Sudan Collection of the Khartoum University library.

Finnegan, W. 1998. *Cold New World: Growing Up in a Harder Country*. New York: Random House.

Fiscal Policy Institute. n.d. *Rhetoric vs. Reality: Assessing New York's 1997–98 Executive Budget in the Context of the "Devolution Revolution."* A Fiscal Policy Institute Briefing. Latham, N.Y.: Fiscal Policy Institute.

———. 1999. The State of Working New York. The Illusion of Prosperity: New York in the New Economy. Latham, N.Y.: Fiscal Policy Institute.

Fitch, R. 1993. *The Assassination of New York.* London and New York: Verso.

Fluehr-Lobban, C., R. A. Lobban Jr., and J. O. Voll. 1992. *Historical Dictionary of The Sudan,* 2d ed. Metuchen, N.J., and London: The Scarecrow Press.

Fortes, M. 1970. Social and Psychological Aspects of Education in Taleland. In *From Child to Adult,* ed. J. Middleton, 14–74. Austin: University of Texas Press. (Orig. pub. 1938.)

Freire, P. 1970. *Pedagogy of the Oppressed.* New York: Seabury Press.

———. 1985. *The Politics of Education.* Trans. Donaldo Macedo. South Hadley, Mass.: Bergin and Garvey Publishers.

Galal el Din, Mohamed el Awad. 1977. The Economic Value of Children in Rural Sudan. In *The Persistence of High Fertility in the Third World,* ed. J. C. Caldwell, 617–32. Canberra: Department of Demography.

———. 1978. A Preliminary Note on Sudanese Migration to Oil-Rich Arab Countries. *Sudan Journal of Economic and Social Studies* 2, no. 2:55–59.

Gaster, S. 1991. Urban Children's Access to Their Neighborhood: Changes over Three Generations. *Environment and Behavior* 23, no. 1:70–85.

Gelal el Din, al Tayib. 1970. *The Southeastern Funj Area: A Geographical Survey.* Khartoum: Sudan Research Unit, Faculty of Arts, Khartoum University. Funj Project Paper 1.

Godlewska, A., and N. Smith, eds. 1994. *Geography and Empire.* Oxford: Blackwell Publishers.

Goody, J., and I. Watt. 1968. The Consequences of Literacy. In *Literacy in Traditional Societies,* ed. J. Goody. Cambridge: Cambridge University Press.

Gould, S. J. 1982. The Importance of Trifles. *Natural History* 91, no. 4:16–23.

Gramsci, A. 1971. *Selections from the Prison Notebooks.* Ed. and trans. Quintin Hoare and Geoffrey Nowell Smith. New York: International Publishers.

Gregory, D. 1994. *Geographical Imaginations.* Oxford: Blackwell Publishers.

Gruenbaum, E. 1979. *Patterns of Family Living: A Case Study of Two Villages on the Rahad River.* Khartoum: Khartoum University, Development Studies and Research Centre, Monograph 12.

Gupta, A. 1998. *Postcolonial Developments: Agriculture in the Making of Modern India.* Durham, N.C.: Duke University Press.

Gurdon, C. G. 1991. Economy of Sudan and Recent Strains. In *Sudan after Nimeiri,* ed. P. Woodward, 18–33. London and New York: Routledge.

Hall, S., and T. Jefferson. 1976. *Resistance through Rituals: Youth Subcultures in Postwar Britain.* London: Hutchinson.

Hart, G. 1991. Engendering Everyday Resistance: Gender, Patronage, and Production Politics in Rural Malaysia. *Journal of Peasant Studies* 19, no. 1:93–121.

———. 2002. *Disabling Globalization: Places of Power in Post-Apartheid South Africa.* Los Angeles and Berkeley: University of California Press.

Hart, R. A. 1986. The Changing City of Childhood: Implications for Play and Learning. Catherine Malony Memorial Lecture. New York: City College Workshop Center.

———. 1997. *Children's Participation: The Theory and Practice of Involving Young Citizens in Community Development and Environmental Care.* London: Earthscan Publications and New York: UNICEF.

Hart, R., and L. Chawla. 1982. The Development of Children's Concern for the Environment. *Zeitschrift für Umweltpolitik* 2:271–94.

Harvey, D. 1989. *The Condition of Postmodernity.* Oxford: Basil Blackwell.

———. 2000. *Spaces of Hope.* Edinburgh: Edinburgh University Press.

Hassan, F. M. A. 1994. Is Adjustment with Equitable Economic Growth Possible? Evidence from a Developing Country. *Canadian Journal of Development Studies* 15, no. 2:219–40.

el Hassan, I. S. 1980. "On Ideology: The Case of Religion in Northern Sudan." Ph.D. diss., University of Connecticut.

Hernandez, C. 2000. Wearing the Colors: A Personal Narrative from a "Die-Hard" Educator. In *Smoke and Mirrors: The Hidden Context of Violence in Schools and Society*, ed. S. U. Spina, 41–48. Lanham, Md.: Rowman and Littlefield.

Hernandez, R. 1996. Critics Attack Pataki Formula for Helping Disabled Students. *New York Times*, 29 February, B1, B5.

Hogbin, I. H. 1970. A New Guinea Childhood: From Weaning Till the Eighth Year in Wogeo. In *From Child to Adult*, ed. J. Middleton, 134–62. Austin: University of Texas Press. (Orig. pub. 1946.)

Human Rights Watch/Africa. 1996. *Behind the Red Line: Political Repression in Sudan.* New York: Human Rights Watch.

Hummaida Abdalla Hummaida. 1977. "The Suki Scheme and Its Socio-Economic Value." B.A. Honours Pt. I diss., Khartoum University.

Hurriez, S., and H. Bell, eds. 1975. *Directions in Sudanese Linguistics and Folklore.* Khartoum: Khartoum University Press.

Hutchinson, S. E. 1996. *Nuer Dilemmas: Coping with Money, War, and the State.* Berkeley and Los Angeles: University of California Press.

Injuryfree.org/harlem.htm. 2000.

International Monetary Fund. 1995. *Sudan-Recent Economic Developments.* IMF Staff Country Report No. 95/12. Washington, D.C.: International Monetary Fund.

Jacobs, J. 1961. *The Death and Life of Great American Cities.* New York: Vintage.

Jakobsen, J. 2002. Can Homosexuals End Western Civilization as We Know It? In *Queer Globalizations: Citizenship and the Afterlife of Colonialism*, ed. Arnaldo Cruz-Malave and Martin F. Manalansan. New York: New York University Press.

Jansen, H-G., and W. Koch. 1982. The Rahad Scheme—The Agricultural System and Its Problems. In *Problems of Agricultural Development in the Sudan*, ed. G. Heinritz, 23–35. Göttingen, FRG: Edition Herodot.

Joseph, M. 1998. The Performance of Production and Consumption. *Social Text* 54:25–61.

Kaplan, A., and K. Ross. 1987. Introduction to *Everyday Life. Yale French Studies* 73:1–4.

Kapur, J. 1999. Out of Control: Television and the Transformation of Childhood in Late Capitalism. In *Kids' Media Culture*, ed. M. Kinder, 122–36. Durham, N.C., and London: Duke University Press.

Karrar, A. S. 1992. *The Sufi Brotherhoods in the Sudan.* Evanston, Ill.: Northwestern University Press.

Kates, R. W., and C. R. Katz. 1977. The Hydrologic Cycle and the Wisdom of the Child. *Geographical Review* 67: 51–62.

Katz, C. 1994. The Textures of Global Change: Eroding Ecologies of Childhood, New York and Sudan. In *Childhood: A Global Journal of Child Research* 2, no. 4: 103–10.

———. 1996. Towards Minor Theory. *Environment and Planning D: Society and Space* 14:487–99.

———. 2000. Fueling War: A Political-Ecology of Poverty and Deforestation in Sudan. In *Producing Nature and Poverty in Africa*, ed. V. Broch-Due and R. A. Schroeder, 321–39. Stockholm: Nordiska Afrikainstitutet.

———. 2001a. Hiding the Target: Social Reproduction in the Privatized Urban Environment. In *Postmodern Geography: Theory and Praxis*, ed. C. Minca, 93–110. Oxford: Blackwell.

———. 2001b. On the Grounds of Globalization: A Topography for Feminist Political Engagement. *Signs* 26, no. 4:1213–34.

———. 2001c. Vagabond Capitalism and the Necessity of Social Reproduction. *Antipode* 33, no. 4:708–27.

Katz, C., and R. Hart. 1990. *The Participatory Design of Two Community Elementary School-yards in Harlem P.S. 185 and P.S. 208.* New York: Children's Environments Research Group, the City University of New York.

Kershaw, S. 1996. At Some Schools, It's Hard to Curl Up with a Good Book. *New York Times,* 11 March, B2.

Kevane, M. 1994. Village Labor Markets in Sheikan District, Sudan. *World Development* 22, no. 6:839–57.

Khalid, M. 1990. *The Government They Deserve: The Role of the Elite in Sudan's Political Evolution.* London and New York: Kegan Paul International.

King, D. L. 1995. *Doing Their Share to Save the Planet: Children and Environmental Crisis.* New Brunswick, N.J.: Rutgers University Press.

Krenichyn, K. 1999. Messages about Adolescent Identity: Coded and Contested Spaces in a New York City High School. In *Embodied Geographies: Spaces, Bodies, and Rites of Passage,* ed. Elizabeth Teather, 43–58. London: Routledge.

Landy, D. 1959. *Tropical Childhood.* Chapel Hill: University of North Carolina Press.

Laraque, D., B. Barlow, L. Davidson, and C. Welborn. 1994. The Central Harlem Playground Injury Prevention Project: A Model for Change. *American Journal of Public Health* 84, no. 10:1691–92.

Lave, J., and E. Wenger. 1991. *Situated Learning: Legitimate Peripheral Participation.* Cambridge and New York: Cambridge University Press.

Leavitt, J., and S. Saegert. 1990. *From Abandonment to Hope.* New York: Columbia University Press.

Lebon, J. H. G. 1965. *Land Use in Sudan.* London: Geographical Publications, Ltd.

Lefebvre, H. 1984. *Everyday Life in the Modern World.* New Brunswick, N.J.: Transaction Books.

———. 1987. The Everyday and Everydayness. *Yale French Studies* 73:7–11.

Lesch, A. M. 1998. *Sudan: Contested National Identities.* Bloomington and Indianapolis: Indiana University Press.

Levine, S. 1996. "Picannin" Wages and Child Labor in the South African Agriculture, Mining, and Domestic Service Industries: 1658 to the Present. *Anthropology of Work Review* 17, nos. 1 and 2:42–50.

Levitan, M. 2000. *More Work, More School, More Poverty? The Changing Face of Poor Families in New York City.* New York: Community Service Society of New York.

MacDonald, Sir M., and Partners. 1964. *Roseires Soil Survey, Report 9: Dinder-Blue Nile Gezira Sennar to Confluence, Semi-Detailed Soil Survey and Land Classification.* London: Hunting Technical Services.

Mahmoud, F. B. 1984. *The Sudanese Bourgeoisie: Vanguard of Development?* London: Zed Books and Khartoum: Khartoum University Press.

Mahmoud Yagoub Ahmed. 1977. "Production Relations in Suki Scheme." B.A. diss., Khartoum University.

Males, M. A. 1996. *The Scapegoat Generation: America's War on Adolescents.* Monroe, Maine: Common Courage Press.

Marris, P. 1974. *Loss and Change.* New York: Pantheon Books.

Marston, S. A. 2000. The Social Construction of Scale. *Progress in Human Geography* 24, no. 2: 219–42.

Marx, K. 1967. *Capital,* 3 vols. Ed. F. Engels, trans. S. Moore and E. Aveling. New York: International Publishers.

———. 1973. *Grundrisse.* Trans. M. Nicolaus. Harmondsworth and Baltimore: Penguin.

Mascarenhas, A. 1977. *The Participation of Children in Socio-Economic Activities: The Case of the Rukwa Region.* Dar es Salaam: University of Dar es Salaam, BRALUP. Research Report 20–1.

McCord, C., and H. P. Freeman. 1990. Excess Mortality in Harlem. *New England Journal of Medicine* 322:173–77.

Mead, M. 1970. Our Educational Emphases in Primitive Perspective. In *From Child to Adult: Studies in the Anthropology of Education,* ed. J. Middleton, 1–13. Austin: University of Texas Press. (Orig. pub. 1942–43.)

Medrich, E. A., J. A. Roizen, V. Rubin, and S. Buckley. 1982. *The Serious Business of Growing Up: A Study of Children's Lives Outside School.* Berkeley and Los Angeles: University of California Press.

Middleton, J., ed. 1970. *From Child to Adult: Studies in the Anthropology of Education.* Austin: University of Texas Press.

Miller, V., M. Hollstein, and S. Quass. 1996. Feminist Politics and Environmental Justice: Women's Community Activism in West Harlem, New York. In *Feminist Political Ecology: Global Issues and Local Experiences,* ed. D. Rocheleau, B. Thomas-Slayter, and E. Wangari, 62–85. London and New York: Routledge.

Millstein, I. M. 1995. "Let Neighborhoods Tax Themselves to Rescue their Parks." Letter to *New York Times,* February 4.

Mintz, S. W. 1985. *Sweetness and Power: The Place of Sugar in Modern History.* New York: Penguin Books.

Mitchell, K. 1997. Different Diasporas and the Hype of Hybridity. *Environment and Planning D: Society and Space* 15, no. 5:533–53.

Modiano, N. 1973. *Indian Education in the Chiapas Highlands.* New York: Holt, Rinehart, and Winston.

Moore, D. S. 1998. Subaltern Struggles and the Politics of Place: Remapping Resistance in Zimbabwe's Eastern Highlands. *Cultural Anthropology* 13, no. 3:344–81.

Nag, M., B. White, and R. C. Peet. 1978. An Anthropological Approach to the Study of the Economic Value of Children in Java and Nepal. *Current Anthropology* 19:293–306.

Nevarez de Jesus, J. 1999. Landscapes of Public Value: A Study of Public Space and Public Safety in a New York City Playground. Ph.D. diss., Graduate Center of the City University of New York.

Newman, M. 1996. Queens School Is Succeeding on a Shoestring. *New York Times,* 23 February, B3.

New York City Board of Education. 1958. *Special Census of School Population.* Brooklyn, N.Y.: New York City Board of Education, Bureau of Educational Program Research and Statistics.

———. 1984. *Students in New York City Public Schools, 1970–1981. Discussion of Data.* Brooklyn, N.Y.: New York City Board of Education.

———. 1989. *A New Direction: 1989/90 Budget Request.* Brooklyn, N.Y.: New York City Board of Education.

———. 1991. *The Chancellor's Budget Estimate 1991–92.* Brooklyn, N.Y.: New York City Board of Education.

———. 1993. *The Chancellor's Budget Estimate 1993–94.* Brooklyn, N.Y.: New York City Board of Education.

———. 1994. *The Chancellor,s Budget Estimate 1994–95.* Brooklyn, N.Y.: New York City Board of Education.

———. 1995. *The Chancellor's Budget Estimate 1995–96.* Brooklyn, N.Y.: New York City Board of Education.

———. 1998a. *1996–1997 Annual School Report.* Brooklyn, N.Y.: New York City Board of Education, Division of Assessment and Accountability.

———. 1998b. *Building Condition Survey.* Brooklyn, N.Y.: New York City Board of Education.

New York City Mayor's Office. 1994. *Green Book: Official Directory of New York 1994–95.* New York: Citybooks.

New York Times. 2000. A Metropolis of Poor Children. 17 August, A28.

Niblock, T. 1987. *Class and Power in Sudan: The Dynamics of Sudanese Politics 1898–1985.* Albany: State University of New York Press.

O'Brien, J. 1978. How Traditional Is Traditional Agriculture? *Sudan Journal of Economic and Social Studies* 2:1–10.

———. 1983. The Formation of the Agricultural Labour Force in Sudan. *Review of African Political Economy* 26:15–34.

———. 1984. The Social Reproduction of Tenant Cultivators and Class Formation in the Gezira Scheme, Sudan. *Research in Economic Anthropology* 6:217–41.

O'Connor, J. 1994. Is Sustainable Capitalism Possible? In *Is Capitalism Sustainable?* ed. M. O'Connor, 152–75. New York: Guilford.

O'Laughlin, B. 1977. Production and Reproduction: Meillassoux's "Femmes, Greniers et Capitaux." *Critique of Anthropology* 2:3–32.

Ong, A. 1987. *Spirits of Resistance and Capitalist Discipline: Factory Women in Malaysia.* Albany: State University of New York Press.

Ortner, S. B. 1995. Resistance and the Problem of Ethnographic Refusal. *Comparative Study of Society and History* 37, no. 1:173–93.

Passell, P. 1998. Benefits Dwindle along with Wages for the Unskilled. *New York Times,* 14 June, 1.

Peluso, N. L. 1992. *Rich Forests, Poor People: Resource Control and Resistance in Java.* Berkeley and Los Angeles: University of California Press.

Piaget, J. 1954. *The Child's Construction of Reality.* New York: Basic Books.

———. 1963. *The Psychology of Intelligence.* Totowa, N.J.: Littlefield Adams & Co.

———. 1975. *The Child's Conception of the World.* Totowa, N.J.: Littlefield Adams & Co.

Porter, K. 1996. The Agency of Children, Work, and Social Change in the South Pare Mountains, Tanzania. *Anthropology of Work Review* 17, nos. 1 and 2:8–19.

Powell, M. 1995. Public Schools' Lobby Is Weak. *New York Newsday.* 19 June, A22.

Pred, A., and M. J. Watts. 1992. *Reworking Modernity: Capitalisms and Symbolic Discontent.* New Brunswick, N.J.: Rutgers University Press.

Primus, W. E., K. Porter, M. Ditto, and M. Kent. 1996. *The Safety Net Delivers: The Effects of Government Benefit Programs in Reducing Poverty.* Washington, D.C.: Center on Budget and Policy Priorities.

Ramirez, A. 1999. Rise in Number of Children Born into Poverty in New York City. *New York Times,* 4 February.

Raum, O. 1940. *Chaga Childhood.* London: Oxford University Press.

Regional Plan Association. 1996. A Region at Risk. In *The Third Regional Plan for the New York-New Jersey-Connecticut Metropolitan Area.* Washington, D.C.: Island Press.

Reynolds, P. 1996. *Traditional Healers and Childhood in Zimbabwe.* Athens, Ohio: Ohio University Press.

Rodgers, G., and G. Standing, eds. 1981. *Childwork, Poverty, and Underdevelopment.* Geneva: International Labour Organisation.

Rogoff, B., and W. Gardner. 1984. Adult Guidance of Cognitive Development. In *Everyday Cognition: Its Development in Social Context,* ed. B. Rogoff and J. Lave, 95–116. Cambridge, Mass.: Harvard University Press.

Rose, G. 1993. *Feminism and Geography: The Limits of Geographical Knowledge.* Minneapolis: University of Minnesota Press.

Rubin, K., G. G. Fein, and B. Vandenberg. 1983. Play. In *Socialization, Personality and Social Development,* ed. E. M. Hetherington, 693–774. Vol. 4 of *Handbook of Child Psychology,* ed. P. Mussen. New York: John Wiley and Sons.

Ruddle, K., and R. Chesterfield. 1977. *Education for Traditional Food Procurement in the Orinoco Delta.* Berkeley and Los Angeles: University of California Press.

Sachs, P. 1993. Old Ties: Women, Work, and Aging in a Coal-Mining Community in West Virginia. In *Full Circles: Geographies of Women over the Lifecourse,* ed. C. Katz and J. Monk, 156–70. London and New York: Routledge.

Salih, K. O. 1991. The Sudan, 1985–89: The Fading Democracy. In *Sudan after Nimeiri,* ed. P. Woodward, 45–75. London and New York: Routledge.

Samuel, R. 1975. *Village Life and Labour.* London: Routledge and Kegan Paul.

Scheuer, J. 1993. *Unequal State Aid for Public Schools.* New York: Educational Priorities Panel.

Schildkrout, E. 1981. The Employment of Children in Kano (Nigeria). In *Child Work, Poverty and Underdevelopment,* ed. G. Rodgers and G. Standing, 81–112. Geneva: International Labour Office.

Schwartzman, H. 1978. *Transformations: The Anthropology of Children's Play.* New York: Plenum.

Scott, J. 1985. *Weapons of the Weak: Everyday Forms of Peasant Resistance.* New Haven, Conn.: Yale University Press.

———. 1990. *Domination and the Arts of Resistance: Hidden Transcripts.* New Haven, Conn.: Yale University Press.

Seiter, E. 1993. *Sold Separately: Parents and Children in Consumer Culture.* New Brunswick, N.J.: Rutgers University Press.

Sidahmed, A. 1996. *Politics and Islam in Contemporary Sudan.* New York: St. Martin's Press.

Smith, N. 1984. *Uneven Development: Nature, Capital and the Production of Space.* Oxford: Basil Blackwell.

———. 1996. *The New Urban Frontier: Gentrification and the Revanchist City.* London and New York: Routledge.

Soja, E. W. 1989. *Postmodern Geographies: The Reassertion of Space in Critical Social Theory.* London and New York: Verso.

Spradley, J. P. 1979. *The Ethnographic Interview.* New York: Holt, Rinehart & Winston.

Stack, C. B. 1975. *All Our Kin: Strategies for Survival in a Black Community.* New York: Harper Colophon.

Steedman, C. 1986. *Landscape for a Good Woman.* London: Virago.

Steedman, C., C. Urwin, and V. Walkerdine, eds. 1985. *Language, Gender and Childhood.* London: Routledge and Kegan Paul.

Sudan, Democratic Republic of. Department of Statistics. 1965. *The Household Budget Survey in the Gezira-Managil Area.* Khartoum: Government of Sudan Department of Statistics.

Sudan, Democratic Republic of. Ministry of Education and Guidance. 1981. Education in the Sudan, Sector Review Paper. Prepared for UNICEF preview meeting, 22 October 1980.

Sudan, Democratic Republic of. Ministry of National Planning, Department of Statistics. n.d. *Second Population Census, 1973: Population Dynamics,* vol.2. (Unpublished manuscript.)

Suki Agricultural Corporation. 1981. Annual Cotton Production Records available from Project Headquarters, Wad Tuk Tuk.

————. 1997. Irrigation Problems in the Suki Agricultural Project. Unpublished report, June.

Taussig, M. 1993. *Mimesis and Alterity: A Particular History of the Senses*. New York and London: Routledge.

Thompson, E. P. 1967. Time, Work-Discipline, and Industrial Capitalism. *Past and Present* 38.

Tienda, M. 1979. Economic Activity of Children in Peru: Labor Force Behavior in Rural and Urban Contexts. *Rural Sociology* 44:370–91.

Tothill, J. D., ed. 1948. *Agriculture in the Sudan*. London: Oxford University Press.

Trouillot, M.-R. 1996. Theorizing a Global Perspective: A Conversation with Michel-Rolph Trouillot. *Crosscurrents in Culture, Power and History: A Newsletter of the Institute for Global Studies in Culture, Power and History, Johns Hopkins University* 4, no. 1:1–4.

Tully, D. 1988. *Culture and Context in Sudan: The Process of Market Incorporation in Dar Masalit*. Albany: State University of New York Press.

Vågenes, V. 1998. *Women of Interior Men of Exterior: The Gender Order of the Hedendowa Nomads, Red Sea Hills-Sudan*. PhD diss., University of Bergen.

Valentine, G. 1997. "Oh yes I can." "Oh no you can't.": Children's and Parents' Understanding of Kids' Competence to Negotiate Public Space Safely. *Antipode* 29, no. 1:65–89.

Van Vliet, W. 1983. Exploring the Fourth Environment: An Examination of the Home Range of City and Suburban Teenagers. *Environment and Behavior* 15, no. 5:567–88.

Vigil, J. D. 2002. *A Rainbow of Gangs: Street Cultures in the Mega-City*. Austin: University of Texas Press.

Vygotsky, L. S. 1978. *Mind in Society: The Development of Higher Psychological Processes*. Ed. M. Cole, V. John-Steiner, S. Scribner, and E. Souberman. Cambridge, Mass.: Harvard University Press.

Walton, J., and D. Seddon. 1994. *Free Markets and Food Riots: The Politics of Global Adjustment*. Cambridge, Mass., and Oxford: Blackwell.

White, S. H., and A. W. Siegel. 1984. Cognitive Development in Time and Space. In *Everyday Cognition: Its Development in Context,* ed. B. Rogoff and J. Lave, 238–77. Cambridge, Mass.: Harvard University Press.

Williams, T., and W. Kornblum. 1994. *The Uptown Kids: Struggle and Hope in the Projects*. New York: G. P. Putnam's Sons.

Willis, P. 1977. *Learning to Labor*. New York: Columbia University Press.

Willner, R., and S. Amlung, eds. 1985. *Ten Years of Neglect: The Failure to Serve Language Minority Students in the New York City Public Schools*. New York: Educational Priorities Panel.

Wilson, W. J. 1996. *When Work Disappears: The World of the New Urban Poor*. New York: Alfred A. Knopf.

World Bank. 1984. *World Development Indicators 1984*. Washington, D.C.: World Bank.

Woodward, P. 1990. *Sudan 1898–1989: The Unstable State*. Boulder, Colo.: Lynne Rienner Publishers.

Wridt, P. 2000. Growing Up in Williamsburg, Brooklyn: Young People's Perspectives about their Environment. In *From the Hudson to the Hamptons: Snapshots of the New York Metropolitan Area*, ed. I. Miyares, M. Pavlovskaya, and G. Pope, 70–78. Washington, D.C.: Association of American Geographers.

Wyatt, E. 2000. School Laptops Paid with Ads Called Feasible. *New York Times,* 20 September, B1, B8.

Index

agricultural labor: birth order and, 16, 66, 73; children's play and, 11–13, 83–86, 88, 122–23; commodification of, 140–43; environmental knowledge/learning, 118; families and, 34, 38–39, 121; requirements of, 33–34, 38–39, 49, 83–88; wage workers, 43; of women, 39, 120–22, 141, 216, 278n1

agriculture: *bildat* (rain-fed), 11–13, 24–25, 29, 39, 188, 192; cash cropping, 25, 48, 192; crop mortgaging (*shayl*), 32, 45, 277n6, 289n4; Dinder Town, 28; education and, 281n1; gardening, 192; irrigated cultivation, 29, 39–40, 83–88; *jeref* (riverbank gardens), 23–25, 27–28; non-mechanized, 36, 38, 181; planting/harvest, 39, 65–66, 87; subsistence, 188, 192; seasons in, 5, 88; soil fertility, 25; traditional, 39; weeding, 56–60, 86–87. *See also* tenancies

Ahmed, Mohamed, 189, 191

Ali, Taiser Mohamed, 278n10

Amlung, S., 165

Anglo-Egyptian Condominium, 23

animal husbandry, 25, 47, 61–62, 68–72, 120–22, 192–93, 253, 275n1. *See also* herding; pastoralism

animal wealth, 140, 193 200–201, 208–9, 233–34, 253, 290n11

antipoverty programs, 285n3

antiurbanism, 243

apprenticeships, 145–46

"arab" identity, 202, 215

artisans, 52–53

Asociación Madres de Plaza de Mayo, 255

Austen, Jane, 133

bakeries, 27–28, 52, 290n13

banking, 190–91, 289n4

Barbour, Kenneth, 26

Barlow, Barbara, 175, 247

Barnett, Tony, 277n5

Bashir, 'Umar Hasan Ahmad al-, xii, 188, 289n2

Bashir government, xii

Bateson, Gregory, 97

Benjamin, Walter, 96, 97–98, 100–101, 111, 240, 257–58, 279n11

Berger, John, xiv, 156

Bernal, Victoria, 43, 278n10, 282n3, 284n8

Bernstein, Henry, 31, 47, 276n3

Bey-Grecia, Aissatou, 175

bildat (rain-fed agriculture), 11–13, 24–25, 188, 192

Cindi Katz is professor of geography in the environmental psychology and women's studies departments at the Graduate Center of the City University of New York. She has published widely in edited collections and in journals such as *Society and Space, Social Text, Signs, Feminist Studies, Annals of the Association of American Geographers, Social Justice,* and *Antipode.* She is the coeditor (with Janice Monk) of *Full Circles: Geographies of Gender over the Life Course* and (with Sallie Marston and Katharyne Mitchell) of *Life's Work.*